# THE

All New

# SCRIPTURE
# SOURCE BOOK

## *for Catholics*

Harcourt Religion Publishers

Imprimatur     ✠ Most Rev. Bernard J. Harrington, DD
           Bishop of Winona
           July 6, 2007

The imprimatur is an official declaration that a book or pamphlet is free of doctrinal or moral error. No implication is contained therein that the person who granted the imprimatur agrees with the contents, opinions, or statements expressed.

For permission to reprint copyrighted material, grateful acknowledgment is made to the following sources:
*The American Bible Society:* From *The New Testament of the Contemporary English Version.* Text copyright © 1995 by The American Bible Society.
*Baker Academic, a division of Baker Publishing Group:* From *The Bible in Translation: Ancient and English Versions* by Bruce M. Metzger. Text © 2001 by Bruce M. Metzger.
*Catholic Biblical Association, Washington, D.C.:* From *The Historical Truth of the Gospels/Instructio de Historica Evangeliorum Veritate* (Latin-English text), translated by Benjamin N. Wambacq, O. Praem in *Catholic Biblical Quarterly,* July 1964. Text © 1964 by Catholic Biblical Association.
*Catholic Book Publishing Company:* From *New Catholic Edition of the Holy Bible,* Douay and Confraternity Editions. Text copyright 1949, 1951 by the Catholic Book Publishing Co.
*Confraternity of Christian Doctrine, Washington, D.C.:* Scriptures from *The New American Bible.* Text copyright © 1970 by the Confraternity of Christian Doctrine, Inc. Scriptures from *The New American Bible with Revised New Testament and Revised Psalms.* Text copyright © 1991, 1986, 1970 by the Confraternity of Christian Doctrine, Inc. No portion of The New American Bible may be reprinted without permission in writing from the copyright holder.
*Costello Publishing Company, Inc., Northport, NY:* From *Companion to the New Breviary,* edited by Austin Flannery, O.P. From *Vatican Council II, The Basic Sixteen Documents,* edited by Rev. Austin Flannery, O.P. Text copyright © 1996 by Reverend Austin Flannery, O.P.
*Division of Christian Education of the National Council of the Churches of Christ in the U.S.A.:* Scripture quotations from the *New Revised Standard Version Bible: Catholic Edition.* Text copyright © 1993 and 1989 by the Division of Christian Education of the National Council of the Churches of Christ in the U.S.A.
*Doubleday, a division of Random House, Inc.:* From *The Jerusalem Bible.* Text copyright © 1966 by Darton, Longman & Todd, Ltd. and Doubleday & Company, Inc. From *The Lamb's Supper* by Scott Hahn. Text copyright © 1999 by Scott Walker Hahn.
*GIA Publications, Inc.:* From the Grail Psalms in *The Liturgy of the Hours.*

Acknowledgments continued on page 417.

Printed in the United States of America
ISBN 0-15-901882-X
ISBN 978-0-15-901882-8
1 2 3 4 5 6 7 8 9 10  076  12 11 10 09 08 07

# Contents

# Introduction

" **L** et your Word, Father, be a lamp for our feet and a light to our path, so that we may understand what you wish to teach us and follow the path your light marks out for us."

This is the Church's prayer in the Liturgy of Hours following Psalm 119:105–112, which begins, "Your word is a lamp for my steps, / and a light for my path."

This verse inspired the title of the last chapter in this book: "Light of the Faithful." May this book help lead the reader to a new experience of Scripture as the light of the faithful.

## The Readers

The *Scripture Source Book for Catholics* is intended especially for catechists, those responsible for the evangelization and catechesis of children, inquirers, catechumens, and candidates for full communion. It is also intended for Catholics of all backgrounds seeking to learn more about Scripture, as well as for inquirers, catechumens, and candidates.

## The Purpose

This is an entry-level book, but with enough inroads for readers to appreciate the breadth and depth of the many aspects of Scripture. These roads lead to what may only be overviews for some, providing a glimpse of the panorama of biblical criticism, for example, and the world of Scripture translation. For others, the roads will lead to entrances into the world of Scripture where readers can explore and make discoveries of their own.

The purpose of this book is to help Catholics become more confident and competent in their faith. Traditionally, many Catholics have not been confident because they did not realize how scriptural the Catholic Church really is. Others have simply not been knowledgeable enough about the Bible to feel confident and competent in a discussion.

This book was written not only to provide scriptural information, but also to introduce the readers to the scriptural richness of the Catholic Church and to provide resources for using and understanding Scripture. It is a comprehensive introduction and invitation to the Scripture topics and worlds of ideas in the Catholic Tradition.

## The Structure

The chapters in this book and their arrangement follow the lead of Vatican II's *Constitution on Divine Revelation,* which consists of six chapters (see below). However, there are seven chapters in the *Scripture Source Book for Catholics.*

The first four chapters answer the question, "What is Scripture, from the Catholic point of view?"

• Scripture is "the word of God" (Chapter 1).

• Scripture is in "the words of people" (Chapter 2).

• Scripture is "a book of covenants" (Chapter 3).

• Scripture is "a journal of God's people" (Chapter 4).

The last three chapters answer the question, "What is the place of Scripture in the life of the Catholic Church?"

• Scripture is "the word of the Liturgy" (Chapter 5).

• Scripture is "the prayer book of the Church" (Chapter 6).

• Scripture is "the light of the faithful" (Chapter 7).

## The Chapters

Sacred Scripture is many things. Each of the seven chapters of this book uses a description of the Bible as its title; in this way the text covers seven different aspects of the Bible.

Scripture is "the word of God" (Chapter 1) because it was inspired by God, and so it stands apart from all other literature.

Scripture was written by human authors, and so it is "the words of people" (Chapter 2). Its eternal and universal message is clothed in the languages, styles, context, and culture of people of specific places, times, and talents. Many parts of it existed as an oral tradition before it was written, collected, and recognized as the word of God.

This word of God in the words of people is "a book of covenants" (Chapter 3), telling the story, from the beginning, of God's intervention in the world and his choice to enter into a covenant with the Jewish people and ultimately the covenant fulfilled in Jesus, the Son of God, for the purpose of redeeming the world.

This book of God's covenants is also "a journal of God's people" (Chapter 4) that has required, through the course of centuries, translation from one language to another and interpretation from one culture to another and one generation to the next. Different kinds of "biblical criticism" and commentary have developed with the passage of time to resource the translation and interpretation of the word.

In the life of the faithful, Scripture, first and foremost, is "the word of the liturgy" (Chapter 5), the prayer of the Church made up of word and sacrament.

Scripture is "the prayer book of the Church" (Chapter 6), prayed traditionally and formally in the Liturgy of the Hours.

Scripture is "the light of the faithful" (Chapter 7), read, prayed, and studied by the faithful as a "lamp" and "light" for the pilgrimage of faith.

## The Content

This resource includes answers to typical questions (like the following) often asked by Catholics. It provides information and context for topics that commonly come up in the course of the Rite of Christian Initiation of Adults (RCIA—the traditional process, including inquiry and catechesis, for initiation or reception into full communion in the Catholic Church).

1. What's the difference between one Bible and another? (This question refers to the various translations and editions of Scripture.)
2. Why is there a "Catholic Bible" and a "Protestant Bible," and what's the difference?
3. Where can you find Catholic beliefs and practices in the Bible?

4. Why do Catholics include Tradition along with Scripture in the foundation of Christian faith?
5. What is meant by "magisterium" and why is it only in the Catholic Tradition?
6. Where did fundamentalism come from; what is it; why is it appealing; and what's the problem with it?
7. How can you pray with Scripture?
8. How can you believe everything that's in the Bible?
9. What makes the Bible different from other great religious works?
10. What's the difference between the Bible and the Lectionary?

## The Format

Outlines and lists are great tools to help us organize our thoughts. The outlines and lists throughout this book help to order the vast array of Catholic ideas and teachings about Scripture.

## Bibliography

The information in this book and its arrangement are based on two primary resources.

- *The Dogmatic Constitution on Divine Revelation ("Dei Verbum")* of Vatican II (1965). It is divided into six chapters:

1. Revelation Itself
2. The Transmission of Divine Revelation
3. The Divine Inspiration and the Interpretation of Sacred Scripture

4. The Old Testament
5. The New Testament
6. Sacred Scripture in the Life of the Church

- *The Catechism of the Catholic Church* (1994). In the 1985 Synod of bishops for the twentieth anniversary of the close of Vatican II, the Synod Fathers expressed a desire for a catechism. "The presentation of doctrine must be biblical and liturgical," they said. In all four parts of the catechism that was eventually published (the creed, the sacred liturgy, the Christian way of life, prayer), as in all aspects of its life, the Church is biblical. Scripture as a topic is treated in paragraphs 101–133 of the *Catechism*:

1. Christ—The Unique Word of Sacred Scripture, 101–104
2. Inspiration and Truth of Sacred Scripture, 105–108
3. The Holy Spirit, Interpreter of Scripture, 109–119
4. The Canon of Scripture, 120–130
5. Sacred Scripture in the Life of the Church, 131–133

In particular, Chapters 5 and 6 in this book, "Word of the Liturgy" and "Prayer Book of the Church," are based on the Lectionary and the Liturgy of the Hours.

- The *Lectionary for Mass* of *The Roman Missal*. The *Scripture Source Book for Catholics*, especially in Chapter 5, includes information from the "General Instruction" of the *Roman Missal* as well as from the "Introduction" of the *Lectionary* itself.

- The 1970 *General Instruction of the Liturgy of the Hours* (GILH) along with the Apostolic Constitution of Pope Paul VI, *Laudis Canticum* (LC)—"Canticle of Praise," that approved the Liturgy of the Hours revised by decree of the Second Vatican Ecumenical Council for use by the Roman Catholic Church. It is a wealth of information, not only about the Liturgy of the Hours, but also about prayer and the prominent place of Scripture in the life of the Church, as Chapter 6 in this book attests.

Various other authorities are cited and quoted throughout this book.

- Scripture commentaries, especially *The New Jerome Biblical Commentary* (1990) and *The Collegeville Bible Commentary* (1992).

- The study guide essays in "The Catholic Study Edition" of *The New American Bible* and the articles in *The New Jerome Biblical Commentary.*

- The preface to the Old Testament of *The New American Bible*, the preface to the First Edition and the preface to the Revised Edition of the New Testament of *The New American Bible*, and the introductions to the books of *The New American Bible.*

- Statements of The Pontifical Biblical Commission. In 1902, Pope Leo XIII established this Commission with the twofold purpose of promoting Scripture study and protecting it from error. It was to consist of members drawn from the College of Cardinals with consulters chosen from Scripture scholars the world over. In its recent history, the Commission's work has been mainly the encouragement of the scientific work of Scripture scholars.

Scripture itself is used. In many instances, this book refers to a Scripture passage not only by chapter and verse, but also by translation. There is only one Bible, but Bible translations abound. One of the purposes of this book is to explain and illustrate the differences (particularly in Chapter 4). The Bible is often referred to by the name of a particular translation—*The New American Bible, The King James*, for example—or just by the initials of a particular translation —"the RSV," for example. Throughout this book, the following abbreviations are used for those translations and their revisions. (Descriptions and publication dates for all these translations can be found in Chapter 4 of this book, with more historical information appearing in the appendix.)

- DR: Douay-Rheims

- CEV: Contemporary English Version

- JB/NJB: The Jerusalem Bible/The New Jerusalem Bible

- KJV/NKJV: The King James Version/The New King James Version

- NAB (1970)/NAB, revised: The New American Bible/The New American Bible with a Revised Edition of the New Testament
- NEB/REB: New English Bible/Revised English Bible
- NIV: The New International Version
- NLT: The New Living Translation
- RSV/NRSV*: The Revised Standard Version/The New Revised Standard Version
- TEV: Today's English Version
- TM: The Message

* In cases where Scripture has been quoted but not identified, the NRSV text has been used.

## CHAPTER 1

# Word of God

## Revelation

"It pleased God, in his goodness and wisdom, to reveal himself and to make known the mystery of his will."[1] The divine will is that we should come to the Father through Christ, the Word made flesh, and, in the Holy Spirit, become sharers in the divine nature (*theosis*). Divine Revelation, then, is the supernatural manifestation of the inner life of God: Father, Son, and Holy Spirit. God's desire to communicate himself to us is entirely his own initiative. God's self-revelation aims to bring about our participation in the life of the Blessed Trinity, something so wondrous that it is impossible for us even to imagine.

—*National Directory for Catechesis*, p. 42

## The Word of God

Years ago there was a Broadway play called *The Royal Hunt of the Sun*. It was about Spain's conquest of the Indians in Peru in the 16th century. In one scene someone gave the Indian chief a Bible and told him, "This is God's word. He speaks to us through it." The chief took the Bible cautiously. He studied it carefully and gently raised it to his ear. He listened and listened, but he heard nothing. Then, feeling insulted, he slammed the Bible down angrily.

# Revelation

This is the beginning: God's choice; God's initiative; God's self-manifestation. "*By his Revelation*, 'the invisible God, from the fullness of his love, addresses men as his friends, and moves among them, in order to invite and receive them into his own company.' The adequate response to this invitation is faith" (*CCC*, 142, quoting Vatican II's *The Dogmatic Constitution on Divine Revelation* [edited by Austin Flannery, O.P.] and citing *Colossians 1:15, 1 Timothy 1:17, Exodus 33:11, John 15:14–15, Baruch 3:38 (Vulg.)*).

The *Constitution on Divine Revelation* (sometimes called by its first two words in Latin *"Dei Verbum,"* Word of God) has six chapters. It begins its first chapter, "Divine Revelation Itself," with the following sentences: "It pleased God, in his goodness and wisdom, to reveal himself and to make known the mystery of his will (see *Ephesians 1:9*), which was that people can draw near to the Father, through Christ, the Word made flesh, in the holy Spirit, and thus become sharers in the divine nature (see *Ephesians 2:18, 2 Peter 1:4*). By this revelation, then, the invisible God (see *Colossians 1:15, 1 Timothy 1:17*), from the fullness of his love, addresses men and women as his friends (see *Exodus 33:11, John 15:14–15*), and lives among them (see *Baruch 3:38*), in order to invite and receive them into his own company."

### Word

The "Word of God" is mentioned in the next paragraph of the *Constitution* (#3), "God, who creates and conserves all things by his Word (see *John 1:3*), provides constant evidence of himself in created realities (see *Romans 1:19–20*)." The document proceeds to outline how God, ". . . wishing to open up the way to heavenly salvation . . ." revealed himself through the course of history, beginning with "our first parents," through a promised redemption, Abraham and the patriarchs, Moses and the prophets, and the promise of a Savior.

### Christ

The Word is named in the next paragraph (#4): "After God had spoken many times and in various ways through the prophets, 'in these last days he has spoken to us by a Son' (*Hebrews 1:1–2*). For he sent his Son, the eternal Word who enlightens all humankind, to live among them and to tell them about the inner life of God."

## Preaching

The preaching (not writing) of the Apostles comes next in the *Constitution*, in its second chapter, which is entitled "The Transmission of Divine Revelation." It begins, "God graciously arranged that what he had once revealed for the salvation of all peoples should last for ever in its entirety, and be transmitted to all generations. Therefore, Christ the Lord, in whom the entire revelation of the most high God is summed up (see *2 Corinthians 1:20, 3:16—4:16*), having fulfilled in his own person and promulgated with his own lips the Gospel promised beforehand by the prophets, commanded the apostles to preach it to everyone as the source of all saving truth and moral law . . ." (#7).

## Scripture

In explaining the transmission of divine revelation and after noting the primacy of preaching, the *Constitution* now describes the Apostles "handing on" the message of Christian faith. It mentions three methods: In preaching the gospel, the Apostles were to communicate the gifts of God to all men. "This was faithfully done: it was done by the apostles who handed on, by oral preaching, by their example, by their dispositions, what they themselves had received . . ."

"Tradition" in the New Testament and in theological use in the Catholic Tradition is rooted in the way the teachings of the rabbis were handed on from one generation to the next. It was an "oral tradition." The apostolic Church communicated its faith in this same way, so familiar in Judaism. For the Church, as for the Apostles in the beginning, the object of tradition is Christian belief.

The *Constitution*, after mentioning the preaching, the example, and the "institutions" of the Apostles, says, "it was done by those apostles and others associated with them who, under the inspiration of the same holy Spirit, committed the message of salvation to writing."

The term "Scripture"—finally—is used specifically, in this great context of Revelation, Word, Christ, and preaching. This paragraph (#7) ends with a mention of a "living" (not written) Gospel and "Scripture." "In order that the full and living Gospel might always be preserved in the church the apostles left bishops as their successors. They gave them 'their own position of teaching authority' (Saint Irenaeus). This sacred tradition, then, and the sacred scripture of both Testaments, are like a mirror, in which the church, during its pilgrim journey here on earth, contemplates God, from whom [she] receives everything, until such time as [she] is brought to see him face to face as he really is (see *John 3:2*)."

The next paragraph (#8) gives a kind of definition and context to the relationship of tradition and "Scripture": "Thus, the apostolic preaching, which is expressed in a special way in the inspired books, was to be preserved in a continuous line of succession until the end of time."

## The Book of Revelation

The last book of the Bible used to be called the Apocalypse. That's not the term used anymore for the Book of Revelation, but it could be. It could, in fact, be used for the whole Bible: The Book of Apocalypse. The word means "revelation" ("to reveal" when it's serving as a verb in Greek).

• "Unveiling" is what *apokalypsis* means, and is usually translated as "revelation."

• It is the first word of the last book of the Bible: "*Apokalypsis* of Jesus Christ . . ."

• It is sometimes confused with the word *apocrypha*, and *apocryphal*, but it is not even related, except for the *apo-* part.

## The Five Stages of Revelation Outlined in the *Catechism*
### 1. From the very beginning
God invited Adam and Eve to intimate communion, clothing them with "grace and justice" (54).

### 2. The covenant with Noah
God determined to restore humanity after the fall, a covenant that "remains in force during the times of the Gentiles, until the universal proclamation of the Gospel"[2] (58).

### 3. The call of Abraham
The descendants of this Chaldean, the Chosen People, would be "trustees of the promise made to the patriarchs" (60).

### 4. The formation of Israel
The people freed from slavery in Egypt were bound in a covenant of Mt. Sinai through Moses.

### 5. The Incarnation of the Son of God
The Christ, "the Father's one, perfect, and unsurpassable Word" (65), is God's ultimate choice for self-disclosure. God is "summed up" [3] (75) in Christ.

# Word

## What's the Good Word?

The author Rudyard Kipling (born, 1865) was at the height of his popularity during the late 19th century. Some students at Cambridge University read that he was being paid a shilling per word for his writing. That was a lot of money for an author to earn in those days, even for one as famous and widely read as Kipling. As a prank, the students sent him a shilling along with a request for one word. To their surprise, Kipling responded. His reply? "Thanks."

## Word

"Word" has many meanings.

1. A sound that has meaning ("Huh?")
2. A message ("Any word about dad?")
3. A promise ("I give you my word.")
4. The Bible, the message of the Gospel ("The word of the Lord")
5. Jesus Christ, the Word (*logos*, in Greek) of God ("The Word was made flesh")

## The Word of God

1. In theology generally, "word of God" is an expression for "revelation."
2. In the biblical tradition, "word of God" was first applied to prophecy and later to the Law as communication from God.
3. In the New Testament, "word of God" sometimes refers to Jewish Scripture: "You have nullified the word of God for . . . your tradition" (*Matthew 15:6*).
4. In the New Testament, "word of God" also refers specifically to the Gospel message of salvation through Jesus.
   - "The sower sows the word." (*Mark 4:14* and parallels, Jesus' own use)
   - "Be eager to present yourself as acceptable to God, a work-man who causes no disgrace, imparting the word of truth without deviation." (*2 Timothy 2:15*)
   - Some Jews receive "the word" and examine "the Scriptures"

to "determine whether these things were so." (*Acts 17:11*)

5. In the New Testament, "word of God" also refers to Jesus, the divine Word incarnate (before there was a sound, before there was a message, before there was a Bible). In its first use of the term "Word," the *Catechism* is referring to Christ (*CCC, 53*).
   - "In the beginning was the Word, / and the Word was with God, / and the Word was God. / . . .And the Word became flesh / and made his dwelling among us . . ." (*John 1:1, 14*).
   - In *Hebrews 4:12* also, "the word" refers to the person of Jesus, "Indeed, the word of God is living and effective, sharper than any two-edged sword. . . ."
6. In Catholic faith and liturgy, "word of God" also refers to Sacred Scripture.
   - "Through all the words of Sacred Scripture, God speaks only one single Word, his one Utterance in whom he expresses himself completely [Cf. Heb.]" (*CCC, 102*).
   - "You recall that one and the same Word of God extends throughout Scripture, that it is one and the same Utterance that resounds in the mouths of all the sacred writers, since he who was in the beginning God with God has no need of separate syllables; for he is not

subject to time[4]" (Saint Augustine, quoted in *CCC*, 102).

- "The Word of the Lord" is the lector's statement after each of the first two Scripture readings at Mass.

7. In Christian history, "word of God" is a popular and pious synonym for the Bible.
   - The Catholic Church is careful about the distinction between Christ "the Word of God" and Scripture "the word of God": "[T]he Christian faith is not a 'religion of the book.'[5] Christianity is the religion of the 'Word' of God, . . . 'not a written and mute word, but . . . incarnate and living.' If the Scriptures are not to remain a dead letter, Christ, the eternal Word of the living God, must, through the Holy Spirit, 'open [our] minds to understand the Scriptures' (compare *Luke 24:45*)" (*CCC*, 108).

   - Scripture as the word of God in the words of people is God's gift in the Judeo-Christian tradition, a unique revelation in preserved written form. As explained below, this unique word of God is recorded in the words of people. This is the Catholic understanding that gives due regard to the human element. The word of God has become a journal (a library, in fact) of God's relationship with Israel and with the early Church.

# The Transmission of Divine Revelation

This is the name of the second chapter of Vatican II's *Constitution on Divine Revelation* and these are its opening words: "In His gracious goodness, God has seen to it that what He had revealed for the salvation of all nations would abide perpetually in its full integrity and be handed on to all generations."

## The Responsibility of the Church

The "sacred deposit" of the faith, contained in Sacred Scripture and Tradition, is entrusted to the whole of the Church (*CCC*, 84), which never ceases its response.

1. Welcoming it
2. Penetrating it more deeply
3. Living it more fully
4. Handing it on

## "What I First Received"

What is handed on—"transmitted" —must first be received, as Saint Paul says, "For I handed on to you as of first importance what I also received . . ." In this passage (*1 Corinthians 15:3*), Paul is describing his own experience as well as the Apostles' experience. Specifically, the *Catechism* explains the three ways the Apostles received the message.

1. From Christ's lips
2. From Christ's works and way of life
3. At the prompting of the Holy Spirit

## "I Handed on to You."

In 1 Corinthians 15:3, Paul speaks of handing on what he had first received. Vatican II begins its chapter on the transmission of revelation (with paragraph #7) with the words quoted above, and then cites 2 Corinthians 3:16—4:6. That passage ends, "For God who said, 'Let light shine out of darkness,' has shone in our hearts to bring to light the knowledge of the glory of God on the face of Jesus Christ." The *Catechism* explains (76–79) the two-fold way this happened:

1. In the apostolic preaching
   - In the spoken word—"by the spoken word of the apostles' preaching, by the example given by the apostles, and by the institutions established by the apostles"—*Dei Verbum* #7.
   - In the written word—"by those apostles inspired by the Holy Spirit and by others associated with the apostles inspired by the Spirit"—*Dei Verbum* #7.

2. In the apostolic succession— "God, who spoke in the past, continues to converse with the Spouse of his beloved Son[6]" (*CCC*, 79):
   - "the full and living gospel[7]" (77), a "living transmission" (78)
   - because the Gospel was not for one generation only, but is for all
   - so the Gospel might always be preserved in the Church

### Apostolic Church Preaching

There are eight "kerygmatic" sermons in the Acts of the Apostles. In 1 Corinthians 15:1-11 Paul wrote of Christ's Resurrection as the core of the message and called it "the preaching" and "the proclamation" (in Hebrew, *kerygma*). Of these sermons in Acts, the first six are directed toward Jews, the last three to the Gentiles. The first five are by Peter, the last three by Paul. (The Scripture citations are all from the Acts of the Apostles.)

1. On the day of Pentecost–*2:14-36*
2. After the cure, with John, of a cripple–*3:12-26*
3. The next day before the sanhedrin after a night in jail with John–*4:8-12*
4. At a second trial after another night in jail–*5:29-32*
5. In Caesarea, after a vision, leading to Cornelius' baptism–*10:34-43*
6. On a mission of Barnabas and Paul, at an Antioch synagogue–*13:16-41*
7. After a cure, acclamation in Lystra, "Gods have come to us . . ."–*14:15-17*
8. In the Athens Areopagus, referring to "A God Unknown"–*17:22-31*

## The Two Distinct Modes of Transmission

These two modes described below are not in order of priority but occurrence: ". . . Tradition . . . comes from the apostles and hands on what they received from Jesus' teaching and example and what they learned from the Holy Spirit. The first generation of Christians did not yet have a written New Testament, and the New Testament itself demonstrates the process of living Tradition" (CCC, 83).

### Tradition

"*Tradition* transmits in its entirety the Word of God which has been entrusted to the apostles by Christ the Lord and the Holy Spirit. It transmits it to the successors of the apostles so that, enlightened by the Spirit of truth, they may faithfully preserve, expound, and spread it abroad by their preaching" (*Dei Verbum* #9). Together with Sacred Scripture, it forms the word of God (CCC, 81).

### Scripture

Sacred Scripture, a "special expression" of the apostolic preaching, is "the speech of God as it is put down in writing under the breath of the Holy Spirit" (*Dei Verbum* #9). Together with Tradition, it forms the word of God (CCC, 81).

"As a result the Church, to whom the transmission and interpretation of Revelation is entrusted, 'does not derive her certainty about all revealed truths from the holy Scriptures alone. Both Scripture and Tradition must be accepted and honored with equal sentiments of devotion and reverence'" (CCC, 82, quoting *Dei Verbum* #9).

## Tradition

In English, "tradition" is a noun. It means something handed on or handed down.

When Saint Paul said, "For I handed on to you as of first importance what I also received . . ." (*1 Corinthians 15:3*), he used a verb (*tradidi* in Latin) from which the English noun "tradition" evolved.

- Saint Paul calls the Gospel something handed on ("the tradition"): "Now I am reminding you, brothers, of the gospel I preached to you, which you indeed received and in which you also stand. Through it you are also being saved, if you hold fast to the word I preached to you, unless you believed in vain" (*1 Corinthians 15:1–2*).

- Saint Paul then proceeds to recall the tradition itself: "For I handed on to you as of first importance what I also received: that Christ died for our sins in accordance with the Scriptures; that he was buried; that he was raised on the third day in accordance with the Scriptures; that he appeared to Cephas, then to the Twelve" (*1 Corinthians 15:3–5*).

- This basic Gospel message is the common ground and foundation on which Saint Paul then builds his teaching on the truth of the Resurrection of Christ and the

## Tradition

*"Even if the apostles had not left their Scriptures to us"*

Saint Irenaeus of Lyons, a major figure of the early Church, was an early third-century pastor, missionary, and heroic writer in defense of the Church. Born about the year AD 130, he was a disciple of Saint Polycarp who was in turn a disciple of Saint John the Evangelist. This is what he wrote about the importance of the tradition of the Apostles:

*"Since there are so many clear testimonies, we should not seek from others for the truth which can easily be received from the Church. [It was] there, [in the Church, that] the apostles, like a rich man making a deposit, fully bestowed everything that belongs to the truth. . . . She is the entrance to life; all the others are thieves and robbers.*[5] *Therefore we ought to avoid them, but to love with the greatest zeal the things of the Church, and so to lay hold of the tradition of the truth. What if there should be a dispute about some matter of moderate importance? Should we not turn to the oldest churches, where the apostles themselves were known, and find out from them the clear and certain answer to the problem now being raised? Even if the apostles had not left their Writings to us, ought we not to follow the rule of the tradition which they handed down to those to whom they committed the Churches?*

*Many barbarian peoples who believe in Christ follow this rule, having [the message of their] salvation written in their hearts by the Spirit without paper and ink. Diligently following the old tradition, they believe in one God, maker of heaven and earth and of all that is in them, through Christ Jesus the Son of God, who on account of his abundant love for his creation submitted to be born of a virgin, himself by himself uniting man to God, and having suffered under Pontius Pilate, and risen, and having been received up into splendor, is to come in glory as the Savior of those who are saved, and the judge of those who are judged, and will send into eternal fire those who alter the truth, and despise his Father and his coming. Those who believe in this faith without written documents are barbarians in our speech, but in their convictions, habits, and behavior they are, because of their faith, most wise, and are pleasing to God, living in all righteousness and purity and wisdom."*

nature of bodily resurrection (see *1 Corinthians 15:12–58*).

- At other times the Gospel is known as the "deposit of faith" and the *kerygma* (message). A revised NAB footnote calls it the "fundamental content of all Christian preaching and belief."

### The Basic Gospel Message

Paul's description of the heart of the Tradition, the "gospel" (*1 Cor-inthians 15:1*), is not his own but is taken from primitive expressions of the fundamental Christian Creed.

1. Jesus' death for our sins (confirmed by his burial)
2. Jesus' Resurrection (confirmed by his appearances)
3. The fulfillment of prophecy ("In accordance with the Scriptures")

### Primitive Expressions

Apostolic Church hymns and

## Coming to Terms

One of the distinguishing marks of the Church is its possession of truth.

### 1. Mystery of the Faith

This phrase (in the Greek original: *musterion tas pisteos*; in Latin translation: *mysterium fidei*) is used in 1 Timothy 3:9 (see also 1 Timothy 4:1). It is also used in the liturgy, following the consecration, "Let us proclaim the mystery of faith," to which there are four optional responses:

–"Christ has died. Christ is risen. Christ will come again."

–"Dying you destroyed our death, rising you restored our life. Lord Jesus, come in glory."

–"When we eat this bread and drink this cup, we proclaim your death, Lord Jesus, until you come in glory."

–"Lord, by your cross and resurrection you have set us free. You are the Savior of the world."

### 2. Truth

Soon after speaking of "the mystery of the faith," 1 Timothy 3:15 refers to the Church as the "pillar and foundation of truth," the Greek word *alatheias* (*veritatis* in the Latin translation) referring to the essence of God's revealed truth in Christ.

### 3. Mystery of Devotion

In the next phrase (3:16), 1 Timothy uses a slightly different wording, *eusebeias musterion* (*pietatis sacramentum* in the Latin translation). The Latin word *pietatis* is transliterated "piety." Translations vary slightly: "the mystery of devotion" (NAB, revised); "the mystery of faith" (NAB, 1970); "the mystery of our religion" (NRSV and CEV); "the mystery of godliness" (NKJV and NIV).

creedal statements can be gleaned from the New Testament.

1. The full hymns in the Pauline letters are used regularly in the Liturgy of the Hours:
   - Philippians 2:6–11 (used during Evening Prayer I of Sunday)
   - Ephesians 1:3–10 (used during Evening Prayer of Monday)
   - Colossians 1:12–20 (used during Evening Prayer of Wednesday)

2. There are many fragments of hymns and confessions of faith, especially in the Pastoral Epistles. The following are examples.
   - "He was revealed in flesh,/ vindicated in spirit,/ seen by angels,/ proclaimed among Gentiles,/ believed in throughout the world,/ taken up in glory." (*1 Timothy 3:16*)
   - "If we have died with him, we will also live with him;/ if we endure, we will also reign with him;/ if we deny him, he will also deny us;/ if we are faithless,/ he remains faithful—/ for he cannot deny himself." (*2 Timothy 2:11–13*)

## A Sacred Tripod

The *Catechism* speaks of the following aspects of the Catholic faith as foundational and as so related that "one cannot stand without the others" (95).

**1.** Sacred Tradition
**2.** Sacred Scripture
**3.** The magisterium of the Church ("Magisterium," which is discussed in more detail in Chapter 4 of this book, is the Latin term for what the *Constitution on Divine Revelation* calls the "living, teaching office of the Church," 10.)

## Properties of the Sacred Tripod
(See *CCC*, 95.)

**1.** They connect and associate "in the supremely wise arrangement of God."
**2.** They collaborate because of the action of the Holy Spirit.
**3.** They contribute effectively to the salvation of souls.

# Inspiration

## "The Divine Inspiration and the Interpretation of Sacred Scripture"

This heading is the title of Chapter 3 of the *Constitution on Divine Revelation*. The first sentence of the first paragraph reads, "Those things revealed by God which are contained and presented in the text of sacred scripture have been written under the inspiration of the holy Spirit" (11).

## Inspiration

This word has a specific meaning in the context of Scripture. (About inspiration in a secular context, the American composer Aaron Copland said, "Inspiration may be a form of super-consciousness, or perhaps of sub-consciousness. I wouldn't know. But I am sure it is the antithesis of self-consciousness.")

**1.** Inspiration literally means "to breathe into."
**2.** Inspiration commonly means to motivate.
**3.** Inspiration theologically means "to communicate or suggest by a divine influence." In its formal teaching documents, the Catholic Church doesn't attempt to explain how inspiration happens (except to say that biblical authors are real authors).

## What the Scriptures Say

The first two passages below are the classic texts quoted most often.

### 2 Timothy 3:14-17

"But as for you, continue in what you have learned and firmly believed, knowing from whom you learned it, and how from childhood you have known the sacred writings that are able to instruct you for salvation through faith in Christ Jesus. All scripture is inspired by God and is useful for teaching, for reproof, for correction, and for training in righteousness, so that everyone who belongs to God may be proficient, equipped for every good work."

### 2 Peter 1:20

"First of all you must understand this, that no prophecy of scripture is a matter of one's own interpretation, because no prophecy ever came by human will, but men and women moved by the Holy Spirit spoke from God."

### 1 Thessalonians 2:13

"We also constantly give thanks to God for this, that when you received the word of God that you heard from us, you accepted it not as a human word but as what it really is, God's word, which is also at work in you believers."

### 2 Peter 3:15-16

"[A]nd regard the patience of our Lord as salvation. So also our beloved brother Paul wrote to you according to the wisdom given him, speaking of this as he does in all his letters. There are some things in them hard to understand, which the ignorant and unstable twist to their own destruction, as they do the other scriptures."

### John 20:30-31

"Now Jesus did many other signs in the presence of his disciples, which are not written in this book. But these are written that you may come to believe that Jesus is the Messiah, the Son of God, and that through believing you may have life in his name."

## What the *Catechism* Says

1. Scripture is the word of God in human language. "*Sacred Scripture* is the speech of God as it is put down in writing under the breath of the Holy Spirit" (*CCC* 81, quoting the *Constitution on Divine Revelation*, #9).

2. God is the principal author. "The divinely revealed realities, which are contained and presented in the text of Sacred Scripture, have been written down under the inspiration of the Holy Spirit" (*CCC* 105, quoting the *Constitution on Divine Revelation*, #11).

3. The human writers are true authors. The human collaborators "made full use of their own faculties and powers so that, though [God] acted in them and by them, it was as true authors that they consigned to writing whatever [God] wanted written, and no more" (*CCC* 106, quoting the *Constitution on Divine Revelation*, #11).

## Rejected Theories of Inspiration

Inspiration has sometimes been explained in ways the Catholic Church rejects as being not only inaccurate but also unworthy of God and unworthy of the human authors.

### Divine dictation (literalist approach)

- This theory makes God alone responsible, as an executive dictating a letter, and relegates the human authors to being mere recorders or writers as if in a trance, unconscious of what they were writing.

- It does not account for God's respect for human freedom or for the clear variety of styles and purposes for writing in the various books of the Bible. See for example *Luke 1:1–3*: "Since many have undertaken to compile a narrative of the events that have been fulfilled among us, just as those who were eyewitnesses from the beginning and ministers of the word have handed them down to us, I too have decided, after investigating everything accurately anew, to write it down in an orderly sequence for you. . . ."

- This theory minimizes the human role (typical in literalist traditions) in order to reinforce Scripture's lack of error and fullness of knowledge, including historical and scientific. In a 1993 statement, "The Interpretation of the Bible in the Church," the Pontifical Biblical Commission said that, because the literalist approach does not allow for the possibility that God would work in history and through human authors, "it makes itself incapable of accepting the full truth of the incarnation itself. As regards relationships with God, fundamentalism seeks to escape any closeness of the divine and the human." (For more on fundamentalism, see Chapter 4.)

**Negative assistance**
- This theory portrays God in a passive role, intervening only to protect the writing from error.
- It exaggerates the human authors' role.

**Subsequent approbation**
- According to this theory, God only approves the final work (like

granting an imprimatur after the fact).

- This theory redefines the whole concept of inspiration and does not account for Jeremiah's experience, for example, of the word "within me there is something like a burning fire" (*Jeremiah 20:9*).

- It also exaggerates the human authors' role.

### Effects of Inspiration

## Scripture Is Revelation
See the copy under The Transmission of Divine Revelation, earlier in this chapter.)

## Scripture Is Unified
Scripture, though composed over the course of more than one thousand years, has a unity (because of its divine author) that transcends its diversity (because of its human authors).

- **Diversity**
A wide variety of human authors described God and God's activity in history, all from their own communities' experience of God.

- **Independence**
There is no indication in Scripture itself that the authors of Amos or Hosea, for example, knew what the other was saying, even though they were prophesying at generally the same time.

- **Development**
Within Scripture's unity there is not only diversity among authors'

styles and viewpoints, but also development in understanding of God and truths God has revealed. In the words of the *Letter to the Hebrews (1:1–2)*: "Long ago God spoke to our ancestors in many and various ways by the prophets, but in these last days he has spoken to us by a Son, whom he appointed heir of all things, through whom he also created the worlds."

There are many, many examples of biblical authors citing Scripture itself. Some of these citations are direct quotations; in other cases, biblical authors are interpreting or reinterpreting earlier Scripture to understand and explain their own situation. In *1 Corinthians 2:9*, for example, when Saint Paul writes, "But, as it is written, 'What no eye has seen, nor ear heard,/ nor the human heart conceived,/ what God has prepared for those who love him'—/ these things God has revealed to us through the Spirit; . . ." he is citing Isaiah 64:3. Saint Paul is here describing the basis of faith as true wisdom (not human wisdom but the power of God). The verse in Isaiah actually says, "no ear has perceived, no eye has seen any God besides you,/ who works for those who wait for him." This is from a prayer that probably originated at the end of the Jewish exile (587–537 BC) and included recollections of God's favor in Israel's history, especially in the exodus.

There is an especially vivid example of one author interpreting another in the account in Matthew

2:16–18 called "the slaughter of the innocents." The author includes a poignant verse about Rachel's tears from Jeremiah 31:15, a passage that was interpreting in a new situation Genesis 35:16–20 in which Rachel grieved not the death of her son but her own death in birthing him (see Chapter 7 in this book).

Bibles with cross-references reveal this richness in Scripture's unity and enable the reader to experience it. (For more on the development in biblical authors' understanding, see the examples treated in Chapter 4 in the section "Historical-Cultural Context:" slavery, polygamy, and the afterlife.)

## Scripture Is Complete

Although the canon is "closed" (see Chapter 2) and revelation is "complete," understanding is continuing.

- God's definitive self-revelation was complete when the final graced oral interpretation was put in writing. To say Scripture is "complete" means that it includes all that God chose to reveal of the divine nature and plan in this inspired form. In the words of Vatican II's *Constitution on Divine Revelation*,[4] "The christian dispensation, therefore, since it is the new and definitive covenant, will never pass away; and no new public revelation is to be expected before the glorious manifestation of our Lord, Jesus Christ (see 1 Timothy 6:14 and Titus 2:13)."

- God's self-revelation continues in this world even after the composition of Scripture is complete. This is not new revelation but a deeper understanding of what Jesus taught and the Apostles proclaimed. "The full and living gospel" of tradition is the language used by the Church in explaining the "living transmission" of revelation in the apostolic succession (see Vatican II's *Constitution on Divine Revelation* 7 and *CCC*, 77 and 78).

- About this tension between complete revelation and continuing revelation, Fr. Eugene Maly writes in an article in *The New American Bible*, "We do not live in, and cannot recapture, the biblical period. That period had its own history, its social and cultural and political background that is now gone. We live in a new period, a new time and history where the *biblical* God must be seen in a new light, against a completely different background. It is in and through Tradition that the biblical God lets himself be constantly revealed anew. And yet, always, it is the same biblical God, which is why we say the Bible is complete" (NAB, p. ix).

## Scripture Is Effective

In Scripture, a person's word unfailingly moves from one heart to another, cannot be retracted (as Isaac's word to Jacob instead of Esau), and brings about what it says. Reading or hearing Scripture is effective in a way that is comparable to the seven sacraments, which are encounters with God in Christ. There are two Scriptures that speak especially eloquently of the effective power of God's word.

- "For as the rain and the snow come down from heaven,/ and do not return thee until they have watered the earth,/ making it bring forth and sprout,/ giving seed to the sower and bread to the eater,/ so shall my word be that goes out from my mouth;/ it shall not return to me empty,/ but it shall accomplish that which I purpose,/ and succeed in the thing for which I sent it" (*Isaiah 55:10–11*).

- "Indeed, the word of God is living and active, sharper than any two-edged sword, piercing until it divides soul from spirit, joints from marrow; it is able to judge the thoughts and intentions of the heart" (*Hebrews 4:12*).

## Scripture Is True

Inerrancy ("without error") means that the inspired books teach the truth. "Since, therefore, all that the inspired authors, or sacred writers, affirm should be regarded as affirmed by the holy Spirit, we must acknowledge that the books of scripture, firmly, faithfully and without error, teach that truth which God, for the sake of our salvation, wished to see confided to the sacred scriptures" (*Constitution on Divine Revelation*, 11).

- The Catholic tradition easily recognizes the scientific limitations and appreciates the poetic license of the human author in passages like this one from "Joshua's Victory" (*Joshua 10:12–14*): "On the day when the LORD gave the Amorites over to the Israelites, Joshua spoke to the LORD; and he said in the sight of Israel, 'Sun, stand still at Gibeon, / and Moon, in the valley of Aijalon." / And the sun stood still, and the moon stopped, / until the nation took vengeance on their enemies. / Is this not written in the Book of Jashar? The sun stopped in mid-heaven, and did not hurry to set for about a whole day. There has been no day like it before or since, when the LORD heeded a human voice; for the LORD fought for Israel."

- Even unstudied readers in the Catholic tradition understand the principles of "biblical criticism" which are recognized in the *Catechism*: "[T]ruth is differently presented and expressed in the various types of historical writing, in prophetical and poetical texts, and in other forms of literary expression [9]" (*CCC*, 110). See "Interpreting" and "Criticizing" in Chapter 4 of this book.

- The words "true" and "factual" are not synonymous. The truth of a fictional work, like a parable of Christ, can be more reliable than fact. It's what's called the moral of the story. "Truth" pertains to the larger questions of life and its meaning: "Why are we here?" "Why do we suffer?" "What is our destiny?" "What does God wish for our happiness?" "Fact" pertains to things of life that are measurable and observable. An event described in Scripture that reveals the place of God in life is no less dependable because it includes inaccurate scientific or historical elements, whether the human author includes this intentionally or not. According to divine plan, God provided a living tradition and a teaching office (magisterium) along with Scripture, three parts of one whole so related, as a "sacred tripod," that "one of them cannot stand without the others [10]" (*CCC*, 95).

# The Authority of Scripture

The truth of Scripture leads to claims about its authority and to applications of that authority that differ with and even contradict another application. In reference to a certain topic that was contentious in American history, Stephen A. Marini wrote in *The Oxford Companion to the Bible* that the Bible would never completely recover its authoritative stature in American discourse again. What was the event, the issue, after which the Bible would never recover its authority? Slavery. This "failing" of scriptural authority occurred in the eyes of Christian faith communities that do not give priority of place to Tradition and the magisterium.

## Slavery in the Scriptures

There is much "casual" reference to slavery in Scripture and a seeming neutrality and tolerance about it. This is especially troubling for Christian groups that remove Scripture from its context in the faith community, making it stand on its own (the so-called *Sola Scriptura*, Scripture Alone, position). In the faith community, Scripture stands with the "living tradition" and a teaching office for authoritative interpretation. In Scripture Alone, there is a striking absence of a critique of the morality of slavery.

That is troublesome for the Scripture Alone position, in which there is no faith community context for it ("tradition") and no magisterium for authoritative interpretation. This is especially difficult for a fundamentalist position, suspicious of "biblical criticism" (see Chapter 4).

### The Old Testament

There are passages, for example, that define and regulate the treatment of slaves (see *Exodus 21:1–11, Leviticus 25:39–55, Deuteronomy 15:12–18*).

### The New Testament Letters

There is often advice about the conduct of masters and slaves (see *Ephesians 6:5–9; Colossians 3:22 — 4:1; 1 Timothy 6:1–2; Titus 2:9–10; 1 Peter 2:18–19;* and *Philemon 16–17*, a letter about Saint Paul sending the runaway slave, Onesimus, back to his owner, Philemon).

### The Gospel

There are events and teachings recorded that reveal the presence of slaves and the institution of slavery (see *Luke 7:1–10, 12:37–46; Matthew 24:45–51, 25:14–30, 26:51*).

## Slavery in New Spain

Slavery in the New World caused one of the great Scripture controversies of early modern times within and among Protestant traditions. ("New Spain" refers here to the former Spanish possessions in the Western Hemisphere, including South America, except Brazil; Central America; Mexico; the West Indies; Florida; and most of the land in what is today the United States west of the Mississippi River.)

To justify the labor slavery imposed on the natives of New Spain, Spanish government spokesmen cited three passages of Scripture to justify themselves:

- Deuteronomy 20 (the conquest of Canaan)

- Genesis 18:16—19:29 (the destruction of Sodom)

- Matthew 22:1–14 (Jesus' parable of the wedding feast)

Forces on the other side, notably the Dominican missionary and bishop of Chiapas in Mexico, Bartolome de Las Casas (1474–1566), condemned the practice as unjust and rejected a scriptural justification by explaining that those passages were historically conditioned and transcended by the teaching of Jesus.

## Slavery in the United States

In the United States between the early 1700s and the Civil War, Scripture was used by both the "pro-choice" position (the choice of the owners, that is) and the abolitionists.

In the colonies' early life, slavery supporters sought scriptural authority in the following:

• Africans depicted as bearers of the mark of Cain (see *Genesis 4:10–15*)

• Africans depicted as children of Ham, cursed by Noah to be the "lowest of slaves" (see *Genesis 9:25*)

In the 1730s British and American evangelicals began a serious scriptural critique of the slavery that had prevailed unchallenged. Founders of Methodism labeled slavery a grave sin that was incompatible with their theology:

• about spiritual rebirth (see *John 3:1–8*)

• about sanctification (see *Matthew 5:48*)

• about evangelism (see *Mark 16:15*)

During the era of the Revolution, evangelical Calvinists joined the anti-slavery movement of the Methodists. Congregationalists, Presbyterians, and Baptists brought the vision of the United States' new covenant with God as a new chosen people. More Scripture was invoked:

• about the prophets' vision of justice and mercy (see *Isaiah 1:16–18,*

*33:15–16, 58:6; Jeremiah 7:1–7, 22:3–5; Amos 5:24*)

• about the prophets' word of judgment (see *Jeremiah 21:12, Ezekiel 22:29–31, Amos 2:6, Zechariah 7:9–12*).

During that same period, the Society of Friends (Quakers) increased the resistance to slavery with their interpretation of Scripture:

• Jesus' warnings against materialism and greed (see *Matthew 6:19*)

• Jesus' condemnation of the neglect of the poor and strangers (see *Matthew 25:44*)

The slavery position, however, persisted as Church members continued to appeal to Scripture that supported slavery, especially as southern cotton plantations thrived in the 1820s. Armed with scores of still more Scripture verses, preachers of the Book made bold proclamations:

• God sanctioned slavery through Noah, Abraham, and Joseph (see *Genesis 9:25–27, 14:14, 16:9, 17:12–13, 24:35–36, 26:13–14, 47:14–25*).

• Slavery was "incorporated" in the Law of Moses (see *Exodus 20:17, 20–21, 21:2–4; Leviticus 25:39–46*).

• Jesus and the Apostles recognized slavery as a "lawful institution among men" (*2 Corinthians 11:20, Ephesians 6:5, Colossians 3:22*).

Evangelical abolitionists countered evangelicals on the slaveholder side in a pitched battle of verse versus verse. There were new arguments, all "proven" scripturally:

- Slavery in the Bible was different from slavery on the plantations so could not be used for support.
- Paul's position in the context of his day could not be used to authorize a similar position in a new context.

Blacks themselves, slave and free, brought their own vision of evangelical Christianity, cast in terms of Israel in Egypt, exodus, and freedom. As slave owners used Scripture to keep slaves in their place, preachers and storytellers arose among slave communities who told the stories of Moses' escape from Egypt and God's protection of the Hebrew peoples as he led them to the promised land. Preachers and participants who were caught were punished and even killed, but the message lived.

## Conclusions

A new era for Scripture interpretation arose in the Protestant traditions of the United States.

In the United States the question of slavery divided some Protestant denominations— including Baptists and Methodists—into northern and southern parts. Such sectarian disunity culminated in the Civil War. One of the by-products of the dispute over slavery was its demonstration that without the guidance of the Church's magisterium, the Bible could be used to argue against itself. As Stephen A. Marini's "Slavery and the Bible" article from *The Oxford Companion to the Bible* points out, the Bible would never completely recover its authoritative stature in American discourse again.

A reminder about Scripture interpretation in the Catholic Tradition on the question of slavery: "Allusions to slavery in the Gospels are casual and describe the inferior position of slaves. . . . Those who are dissatisfied with this neutrality fail to observe the true character of Christian social reform, which is very well illustrated in slavery. The New Testament does not attack the institution directly, but attacks the principle of inequality on which chattel slavery was based. . . . The principles of Christian love and unity made it impossible for the Christian to regard another man as a chattel, and thus made slavery impracticable. Historically, Christianity has been the only effective destroyer of slavery" (John McKenzie, S.J., *Dictionary of the Bible*, 1965, p. 825). Note: *Christianity* was the destroyer, not the Bible.

# 2

# Words of People

## Sacred
## Scripture

Sacred Scripture, the word of God written under the inspiration of the Holy Spirit, has the preeminent position in the life of the Catholic Church and especially in the ministry of evangelization and catechesis. . . . Through all the ages of the Church, the study of Sacred Scripture has been the cornerstone of catechesis. . . . Sacred Scripture . . . strengthens faith, nourishes the soul, and nurtures the spiritual life.

—*National Directory for Catechesis*, p. 70

## Bearers of the Torah

During World War II, the Germans established a work camp in the town of Yanov in Poland. Yanov later became a concentration camp; but during the period that it was a work camp, prisoners were occasionally allowed to leave the camp, provided a family member was left behind to insure the prisoners' return.

While on pass, a group of devout Jews decided to smuggle a Torah into camp. They dismantled the Torah piece by piece, hiding parts of it in their bodies and clothing and returned to camp. The exact whereabouts of the various hiding places were handed down by word of mouth. God's Word lived among the persecuted but persevering community, its beloved Torah whole in spirit if physically divided into pieces.

When the camp was finally liberated, the precious fragments of the Torah were pieced back together. Over the years the holy scroll remained with the oldest living survivor of Yanov. The last survivor arranged for it to be taken to America, where it travels from congregation to congregation as an important symbol of hope and courage.

*From Stacey Roberts, Jewish Federation of Greater New Orleans (quoted in* Connections, *2/4/01, 5c).*

# From Word to Words

"Hearing the word of God with reverence and proclaiming it confidently, this most sacred Synod takes its direction from the words of Saint John, who says: 'We proclaim to you the eternal life which was with the Father and was made manifest to us—that which we have seen and heard we proclaim also to you, so that you may have fellowship with us; and our fellowship is with the Father and with his Son Jesus Christ.' (*1 John 1:2–3*)."

That sentence begins Vatican II's *Constitution on Divine Revelation.* "Word of God" (*Dei Verbum* in Latin) is the opening phrase. Hearing that word and proclaiming that word, the Council then quoted the words of a man, Saint John, as its source of "direction." The words of Saint John are from the Bible, the word of God—a word spoken and heard before it was recorded in words written and read.

## The Vatican Council's Document on the Bible

This document, *Dei Verbum*, is "in fact, if not in name, the Second Vatican Council's pronouncement on the Bible. Four of its six chapters (3 to 6) expressly deal with sacred Scripture. Chapters 1 and 2 set the Bible in the context of the whole Christian doctrine of salvation, and in this light explain its origin and its function."

## The Origin of Scripture in Revelation

"The document's main subject is revelation. This is a manifestation by God—primarily, of Himself; secondarily, of His will and intentions—granted to particular men at particular times . . . Revelation by its nature is public. . . . Therefore it has to be made known to others by the testimony of its recipient. Passed on orally, it becomes tradition; recorded in writing, it becomes Scripture."

## The Writing in the Human Heart

The *Catechism of the Catholic Church* uses the image and language of writing to describe the core condition of the human person: "The desire for God is written in the human heart, because man is created by God and for God; and God never ceases to draw man to himself. Only in God will he find the truth and happiness he never stops searching for . . ." (*CCC*, 27).

## The Experience of God

This is all context for understanding Scripture as "the words of humans." Through the design and initiative of God (revelation), a religious awareness emerged in people of the presence and loving kindness and justice of God. A community gradually recognized the revelation of God and began an accurate religious interpretation of life experience as salvation history.

## The Conception and Birth of Scripture

The Bible did not appear all at once, in full maturity, as we know it today. It began with an experience of God who intervened in the world and became involved in its history.

The Jewish people experienced "saving events and significant realities" (*CCC*, 1093). They came to understand, under the influence of grace, that this was an experience of God.

This is the Church's experience too, since she was "prepared in marvelous fashion in the history of the people of Israel and in the Old covenant"[1] (*CCC*, 1093).

# An Oral Tradition

"God graciously arranged that what he had once revealed for the salvation of all peoples should last for ever in its entirety and be transmitted to all generations." So begins Chapter 2 of the *Constitution on Divine Revelation*, "The Transmission of Divine Revelation."

## Remembering the Experience

Moses often exhorted Israel to remember and to hand on their experience: "Take care and be earnestly on your guard not to forget the things which your own eyes have seen, nor let them slip from our memory as long as you live, but teach them to your children and to your children's children"

(*Deuteronomy 4:9*; see also *Deuteronomy 6:20–25, 11:18–21*). In a reminiscence, Moses then reviews the revelation at Horeb that the Israelites should recall and relate to their children (*Deuteronomy 4:10–14*).

1. In remembering, people who were not present participate.
2. In remembering, the unfaithful are recalled to fidelity.
3. In remembering, the full understanding of the experience is realized.

## Endowing the Next Generation

"But it is not with you alone that I am making this covenant, under this sanction of a curse; it is just as much with those who are not here among us today as it is with those of us who are now there present before the Lord, our God" (*Deuteronomy 29:13–14*).

1. Among the people of the exodus and later the nation of Israel and still later the disciples of Christ, experiences of God's intervention were shared and remembered and passed on to the next generation by those who were there.
2. The religious interpretation of life by the people of Moses' day became a living tradition. Stories were repeated, sayings became familiar, commemorations became rituals, insights of one were claimed by others, proverbs and poetry were inspired, narratives were formed and reformed by the telling.

Descendants, endowed with their forebearers' recollections, came to share the historical experience.

## Salvation History

Within human history, Abraham and his descendants, under the influence of the grace of God, discerned salvation history (which can be described as the story of God's personal and saving engagement with humanity and the rest of God's creation, bringing it finally to wholeness and restored relationship to God).

### Themes of salvation history

Under the influence of divine inspiration, Jews, and later Christians, came to interpret their experience of "saving events and significant realities" in terms of certain themes and patterns in their life:

- promise and covenant
- exodus and Passover
- kingdom and temple
- exile and return

### Stages of salvation history

- The lives of the patriarchs
- The saving events of the Exodus
- The history of Israel, the people of God
- The life, death, and Resurrection of Jesus Christ, the Son of God

## The Texture of Scripture

The texture of fabric is something a person can feel through its threads and the weave. So too is the texture of a book felt, especially a book of Scripture. The word "texture" comes from the Latin past participle *textus*, "something woven or constructed," from the verb *textere*, to weave or construct.

The word "text" came to be used, naturally, for passages of Scripture as well as other religious works in which spoken words were used to weave the stories that were, in turn, woven into the large fabric of Scripture. The reader can still feel the unique thread and weave of its various parts.

## The Old Testament Oral Tradition

Psalm 78 illustrates the place of the oral tradition in the Jewish generations of faith: "Give ear, O my people, to my teaching;/ incline your ears to the words of my mouth./ I will open my mouth in a parable;/ I will utter dark sayings from of old,/ things that we have heard and known,/ that our ancestors have told us./ We will not hide them from their children;/ we will tell to the coming generation/ the glorious deeds of the LORD, and his might,/ and the wonders that he has done." (*Psalm 78:1–4*). The psalm continues through its 72 verses to recount God's gracious acts and people's infidelity.

## The New Testament Oral Tradition

In a similar way, centuries later, disciples of Christ remembered and handed on their experience of "the praiseworthy and mighty deeds of the Lord," now including the experience of Christ. Their remembering had the same result it always had in the Jewish tradition.

"Remembering" is the way the New Testament speaks of understanding, after the Resurrection, the true significance of words and events in the life of Christ. The Holy Spirit does not bring new teaching but a true interpretation of what Jesus had taught. Following are three examples.

### After the cleansing of the temple

Jesus said, "Destroy this temple, and in three days I will raise it up" (*John 2:19*). John concludes the episode by saying, "After he was raised from the dead, his disciples remembered that he had said this; and they believed the scripture and the word that Jesus had spoken" (*John 2:22*).

### During Jesus' entry into Jerusalem

"Jesus found a young donkey and sat on it; as it is written: 'Do not be afraid, daughter of Zion./ Look, your king is coming, sitting on a donkey's colt!'" (*John 12:14–15*). John also says, "His disciples did not understand these things at first; but when Jesus was glorified, then they remembered that these things had been written of him and had been done to him." (*John 12:16*).

### During Jesus' last discourse

Jesus said, "I have said these things to you while I am still with you. But the Advocate, the Holy Spirit, whom the Father will send in my name, will teach you everything, and remind you of all that I have said to you." (*John 14:25–26*).

## The Place of Preaching in the Formation of Scripture

"The teachings and the life of Jesus were not simply recounted for the mere purpose of being kept in remembrance, but were 'preached' in such a way as to furnish the Church with the foundation on which to build up faith and morals" (Pontifical Biblical Commission, "Historical Truth of the Gospels" #2, 1964).

### Preaching

In the beginning, preaching had a central place in Christianity. In continuity with Jesus' proclamation, the preaching of Peter and Paul and the others who had been sent was foundational and formative and authoritative for the first Christians. The Christian Church was a Church of the Word for many years before there was a "word of God" (Bible) as we know it.

### Faith sharing

In the first years of the Church (AD 30-50), there is no clear evidence of important Christian writing. The Christian faith was communicated, received, and nurtured by word of mouth (see *Romans 10:14–15*). "Faith comes from what is heard," Saint Paul said in *Romans 10:17*.

### Writings

For approximately the first 100 years, the Sacred Scripture of the early Christians as a whole was that of their Jewish heritage. The term "Old Testament" was not used then, since there was not a clearly established "New Testament" from which to distinguish it. (Jews today, not recognizing Christian Scripture as their inspired text, do not speak of it as a New Testament or of their own Scripture as old.)

## Historical Truth in the Oral Tradition

The Pontifical Biblical Commission, in a 1964 document "Historical Truth of the Gospels," directs the interpreter of Scripture to the three stages of tradition by which the Good News has come down to us (the life and teaching of Jesus, the oral tradition, and the written Gospels) and makes two fundamental points.

1. The Apostles handed on things that were actually said and done by Jesus Christ.
2. The Apostles understood things in a fuller light than when they had first received them.

## Causes of the Apostles' Fuller Understanding

1. They were "schooled by the glorious things accomplished in Christ."
2. They were illumined by the Spirit of Truth.

## Interpretation in the Oral Tradition

1. After his Resurrection, Jesus had "interpreted to them" (*Luke*

24:27) not only words of Scripture (the Old Testament), but also words that he himself had spoken.

2. Likewise, the Apostles, after Pentecost, interpreted the words and deeds of Christ according to their own purposes and the needs of those who heard them.

### Resources of the Oral Tradition

1. There was a variety of material available in various literary forms in the Apostolic Church. As the Apostles carried on their ministry of the word (see *Acts 6:4*), they needed to make full use of this common fund of formulations that included liturgical and catechetical traditions, "obligated" as they were, as Saint Paul said, "to Greeks and barbarians, both to the wise and to the foolish" (*Romans 1:14*).

2. The Catholic Church recognizes the importance of understanding and "criticizing" these resources in the oral tradition that ended up in Scripture: "These varied ways of speaking which the heralds of Christ made use of in proclaiming Him must be distinguished one from the other and carefully appraised: catecheses, narratives, testimonies, hymns, doxologies, prayers and any other such literary forms as were customarily employed in Sacred Scripture and by people of that time" (Pontifical Biblical Commission, "Historical Truth of the Gospels," #2, 1964). The nature and methods of "biblical criticism" are covered in Chapter 4 of this book.

# The Writing of Tradition

In the course of time, some members of the community began to give written form to some of the wide variety of material that had become an oral tradition, so the religious interpretation of one generation could be surely and accurately transmitted for the generations to come. This "Sacred Scripture" became a foundational and formative record of God the Father's self-revelation in the history of Israel and in the life, death, and Resurrection of his Son.

As explained in the pages ahead, writing and editing are not always distinguishable and often merge.

## Scripture's Infancy

The descendants of Abraham were nomads. Their library was within them. There are only fragments of a written literature that can be traced to the period of the Exodus, notably:

- The Song of Miriam in Exodus 15 may date from the Exodus from Egypt around 1300 BC.

- The Song of Deborah in Judges 5 may have been composed shortly before 1100 BC. (Both of these are hymns praising God for victory in battle.)

This process and purpose of writing is sometimes mentioned in the

Scriptures themselves. Before the great Song of Moses, for example, God commanded him, "Now therefore write this song, and teach it to the Israelites; put it in their mouths, in order that this song may be a witness for me against the Israelites. For when I have brought them into the land flowing with milk and honey, which I promised on oath to their ancestors, and they have eaten their fill and grown fat, they will turn to other gods and serve them, despising me and breaking my covenant. And when many terrible troubles come upon them, this song will confront them as a witness, because it will not be lost from the mouths of their descendants. For I know what they are inclined to do even now, before I have brought them into the land that I promised them on oath" (*Deuteronomy 31:19–22*). The poetic sermon of The Song of Moses follows (see *Deuteronomy 32:1–43*). Following the song is his blessing on the tribes and death.

## Authorship

The ancients did not understand authorship the way modern people do. We cannot speak of the authors of scriptural books in the same way we speak of authors of books today.

### In Judeo-Christian History

1. Few of the books in the Bible, especially in the Old Testament, have come to us from the hand of an individual author. Today, most books do. Today, a book "belongs" to its author, but scriptural books are the product and property of the community. We still use terms like "Moses' Pentateuch," "David's Psalms," "Solomon's Song of Songs," and "Isaiah's prophecies," but not in the same literal way we speak of literature today.

2. The identity of a book's author and "copyright protections" were not the concerns then that they are today. Scripture arose from the midst of the community of faith to serve the community of faith. Before an individual became responsible for authoring or editing some part of the word of God, the Word was in the life of God's people.

3. Normally, scriptural books came together and were edited and re-edited over the course of generations (in the case of the Old Testament). It was a long and uneven development that brought various written material together to form what is known today as the Old Testament.

### In Biblical Scholarship

God is the author and the authority behind the Scriptures. The community authorized the Scriptures. Individuals put oral traditions into written form. Other individuals edited written traditions.

## The Authority of Moses

The first five books of the Bible, the Pentateuch, are often called "the books of Moses." In the Bible itself, there are numerous references to "the law of Moses." Jesus used this term.

It appears that, through the course of the history of biblical interpretation, this phrase was sometimes understood in a literal way: that Moses himself wrote those books. However, among the ancients, this phrase was used more broadly than it was used later in history. For them, the Pentateuch was deeply associated with Moses. It has the authority of Moses behind it. Today there is a more careful distinction between someone actually authoring a book and the traditions standing behind a book. The interest for the ancients was the authority of Moses, not authorship in today's terms. The interpretation of authorship in a literal way, anachronistically, by generations far removed, would be foreign to them.

It should pose no problem to the reader of Scripture to learn that many scholars today believe the Pentateuch did not exist in its present condition until approximately 450 BC—nearly 800 years after Moses' death. It should not be confusing to learn that Moses own death is recorded in "the books of Moses" (*Deuteronomy 34:5-12*) or the "Law of Moses" includes laws regarding conditions that did not exist at the time Moses led the people through the desert.

So we still call the Pentateuch "the Books of Moses." Some have little interest in the scholarly work of dating the process through which the Pentateuch came into the form as we know it today. Some are very interested and are greatly served by scholars as their appreciation for the Bible grows and their understanding of God's ways deepens. How could this not serve faith?

### Autograph

An autograph is not just a signature; it also refers to something written by one's own hand. It is an anachronism to apply the term to the Scriptures as if its meaning and significance were the same then as it is now.

### Anonymous

"Unknown name" (*an-* not, without; *-onym*, name). The word is also used to describe something that lacks individuality.

### Pseudonymous (sue-don-eh-mehss)

Literally, a pseudonym is a false or fictitious name. In biblical studies it is used of a work that was written in the name of a famous person like Moses to honor his memory and continue his teaching for a new generation. In the New Testament, for example, 1 Timothy (the First Letter of Paul to Timothy) was written under the pseudonym of Paul. The actual author is unknown, but we can say that he was writing to honor Paul's memory and to relate Paul's teaching to a later generation of Christians.

### Eponymous (eh-pon-eh-mehss)

An eponymous work is named after someone or something. Its root is "name" (as in anonymous and pseudonymous) plus a prefix meaning "upon," "above," or "in addition." An eponym is a person, who could be real or imaginary, from whom something takes its name. Among Scripture scholars, the word pseudonym is commonly used instead, with similar connotations.

## Stages in the Written History of the Old Testament

Over time, the need arose for writing and documentation. Written records were generated by the development of various cultures at the time of the establishment of David's capital in Jerusalem (1000 BC). On the secular side, there was the need to document the economic, legal, and military affairs of the nation. At the same time, and drawing on a growing archive of resources, inspired writing blossomed that ultimately became Sacred Scripture.

1. There was a great emergence of religious poetry and song, if not by the hand of David, certainly with his inspiration.

2. A court history also came from this period, composed by an unknown, gifted composer using the available documents of the kingdom along with his own eyewitness accounts. There are vestiges preserved in 2 Samuel 9—20 and 1 Kings 1—2, telling the story of the passing of the crown from David to Solomon.

3. In this same period, possibly during the reign of Solomon (970–931), an account in writing of Israel's origin and growth as a people emerged. "The Yahwist" is the name given to this tradition. It's not an author's name, it's God's name, "Yahweh," because the account refers to God by this holy name that was revealed to Moses at the burning bush (see *Exodus 3:14–15*). The Yahwist calls God Yahweh even in its version of the creation story. There isn't a particular book authored by the Yahwist.

It is a whole tradition, making up much of the Pentateuch (the first five books of the Bible), that took centuries to develop. The final form of the Pentateuch emerged only after the exile (587–537) in the fifth century before Christ.

### Four Threads, One Fabric

Most scholars agree that there are probably four traditions of written material that became strands woven into the narrative we have today:

- Yahwist, already mentioned

- Elohist (from Elohim, the Hebrew name for God before the revelation to Moses)

- Deuteronomist (from the word "deuteronomy," which also became the name of the last book of the Pentateuch with its emphasis on the reform of the nation's religious law and justice)

- Priestly (from a priestly emphasis on religious ritual, covenants, and genealogy)

**4.** Somewhat later than the Yahwist, the Elohist was also generating a written tradition, but in very different circumstances. It's the ninth century and the Kingdom is now divided. The Elohist tradition comes from the Northern Kingdom and has as a starting point God's covenant with Abraham. In the stories of the patriarchs and Moses, some of the Elohist writing parallels the Yahwist. The two were combined by a later editor at about the same time that two other traditions were forming: Deuteronomist and Priestly.

**5.** At this same time (about the ninth century BC), there were prophets emerging, like musicians who would one day find themselves in one orchestra playing one symphony.

- Elijah and his successor Elisha were rising up, also in the Northern Kingdom ("Israel"), and a prophetic tradition was born.

- In the eighth century, the first so-called "writing prophets" appeared: Amos and Hosea. More properly, they were the first prophets whose oracles were put into written form— finally the books we know today, not necessarily by the prophets themselves.

- More prophets followed, in both Israel and Judah (the Southern Kingdom).

**6.** Assyria's overthrow of Israel's royal city of Samaria in 721 BC became the context (but not the locale) of the work of priestly descendants of Levi. Escaping to Judah, they supported the movement to purify the Southern Kingdom by reforming its worship and centralizing it in the temple of Jerusalem. The teachings of these priest-refugees to Judah, supporting the reforms of King Hezekiah (716–687), came to have an extensive influence in the formation of Scripture. They became the core of the Deuteronomic tradition from which came the Book of Deuteronomy and the "Deuteronomic historians" who edited Joshua, Judges, 1 and 2 Samuel, and 1 and 2 Kings.

**7.** A new era of religious fervor— and literary activity—came with another king: Josiah (640–609). After Hezekiah's corrupt successors, the stage was set for renewal. It was triggered by the discovery of "the Book of the Law" in the Temple, led by Josiah, and fueled by more prophets (like Zephaniah, Nahum, Habakkuk, and the great Jeremiah). That Book of the Law was probably what is known as "the Deuteronomic Code" (see *Deuteronomy 12—26*) written during the time of King Hezekiah and "lost" by his successors.

**8.** Another tragedy, the defeat of Judah and the destruction of Jerusalem by Babylon (and King Nebuchadnezzar), brought darkness in the national experience but light in terms of sacred writing. When the Israelites rose from the ashes of exile (587–537), they brought with them the core of the Old Testament:

- There were psalms written in exile.

- There were lamentations in the ruins of Jerusalem.

- There were old traditions from the desert wandering collected in exile and accounts recorded of the order of worship when the Jerusalem temple was the center of worship.

It was in the early 500s BC that a school of writers compiled the narratives of "Deuteronomic history."

- This collection includes the books of Joshua, Judges, 1 and 2 Samuel and 1 and 2 Kings.

- Christians refer to this collection as "history books." They are mainly about the history of the Chosen People from the settlement of the Promised Land and include the period of the judges, the establishment of the monarchy, the divided kingdom after the reign of King Solomon, the story of the divided kingdom, the exile into Babylon, and finally the return to Judah and Jerusalem (including the temple rebuilding and the covenant renewal).

- Jews refer to this collection under the broad heading "prophets" ("former prophets," distinguishing it from the "latter prophets" which include most of the figures associated with prophecy —the "literary" prophets whose names are on books of Scripture). "Oral" prophets like Samuel, Elijah, and Elisha play major roles in these books.

- Scholars refer to this collection as "Deuteronomic history" because its compilers worked from the basis and principles of the Book of Deuteronomy.

9. After the return from exile the rebuilding of the temple and national life is recorded in the writings of the prophets Haggai and Zechariah and in the books of Ezra and Nehemiah.

10. An anonymous author, called "the Chronicler" in two books named after him, describes Israel's history in terms of the unfolding of God's will.

11. In the fifth century, authors known collectively as "the priestly tradition" edited the Pentateuch into the form we have it today, including as a conclusion the book of Deuteronomy, which had become an introduction to the history of Joshua, Judges, Samuel, and Kings. The writing of prophetic literature declined gradually through the fifth and fourth centuries before Christ.

12. The largest collection of inspired writing after the exile belongs to a broad category called "Wisdom Literature." It is associated with Solomon, the "wisest of men."

- The books of Ecclesiastes (Qoheleth), Song of Songs, and Wisdom, although written after the exile (four centuries after Solomon) were attributed to him (in much the same way that the Pentateuch was credited to Moses and the psalms to David).

- Other books of Wisdom Literature, also associated with Solomon, include Proverbs, Sirach, Song of Songs, Job, and Ecclesiastes (Qoheleth).

13. When Alexander the Great and the Greeks conquered Syria and Palestine in 333 BC, as Assyria had centuries before and as Babylon had, a whole new era began with its own influences and threats. There was new writing inspired to counter the Greek ("Hellenizing") influence. In particular, it was the severe persecution of the Syrian ruler Antiochus IV Epiphanes, committed to crushing the worship of Yahweh, that inspired the Maccabean revolt of 167–164 BC.

- The Book of Daniel, inspiring hope and faithfulness and using apocalyptic language (see below), came out of this period.

- The Maccabean revolt was described by historians inspired fifty to seventy-five years later in the two books of Maccabees.

- The books of Esther, Tobit, and Judith, in the style of

historical novels, also appeared at this late point.

## Stages in the Written History of the New Testament

The Old Testament evolved over centuries; the New Testament, over decades.

## Writing Destined for a "New Testament"

In the first decades of the life of the Christian community, we have to assume that there were things being written. The process of passing on a New Testament in an oral tradition was not only like that of the Old Testament—it was part of it.

1. Just as in Israel, so in the Christian community, liturgy was a mix of songs, creeds, psalms, and other prayers.
   - "Let the word of Christ dwell in you richly; teach and admonish one another in all wisdom; and with gratitude in your hearts sing psalms, hymns, and spiritual songs to God" (*Colossians 3:16*).

   - "Be filled with the Spirit, as you sing psalms and hymns and spiritual songs . . ." (*Ephesians 5:18–19*).

2. Some of these liturgical ingredients appeared full blown in the letters of Saint Paul.
   - "Though he was in the form of God,/ [he] did not regard equality . . ." (the hymn in *Philippians 2:6–11*).

- "He is the image of the invisible God, / the firstborn of all creation" (the hymn in *Colossians 1:15–20*).

3. There were also sayings of Jesus written down in the first decade after his death and Resurrection that were put down in some order that circulated probably first in Aramaic then in Greek. There are strands of this source (*quelle*, in German; "Q" in academic circles) woven into the Gospel versions of Matthew and Luke.

4. There were probably other collections and fragments—proof texts from the Old Testament, records of parables, notes on deeds of Jesus—that were used by first-generation evangelists and catechists.

5. There was a primitive account of the suffering and death of Christ in writing.

6. The letters of Paul became the first body of Christian writing. He wrote for the same reason people write today: to bridge the distance between one person and another—between an evangelist and a community of faith in Paul's case.

   - Authorship by Saint Paul himself is not always certain: Ephesians is unique enough in style and vocabulary to cast doubt on his personal authorship. It is still certainly "Pauline" but possibly written by a disciple of Paul. Likewise, Colossians, 2 Thessalonians, and 1 Timothy are thought by most scholars to be "deuteropauline" books (*deutero*- meaning secondary, literally). The letter long-called "Paul's Letter to the Hebrews" is now called simply "the Letter to the Hebrews" and thought by most scholars to have had little or no connection to Paul himself.

   - In approximately AD 50, Saint Paul wrote the earliest of these letters, 1 Thessalonians, in a style that would become familiar in the later ones: encouraging, admonishing, instructing.

   - The actual letters of Paul himself are earlier in date than any of the New Testament's written Gospels. The dates of the other New Testament letters are more difficult to determine, but there is general agreement that they do not belong to the first generation of the Christian Church but to the second or third.

   - In the middle 50s of the first century, he wrote his main doctrinal letters, Galatians, 1 and 2 Corinthians, and Romans.

   - At various times, Philippians and Philemon, written by Paul, and Colossians and Ephesians, attributed to Paul, were written and have been called "captivity letters" because of Paul's imprisonment variously in Caesarea, Ephesus, and Rome.

- 1 and 2 Timothy and Titus, called "pastoral" epistles because they are addressed to pastors not communities, are concerned about more settled and formally organized Christian communities.

- Since the New Testament letters can be attributed to a single author writing over a relatively short period of time, they did not undergo the creative and extensive editing process that is part of the very nature of the Gospels. Strictly speaking, the author of a New Testament letter is a writer; the author of a Gospel is an editor.

## Gospels

Unlike a letter of Paul or his disciple, the Gospels by their very nature emerged only in the editing stage. They are the work of an editor (evangelist) who creatively, artistically, and faithfully brought together existing materials according to his own purposes and the needs of his audience (which was usually broader than the community or pastor that received a letter of Paul). Chronologically, they are later than the New Testament letters, even though they come first in the New Testament canon. (Paul was probably dead before the Gospel of Mark—the first—was in circulation.)

### Gospel and Gospels

When the word "gospel" appears in the New Testament, it is referring to the proclamation of faith: the "good news" of Jesus Christ. Nowhere does the New Testament use the word Gospel to designate a writing. Mark begins, for example, "The beginning of the gospel of Jesus Christ [the Son of God]." The Gospel writers did not call their books gospels.

Nevertheless, very early in the Christian tradition, Church writers began calling Matthew, Mark, Luke, and John "gospels" (as a genre). They were, after all, not biographies of Jesus of Nazareth but collections of material presented as "proclamations of faith" in Jesus as the Christ (the Messiah).

In the table of contents of the revised New American Bible, this dual use of the word "gospel" is illustrated: There is a heading "The Gospels" followed by the titles of four books beginning with "The Gospel according to Matthew" (not "the Gospel of Matthew").

Likewise, in the Catholic liturgy, the proclamation of the Gospel is announced by the phrase, for example, "A reading from the Gospel according to Matthew" (not of Matthew). And after the proclamation is the statement, "The Gospel of the Lord" (not "The Gospel of Matthew").

There may be four "gospels" that are written works of a particular literary style, but there is only one Gospel that is a proclamation of faith. As some teachers say, there is only one Gospel; there are four "according to's."

## The Formation of the Gospels

(See *CCC*, 126.)

The editing of the Gospels was the third of three stages in their formation. Just as Christ did not begin his life on earth as a full-grown man, so the Gospels did not begin their life in the form we know them today. Jesus, like every human being, began life in the womb, was born, grew as an infant and then as a child, and finally grew to adulthood. Stages can be discerned in the incarnation of the Gospel too. In the traditional language of "form criticism" of Scripture scholarship (see Chapter 4), these stages have each been called a "situation in life" (*Sitz im Leben* in its German original).

### The life and teaching of Jesus

The "situation in the life of Jesus" is about the context and meaning of individual stories and sayings in the earthly ministry of Jesus.

### The oral tradition

The "situation in the life of the Church" is about the context and meaning of these component stories and sayings in the life of the early Church. Why were these particular reminiscences preserved and what was their significance in the first community?

### The written Gospels

The "situation in the Gospel" is about the context and meaning of these stories and sayings of Christ in the text of the Gospel as we know it. What was the purpose of the evangelist in recording particular stories and sayings in particular settings?

## Motivation for Written Accounts

In the various communities of Christians, there were pastors and preachers who kept alive the memory of Jesus' words and deeds. Each community was unique and the accounts of Jesus varied. The emphasis in a particular story was not the same in Ephesus as it was in Jerusalem or Rome. Corinth might have had an incident in its memory that had never been heard in Alexandria.

### Saint Luke's Motivation

Saint Luke, not one of the Twelve but a second- or third-generation Christian, recognized his debt to "eyewitnesses" and "servants of the word" (*Luke 1:2*). He also declares in the following verses that his part in this developing tradition is "accurate" so that his readers will have certainty and clarity about the earlier teachings they have received. ("Accurate" in the Catholic tradition means "trustworthy" for the sake of salvation.)

"Since many have undertaken to set down an orderly account of the events that have been fulfilled among us, just as they were handed on to us by those who from the beginning were eyewitnesses and servants of the word, I too decided, after investigating everything carefully from the very first, to write an orderly account for you, most excellent Theophilus, so that you may know the truth concerning the things about which you have been instructed." (*Luke 1:1-4*, addressing himself to Theophilus–"friend of God").

1. There were concerns that important material or its interpretation would be lost.
2. There were requests for a systematic presentation of the Jesus story by new converts.

In response to these concerns and requests, the Gospel as a literary form emerged, a form or genre that was not a documentary, a history of the life of Christ, or a biography, but a proclamation by the Church of its faith in Jesus and what it means to call him the Christ.

## A Chronology of the Writing of the Gospels

The letters that Saint Paul himself wrote pre-date the written Gospels. They are an example of first-generation Christian writing. There is much uncertainty and debate about the dates of composition of Colossians, Ephesians, 2 Thessalonians, and the "Catholic" letters. Mainly, they are second- and third-generation Christian writings.

1. Around AD 70, the Gospel according to Mark appeared, probably in Rome, soon after the martyrdom of the pillars Peter, Paul, and James of Jerusalem. His Gospel, like those that followed, was not a "life of Christ." It was not a biography. It dealt only with Jesus' public life and ministry. It begins with the words, "The beginning of the good news of Jesus Christ. . . ." And what follows immediately is not an account of Jesus' birth but a quotation from Isaiah ("I am sending my messenger ahead of you") and the preaching of John the Baptist. As explained earlier, the Gospels are not biographical or historical works in the modern sense.

2. Around AD 85, the Gospel according to Matthew was written. Its original audience was Jewish Christians of Palestine and Syria. It contains material in common with that of Mark, but is nearly twice as long because of material designed to illustrate for Jewish converts that Jesus' mission and their Christian faith are the fulfillment of Judaism and the Old Testament (which is quoted more than 60 times in Matthew). Like the other Gospels, it was written in Greek, although there is speculation that there was an Aramaic version behind it.

3. Also around AD 85, the Gospel according to Luke and its sequel, the Acts of the Apostles, were written by a Greek Christian convert of Asia Minor. Unlike Matthew's Gospel, Luke's was intended for the Roman Empire's Greek-speaking communities whose interests and needs were different from Matthew's Jewish Christian audience. For them, the Gospel provided the basis of Jesus' words and deeds for their Christian faith, which had come to them from missionary preaching.

4. Probably in the 90s, the Gospel according to John was

composed, probably also in Asia Minor, near Ephesus. Aside from the passion account, John repeats almost nothing from the synoptics. It came from a community that claimed the Beloved Disciple, "the one whom Jesus loved" (*John 13:23*), as its founder. The Book of Revelation and the three letters of John followed the Gospel by a few years.

## The Lips of Jesus and the Hand of the Evangelist

"Redaction criticism" (see Chapter 4) is the name of professional Scripture scholarship that studies what the evangelist did with sources in editing and combining them. The cleansing of the temple episode (see *John 2:13–22*) is an example: After Jesus' declaration, "Stop making my Father's house a marketplace," it says, "His disciples remembered that it was written, 'Zeal for your house will consume me.'" That Scripture is Psalm 69:10—almost. The evangelist changes the wording to the future tense. In this way, what the psalmist said of himself is made to refer to Jesus, ultimately his death as the price of his zeal for doing the work of the Father. Immediately following this, the Gospel of John referred to "the Jews" demanding a sign, a

### The Evangelists and the Jews

The document of the Second Vatican Council on the relationship of the Church to non-Christian religions (*Nostra Aetate*) includes fundamental Catholic teaching:

• Jews are and always will be God's Chosen People.

• Any teaching or preaching of Scripture that justifies persecution of the Jewish people is condemned.

In an application of *Nostra Aetate*, the Vatican Commission for Religious Relations with the Jews published a statement in 1985, "Notes on the Correct Way to Present the Jews and Judaism in Preaching and Catechesis in the Roman Catholic Church." It is based on the Church's understanding that the Gospels went through three stages before emerging as we have them today. It says, for example, ". . . it cannot be ruled out that some references hostile or less than favourable to the Jews have their historical context in conflicts between the nascent Church and the Jewish community. Certain controversies reflect Christian-Jewish relations long after the time of Jesus. To establish this is of capital importance if we wish to bring out the meaning of certain Gospel texts for the Christians of today" (IV.1.A).

For example, in the story of the healing of the man blind from birth, the evangelist says "the Jews" confronted the parents of the man newly healed of his blindness. Their response was, "'We do not know . . . who opened his eyes. Ask him, he is of age; he can speak for himself.' His parents said this because they were afraid of the Jews, for the Jews had already agreed that if anyone acknowledged him as the Messiah, he would be expelled from the synagogue." (A revised NAB footnote on John 9:21 points out, "Rejection/excommunication from the synagogue of Jews who confessed Jesus as Messiah seems to have begun around AD 85 . . .")

proof of his authority in doing and saying what he did.

## Diversity Among the Evangelists

As described above ("New Testament Oral Tradition"), there was a rich resource of tradition, liturgical and catechetical, from which the sacred authors drew "for the benefit of the churches." From this earliest body of material, which had first been handed on orally and then in writing, the Evangelists produced four Gospels. As the Pontifical Biblical Commission explains in "Historical Truth of the Gospels" (1964):

1. Each one "followed a method suitable to the special purpose which he had in view."
2. Each one chose certain elements of the many that had been handed on: some they synthesized and some they explained in terms of the situation of the churches and the varied circumstances of the faithful.

## Truth in the Gospels

The Pontifical Biblical Commission's 1964 "Historical Truth of the Gospels" is an important document for understanding truth in the Gospels. The following teachings come from section #2.

1. "[T]he truth of the narrative is not affected in the slightest by the fact that the Evangelists report the sayings or the doings of our Lord in a different order, and that they use different words to express what He said, not keeping to the very letter, but nevertheless preserving the sense."
2. In their diversity, the Evangelists are all the same in the way they "painstakingly [used] every means of bringing home to their readers the solid truth of the things in which they had been instructed."
3. In quoting Saint Augustine, the Commission also teaches the Catholic understanding of inspiration (see Chapter 1 for more on this): "Where it is a question only of those matters whose order in the narrative may be indifferently this or that without in any way taking from the truth and authority of the Gospel, it is probable enough that each Evangelist believed he should narrate them in that same order in which God was pleased to suggest them to his recollection. The Holy Spirit distributes His gifts to each one according as He wills; therefore, too, for the sake of those Books which were to be set so high at the very summit of authority, He undoubtedly guided and controlled the minds of the holy writers in their recollection of what they were to write; but as to why, in doing so, He should have permitted them, one to follow this order in his narrative, another to follow that—that is a question whose answer may possibly be found with God's help, if one seeks it out with reverent care."

4. The Commission also touches on the topic of context and "the literal sense." (See Chapter 4 in this book for more on both of these topics.) "Literal" is used here not in the common sense of a "literalist reading," but in a technical sense. The distinction is critical. The "literal sense" of a passage is the historical meaning of the text insofar as what the human author intended to say.) The Commission states, ". . . since the meaning of a statement depends, amongst other things, on the place which it has in a given sequence, the Evangelists, in handing on the words or the deeds of our Savior, explained them for the advantage of their readers by respectively setting them, one Evangelist in one context, another in another. For this reason the exegete must ask himself what the Evangelist intended by recounting a saying or a fact in a certain way, or by placing it in a certain context." (An exegete is a trained interpreter of Scripture.)

## Interpreting the Gospels as Their Authors Intended

A reader can resolve what can appear to be inconsistencies in Gospel passages with some education (like that given above from the Pontifical Biblical Commission), some help (like good footnotes and commentaries), and a little practice. Even a novice reader can understand that the Gospel writers adapted Jesus' traditions to make a proclamation of faith that was meaningful for the community for which each was writing. See the following examples.

## Passover and the Last Supper
### An apparent discrepancy

- In the synoptics (Matthew, Mark, and Luke), Jesus shares a last supper with disciples at their Jewish Passover celebration and then shares the first Eucharist with them.

- In John, the Last Supper takes place on the day before Passover began, while the lambs for the Passover were being slaughtered in the temple. There is no scene in which Jesus shares the first Eucharist with his disciples.

### The question

The question is not which version is more historical but what theological statement is the Gospel writer making by crafting the story in this way?

### The resolution

The Evangelists are offering a new interpretation of Passover.

- In the synoptics, the Last Supper is the Passover celebration, a placement that emphasizes the connections between the Passover and the Last Supper and the Eucharist.

- John emphasizes the connections between the crucifixion and the slaughter of the Passover lamb.

## The Ascension
### An apparent discrepancy

- Luke ends his Gospel with the

Easter-day Ascension of Jesus: "Then he said to them, . . . 'stay here in the city until you have been clothed with power from on high.' Then he led them out as far as Bethany, and, lifting up his hands, he blessed them. While he was blessing them, he withdrew from them and was carried up into heaven" (*Luke 24:44, 49–51*).

• Luke begins the Acts of the Apostles by mentioning a 40-day period between the Resurrection and the Ascension: "In the first book, Theophilus, I wrote about all that Jesus did and taught from the beginning until the day when he was taken up . . . he presented himself alive to them by many convincing proofs, appearing to them during forty days . . ." (*Acts 1:1–3*).

### The question

The question is not which version is more historical, but what theological statement is the Gospel writer making by crafting the story in this way?

### The resolution

In the Acts of the Apostles, when Luke describes the Ascension as happening forty days later and Pentecost nine days after that, it's called "historicizing" what was probably one climactic event: the Resurrection, glorification, and Ascension of Christ and the outpouring of the Holy Spirit. Using the number forty could have been Luke's way of describing this sacred period of the risen Jesus' appearances and instructions. The number forty, the number of transition and transformation, has enormous symbolic power and alludes to the exodus itself. Recall the words of Moses, "Remember the long way that the LORD your God has led you these forty years in the wilderness, in order to humble you, testing you to know what was in your heart, whether or not you would keep his commandments" (*Deuteronomy 8:2*).

## Differences in Audiences

### The Principle

Most New Testament books were addressed to particular Christian communities. Some of them, the letters for example, were even specifically addressed to them and bear their name. Other books too, certainly the four versions of the Gospel, had specific communities of believers in mind.

### An Example

The infancy narratives developed in the early Church and are rooted in the Church's understanding of Christ. Matthew and Luke are the only two Evangelists who include the Christmas story. They are not identical. Their differences reveal each Evangelist's emphasis and style that comes through in the course of their version of the Gospel. Their differences also illustrate the awareness each had of his audience: Matthew wrote for newly converted Jews while Luke wrote for newly converted

Gentiles. Central in both versions is the virginal conception emphasizing to both Jews and Gentiles the divine origin of Jesus.

- Matthew brings the conviction that Jesus is the promised Messiah fulfilling the Old Testament prophecies.

- Luke presents the good news that Jesus is truly the Savior of all the poor and downtrodden in the world.

- Matthew traces Jesus' genealogy back to Abraham, the father of the Jewish people.

- Luke traces Jesus' genealogy back to Adam, the father of the human race.

- Matthew positions Jesus' birth in the Jewish tradition. Joseph is given a central role symbolic of all faithful Jews of the Old Testament exemplifying obedience to God and trust in him.

- Luke positions Jesus' birth within the context of the larger world. He makes reference to Augustus Caesar and the universal power Rome represented at the time.

- Matthew tells the stories about the star that drew the magi (the star of Jacob spoken of in the Old Testament, see *Numbers 24:17*), the slaughter of the innocents, and the flight into Egypt which echo the Old Testament pharaoh's attempt to thwart God's saving action.

- Luke perhaps knows that many events recorded in the Old Testament would have been less familiar to the Gentiles so he does not speak of the magi, the holy innocents, or the flight. He stresses instead Jesus' birth in a manger and the visit of humble shepherds who are the first to hear the good news. He contrasts the peace on earth that an infant in a manger is destined to bring to the poor and downtrodden with the order imposed by brutal armies.

## Differences in Evangelists

There are many other unique characteristics of each Evangelist that come not from the needs of their audience but from the writer's own style and purpose. The following are three examples.

## The Demands of Discipleship

The Gospel of Luke is called "the gospel of absolute renunciation" by some commentators.

### Call of Peter, James, and John

- According to Luke (see *5:1–11*), disciples must leave everything. Mark (see *1:16–20*) and Matthew (see *4:18–22*) say the disciples leave only their nets and their father.

### Call of Levi

- According to Luke (*5:28*), "And he got up, left everything, and followed him." Matthew (*9:9*) and Mark (*2:14*) say, "And he got up and followed him."

### Treasure in heaven

- Only Luke mentions selling all and giving to the poor: "Sell your posessions, and give alms. Make purses for yourselves that do not wear out, an unfailing treasure in heaven, where no thief comes near and no moth destroys. For where your treasure is, there your heart will be also" (12:33–34). Matthew only says, "Do not store up for yourselves treasures on earth, where moth and rust consume and where thieves break in and steal; but store up for yourselves treasures in heaven, where neither moth nor rust consumes and where thieves do not break in and steal. For where your treasure is, there your heart will be also" (6:19–21).

### Demands of discipleship

- Only Luke uses the Semitic exaggeration (hyperbole) "hate": "Whoever comes to me and does not hate father and mother, wife and children, brothers and sisters, yes, and even life itself, cannot be my disciple" (14:26). Also, only Luke includes "wife" in the description of renunciation. There is no synoptic parallel for Luke's conclusion to these sayings on discipleship (14:33), "So therefore, none of you can become my disciple if you do not give up all your possessions." Instead, Matthew says, "Whoever loves father or mother more than me is not worthy of me; and whoever loves son or daughter more than me is not worthy of me . . ." (10:37).

### The rich official

- In his account, Matthew quotes Jesus, "If you wish to be perfect, go, sell your posessions and give the money to the poor . . ."

(19:21). In Mark, the parallel is, "go, sell what you own, and give the money to the poor . . ." (10:21). Only Luke makes the detachment even more demanding by adding "all": "Sell all that you own and distribute the money to the poor . . ." (18:22).

## The Humanity of Jesus

Matthew changes little things in the Gospel of Mark when he gives his own version, as if God's Son in Mark's Gospel sounds too much like anybody's son.

- Mark wrote that when Jesus healed the leper he was "moved with pity" (1:41). Matthew does not mention pity and just says he cleansed him (8:3).

- Mark says that Jesus looked at the people who disapproved of a miracle on the Sabbath "with anger . . . grieved at their hardness of heart" (3:5). Matthew doesn't mention the look, the anger, or the grief (12:13).

- Mark says that Jesus, when asked for a sign, "sighed deeply in his spirit . . ." (8:12). Matthew records the dialogue (12:38–42) but does not let Jesus "sigh deeply."

- The Gospel of Mark says, "And he could do no deed of power there (his home town) . . ." (6:5). Matthew just says "he *did* not" (13:58).

## The Details of Storytelling

No Evangelist includes all of Christ's parables. Some are

recorded only by one. Even when they are repeated by more than one, they are not told exactly the same way. The Parable of the Tenants is an example. There is also an example below of the value of footnotes and commentaries (for more, see Chapter 4).

### The text

- At the end of Mark's version (*12:1–12*), it says, "So they seized him, killed him, and threw him out of the vineyard. What then will the owner of the vineyard do? He will come and destroy the tenants and give the vineyard to others."

- At the end of Luke's version (*20:9–19*), it says, "So they threw him out of the vineyard and killed him. What then will the owner of the vineyard do to them? He will come and destroy those tenants and give the vineyard to others."

- At the end of Matthew's version (*21:33–46*), it says, "'So they seized him, threw him out of the vineyard, and killed him. Now when the owner of the vineyard comes, what will he do to those tenants?' They said to him, 'He will put those wretches to a miserable death, and lease the vineyard to other tenants who will give him the produce at the harvest time.'"

### Some differences

- The Gospel of Luke is different from that of Mark in a detail that a revised NAB footnote brings to the reader's attention: "Luke has

altered his Marcan source and reports that the murder of the son takes place outside the vineyard to reflect the tradition of Jesus' death outside the walls of the city of Jerusalem (see Hebrews 13:12)."

- The story in the Gospel of Matthew is different from Mark's and Luke's in a more significant way, pointed out by the NJBC, "Matthew creates a dialogue in which the harsh answer is ironically given by the very chief priests incriminated by the story. . . . This conclusion is milder than the parable; the wicked tenants are not destroyed, but the promise is taken from them."

*"Now there are varieties of gifts but the same Spirit . . ."*

Paul's observation (*1 Corinthians 12:4*) is certainly illustrated in the work of the Evangelists. Scripture is the word of God in the words of people. Although God is the author of the Bible, the inspired human authors are real authors, writing from within their historical and cultural contexts. Each is uniquely gifted, each humanly limited, each differently motivated, but ultimately the methods and purposes of all find harmony and unity in the one word, the one book of books, the one Bible.

# The Scripture as Canon

This chapter has traced the origins of Scripture from God's

intervention in human history to the response of human beings in faith: recognizing experiences of God and salvation, celebrating them, endowing the following generations through an oral tradition, writing, and, later, collecting the writings. "Canonical recognition" is the ultimate phase of this centuries-long process that resulted in "the Bible."

## "The Canon of Scripture"

(See *CCC*, 120-130.)

This is the fourth of five topics the *Catechism of the Catholic Church* discusses in its teaching on Sacred Scripture (101–141).

1. Christ—The Unique Word of Sacred Scripture
2. Inspiration and Truth of Sacred Scripture
3. The Holy Spirit, Interpreter of Scripture
4. The Canon of Scripture
5. Sacred Scripture in the Life of the Church

## The *Catechism* Teaches about the Formation of Canon

An introductory paragraph (120) begins: "It was by the apostolic Tradition that the Church discerned which writings are to be included in the list of the sacred books."[2] It then includes a list of the 73 books (46 in the Old Testament, 27 in the New).

It then has three paragraphs on the Old Testament (121–123), four

paragraphs on the New Testament (124–127), and three paragraphs on the Unity of the Old and New Testaments (128–130). (These topics are treated in Chapter 3 of this book.)

## Canon

This rich word has an ancient history and a large family.

1. The Greek word *kanon* comes from a Semitic word meaning "reed."
2. "Canon" referred to a measuring stick, the straight bar or rod used by carpenters and masons.
3. Like the word "yardstick" today, "canon" came to be used (as a metaphor) for a standard or norm.
4. Today, the dictionary includes several definitions for "canon." The first two that follow are the ones used in this chapter; the third shows up in Chapter 5; the fourth is used in Chapter 6.
   - The first meaning given for canon is a general law or rule or standard.
   - Another meaning is the list or collection of sacred writings included in Scripture.
   - Another meaning is the Eucharistic Prayer of the Mass.
   - And yet another meaning is a law of the Church, whose body of law is called canon law. Chapter 6 of this book explains, for example, that the times established by canon

law for the Liturgy of the Hours to be prayed are called "canonical hours."

## The Canon of the Christian Church

The earliest use of the term "canon" in Christian settings was in reference to the Creeds as the "rule" (canon) of faith. Irenaeus (AD 180) wrote that the orthodoxy (truth) of teaching could be judged by its conformity to the Creeds and the authority of teachers by apostolic succession (teachers who could trace the source of their teaching back to the Apostles).

## The Canon of Scripture

In the present context, canon has two specific meanings.

### 1. List

The canon of Scripture is the list of inspired books in the Bible.

- Over time, the Church discerned by apostolic Tradition which writings are included as inspired and normative for faith.

- Through a similar process, Israel distinguished and developed its canon of sacred writings, which the Church also accepted as what became known as its Old Testament.

- The Roman Catholic canon includes, in the Old Testament, 46 books (45 if Lamentations is included with Jeremiah).

- The Roman Catholic canon includes, in the New Testament, 27 books.

### 2. Norm

A canon is the regulating value of writings for faith and morals. They are "normative." Certain books are reflective of the Church's faith.

## The Charism (Gift) of Inspiration

As noted earlier in this chapter, scholars are now recognizing a strong community component in the development of Scripture, from its inspiration to its canonization.

1. God was first inspiring the community in which divine revelation was recognized and oral interpretation of religious history was spoken.
2. He then inspired individual authors to put in writing the inspired oral interpretation.
3. And last, God inspired the community (the institutional Church, finally) to recognize which writing was inspired and authoritative for faith.

### The Old Testament Canon

#### Principles

The development of a canon was a process that lasted more than 1,000 years.

- The earliest elements probably originated in the twelfth or thirteenth century. Examples are the poetry of the Song of Miriam (see *Exodus 15:1–18*) and the Song of Deborah (see *Judges 5*).

- The latest parts of the canon were recognized in the second and first centuries BC (the books of Daniel, Esther, and Wisdom).

The process was gradual as material familiar in an oral tradition was preserved in individual books and in collections of books.

The original authors did not think of themselves as divinely inspired writers of literature that would be normative for succeeding generations. Rather, they most likely saw themselves as compilers and preservers of oral and written traditions that encompassed their communities' experience of encounters with God. Only gradually did it gain status as sacred literature, confirmed by the fact that it was read and studied in the synagogue. The earliest Christians inherited this Scripture from their Jewish brothers and sisters.

There were other written materials besides those mentioned above, some of which were lost and some that were preserved but not considered canon.

## A Chronology

The acronym TNK ("*tanak*") comes from the first letters of the Hebrew names of the following three parts of the Old Testament. It is the name given to Jewish Sacred Scripture.

### 1. The Law (Torah)

- Many today think that a written form of the earliest parts of the Pentateuch—the law codes—date to the twelfth and eleventh centuries.

- What we know as an Old Testament canon probably began with the discovery of the Deuteronomic Code in the temple in 621

BC. Because it was attributed to Moses, this writing had authority in driving Josiah's reform (see above).

- This was the first instance of sacred writing being recognized as "the word of God."

- Through the course of the next 200 years, other material (described above), including narratives of Israel's origins, was added to this core and became the five books ("pentateuch") known as the Law (*torah*). It was literature recognized as authoritative for what it meant to live as a Jew. This collection was complete by around 400 BC.

### 2. The Prophets (Nebiim)

By the second century BC the whole collection of prophets was accorded the status of sacred books, "the Law and the Prophets" commonly referred to in one phrase.

- The "Deuteronomic history," the so-called "Former Prophets" (Joshua, Judges, Samuel, and Kings) is a collection commonly known today as "Deuteronomic History" and was probably completed around 600–560 BC. Through the years it grew in stature as a definitive record of Israel's religious history.

- "Latter Prophets" (Isaiah, Jeremiah, Ezekiel, and the twelve "minor prophets") is a more mixed collection and was probably composed between 750 and 400–300 BC. These writings too were being used by the Jewish community and recognized as part of God's authentic message and their record of faith.

### 3. The Writings (Ketubim)

The precise identity of "the rest of the books" was not clear from the beginning. Their heading is generic. They are referred to with vagueness even into the first Christian century. A clearly defined collection of Scripture beyond the Law and the Prophets had not yet emerged in Judaism at this time. The familiarity and longevity of the Law and the Prophets were rewarded with respect sooner than the later Writings. All three, finally, enjoyed sacred status.

- This is the most mixed collection of books. The sacred status of these writings was most disputed. All were probably composed between the exile (587–537 BC) and the second century BC.

- The book of Sirach testifies to this collection (and more) when it says in its Forward, "For words spoken originally in Hebrew are not as effective when they are translated into another language. That is true not only of this book but of the law itself, the prophets and the rest of the books, which differ no little when they are read in the original."

- Even at the time of Christ, there was disagreement about the canonicity of some of these books.

## "Protocanonical" and "Deuterocanonical" Books

This terminology and distinction for Old Testament books probably originated in the mid-sixteenth century. It generalizes the "Protestant" position: The Anglican Church (Episcopalian), for example, is not labeled "Protestant" by all and has not officially made a declaration on the number of Old Testament books. Furthermore, there has been some agreement in the non-Catholic (and non-Protestant) Orthodox and Eastern Churches about the longer Catholic canon (and even proposals of an even more inclusive canon).

There are 39 protocanonical books. *Proto* means "first" but in this case means "accepted as canonical with little or no debate" (the first of the categories used by Eusebius, cited above).

There are seven deuterocanonical books. *Deutero* means "second" but in this case means "accepted after debate" (the second of the categories used by Eusebius, cited above).

- They are Tobit, Judith, 1 and 2 Maccabees, Wisdom, Sirach (also known as Ecclesiasticus), and Baruch (including the "Epistle of Jeremiah").

- There are also parts of the books of Esther and Daniel considered deuterocanonical.

- Deuterocanonical means fully canonical.

- It does not mean the books are less inspired than those in the "first" canon.

- It also does not mean they were canonized after those on the "first" list.

Why are these seven books singled out?

- These Jewish books, uniquely, were preserved in Greek, not in Hebrew or Aramaic like other Old Testament books. (It was once thought that all were written in Greek originally; we know now that much of this body of literature was written originally in Palestine's sacred languages: Sirach, Judith, and 1 Maccabees in Hebrew, for example, and Tobit in Aramaic.)

- The Greek translation of the Old Testament known as the Septuagint was done by Jews before the time of Christ and was the commonly accepted Bible of the Early Church.

- Saint Jerome, in the fifth century, included the deuterocanonical books in the Vulgate (his Latin translation of the Septuagint and the Greek New Testament), but said that they were not authoritative for doctrine. Nevertheless, since the Vulgate was used as the official Latin translation of the Bible for much of the Middle Ages, these books held a quasi-canonical status.

- The proliferation of vernacular translations of the Bible at the time of the Protestant Reformation was fueled by new interest in and knowledge of ancient languages. There was some suspicion and even rejection among reformers of the deuterocanonical Scriptures that were not available in Hebrew or Aramaic.

- Canonicity aside, the deutero-canonical books are valuable for understanding Judaism after the Babylonian Exile (587–539 BC). Compared to much of the Old Testament, they were written closer to the actual time of Jesus and include ideas that became central Christian truths (like belief in the afterlife). One of the seven, Sirach, was second only to the Psalms among Old Testament Scriptures used by the Church Fathers for ethical teachings in their Christian instruction.

- These seven books are seldom used in the Sunday lectionary (Tobit never).

## "Apocryphal" Books

The word "apocrypha" (a Greek word meaning "hidden") has two meanings or applications, the first more common.

1. In the Protestant tradition, the word refers to books considered non-canonical in the Protestant tradition, including the books called "deuterocanonical" (secondary canon) in the Catholic tradition. When the word appears on the cover of a Bible published in Protestant traditions ("including apocrypha"), it's referring to the seven deuterocanonical books.

2. In the Catholic tradition, the word refers to non-canonical books that are in some way connected with Old or New Testament writings. (For more about this category, see the section

on "Apocrypha" beginning on p. 64.)

## Apocryphal/Apocalyptic

There is another word that has added to the confusion of the two uses of the word "apocryphal." Apocalypse, which happens to have the same prefix as apocryphal, is what the Book of Revelation was formerly called. The word means "revelation" ("reveal" or "unveil" when it's serving as a verb in Greek).

When Saint Paul wrote, "For the wrath of God is revealed from heaven . . ." (*Romans 1.18*), for example, the Greek word for "revealed" is *apokalyptetai*. The noun is *apocalypsis* from which comes our English words "apocalypse" and "apocalyptic."

## Closing of the Jewish Canon

Most agree today that the canon of books of Judaism was not established ("closed") until the Christian era. A "canon" of sacred writings, as understood in the early Church, was a distinctively Christian concept and not part of Jewish thinking in the first century.

### Motive

Father Ray Brown (*The New Jerome Biblical Commentary*, "Canonicity," 66:35) makes this observation, "[M]any (critical scholars) suggest that the rivalry offered by Christian books was a spur for the closing of the Jewish canon. Others prefer to find the stimulus in the disputes within Judaism, particularly between the Pharisees and some of the more apocalyptically minded Jewish sects."

### A traditional view

• It had been broadly accepted that a version of the Jewish canon was determined by a council of rabbis at Jamnia (a town west of Jerusalem) around AD 90 or 100.

• This view is seriously disputed today.

### The safest statement

• In the first Christian century, there was probably a collection of 22 or 24 books considered sacred. But there was probably not a formally fixed and exclusive Hebrew canon until the end of the second century AD, before which time various groups within Judaism read as sacred certain books not included in the 22/24 count.

• The discovery of the Dead Sea Scrolls (1947–1956) supports the view that there was no uniformity among Jews in the first century BC and the first century AD about the books in the canon. In libraries like Qumran, it isn't certain whether a strict distinction was made between what are today called canonical, deuterocanonical, and non-canonical sectarian works. (Qumran, near the Dead Sea, was the home of a sect or sects of Jews.)

## The New Testament Canon

Even as the Church was generating inspired writings, she was inwardly recognizing them as part of the "apostolic tradition." They were valued in the communities of faith as the "rule of faith" but not named as such prior to Irenaeus (AD 180), as noted above.

1. The preaching of Peter and Paul and the others who had been sent was understood as "canonical."
2. An inward, un-proclaimed appreciation of Sacred Scripture existed before any need to make a formal declaration of it.

## The Christian Canon

"If one no longer thinks of inspiration solely as God's moving an individual scribe isolated at a writing table, and if one does not define meaning solely as what that scribe intended and conveyed at the moment he wrote, so one does not think that at a given moment in the first century the apostles could list inspired books by title" (Raymond F. Collins, *The New Jerome Biblical Commentary*, "Canonicity," 66:16).

"[F]or the first Christians what was 'canonical' was what Peter (Cephas), James, and Paul preached in continuity with what Jesus had proclaimed (1 Corinthians 15:11)" (Raymond Brown, *The New Jerome Biblical Commentary*, "Canonicity," 66:49).

Christianity is not first of all a religion of the book but of a person.

- Christians believe "in Christ God was reconciling the world to himself . . . and entrusting the message of reconciliation to us" (*2 Corinthians 5:19*).

- The apostolic Church followed the example of the Lord himself who wrote nothing, who like the rabbis of his day taught not by written word but word of mouth.

- The word was written in the hearts of disciples who remembered it with the help of the promised Spirit (see *John 14:25–26*) and proclaimed it in the form of public discussion, preaching, and evangelization—apostolic tradition (see Chapter 1).

In the first generation, there was less need for a written word (that is, Christian Scripture, beyond the Scriptures of Judaism) than there was later.

- There was a close presence (geographically and chronologically) of the living link, the Apostles, between the community of faith and the living Word, Jesus Christ.

- There was an expectation of an immanent return of Christ that made the written preservation of the word, if not faithless, pointless.

- Christians claimed the Jewish Scripture (the Old Testament) as their heritage too. It was ultimately included in the Christian canon.

## Motivation for Developing a New Testament Canon
### Geography

The importance of the written word increased along with the distances between believers and between Churches of believers.

- The decision to initiate Gentiles as Christians without circumcision transformed the community of the faithful from a Jewish sect into a universal Church (see *Acts 15*).

- The Apostles' instruction, one of the four characteristics of the early Church along with the communal life, the breaking of the bread, and the prayers (see *Acts 2:42*), now made the written word essential. Not surprisingly, the first Christian Scriptures were letters—the writings of Paul and others.

### Chronology

The importance of the written word also increased because of the passage of time and the death of eyewitnesses, since the living memory needed to be preserved. Writing was also specially suited to organizing the presentation of the message that was something to be handed on (apostolic tradition).

### Heresy

Around AD 150, Marcion, a Christian heretic, rejected the Jewish-inspired writings (the Old Testament) and most of what was later recognized as New Testament Scripture. This error fueled the need felt by the Church to define the canon more formally.

## Criteria for Development of the Canon of the New Testament

The final assurance that books in the Bible are the word of God rests on faith in the Holy Spirit's guidance and inspiration of the Church. This is the same faith that believes the Holy Spirit inspired any writing in the first place.

### A book's apostolic origin

When doubts arose about the apostolic authorship of Hebrews and Revelation, for example, so did they arise about the canonicity of these books.

- Formerly, "apostolic origin" meant "written by an apostle." Today we realize that authorship was understood in quite a different way at the time of the early Church from the way it is today.

- For the early Church, interest in the sacred writings did not include authorship in terms as individualistic and precise as ours are today. For them, "apostolic" meant associated with Apostles, not specifically written by Apostles.

- This is not to say that the names on many of the New Testament's works are meaningless. Every name, at the very least, indicates a connection to the apostolic tradition, which is authoritative for faith.

- So in more scholarly circles, the broader term "Pauline letters," for example, and "Pauline corpus" are commonly used instead of the specific term "Paul's letters," which implies the letters were written personally by Paul as personal letters are written by individuals today. Likewise, Matthean, Markan, Lukan, and Johannine are technical terms sometimes used today, certainly among scholars, so as not to imply that four individuals with those names actually wrote these Gospels in the way we understand authorship today.

### A book's acceptance by local Christian communities

Most New Testament books were addressed to particular Christian communities, the importance of which influenced the status and preservation of certain writings. Some of them, the letters, for example, were even specifically addressed to them and bear their name. Other books too, certainly the four versions of the Gospel, had specific communities of be-lievers in mind.

### Conformity to the "rule of faith"

Some religious writings were rejected because they seemed not to be compatible with the creeds of the early Church.

## History of the New Testament Canon

The organizational structure of the Catholic Church in the first centuries was not as developed and formalized as it is today. The list of inspired books in the Bible emerged out of common usage by the churches and pastoral advice of the leaders of the churches.

### 1. The First Century (AD 30-100)

- In the first years of the Church, there is no clear evidence of important Christian writing. The Christian faith was communicated, received, and nurtured by word of mouth (see *Romans 10:14–15*).

- In the beginning, preaching had a place in Christianity more central than it ever had in Judaism. In continuity with Jesus' proclamation, the preaching of Peter and Paul and the others who had been sent was "canonical" for the first Christians.

- The first complete Christian written document was 1 Thessalonians, dating from approximately AD 50 (twenty years after the death of Christ).

- It was another twenty years— approximately AD 70—before a version of the Gospel appeared (Saint Mark).

- The sacred writings of the early Christians were those that were part of their Jewish heritage. (The term "Old Testament" was not used then, since there was not a clearly established "New Testament" from which to distinguish it. Jews today, not recognizing Christian Scripture as inspired, do not speak of it as a New Testament or their own as old.)

- Some writings of the first century were not preserved. Some preserved first-century writings were not canonized.

### 2. The 100s

- In the early 100s, Clement of Rome (died about AD 97) and Ignatius of Antioch (about 50–107) referred to books in what we now call the New Testament as the standard of faith and practice. These were writings that had been composed for first-century churches (Christian communities), but the whole Christian body preserved them and put them into collections for use in her liturgy.

- Some Church writers referred to certain Christian written works, destined for the New Testament, as "scripture." At the same time, they quoted them alongside other Christian writings that would not be canonized.

- Meanwhile, other writings were being rejected as not being rooted in apostolic times or as including views not in harmony with the rule of faith.

- Still, Christian preaching was based on the Old Testament, interpreted in the light of the words and deeds of Jesus the Messiah, and on the living tradition of Jesus, which was passed on by word of mouth. This personal witness was held in high regard in the early Church. The second-century apostolic Father Papias, for example, wrote of his disdain for books and his esteem for "the living and abiding voice" of tradition ("things handed on"). This vital and sacred record was carried in living persons.

- At this same time, there was a similar process in Israel regarding its sacred writings, which the Catholic Church later accepted as its Old Testament.

- In AD 150, the apologist Saint Justin, in describing the Lord's Day Eucharist, mentioned reading the Gospels and the writings of the Apostles along with what came to be called the Old Testament.

- Melito of Sardis (170–190) termed the Jewish Scriptures "books of the Old Covenant" (which is not to say that this understanding is the same as what is meant by the terms "Old Testament" and "New Testament" today).

- Marcion, a Christian heretic who lived in the middle of the second century, rejected the Jewish-inspired writings (the Old Testament) and most of what was later recognized as New Testament Scripture.

### 3. About 200

- The term "New Testament" was used for the first time by a Christian writer named Tertullian, who was developing a vocabulary of two testaments. The concept of a unified body of Christian Scripture was becoming clear.

- The Gospels, the letters associated with Paul, Acts, 1 Peter, and 1 John were generally regarded as canonical. There was still debate about including the other "catholic letters" (see above) as canonical because of uncertainty about their authorship and the desire for apostolic testimony. The understanding was still not clear that "apostolic witness" did not require literal authorship by an Apostle.

### 4. In the 300s

Around AD 303, Eusebius distinguished three categories.

- undisputed books accepted as canonical

- disputed books

- spurious books ("not being what they pretend to be"; "counterfeit")

In AD 367, Athanasius made a two-fold distinction.

- "Canonical" books—"handed down and credited as divine"
- "Apocryphal" books—"which the heretics mixed up with divinely inspired Scripture"

The 39-book Old Testament canons of Athanasius and Jerome were becoming widely recognized. Although both list 22 books in the Jewish Scriptures (corresponding to the number of letters in the Hebrew alphabet), this number includes all 39 books today recognized as "protocanonical":

- add eleven for the twelve Minor Prophets they considered a single book
- add five for their five "double books" now counted singly (Samuel, Kings, Chronicles, Ezra-Nehemiah, Jeremiah-Lamentations)
- add one for Ruth, which they included with Judges

### 5. About 400

In 396–397, Augustine listed the complete 46-book Old Testament canon (his actual number was 44, but he included Lamentations and Baruch with Jeremiah).

- Augustine's stature in the Church "tended to close discussion" on the extent of the canon.
- At this same time, the 27-book New Testament we know today was generally accepted. Most objections to the inclusion of the "catholic epistles" (except for 1 Peter and 1 John, which were accepted earlier) were overcome. However, even into the fourth and fifth centuries, some writings known today as "sub-apostolic" were considered scriptural—1 and 2 Clement, the *Didache*, Hermes, and Barnabas, for example. (There is more on these writings below.)
- The councils of Hippo in 393, Carthage III in 397, and Carthage IV in 419 plus a letter of Pope Innocent I in 405, all agreed on the canon of 46 books in the Old Testament and 27 in the New.
- There were certainly lists (canons) of scriptural books before this, but by now they had gained a more formal status in the Church, clarifying the very word "canon" with its two-fold meaning, list and norm.
- In 1442, "in continuity with (this) dominant tradition," the ecumenical Council of Florence listed 73 books in the Bible (46 plus 27).
- In 1546 the Council of Trent, responding to Protestant questioning, promulgated a statement, "so that no doubt may remain as to which books are recognized," that listed the 73 books in the Bible as sacred and canonical and inspired by the Holy Spirit.

## Non-Catholic Bibles

This label is used for translations of the Bible done under the auspices of a Protestant Church or organization.

Seven Old Testament books and smaller units of some other books are not included or are put in a section labeled "apocrypha" or "deuterocanonical" (as explained earlier).

At this stage of modern biblical scholarship, this does not necessarily mean that a translation is "theologically slanted" (as once was more common).

# Early Christian Literature

Some of the wealth of writing generated within the early Christian communities and inspired by God was finally canonized as Scripture. There was other writing that was not recognized as authoritative. There was much, much more writing that continued after the canon of Scripture was established. This non-biblical literature, described in the following pages, can be put in three categories: Apostolic Fathers, apologists, and apocryphal.

- It included a great variety of writing.

- It was almost entirely Gentile in authorship (unlike Scripture).

- There was increasing Christian literary activity early in the second century, which became a flood before the end of the century.

- To make a definitive list of "classics" would be difficult and arbitrary. Works mentioned in the text below have been chosen for

their representative character as well as their intrinsic merit.

## The Apostolic Fathers

These writings, like that of the apologists, came out of a new era in the developing life of the Church, following the death of the first-generation, apostolic founders and missionaries. There were at least three prominent features of this new era.

- the threatening emergence of persecution by the Roman state

- the emergence of the heresies of Docetism and Gnosticism (see below)

- the establishment of "monepiscopacy": one "overseer" (*episcopos*, a word designating what came to be known as a bishop) in a local Church (a "diocese" in today's language), responding to the threat to truth and unity brought by heresies

## Letters

They reflect the thinking of the canonical letters, show greater Hellenistic (Greek culture) influence, and foreshadow a "Roman Catholicism."

### 1. Clement's First Letter (about AD 96)

- an anonymous letter of the Church of Rome to the Church of Corinth, a Church in conflict

- traditionally considered the most significant non-canonical writing—at one time and in some places even included in the canon of Scripture

- ascribed to a Clement, identified in an ancient tradition as the third bishop of Rome

### 2. The Letters of Ignatius (about 50-107), bishop of Antioch

- six addressed to Christian communities (Ephesians, Magnesians, Trallians, Romans, Philadelphians, and Smyrnaeans) and one to the bishop Polycarp

- revealing about the person of the author (like some of Paul's frankness and unlike the impersonalism of much early Christian literature)

### 3. The Letter of Polycarp (about 79-155), bishop of Smyrna

- addressed to the Church of the Philippians

- reflecting the condition and concerns of his generation (see below)

### 4. The Letter of the Church of Smyrna

- addressed to the Church of Philomelium

- traditionally called "The Martyrdom of Polycarp" (it describes the martyrdom of Polycarp, bishop of Smyrna)

- the oldest extant account of a Christian dying for the faith (outside of those described in Scripture—like Stephen's)

- the earliest testimony in the Church of what came to be called "the cult of the martyrs" (the traditional memorial observance including a place on the liturgical calendar and the veneration of relics)

## A Church Manual

The *Didache* (this Greek word means "teaching" and is pronounced "*did*-uh-kay") was discovered in 1873 and has been the subject of much discussion and speculation.

- in its present form originating in the 100s (initial opinions dated it as early as 70–90)

- in two parts: a Christian moral code (the "Two Ways") and a manual of Church order (including topics like Baptism, fasting, the Lord's Supper, local ministries of bishops and deacons, and itinerant prophets)

- a piece of literature with a history of stages in its development like some books of Scripture (the Gospels, for example)

## A Sermon

This anonymous work was traditionally called Clement's Second Letter although it is not a letter and it is not by Clement.

- dates from before 150; the earliest preaching document to come down to us

- mentions being presented liturgically "after God's truth" (the Scripture reading) as "an exhortation to heed what was there written, so that you may save yourselves"

- explains a text (Isaiah 54:1) and then exhorts the hearers to moral purity, steadfastness in persecution, and repentance in the face of coming judgment

## An Apocalypse

Called the "Shepherd of Hermas," this document's subject is repentance after Baptism.

## Theological Treatises

### 1. The Letter of Barnabas

Its subject is the value of the Old Testament for Christianity.

### 2. The Letter to Diognetus

It is not so much a letter as a brief for Christianity.

### 3. Papias

It includes fragments of five books called "Explanations of the Lord's Sayings."

### 4. Quadratus

This Christian apology is addressed to the Roman emperor Hadrian.

## The Great Apologists

- The apologists include Aristides, Saint Justin, Tatian, Athenagoras, Theophilus, Clement of Alexandria, and Tertullian.

- The apologists' purpose was to defend Christian faith in the face of prevailing philosophies by explaining the superiority and truth of Christianity.

- The classical apologists' primary theme was monotheism, attacking mainly the weaknesses of ancient mythology. The unity of God (more than the place of Christ) is their main emphasis since they are addressing Gentiles who were not beneficiaries of Old Testament monotheism.

## Apocrypha

## Clarification

As explained earlier, the word "apocryphal" (meaning "hidden") is used in two different ways.

1. More commonly, it is used in the Protestant tradition to designate the books that are called "deuterocanonical" in the Catholic Tradition.
2. In the Catholic Tradition (and in the following pages), the word refers to non-canonical books that are in some way connected with Old or New Testament writings.

## Definition and Explanation

1. These are Jewish and Christian religious books not considered scriptural in either the Catholic or Protestant tradition.
2. In the case of the New Testament, apocryphal literature includes non-canonical Gospels, letters, and collections of sayings attributed to Jesus.
3. Some apocryphal works have been lost.
4. Some apocryphal works have come down to us. The Protevangelion of Saint James, originating in the mid-second century, was widely used through the centuries and influenced Christian thinking in particular about Mary. It includes a creative account of her life before the annunciation, including the names of her parents, Joachim and Anna, her presentation in the temple (portrayed artistically

everywhere), and the portrayal of Joseph as an elderly man, including the legend of the budding staff.

5. Some apocryphal works have been recently discovered, like the famous apocryphal Gospel of Peter (an imaginative version of the passion of Christ). The most well known of these works, like the Gospel of Saint Thomas, were discovered at Nag Hammadi, Egypt, in the late 1940s and are mainly gnostic (heretical) writing. (Not all of the Nag Hammadi library is considered apocryphal.)

## Implication

1. Originally, "apocryphal" may have been a complimentary term, designating sacred writings whose content was beyond ("hidden from") the common reader. They were "esoteric" (intended only for the initiated).

2. Gradually, "apocryphal" became an uncomplimentary term, referring to non-canonical books whose orthodoxy was questionable. Heretical groups often preserved and even composed them and so the term apocryphal came to be used broadly by Church leaders for heretical literature that was not to be read. They were "spurious" (not what they pretend to be). The letter of Jude quotes two apocryphal Jewish works: the *Assumption of Moses* in verse 9 and the *Book of Enoch* in verses 14–15. The introduction to the letter of Jude in the revised NAB comments,

"There was controversy in the early Church about the propriety of citing non-canonical literature that included legendary material."

3. By the time of Saint Jerome (around 400), "apocryphal" had become a more neutral term to designate non-canonical literature. It's still a useful term in this sense.

## Description

- Apocryphal Jewish works include the Assumption of Moses, the Book of Enoch (two works mentioned above), Jubilees, and IV Ezra.

- Most of the very large body of apocryphal writing originates after the 100s and much of it is heretical. There is both Christian-Gnostic literature (little of which has survived) and anti-Gnostic writing. (For more, see "Gnosticism" on p. 67.)

- If not heresy it is often Christian romance authored by "pious novelists." This literature imaginatively filled in the blanks of the New Testament about the life of Christ and the Apostles in order to satisfy curiosity and the appetite for the miraculous. It blends Gospel material with popular folklore in ways the Church Fathers sometimes considered orthodox and sometimes heretical.

- There is some Christian poetry that has survived, including the first Christian hymnbook we possess, the "Odes of Solomon."

**2**

**Words of People**

- There are many stories of martyrdoms, in the vein of Polycarp's described in the Letter of the Church of Smyrna (which is not apocryphal; see above). These include stories of persecution in Lyon and Vienne; the martyrdoms of Perpetua and Felicity (whose names are still mentioned at Mass in Eucharistic Prayer I) in Carthage; the martyrdom of Carpus, Papylus, and Agathonice in Pergamon; and the martyrdom of Apollonius in Rome. There are also court records of the trials and executions of Christians, notably Justin and the martyrs of Scili in North Africa.

- Occasionally an apocryphal Gospel includes a statement of Jesus in a form that is older than the form preserved in a canonical Gospel.

- Rarely does an apocryphal Gospel include an authentic statement of Jesus that has not come down to us in a canonical Gospel.

- Apocryphal Gospels reveal the thinking of Christians about Christ in the second century and later.

- They are good sources for studying the varied Christian groups of the second, third, and fourth centuries.

- They are of virtually no value as resources for historical information about Jesus or the first-generation Church.

- They reveal more of their second-century (and third- and fourth-century) context and theology than the first-generation Church of the years 30–70 (before the death of the Apostles Peter and Paul in the 60s) or of the life of Christ.

- "The idea that recently discovered gospels tell us what the *earliest* Christians (AD 30–70) were like or thought, and that by contrast the canonical gospels represent a highly censored and patriarchal version of Christianity, suppressing the freedom of the earliest Christian movements, is a distortion" (Rev. Raymond E. Brown, *Responses to 101 Questions on the Bible,* Paulist Press, 1990).

## Gnosticism

Gnosticism was both a philosophy and a theology, a vast intellectual movement more ancient than Christianity that blended Asian and Greek ideas into various elaborate systems with the purpose of understanding the world and human beings' relationship to the divine.

Salvation for the Gnostic involved *knowing* where you came from and to what you were destined (the divine realm), hence its name. With this true knowledge, the soul is delivered from the evil prison of the body in which it has fallen and empowered to rise to its original home in the spiritual world.

Gnosticism emerged out of Greek philosophy, which was spread throughout the world with the conquests of Alexander the Great (353-323 BC) and the spread of the Greek empire known as "Hellenization." This was the intellectual climate of the literature of the late Old Testament and the early Christian Church. Sometimes a superficial Christian theology was added to an already complete Gnostic system. In other cases, a fundamental Christian faith took on Gnostic overtones and beliefs.

Regardless of the particular Gnostic system or the degree of its influence, it is at odds with Christian faith and rests on certain "heretical" principles:

1. Gnosticism includes a "dualism" of matter and spirit. The significance of the body, believed to be basically evil, is denied. The material world is the creation of an evil or powerless God.

2. This dualism undermines the Old Testament with its revelation of creation as the act of a good God, contrasting "the Old Testament God" with "the good God" revealed in Jesus.

3. Gnosticism denies the incarnation. Christ was only an intermediary between God and people and only "appeared" to be human, but did not actually take on human flesh. (The Greek word for "appeared" is *dokeo*, the origin of the name of a Gnostic heresy called "Docetism.")

4. Gnosticism in its ethics and morals could go in one of two directions: In some cases, Gnosticism was strictly ascetical, promoting practices that would distance the soul from the material world. In other cases, Gnosticism became antinomian (from the Greek words meaning "against" and "law"), morally indifferent in this world that is not a creation of God. (Moral antinomianism held that Christians are freed from the moral law because of the grace of the Gospel.)

The great exposition of Catholic faith by Saint Irenaeus, traditionally called "Against Heresies" ("Refutation and Overthrow of the Pretended but False Gnosis") is the first full-blown and full-length orthodox reply to the various systems of Gnosticism.

2

Words of People

# The Book
## THE BOOKS OF THE OLD TESTAMENT

Parenthesized words are the former titles/spellings that were used prior to 1970s *New American Bible*, the first Bible in the Catholic tradition to use proper names derived from the Hebrew instead of the Latin and also name books to agree with the more proper usage of Bibles in the Protestant tradition—"Chronicles" instead of "Paralipomenon" for example.

| Pentateuch | *Abbrev.* | *NSRV Abbrev.* | *Chapters* | |
|---|---|---|---|---|
| Genesis | Gn | Gen | 50 | |
| Exodus | Ex | Ex | 40 | |
| Leviticus | Lv | Lev | 27 | **The Torah** (Law) |
| Numbers | Nm | Num | 36 | |
| Deuteronomy | Dt | Deut | 34 | |
| **The Historical Books** | | | | |
| Joshua (*Josue*) | Jos | Josh | 24 | |
| Judges | Jgs | Judg | 21 | |
| Ruth | Ru | Ruth | 4 | |
| 1 Samuel (*1 Kings*) | 1 Sm | 1 Sam | 31 | Primary Group |
| 2 Samuel (*2 Kings*) | 2 Sm | 2 Sam | 24 | (Former Prophets) |
| 1 Kings (*3 Kings*) | 1 Kgs | 1 Kings | 22 | Excluding Ruth |
| 2 Kings (*4 Kings*) | 2 Kgs | 2 Kings | 25 | |
| 1 Chronicles (*1 Paralipomenon*) | 1 Chr | 1 Chr | 29 | |
| 2 Chronicles (*2 Paralipomenon*) | 2 Chr | 2 Chr | 36 | Secondary Group |
| Ezra (*1 Esdras*) | Ezr | Ezra | 10 | |
| Nehemiah (*2 Esdras*) | Neh | Neh | 13 | |
| •Tobit (*Tobias*) | Tb | Tob | 14 | Stories with a historical base |
| •Judith | Jdt | Jdt | 16 | Including Ruth |
| Esther | Est | Esth | 10 | |
| •Maccabees | 1 Mc | 1 Macc | 16 | Later History |
| •Maccabees | 2 Mc | 2 Macc | 15 | |
| **The Wisdom Books** | | | | |
| Job | Jb | Job | 42 | |
| Psalms | Ps(s) | Ps | 150 | |
| Proverbs | Prv | Prov | 31 | |
| Ecclesiastes (*Qoheleth*) | Ecc | Eccl | 12 | **The Writings** |
| Song of Songs (*...of Solomon*) | Sg | Song | 8 | Including Daniel, Ezra, |
| (*Canticle of Canticles*) | | | | |
| •Wisdom | Wis | Wis | 19 | Nehemiah, Chronicles, Ruth, |
| •Sirach (*Ecclesiasticus*) | Sir | Sir | 51 | Lamentations, and Esther |
| **The Prophetic Books** | | | | **Latter Prophets** |
| Isaiah (*Isaias*) | Is | Isa | 66 | |
| Jeremiah (*Jeremias*) | Jer | Jer | 52 | |
| Lamentations | Lam | Lam | 5 | Major Prophets |
| •Baruch | Bar | Bar | 6 | Excluding Lamentations and |
| Ezekiel (*Ezechiel*) | Ez | Ezek | 48 | Baruch |
| Daniel | Dn | Dan | 14 | |
| Hosea (*Osee*) | Hos | Hos | 14 | |
| Joel | Jl | Joel | 4 | |
| Amos | Am | Amos | 9 | |
| Obadiah (*Abdiah*) | Ob | Obad | 1 | |
| Jonah (*Jonas*) | Jon | Jon | 4 | |
| Micha (*Micheas*) | Mi | Mic | 7 | Minor Prophets |
| Nahum | Na | Nah | 3 | Daniel and Jonah being |
| Habakkuk (*Habacuc*) | Hb | Hab | 3 | special cases |
| Zephaniah (*Sophonias*) | Zep | Zeph | 3 | |
| Haggai (*Aggeus*) | Hg | Hag | 2 | |
| Zechariah (*Zacharias*) | Zec | Zech | 14 | |
| Malachi (*Malachias*) | Mal | Mal | 3 | |

•**Deuterocanonical** (Greek: second canon) or **Apocrypha** (Greek: hidden)

Tobit, Judith, 1 and 2 Maccabees, Wisdom, Sirach, Baruch

Called the *Apocrypha* in the Protestant tradition, these books of the Bible found in the Septuagint (ancient Greek translation of the Old Testament), but not the Hebrew canon. Jerome included these books in his Vulgate (Latin translation of the Bible). During the proliferation of published Bibles after the advent of printing, the reformers followed one Jewish tradition of excluding these books. Today in Protestant editions, these books are often included in a section at the end of the Old Testament.

Originally, the word *apocrypha* referred to works claiming a sacred origin but supposedly hidden for generations. Later, a specific body of literature with scriptural or quasi-scriptural pretensions though not canonical or genuine, composed during the two centuries before Christ and the early Christian centuries.

## THE BOOKS OF THE NEW TESTAMENT

### Gospels

|  | *Abbrev.* | *NSRV Abbrev.* | *Chapters* |  |
|---|---|---|---|---|
| Matthew | Mt | Mt | 28 | ⎫ |
| Mark | Mk | Mk | 16 | ⎬ Synoptics |
| Luke | Lk | Lk | 24 | ⎭ |
| John | Jn | Jn | 21 | |

### History of the Early Christian Church

|  | | | |
|---|---|---|---|
| Acts of the Apostles | Acts | Acts | 28 |

### Letters ("Epistles")

|  | *Abbrev.* | *NRSV Abbrev.* | *Chapters* |  |
|---|---|---|---|---|
| Romans | Rom | Rom | 16 | ⎫ |
| Corinthians (2) | (1,2) Cor | 1, 2 Cor | 16,13 | ⎪ |
| Galatians | Gal | Gal | 6 | ⎪ |
| Ephesians | Eph | Eph | 6 | ⎪ |
| Philippians | Phil | Phil | 4 | ⎬ By Paul |
| Colossians | Col | Col | 4 | ⎪ |
| Thessalonians (2) | (1,2) Thes | 1, 2 Thess | 5,3 | ⎪ |
| Timothy (2) | (1,2) Tim | 1, 2 Tim | 6,4 | ⎪ |
| Titus | Ti | Titus | 3 | ⎪ |
| Philemon | Phlm | Philem | 1 | ⎭ |
| James | Jas | Jas | 5 | |
| Peter (2) | (1,2) Pt | 1, 2 Pet | 5 , 3 | ⎫ |
| John (3) | (1,2,3) Jn | 1, 2, 3 Jn | 5, 1, 1 | ⎬ Synoptics |
| Jude | Jude | Jude | 1 | ⎭ |
| Hebrews | Heb | Heb | 13 | ⎫ Unknown or |
| Ephesians | Eph | Eph | 6 | ⎭ uncertain |

### Apocalyptic

|  | | | |
|---|---|---|---|
| Revelation or Apocalypse | Rv | Rev | 22 |

CHAPTER 3

# Book of Covenants

## Moral Formation
### in the Old
### and New Testaments

The Ten Commandments (or Decalogue) and the Beatitudes are the primary reference points for the application of Christian moral principles. The Decalogue, the expression of God's covenant with his people, is also a privileged expression of the natural law that sums up love of God and neighbor. In the Sermon on the Mount, Jesus took up the Ten Commandments and challenged his disciples to live them in the spirit of the Beatitudes. The Beatitudes proclaim the salvation brought about through the Kingdom of God.

—*National Directory for Catechesis*, p. 172

## The Word Speaks to Francis

There were three Scriptures that played a major role in the transformation of Francis of Assisi. Because of events earlier in life, he had already left home and inheritance, putting aside his worldly ways in favor of the life of a hermit. He spent hours alone in prayer, which caused a deep love and concern to develop in his heart for the rejects and outcasts of society.

His inspiration came from the Book of Genesis, which teaches that every person is created in the image and likeness of God, and from Jesus' teaching on the final judgment: ". . . just as you did it to one of the least of these who are members of my family, you did it to me." (*Matthew 25:31-46 [verse 40]*)

A further change was triggered in Francis when he was at Mass and he heard the Gospel passage of Jesus commissioning the Apostles. He was touched by the Lord's instruction to go and preach the Gospel, taking nothing for the journey, not even food or money. It prompted a still deeper conversion in Francis' life.

# Judea-Christian Spiritual Ties

Pope Pius XI said it succinctly: "Spiritually, we are Semites." In Vatican II's *Declaration on the Relationship of the Church to Non-Christian Religions*, paragraph four (of its five paragraphs) begins with a statement of unity, proceeds with a list of points describing that relationship between Christians and Jews, which "the Church of Christ acknowledges," and then recalls Paul's esteem for Judaism.

## A Statement of Unity

"Sounding the depths of the mystery which is the church, this sacred council remembers the spiritual ties which link the people of the new covenant to the stock of Abraham."

## The Church's Relationship to Judaism

1. The origins of her faith and election are found in the patriarchs, Moses, and the prophets.
2. All Christ's faithful, people of faith and so children of Abraham (see *Galatians 3:7*), are included in the call of the same patriarch.
3. "[T]he salvation of the Church is mystically prefigured in the exodus of God's chosen people from the land of bondage."
4. The Church has received the revelation of the Old Testament through that people with whom God mercifully made the ancient covenant.
5. The Church "draws nourishment from that good olive tree onto which the wild olive branches of the Gentiles have been grafted (see *Romans 11:17–24*)."

**6.** Christ our peace has reconciled Jews and Gentiles through his cross and made them one in himself (see *Ephesians 2:14, 16*).

## A Recollection of Paul's Esteem

After making the list above, the *Declaration on the Relationship of the Church to Non-Christian Religions* recalls a list of Paul's: "Likewise, the church keeps ever before [her] mind the words of the apostle Paul about his kin. . . ." (paragraph 4). These are the so-called privileges or prerogatives of the Jews from Romans 9:4–5:

**1.** The sonship
**2.** The glory
**3.** The covenants
**4.** The giving of the law
**5.** The worship
**6.** The promises
**7.** The patriarchs
**8.** From them, according to the flesh, is the Messiah

# The Value of the Old Testament

The *Constitution on Divine Revelation* (#14–16) and the *Catechism* (121–123, often quoting the *Constitution*) explain the list above that describes the Church's relationship to Judaism, specifically as it relates to the Old Testament.

## The Old Testament

The Old Testament

• is an indispensable part of Sacred Scripture

• is divinely inspired and the true Word of God

• retains a permanent value

• has never been revoked or rendered void

• bears witness to "the whole divine pedagogy" of God's redeeming love

• is a storehouse of sublime teaching on God and of sound wisdom on human life

• has a wonderful treasury of prayers

• includes the mystery of our salvation "in a hidden way" (". . . when the Church reads the Old Testament, she searches there for what the Spirit, 'who has spoken through the prophets,' wants to tell us about Christ"[1] *CCC*, 702.)

## The Intrinsic Value of the Old Testament

*The* Catechism *says the New Testament "has to" be read in light of the Old. The* Catechism *does not say that the Old Testament "has to" be read in light of the New. The Old Testament can stand alone; the New Testament cannot.*

**1.** The value of the Old Testament does not come from a New Testament "typological" reading. (Typology is discussed later in this chapter.)
**2.** The value of the Old Testament is "intrinsic." Inherent. Essential. In itself. (See *Mark 12:29–31*.)

3. The value of the call of the patriarchs and the exodus (for example) is not lost by "the mere fact" that they were "intermediate stages."

4. "Besides," the New Testament "has to" be read in light of the Old.

## Catholic Reverence for the Jewish Bible

1. There is strong scholarly opinion that Vatican II's view of the Old Testament in its *Constitution on Divine Revelation* was "heavily christological" (see par. #15):

   • The Old Testament prepares for the New.

   • The Old Testament through its prophecies announces the coming of the messianic kingdom.

2. The *Catechism* (1994) goes further than Vatican II (1965) in recognizing the "intrinsic" value of the Old Testament (see above) and brings a sensitive balance (see paragraph #129):

   • Of course the Christian reads the Old Testament in terms of the Gospel.

   • Nevertheless, the Old Testament can stand on its own. (The writers of the *Constitution on Divine Revelation*, one of the watershed documents for modern Catholic biblical interpretation, were still thinking in terms of the scholarship of the past; by comparison, the *Catechism* reflects more current scholarship.)

3. In the long history of interpretation, this is a relatively new sensitivity. For example, in Psalm 80, a prayer for the restoration of God's vineyard says, "May your help be with the man at your right hand, / with the one whom you once made strong" (verse 18).

   • A footnote in the old Catholic translation (Challoner's eighteenth-century revision of the *Douay-Rheims*) says flatly about verse 18: "*The man of thy right hand*: Christ."

   • About the same verse, a *New American Bible* (1970) footnote says, "*The man at your right hand . . . the one*: the Davidic king who will lead the army in battle."

(The comment in the 1970 NAB recognizes the meaning and significance of the Old Testament reference in its own historical context while Challoner only and flatly interprets it in light of the New Testament.)

# The Place of the New Testament

## The New Testament (See *CCC*, 124.)

1. The word of God is set forward in the New Testament and it "displays its power in a most wonderful way.[2]"

2. The New Testament hands on the "ultimate truth of God's Revelation."

3. The New Testament is about the acts, teaching, passion, and glorification of Jesus Christ, God's incarnate Son, and the Holy Spirit's guidance in the beginning of Christ's Church.
4. The heart of all Sacred Scripture is the Gospel.

## The Gospel (See CCC, 125-127.)

1. "The *Gospels* are the heart of all the Scriptures 'because they are our principal source for the life and teaching of the Incarnate Word, our Savior.'[2]"
2. "The fourfold Gospel holds a unique place in the Church, as is evident . . . in the veneration which the liturgy accords it . . ." This unique place is evident in the use of a book of the gospels, in the posture of the assembly when it is proclaimed, and in the proclaimer (an ordained minister, not the lector at the liturgy).
3. The Gospel has exercised a "surpassing attraction . . . on the saints at all times."
   - "There is no doctrine which could be better, more precious, and more splendid than the text of the Gospel. Behold and retain what our Lord and Master, Christ, has taught by his words and accomplished by his deeds" (Saint Caesaria the Younger to Saint Richildis and Saint Radegunde,[3] quoted in CCC, 127).
   - "But above all it's the Gospels that occupy my mind when I'm at prayer; my poor soul has so many needs, and yet this is the one thing needful. I'm always finding fresh lights there, hidden and enthralling meaning[3]" (Saint Therese of Lisieux, quoted in CCC, 127).

# The Unity of the Two Testaments

## The Unity of the Old and New Testaments (See CCC, 128-130.)

The *Catechism* teaches that Christians read the Old Testament in light of Christ crucified and risen (129). "Typological" reading, explained later in this chapter, is one of the ways this has been done.

1. This "Christian reading" of the Old Testament discloses its inexhaustible content.
2. Early Christian catechesis made regular use of the Old Testament.
3. According to an old saying, "The New Testament lies hidden in the Old and the Old Testament is unveiled in the New."

## Reconciling Both Testaments of the One Bible

1. It is not uncommon for a Christian with a newly awakened spiritual life to develop an appetite for Scripture, often turning to the pages of the New Testament and to the life and teachings of Jesus Christ.

**2.** There are some who find themselves comparing the person of Jesus—loving and compassionate—to what they thought they knew of "the God of the Old Testament"—distant judge, stern, and demanding.

**3.** With maturity, the comparison gives way to a new discovery of God and a new appreciation of the Old Testament. The words of Jesus, "Whoever has seen me has seen the Father" (*John 14:9*), are borne out. A person does begin to see the Father in a new way, to hear God, and to seek God, the Father of Jesus. A reading in faith of the New Testament brings an invitation to the revelation of the Old Testament too.

## Discovering the Unity and the Continuity

Jesus himself was a Jew who read and studied Jewish Scriptures

### Marcionism

A man named Marcion, who lived in the second century, argued that the Christian Church should not accept as part of its canon the Old Testament as well as parts of what would later be the New Testament, most notably the parts that are very Jewish in character. He made an erroneous distinction between "the God of the Old Testament" and "the God of the New Testament"—one a God of wrath, the other a God of love. The Church disagreed, declaring Marcion a heretic (not teaching the true faith of the Church) and "Marcionism" a heresy. Marcion was not the first and he was not the last to misread the Old Testament and brand it harsh. Read the following Old Testament Scripture quotes, none of which are harsh.

"Can a woman forget her nursing child,/ or show no compassion for the child of her womb?/ Even these may forget,/ yet I will not forget you." (*Isaiah 49:15*)

"He does not deal with us according to our sins," (*Psalm 103:10*)

"The LORD is my shepherd, I shall not want./ He makes me lie down in green pastures;/ he leads me beside still waters;" (*Psalm 23:1-2*)

"[E]veryone who thirsts,/ come to the waters;/ . . . For you shall go out in joy,/ and be led back in peace;/ the mountains and the hills before you/ shall burst into song, . . ." (*Isaiah 55:1, 12*, from "An Invitation to Abundant Life" passage)

"For I am about to create new heavens/ and a new earth;/ the former things shall not be remembered/ or come to mind./ But be glad and rejoice forever/ in what I am creating;/ for I am about to create Jerusalem as a joy,/ and its people as a delight./ I will rejoice in Jerusalem,/ and delight in my people;/ no more shall the sound of weeping be heard in it,/ or the cry of distress." (*Isaiah 65:17-19*)

"For the Lord is compassionate and merciful;/ he forgives sins and saves in time of distress." (*Sirach 2:11*)

It would be hard to find in the New Testament more tender and compassionate descriptions of God and more loving promises than ones like these from the Old Testament.

as the revealed word of God. Likewise, Paul and the Evangelists appealed to Jewish Scriptures to proclaim their faith in Jesus as the Messiah and Son of God. Therefore, in contemporary catechesis we too teach not the contrast but the continuity of the Old Testament and the New Testament.

### Contrast

"In this reactionary, Old Testament world of zero tolerance in which we live, we must find a way to express Christ's New Testament message of forgiveness." This thinking and language perpetuates a heresy called Marcionism that was already condemned in the second century.

### Continuity

Instead of making such a sharp distinction between a harsh Old Testament world and a loving New Testament one, the Fathers of the Church preached continuity.

## Preaching the Continuity of the Old Testament and the New

There are eight sermons recorded in the Acts of the Apostles (see box). The last three of these are Paul's, the first of which is in Acts 13:16–41. Paul, in rooting his preaching in what we know today as the Old Testament, displays the Church's comprehensive understanding of the whole of Scripture.

- Paul begins by saying: "The God of this people Israel chose our ancestors and made the people great during their stay in the land of Egypt" (*Acts 13:17*).

- He continues to summarize the Old Testament, culminating, "And we bring you the good news that what God promised to our ancestors he has fulfilled for us, their children, by raising Jesus; as also it is written in the second psalm, 'You are my Son;/ today I have begotten you.'" (*Acts 13:32–33*).

### The Eight Kerygmatic Sermons in Acts

In 1 Corinthians 15:1-11 Paul writes of Christ's Resurrection as the core of the message (that which has been handed on), the foundation of Christian faith, and calls it "the preaching" and "the proclamation" (*kerygma*, in Hebrew).

Six to Jews (Five by Peter, the sixth by Paul):

**1.** On the day of Pentecost–*2:14-36*

**2.** After the cure, with John, of a cripple–*3:12-26*

**3.** The next day before the sanhedrin after a night in jail with John–*4:8-12*

**4.** At a second trial after another night in jail–*5:29-32*

**5.** In Caesarea, after a vision, leading to Cornelius' baptism–*10:34-43*

**6.** On a mission of Barnabas and Paul, at an Antioch synagogue–*13:16-41*

Two to Gentiles (by Paul):

**1.** After a cure, acclamation in Lystra, "Gods have come to us . . ."–*14:15-17*

**2.** In the Athens Areopagus, referring to "an unknown god"–*17:22-31*

# Fulfillment in the New Testament

There is an old saying, "The New Testament lies hidden in the Old and the Old Testament is unveiled in the New." Jesus of Nazareth said that he came to fulfill the Law, not destroy it. The Paschal Mystery (his life, death, and Resurrection) is a study in fulfillment according to divine plan and difficult to appreciate apart from its Old Testament background and circumstances. As illustrated below, there are many explicit Old Testament references in the New Testament (called "fulfillment citations") as well as countless allusions.

New Testament readers need to bear in mind that the Gospels were written some 40–60 years after the death and Resurrection of Jesus, so these citations are not prophecies in the sense of foretelling the future, but ways of understanding and explaining what was already known about Jesus and his role in God's plan of salvation.

## In The Writings of the Evangelists
### About John the Baptist

- The words of the fourth Gospel describe John's testimony of himself in this way: "I am the voice of one crying out in the wilderness, / 'Make straight the way of the Lord,' as the prophet Isaiah said" (*John 1:23*, with a parallel in all three synoptics).

- He was quoting Isaiah 40:3. But what that Scripture actually says is, "A voice cries out: / 'In the wilderness prepare the way of the LORD, / make straight in the desert a highway for our God!'," (not "a voice cries out *in the wilderness*,"—note also the difference in punctuation).

- In its original context, Isaiah 40:3, with its figurative language, referred to the return of the exiles from Babylon to Jerusalem, with God in the lead, making the way easy for them.

- The Gospel writer thus gave a new interpretation to Isaiah 40:3, re-punctuating it in the process.

### About Jesus

The Gospel writers also describe Jesus as "the fulfillment of Scripture" (the Old Testament).

- In the Gospel of Luke, during Jesus' inaugural preaching (see *Luke 4:16–21*), he proclaimed the beginning of the time of fulfillment of Old Testament prophecy: At the Nazareth synagogue, he read Isaiah 61:1–2, "The Spirit of the Lord is upon me, / because he has anointed me / to bring good news to the poor. / He has sent me to proclaim release to the captives / and recovery of sight to the blind, / to let the oppressed go free, / to proclaim the year of the Lord's favor" (*Luke 4:18–19*). He then declared, "Today this scripture has been fulfilled in your hearing" (*Luke 4:21*).

- In the Gospel of Matthew, during the first of five discourses (according to Matthew) known as the Sermon on the Mount, Jesus declared, "Do not think that I have come to abolish the law or the prophets; I have come not to abolish but to fulfill" (*Matthew 5:17*).

- The Gospel of Luke has a similar saying that it attributes to Jesus: "The law and the prophets were in effect until John came; since then the good news of the kingdom of God is proclaimed . . . But it is easier for heaven and earth to pass away, than for one stroke of a letter in the law to be dropped" (*Luke 16:16–17*).

- There are other times that the Gospels attribute to Jesus a specific reference to the fulfillment of Scripture, as in *Matthew 26:24*: "The Son of Man goes as it is written of him . . ."

- Another allusion to Scripture is unmistakable. When messengers from John the Baptist came to him asking, "Are you the one who is to come, or are we to wait for another?" (*Matthew 11:3*), Jesus responded, "Go and tell John . . ." Then, without mentioning Isaiah by name or using the word "fulfill," Jesus uses language from Isaiah (see *26:19, 29:18–19, 35:5–6, 61:1*) that describes the time of salvation in terms people could "hear and see" in the flesh and blood of Jesus' ministry.

- The Gospel writers even used Scripture to explain the problem of Jesus' betrayal by his disciple. In the Gospel of Mark, for example, we hear: "And when they had taken their places and were eating, Jesus said, 'Truly I tell you, one of you will betray me, one who is eating with me'" (*Mark 14:18*). The phrase "one who is eating with me" was probably an allusion to *Psalm 41:9*: "Even my bosom friend in whom I trusted, / who ate of my bread, has lifted the heel against me."

- Luke used the Old Testament Scripture to explain the necessity of Jesus' death and Resurrection. After his Resurrection, Jesus (unrecognized) joined two disciples on the way to Emmaus. Only later at table did he reveal himself, after responding to their misunderstanding, "'Oh, how foolish you are, and how slow of heart to believe all that the prophets have declared! Was it not necessary that the Messiah should suffer these things and then enter into his glory?' Then beginning with Moses and all the prophets, he interpreted to them the things about himself in all the scriptures. . . . 'Were not our hearts burning within us while he was talking to us on the road, while he was opening the scriptures to us?'" (*Luke 24:25–27, 32*).

- Likewise, in describing Jesus' appearance after the Resurrection to the disciples in Jerusalem, Luke describes Jesus as explaining words he had spoken to the disciples "'. . . while I was still with

3

**Book of Covenants**

you—that everything written about me in the law of Moses, the prophets, and the psalms must be fulfilled.' Then he opened their minds to understand the scriptures" (*Luke 24:44–45*).

### About apostolic preaching

There are eight proclamations of the Good News ("kerygmatic sermons") in the Acts of the Apostles, six to Jews and two to Gentiles (see box on p. 77). In four of the six to Jews there is explicit mention of the fulfillment of prophecy.

- For example, in Luke's description of Peter's speech at Pentecost, he begins by explaining the extraordinary phenomena, "[T]hese are not drunk, as you suppose, for it is only nine o'clock in the morning. No, this is what was spoken through the prophet Joel . . . " (*Acts 2:14–16*). (He then quotes at length—Joel 3:1–5).

- In the course of the same sermon, Luke describes how Peter proclaimed Jesus' Resurrection (see *Luke 2:24*). He then quotes *Psalm 16:8–11*—"I keep the LORD always before me;/ because he is at my right hand, I shall not be moved. . . . For you do not give me up to Sheol,/ or let your faithful one see the Pit." Next he explains the fulfillment: "Since [David] was a prophet, he knew that God had sworn with an oath to him that he would put one of his descendants on his throne. Foreseeing this, David spoke of the resurrection of the Messiah . . ." (*Acts 2:30–31*).

- In a later sermon, Luke describes Paul's address in the Antioch synagogue, "Because the residents of Jerusalem and their leaders did not recognize him or understand the words of the prophets that are read every Sabbath, they fulfilled those words by condemning him" (*Acts 13:27*).

## In the Writings of Saint Paul

Paul roots his writing in Scripture.

- He even includes Scripture in his greeting in the Letter to the Romans: "Paul, a servant of Jesus Christ, called to be an apostle, set apart for the gospel of God, which he promised beforehand through his prophets in the holy scriptures, the gospel concerning his Son . . ." (*Romans 1:1–2* in which "gospel" means "good news" and not a written Gospel).

- In setting the theme of the great letter to the Romans, he makes reference to the Old Testament: "For I am not ashamed of the gospel; it is the power of God for salvation to everyone who has faith, to the Jew first and also to the Greek. For in it the righteousness of God is revealed through faith for faith; as it is written, 'The one who is righteous will live by faith'" (*Romans 1:16–17*).

When you see the phrase "as it is written," you should know that the biblical writer is almost always quoting or paraphrasing Scripture. Although the biblical writer doesn't always give you the source, you can find it in the cross-references or footnotes of your Bible. In this case, Paul is referring to Habakkuk 2:4.

- In his teaching on justification by faith in the Letter to the Galatians, Paul says, "And the scripture, foreseeing that God would justify the Gentiles by faith, declared the gospel before-hand to Abraham, saying 'All the Gentiles shall be blessed in you'" (*Galatians 3:8*, citing *Genesis 12:3* and *18:18*).

## In the Teaching of the Fathers

This is from a sermon by Pope Saint Leo the Great (390–461), quoted in the Liturgy of the Hours in the Office of Readings on the Second Sunday of Lent. This is but one example of many such discussions in the writings of the Fathers. It's an example of how thoroughly scriptural the Fathers were in preaching the Good News, making regular use of the Old Testament and "disclos[ing] the inexhaustible content" (see *CCC*, 129).

"Moses and Elijah, the law and the prophets, appeared with the Lord in conversation with him. This was in order to fulfill exactly, through the presence of these five men, the text which says, *Before two or three witnesses every word is ratified.* What word could be more firmly established, more securely based, than the word which is proclaimed by the trumpets of both old and new testaments, sounding in harmony, and by the utterances of ancient prophecy and the teaching of the

Gospel, in full agreement with each other?"

"The writings of the two testaments support each other. The radiance of the transfiguration reveals clearly and unmistakably the one who had been promised by signs foretelling him under the veils of mystery. As Saint John says: *The law was given through Moses, grace and truth came through Jesus Christ.* In him the promise made through the shadows of prophecy stands revealed, along with the full meaning of the precepts of the law. He is the one who teaches the truth of prophecy through his presence, and makes obedience to the commandments possible through grace."

## In the Teaching of the Church

The Catholic Church recognizes the unity of the two testaments in teaching about the origins of the Church in the people of Israel and elements of the worship of the Old Covenant in the liturgy of the New:

"Since Christ's Church was 'pre-pared in marvelous fashion in the history of the people of Israel and in the Old Covenant,'[4] the Church's liturgy has retained certain ele-ments of the worship of the Old Covenant as integral and irreplace-able, adopting them as her own: notably, reading the Old Testament; praying the Psalms; above all, recalling the saving events and sig-nificant realities which have found

## A Catalogue of New Testament Fulfillment Citations

There are many places in the Gospels where the Evangelists make explicit reference to prophecy. The following is not an exhaustive listing. Not surprisingly, Matthew, with his Jewish audience, provides the most. Many of these are unique to him. Where there are parallels in the other Evangelists' texts, reference is usually not made to Scripture in the same way.

**Jesus would . . .**

be born of a virgin and called Emmanuel–*Matthew 1:23; Luke 1:35; Isaiah 7:14*

be born in Bethlehem–*Matthew 2:1, 5-6; Micah 5:1; 2 Samuel 5:2*

come out of Egypt–*Matthew 2:15; Hosea 11:1*

be called a Nazorean (perhaps reflecting the tradition that he was raised in Nazareth)– *Matthew 2:23;* see *Isaiah 66:19*

make his home in Capernaum, suggesting a Gentile mission–*Matthew 4:12-17;* see *John 7:40- 42; Isaiah 8:11*

bear our infirmities, with reference to his healing powers–*Matthew 8:17; Mark 9:12; Isaiah 53:4*

be meek (but victorious in justice)–*Matthew 12:17-21; Isaiah 42:1-4*

teach a message that would be rejected–*Matthew 13:14-15; Mark 4:11-12; John 12:40; Isaiah 6:9-13, 53:1*

teach by means of parables–*Matthew 13:35; Psalm 78:2*

contend with hypocrisy in his hearers–*Matthew 15:7-9; Mark 7:6-7; Psalm 78:36-72; Isaiah 29:13*

draw to himself all who listen to the Father–*John 6:45; Isaiah 54:13*

enter Jerusalem meek, astride an ass–*Matthew 21:5; Isaiah 62:11; Zechariah 9:9*

be rejected as a stone by builders–*Matthew 21:42; Daniel 2:45; Psalm 118:22-23; Isaiah 28:16*

be betrayed by a companion–*John 13:18; Psalm 41:10*

be abandoned by disciples in time of greatest need–*Matthew 26:31; Zechariah 13:7*

be killed without his bones being broken–*John 19:36; Exodus 12:46; Numbers 9:12; Psalm 34:19-20*

## Allusions in the New Testament to Old Testament Scripture

Some see allusions to Old Testament Scripture in passages like these.

**Jesus would . . .**

be God's son–*Mark 1:1, 11; Psalm 2:7*

be born of a woman–*Luke 2:12; Isaiah 9:5*

be descended from Abraham–*Matthew 1:2, 16, 18-25; Genesis 12:2, 15:5, 17:2*

be descended from David in the tribe of Judah–*Matthew 1:6, 16, 18-25; Mark 11:9-10; Luke 1:32; 2 Samuel 7:8-16; Psalm 89:20-38; Psalm 132; Jeremiah 23:5-6; Genesis 49:10; Isaiah 9:6*

be announced by a star–*Matthew 2:2; Numbers 24:17*

be given homage by Gentiles–*Matthew 2:11; Psalm 72:10-11; Isaiah 60:5-16; Numbers 24:17; Isaiah 49:23*

experience the spirit of the Lord come to rest on him–*Matthew 3:16-17; Isaiah 11:2*

inaugurate the judgment of the reign of God–*Matthew 3:12, 13:42, 50; Isaiah 1:25; Zechariah 13:9; Malachi 3:2; Isaiah 41:16; Jeremiah 7:20, 15:7*

universalize the covenant–*Matthew 2:1-12; Isaiah 60:1-6, 9, 11*; see *Epiphany*

be resisted in certain key cities in Galilee–*Matthew 11:23; Isaiah 14:13-21*

be a good shepherd–*John 10:1-18; Ezekiel 34:11-31; Micah 2:12, 7:14; Zechariah 11:17; Matthew 18:12-14*

administer the key of the house of David–*Matthew 16:19; Isaiah 22:22*

reconcile parents and children, rebellious and wise–*Luke 1:17; Sirach 48:10*

bring grace (living water)–*John 4:10-14; Isaiah 55:1-2*

free people with the truth–*John 8:32; Isaiah 42:7*

open the eyes of the blind–*John 9; Isaiah 42:7*

preach the kingdom of God as a vineyard taken away from Israel–*Matthew 21:33-46; John 15:1-7; Isaiah 5:1-7*

be betrayed for thirty pieces of silver–*Matthew 26:15, 27:9; Zechariah 11:12-13*

be silent before his accusers–*Matthew 26:63; Isaiah 53:7*

be beaten and spat upon as the Suffering Servant–*Matthew 27:30; Isaiah 50:6*

be stripped of his garments, which would be divided–*Matthew 27:35; Psalm 22:19*

endure public humiliation–*John 19:5; Isaiah 52:14*

be insulted–*Matthew 27:39; Psalm 22:8*

be taunted for his reliance on God–*Matthew 27:43; Psalm 22:8; Wisdom 2:12-20*

feel forsaken–*Matthew 27:46; Psalm 22:2*

be abandoned–*Matthew 27:49; Psalm 69:20*

thirst on the cross–*John 19:28-30; Psalm 69:21*

be pierced by a sword–*John 19:34; Psalm 22:20*

be buried in someone else's tomb–*Matthew 27:59-60; Isaiah 53:9*

bear much fruit by dying ("grain of wheat")–*John 12:24; Isaiah 53:10-12* their fulfillment in the mystery of Christ (promise and covenant, Exodus and Passover, kingdom and temple, exile and return)" (*CCC*,1093).

## Typology

The mystery of Christ, hidden under the letter of the Old Testament, is revealed in a Christian understanding of the relationship between the Old Testament and the New Testament.

This understanding is called "typology" because Christ is revealed on the basis of figures (types)— historical persons and events foreshadowing or prefiguring a future person or event— which are thereby explained in their richness and significance by the type. (See *CCC*, 1094, 128–130; *Luke 24:13–35*, the Emmaus event; and *2 Corinthians 3:14–16*.)

## Explanations

1. The *Catechism* offers typology as one way to appreciate the unity of the two testaments (*CCC*, 128). It was used "as early as apostolic times" and regularly in Sacred Tradition to bring to light the unity of God's plan in the two Testaments.
2. Typology "discerns in God's works of the Old Covenant prefigurations of what he accomplished in the fullness of time in the person of his incarnate Son" (*CCC*, 128). Its goal is to "disclose the inexhaustible content of the Old Testament."

3. "Typological catechesis" is explained at the very beginning of part two of the *Catechism* ("The Celebration of the Christian Mystery") as it emphasizes the harmony of the two Testaments as the foundation for the Paschal Mystery itself:

- "... it reveals the newness of Christ on the basis of the 'figures' (types) which announce him in the deeds, words, and symbols of the first covenant. By this re-reading in the Spirit of Truth, starting from Christ, the figures are unveiled."[7]

- "Thus the flood and Noah's ark prefigured salvation by Baptism,[8] as did the cloud and the crossing of the Red Sea. Water from the rock was the figure of the spiritual gifts of Christ, and manna in the desert prefigured the Eucharist, 'the true bread from heaven'[9]" (*CCC*, 1094).

## Caution

Not everyone would agree with the *Catechism's* heavy endorsement of typological interpretation to the neglect of other approaches. The benefits of typological interpretation should never undermine the intrinsic value of the Old Testament. Following are cautions from three different quarters.

1. In 1974, the Vatican Commission for Religious Relations with the Jews published "Guidelines and Suggestions for Implementing the Conciliar Declaration

*Nostra Aetate, #4"* (*Nostra Aetate* is Vatican II's *Declaration on the Relationship of the Church to Non-Christian Religions.*) In section II on liturgy, it included the following statements. (It refers to Vatican II, *Constitution on Divine Revelation*, by its Latin title *Dei Verbum.*) Here are two summary highlights related to interpretation of the Old Testament from the documents above:

- It is important to understand how the Old Testament is related to the New. The Old Testament has intrinsic meaning, and the Old and New Testaments mutually shed light upon one another. These are especially important for Christians to keep in mind when hearing the Old Testament read in liturgy.

- The fact that there are distinct and original elements to Christianity must always be kept in mind; at the same time, the continuity between the Old and New Covenants should also be recognized. The Old Testament's promises were realized in the first coming of Christ, but their complete fulfillment will occur when Christ comes again at the end of time.

2. *The New Jerome Biblical Commentary* (1990). In an article in the NJBC, Rev. Raymond E. Brown, S.J., explains, "Typology in the NJBC has been treated more

briefly than in the [original] JBC (1968) and has been placed under the history of the recent past rather than under the contemporary situation. Although the element of typology is still appreciated, the revival of patristic patterns is not so active now; and the discussion has largely been subsumed under the role of metaphor and symbol in literary criticism" (71:48).

- Brown includes succinct advice: "Good typology does not stress the continuity between the Testaments at the price of obliterating important aspects of discontinuity" (71:47).

- He makes the observation that typology is most reliable when it is related to patterns already suggested in Scripture, citing as examples Davidic typology for Jesus, Exodus typology for aspects of the mystery of Christian salvation, and Melchizedek: "If (the Letter to the Hebrews) saw Melchizedek as a type of Christ, it has been argued that liturgy and patristic exegesis were justified in considering Melchizedek's presentation of bread and wine (Genesis 14:18) as a type of the Christian eucharistic sacrifice" (71:47).

**3 Book of Covenants**

3. After the 1994 publication of *The Catechism of the Catholic Church*, the Christian Scholars Group on Judaism and the Jewish People said that the *Catechism* did not reflect the full development of Catholic-Jewish understanding since Vatican II (citing the above-mentioned 1974 document).

   • Members said that the way the *Catechism* treats the Hebrew Scriptures suggests that "events and persons central to Jewish life and history are simply prefigurations of Christ and Christianity."

   • They saw a particular problem in the *Catechism's* heavy use and endorsement of a typological approach to the Old Testament.

## Typology in Use

### Typology in Apostolic Times
#### 1. In Paul, *1 Corinthians 10:1–13*

"I do not want you to be unaware, brothers and sisters, that our ancestors were all under the cloud and all passed through the sea, and all of them were baptized into Moses in the cloud and in the sea, and all ate the same spiritual food, and all drank the same spiritual drink. For they drank from a spiritual rock that followed them, and the rock was Christ" (*1 Corinthians 10:1–4*).

• In this passage Paul presents a panorama of events associated with the Exodus. He describes God's providence during the wilderness wandering in clearly Christian terms ("baptized," "spiritual food," "spiritual drink"). By interpreting the ancestors' experience in this New Covenant language, Paul is reading the Old Covenant story "typologically." He proceeds to use these Old Testament "types" as warnings to Jews of his day.

• The NAB footnote on verse 4 says, "*A spiritual rock that followed them:* the Torah speaks only about a rock from which water issued, but rabbinic legend amplified this into a spring that followed the Israelites throughout their migration. Paul uses this legend as a literary type: he makes the rock itself accompany the Israelites, and he gives it a spiritual sense. *The rock was the Christ:* in the Old Testament, Yahweh is the rock of his people (see *Deuteronomy 32*, Moses' song to Yahweh the Rock). Paul now applies this image to the Christ, the source of the living water, the true Rock that accompanied Israel, guiding their experiences in the desert."

#### 2. In *Matthew 12:40*

"For just as Jonah was three days and three nights in the belly of the sea monster, so for three days and three nights the Son of Man will be in the heart of the earth."

#### 3. In *John 3:14–15* (citing Numbers 21:9)

"And just as Moses lifted up the serpent in the wilderness, so must the Son of Man be lifted up, that whoever believes in him may have eternal life."

### 4. In *1 Peter 3:18-21*

". . . He was put to death in the flesh, but made alive in the spirit, in which also he went and made a proclamation to the spirits in prison, who in former times did not obey, when God waited patiently in the days of Noah, during the building of the ark, in which a few, that is eight persons, were saved through water. And baptism, which this prefigured, now saves you . . ."

## Typology in the Fathers

Typological interpretations were very popular in the early Church. Here are just three examples.

### 1. "The Passover and the New Passover"

This is from a homily by Saint Gregory Nazianzen (329–390), bishop, quoted in the Liturgy of the Hours, Office of Readings, on Saturday of the fifth week of Lent.

"We are soon going to share in the Passover, and although we still do so only in a symbolic way, the symbolism already has more clarity than it possessed in former times because, under the law, the Passover was, if I may dare to say so, only a symbol of a symbol. Before long, however, when the Word drinks the new wine with us in the kingdom of his Father, we shall be keeping the Passover in a yet more perfect way, and with deeper understanding. He will then reveal to us and make clear what he has so far only partially disclosed. For this wine, so familiar to us now, is eternally new."

### 2. "The First Man and the Second Man"

Saint Gregory the Great (died, 604) explains Christ's temptations in the desert and the result of his victory by comparing and contrasting ("typologically") Adam ("the first man") and Christ ("the second man"). He explains that both Adam and Christ were subject to the same three temptations (gluttony, vain glory, and avarice) and concludes with the following statement.

"The second man overcame him (the devil) by the same means he had boasted that he used to overcome the first man. As a captive he would depart from our hearts by the same avenue which had given him entrance when he possessed us." (cited in *Magnificat*, February, 2005)

### 3. The Cross Prefigured

This is from a sermon by Saint Theodore the Studite (759–826), abbot, quoted in the Liturgy of the Hours, Office of Readings, on Friday of the second week of Easter.

"The wonders accomplished through this tree were foreshadowed clearly even by the mere types and figures that existed in the past. Meditate on these, if you are eager to learn. Was it not the wood of a tree that enabled Noah, at God's command, to escape the destruction of the flood together with his sons, his wife, his sons' wives and every kind of animal? And surely the rod of Moses prefigured the cross when it changed water into blood, swallowed up the false serpents of Pharaoh's magicians, divided the sea at one stroke and then restored the waters to their normal course, drowning the enemy and saving God's own people? Aaron's rod, which blossomed in one day in proof of his true priesthood, was another figure of the cross, and did not Abraham foreshadow the cross when he bound his son Isaac and placed him on the pile of wood?"

## Typology in the Liturgy of the Church

The following example from the Liturgy of the Hours, Evening Prayer of Tuesday, week 4, shows how Psalm 137:1–6 is used. The psalm begins, "By the rivers of Babylon/ there we sat and wept,/ remembering Zion."

### 1. Title

The Liturgy of the Hours entitles it "By the rivers of Babylon" and includes the subtitle, "The Babylonian captivity is a type of our spiritual captivity (Saint Hilary)."

### 2. Prayer

The prayer that follows the psalm reads, "Lord, remember your pilgrim Church. We sit weeping at the streams of Babylon. Do not let us be drawn into the current of the passing world, but free us from every evil and raise our thoughts to the heavenly Jerusalem."

## Traditional Typology Catalog

The following moments are prefigured in the Old Testament Scriptures cited:

### Annunciation

- announcement of the births of Isaac—*Genesis 17:16*; of Samson—*Judges 13:5*; of Samuel—*1 Samuel 1:17*

- God announcing to Moses from a burning bush the delivery of Israel—*Exodus 2:23—4:17*

### Incarnation

- Jacob's ladder—*Genesis 28:12–15*

- divine presence in a dwelling—*Exodus 40:34*; in the temple—*1 Kings 8:10*

- the fleece of Gideon—*Judges 6:36–40*

### Nativity

- birth of Eve—*Genesis 2:18–20*

- Moses in the bulrushes—*Exodus 2:1–10*

- flowering of Aaron's rod—*Numbers 17:16–26*

### Presentation of the child Jesus in the temple

- joy of Jacob at the sight of his long lost son Joseph (prefiguring Simeon and the Messiah)—*Genesis 46:28–30*

- presentation in the temple of Israelite firstborn—*Exodus 13:1–16*; of Samuel—*1 Samuel 1:24–28*

### Epiphany

- Joseph's brothers bowing before him—*Genesis 42:6*

- Abner's visit to David at Hebron—*2 Samuel 3:20*

- Queen of Sheba visiting Solomon—*1 Kings 10:1–13*

### Flight into Egypt

- flight of Jacob to Laban—*Genesis 27:46—28:5*

- Moses concealed from Pharaoh's soldiers—*Exodus 2:1–4*

- two spies' flight from Rahab's house—*Joshua 2*

- David's flight through the window—*1 Samuel 19:11–12*

### Slaughter of holy innocents
- Pharaoh's slaughter of Israelite baby boys—*Exodus 1:15–16*

- Saul's slaughter of the priests—*1 Samuel 22:11–19*

- Athaliah's slaughter of the king's sons—*2 Kings 11:1*

- Rachel mourning Israel's exile—*Jeremiah 31:15–17*

### Holy Family in Egypt
- migration of Jacob's family to Egypt—*Genesis 46:1–4*

### Return from Egypt
- Jacob's return to Israel—*Genesis 50:1–13*

- Moses' return to Egypt—*Exodus 4:18–23*

- David's return to Hebron—*2 Samuel 2:1–4*

### John the Baptist
- faith, parentage, and consecration of Isaac—*Genesis 21:1–8*; of Samuel—*1 Samuel 1*

- Elijah (attire, locale, message, way of life)—*1 Kings 17:1–6*

### Temptation of Jesus
- Adam and Eve—*Genesis 3*

- Esau (over his birthright)—*Genesis 27:1–45*

- Joseph (tempted by Potiphar's wife)—*Genesis 39:1–20*

- Moses overcoming the Egyptians—*Exodus 4—14*

- Moses' forty days and nights on the mountain—*Exodus 24:18*

- Samson overcoming the lion—*Judges 14:5–6*

- David overcoming the lion—*1 Samuel 17:35*

- David defeating Goliath—*1 Samuel 17:32–51*

### Sermon on the Mount
- Moses on Mt. Sinai—*Exodus 19*

### Jesus' rasising of Lazarus
- Elijah's raising of the son of the widow Sarepta—*1 Kings 17:17–24*

- Elisha's raising of the Shunammite's son—*2 Kings 4:8–37*

### Transfiguration of Jesus
- angel appearing to Abraham (as Moses and Elijah appeared with Jesus)—*Genesis 18:1–8*

- Moses' transfiguration—*Exodus 34:29*

- Nebuchadnezzar seeing the three youths in the furnace—*Daniel 3*

### Jesus' messianic entry into Jerusalem
- David's entry in triumph with Goliath's head—*1 Samuel 17:55–58*

- Elisha met at Bethel and Jericho by guild prophets—*2 Kings 2:1–5*

### Jesus laments over Jerusalem
- Jeremiah weeping over Jerusalem—*Jeremiah 8:18–23*

### Cleansing of the temple
- King Darius mandating Ezra to cleanse the temple—*Ezra 6:1–18*

- Judas Maccabeus purging the profaned temple—*1 Maccabees 4:36–61*

### Last Supper
- Melchizedek's bread offering to Abraham—*Genesis 14:18–20*

**3**

**Book of Covenants**

- desert manna—*Exodus 16:4–36*

### Jesus' last discourse

- the farewell of Moses—*Deuteronomy 27:1–33:29*; of Joshua—*Joshua 23:1–24:28*

### Prediction of the passion

- predicted death of Ahab by Micaiah—*1 Kings 22:9–28*; of Ben-hadad by Elisha—*2 Kings 8:7–15*; of Belshazzar by Daniel—*Daniel 5:25–30*

### Agony in the garden

- Abraham escorting Isaac up the mountain—*Genesis 22:1–14*

- angel wrestling with Jacob—*Genesis 32:23–33*

- angel comforting Elijah—*1 Kings 19:1–8*

### Betrayal

- Joseph sold to Ishmaelites—*Genesis 37:25–28*

- Joseph sold to Potiphar—*Genesis 37:36*

- Saul threatening David—*1 Samuel 18*

- Joab murdering Abner—*2 Samuel 3:22–30*

- Absalom plotting against David—*2 Samuel 15:1–12*

- Trypho betraying Jonathan—*1 Maccabees 13:12–24*

### Jesus before Pilate

- Joseph before Potiphar's wife—*Genesis 39:1–20*

- Daniel in Babylon—*Daniel 1:6–21*

- Susanna before corrupt judges—*Daniel 13*

- Elijah threatened by Jezebel—*1 Kings 19:1–2*

- Job tested by the devil—*Job 1:1–2:10*

### Crowning with thorns

- the mistreatment of David's messengers by the king of Ammon—*2 Samuel 10:1–5*

### Jesus mocked by soldiers

- Noah's treatment by Ham—*Genesis 9:20–27*

- Samson taunted by the Philistines—*Judges 16:23–25*

- Elisha taunted by children—*2 Kings 2:23–24*

### Scourging at the pillar

- Job tested by the devil—*Job 1:1–2:10*

### Way of the cross

- Isaac carrying the wood for his own sacrifice—*Genesis 22:6*

### Crucifixion

- Abel's murder—*Genesis 4:8*

- Isaac on Mt. Moriah—*Genesis 22:1–18*

- Joseph's imprisonment with cupbearer and baker—*Genesis 39:20–40:4*

- sacrifice of Moabite king's son—*2 Kings 3:27*

- Moses' lifting the bronze serpent in the desert—*Numbers 21:4–9*

### Jesus' seamless garment

- Joseph's coat—*Genesis 37:3*

### Jesus' pierced side

- Eve created from Adam's side—*Genesis 2:21–22*

- Moses calling forth water from the rock—*Exodus 17:1–7*

### New covenant in Christ's blood

- Old Testament covenant sealed

with the blood of the lamb—
*Exodus 12:1–28*

### Mary's sorrow

- Adam and Eve's loss of Abel—
*Genesis 4:1–16*

- Jacob's loss of Joseph—*Genesis 37*

- Naomi's loss of her sons—*Ruth 1:1–5*

### The descent from the cross

- Rizpah and her sons who were hanged—*2 Samuel 21:8–14*

### Jesus' burial

- Joseph thrown in a cistern—
*Genesis 37:21–24*

- the burial of Jacob—*Genesis 50:1–6*; of Moses—*Deuteronomy 34*; of Abner—*2 Samuel 3:31–34*

- Jonah thrown into the sea—*Jonah 1:15*

### Descent into hell or to the dead

- Moses in Egypt—*Exodus 1:1–2:10*

- Joshua's siege of Jericho—*Joshua 5:13–6:27*

- Samson killing a lion—*Judges 14:5–6*

- David defeating Goliath—
*1 Samuel 17:32–51*

- Elijah's contest with priests of Baal—*1 Kings 18:1–40*

### Resurrection

- Samson carrying off the gates of Gaza—*Judges 16:1–3*

- Jonah spewed up by the fish—
*Jonah 2*

- three youths surviving the fiery furnace—*Daniel 3:1–97*

- Daniel surviving the lion's den—*Daniel 6:2–24*

### Women at the tomb

- Reuben looking for Joseph—
*Genesis 37:29–30*

- Love's search for the beloved—
*Song of Solomon 3:1–3, 5:2B–8*

### Appearance to Mary

- the appearances of Jonah after the fish—*Jonah 2:11*; of the three youths in fiery furnace—*Daniel 3:13*; of Daniel in the lion's den—*Daniel 6:24*

### Appearance to the disciples

- Joseph revealing himself to his brothers—*Genesis 45:3*

- prodigal son, forgiven by his father (as disciples were for their cowardice)—*Luke 15:11–32*

### Thomas

- Jacob's stairway dream at Bethel —*Genesis 28:10–17*

- an angel's appearance to Gideon —*Judges 6:11–24*

- Gideon's dew-and-fleece test—
*Judges 6:36–40*

### Ascension

- the taking up of Enoch—*Genesis 5:24*

- Elijah's fiery chariot—*2 Kings 2:11*

### Pentecost

- stone tablets given to Moses—
*Exodus 24:12*

- descent of fire upon Elijah's altar —*1 Kings 18:38*

### Damnation

- the judgment on and destruction of Sodom—*Genesis 19:1–29*; of Dathan and Abiram—*Numbers 16:25–34*; of Korah—*Numbers 16:35*; of Jericho—*Joshua 5:13–6:27*

**3**

**Book of Covenants**

- expulsion of Hagar and her son Ishmael — *Genesis 21:14–21*
- writing on the wall at Belshazzar's feast — *Daniel 5:5–30*

### Salvation
- Jacob's ladder — *Genesis 28:10–17*
- Joseph's brothers fed during famine — *Genesis 42:18–19*
- blood on the doorposts — *Exodus 12:1–28*
- Israel delivered through the Red Sea — *Exodus 14:10–31*
- feast of Job's sons — *Job 42:11*
- three youths saved from the furnace — *Daniel 3:1–97*
- Daniel saved from the lion's den — *Daniel 6:2–24*

### Church
- eight people saved in Noah's ark — *Genesis 7:6–23*
- Isaac meeting Rebecca (Church, the bride of Christ) — *Genesis 24:1–27*

- Solomon building his temple (Christ building his Church) — *1 Kings 6 — 8*
- laying the cornerstone of the temple (Christ) — *1 Kings 5:31, 6:37; Isaiah 28:16*
- the bridegroom meeting the bride — *Song of Solomon 7:11–14*

### Baptism
- the flood — *Genesis 7:6–23*
- the exodus through the Red Sea — *Exodus 14:10–31*
- water in the desert — *Exodus 17:1–17*
- washing of the leper Naaman the Syrian — *2 Kings 5:13–14*

### The Eucharist
- Melchizedek bringing bread and wine to Abraham — *Genesis 14:18–20*
- manna in the desert — *Exodus 16:4–36*
- Elijah fed by angels — *1 Kings 19:1–8*

# An Old Testament Overview

*The following outline includes many of the well-known stories and passages of the Old Testament as suggestions for the beginning reader.*

*Genesis*

I. **Human Origins** (Genesis 1—11)

- Stories of creation (used at the Easter Vigil)—*Genesis 1:1—2:4, 2:4–25*
- Fall of Adam and Eve—*Genesis 3*
- The first promise of a redeemer—*Genesis 3:15*
- Cain and Abel—*Genesis 4:1–16*
- Generations from Adam to Noah—*Genesis 4:17—6:4*
- The flood—*Genesis 6:5—8:22*
- God's covenant with Noah—*Genesis 9:1–17*
- The tower of Babel (used on Pentecost)—*Genesis 11:1–9*

II. **Jewish Origins** (Genesis 12—50)

A. **Patriarchal Period** (Genesis 12—36)

- Abraham's lineage, call, and migration—*Genesis 11:27—12:9*
- Offering of Melchizedek—*Genesis 14:18–20*
- God's covenant with Abraham—*Genesis 15:1–21*
- Birth of Ishmael—*Genesis 16:1–16*
- Abraham's three visitors—*Genesis 18:1–15*
- Destruction of Sodom and Gomorrah—*Genesis 18:16—19:29*
- Birth of Isaac and the expulsion of Hagar—*Genesis 21:1–21*
- Sacrifice of Isaac (used at the Easter Vigil)—*Genesis 22:1–19*
- The patriarchal burial place—*Genesis 23:120* (for Sarah, Abraham, Isaac, Rebekah, Leah, Jacob; see also *Genesis 25:9, 49:31, 50:13*)
- Isaac and Rebekah—*Genesis 24*
- The Jacob-Esau conflict—*Genesis 25:19—28:9*
- Jacob's dream at Bethel—*Genesis 28:10–22*
- Jacob, Leah, and Rachel—*Genesis 29:1–30*
- Reconciliation of Jacob and Esau—*Genesis 32—33*
- Rape of Dinah—*Genesis 34*

B. **Joseph Stories** (Genesis 37—50)

- Conflict of Joseph and his brothers—*Genesis 37*
- Joseph's temptation (Potiphar's wife)—*Genesis 39*
- Joseph's interpretation of dreams—*Genesis 40—41*

- Joseph's reunion—*Genesis 42—44*
- Judah's speech ("paragon of Hebrew eloquence")—*Genesis 44:18–34*
- Joseph's identity revealed—*Genesis 45*
- Joseph's statement of God's purpose—*Genesis 45:7–9*
- Jacob in Egypt—*Genesis 46—47*
- Jacob's demise, testament, and death—*Genesis 48—50*

## III. Israel

### A. National Origins        *Exodus*

1. In Egypt

   Bondage in Egypt—*Exodus 1—5*

   The plagues—*Exodus 7:8—12:32*

   Exodus from Egypt (used at the Easter Vigil)—*Exodus 12:37—14:31*

   Song of deliverance—*Exodus 15:1–21*

2. In the desert

   Journey from the Red Sea to Sinai—*Exodus 15:22—19:2*

   The quail and manna—*Exodus 16; Numbers 11:1–15, 31–34*

   Water from the rock—*Exodus 17:1–7; Numbers 20:2–13*

   Sinai covenant (used on Pentecost)—*Exodus 19:1—24:11*

   The ten commandments—*Exodus 20:1–17* (see *Deuteronomy 5:6–21*)

   The sanctuary and its furnishings—*Exodus 25—30*

   The golden calf—*Exodus 32*      *Leviticus*

   Israelite sacrificial and other ritual legislation—*Leviticus 1—27*

   Social laws—*Leviticus 19*

   Sabbatical and jubilee year—*Leviticus 25*

   The reward of obedience—*Leviticus 26*

   The first census—*Numbers 1—3*      *Numbers*

   Further legal observances—*Numbers 3:1—10:10*

   Aaron's blessing—*Numbers 6:22–27*

   The 38-year journey from Sinai to Moab—*Numbers 10:11—22:1*

   The jealousy of Aaron and Miriam—*Numbers 12* (see also *Exodus 2:4–9, 15:20–21; Numbers 20:1*)

3. Toward Canaan

   Reconnoitering Canaan—*Numbers 13—14*

   Rebellion of Korah—*Numbers 16*

   The sin of Moses and Aaron—*Numbers 20:2–13*

   Aaron's death—*Numbers 20:22–29*

   The bronze serpent—*Numbers 21:4–9*

Baalam, religious compromiser, and the talking ass—*Numbers 22:2—24:25, 31:16*

The second census—*Numbers 26*

The succession of Joshua—*Numbers 27:12–23*

4. Moses' testament

Historical review—*Deuteronomy 1:1—4:43*          *Deuteronomy*

Exhortation to covenant fidelity—*Deuteronomy 5—11*

The great commandment ("shema"), keynote of the Mosaic Law—*Deuteronomy 6:4–5*

Recapitulation/completion of Exodus 20—23 (second Law)—*Deuteronomy 12—26*

Synopsis of the sacred story ("My father was a wandering Aramean . . .")—*Deuteronomy 26:5–9*

Moses' final words—*Deuteronomy 27—33*

Israel's choice: The two ways—*Deuteronomy 30:15–20*

5. Into Canaan

The Jordan crossing—*Joshua 3*                    *Joshua*

Joshua, military strategist—*Joshua 3, 6, 8*

The fall of Jericho—*Joshua 6*

Rahab and the red rope—*Joshua 2, 6:22–23*

The day the sun stopped—*Joshua 10* (see especially verses 12–14)

Joshua's farewell and death—*Joshua 23—24*

**B. The Period of the Judges**                    *Judges*

1. The Book of Judges

Thesis and interpretation of the Book of Judges—*Judges 2:1—3:6*

Deborah, prophetess and judge—*Judges 4—5*

Jael, deceitful hostess, and the defeat of Sisera—*Judges 4:17–22, 5:24–27*

Gideon the conqueror—*Judges 6:1—8:33*

Abimelech the usurper—*Judges 9*

Jotham's parable of the trees—*Judges 9:7–21*

Jephthah and the fateful vow—*Judges 11:1—12:7*

The "Shibboleth"—*Judges 12:1–6*

The life of Samson—*Judges 13:2—16:31*

Micah and the stolen silver—*Judges 17—18*

2. The Book of Ruth                                *Ruth*

The fidelity of Ruth, Moabite become Israelite—*Ruth 1:1–18*

The Ruth-David lineage—*Ruth 4:18–22*

**3**

**Book of Covenants**

## C. The Monarchy (united about 1000–922 BC)

### 1. Eli and Samuel                                    *1 Samuel*

Birth of Samuel—*1 Samuel 1*

Wickedness of Eli's sons—*1 Samuel 2:11–26*

Call of Samuel—*1 Samuel 3:1–4:1a*

The beginning of prophetic ministry—*1 Samuel 3, 9, 10, 12*

Eli's death—*1 Samuel 4:16–18*

Demand for a king—*1 Samuel 8*

### 2. Samuel and Saul

The anointing of Saul—*1 Samuel 9:1–10:16, 11:12–15*

The disobedience of Saul—*1 Samuel 13–15*

### 3. Saul and David

Anointing of David—*1 Samuel 16*

Challenge of Goliath—*1 Samuel 17:1–18:16*

The Jonathan friendship—*1 Samuel 18, 20; 2 Samuel 1*

Jonathan's son Meribbaal, the lame prince—*2 Samuel 4:4, 9:6–13, 16:1–4, 19:24–30, 21:7; 1 Chronicles 8:34, 9:40*

The widow Abigail—*1 Samuel 25, 30; 2 Samuel 2:2, 3:3; 1 Chronicles 3:1*

Saul pursues David—*1 Samuel 26*

Saul, Samuel, and the Witch of Endor—*1 Samuel 28:3–25*

Saul's death—*1 Samuel 31*

### 4. King David                                    *2 Samuel*

Mourning for Saul and Jonathan—*2 Samuel 1*

The oracle of Nathan ("Magna Carta" of royal messianism)—*2 Samuel 7:8–16*

David's prayers—*1 Chronicles 17:16–27, 29:10–19*

The sin of David (the Bathsheba episode)—*2 Samuel 11*

The parable of Nathan—*2 Samuel 12*

David's son Absalom—*2 Samuel 13–18*

Rizpah and the longest wake—*2 Samuel 21:1–10*

### 5. King Solomon                                    *1 Kings*

Reign of Solomon—*1 Kings 1–5, 9–11*

Solomon's dream—*1 Kings 3:5–15*

Solomon' judgment: the two babies—*1 Kings 3:16–28*

Temple dedication—*1 Kings 8; 2 Chronicles 5–7*

The visit of the Queen of Sheba—*1 Kings 10:1–13*

**D. The Divided Monarchy and the Rise of Prophecy**

  1. From Solomon's death (922 BC) to the fall of the North (721 BC)

    The Division of the Kingdom—*1 Kings 11—16*

    a. The Elijah Cycle

      The widow of Zarapheth—*1 Kings 17:8–24*

      The Baal prophets—*1 Kings 18*

      Jezebel's wrath—*1 Kings 19:1–18*

      Ahaziah and the captains' fate—*2 Kings 1*

      Elijah's ascension—*2 Kings 2:9–14*

---

**Elijah's Empty Chair**

The empty chair for Elijah, placed by Orthodox Jews at the yearly Seder meal, expresses hope in the return of Elijah to prepare the way for the Messiah's coming. It's rooted in two Old Testament passages: the description of Elijah being taken up in a chariot of fire (see *2 Kings 2:11*) and the promise of God that Elijah will return prior to the Messiah's coming to prepare the way for him (see *Malachi 4:5*).

---

      Ahab's reign—*1 Kings 16:29—22:40*

      Naboth's vineyard—*1 Kings 21*

      The exploits of Jezebel—*1 Kings 16:31–32, 18:1—19:3, 21; 2 Kings 9:7–37*

    b. The Elisha Cycle

      The call of Elisha—*1 Kings 19:19–21*

      The prophet's curse—*2 Kings 2:23–25*        *2 Kings*

      Miracles of Elisha

- The poor widow—*2 Kings 4:1–7*
- The rich woman of Shunem—*2 Kings 4:8–37*
- The poisoned stew—*2 Kings 4:38–41*
- Multiplication of the loaves—*2 Kings 4:42–44*
- Naaman the leper and Gehazi—*2 Kings 5:1–27*
- The lost ax—*2 Kings 6:1–7*
- The foiled ambush—*2 Kings 6:8–23*
- Ben-hadad's siege of Samaria—*2 Kings 6:24—7:20*
- The prediction of famine—*2 Kings 8:1–6*
- Hazael and the death of Ben-hadad—*2 Kings 8:7–15*

      Elisha's death and corpse—*2 Kings 13:14–21*

      The purge of Jehu—*2 Kings 9:1—10:27*

      The fate of Jezebel—*2 Kings 9:30–37*

Athaliah, Israel's only queen—*2 Kings 11*

Origin of the Samaritans—*2 Kings 17*

Assyrian invasion—*2 Kings 18—20*

c. **Isaiah prophecies**, 742 to about 690 BC (Judea addressed) *Isaiah*

The call of Isaiah ("In the year King Uzziah died")—*Isaiah 6*

Arraignment of Jerusalem—*Isaiah 1—5*

The sin of Judah—*Isaiah 1:1–20, 5:7*

Messianic oracles—*Isaiah 2:2–4* (see *Micah 4, 9:1–6, 11:1–9*)

The Emmanuel oracle—*Isaiah 7:14*

Israel and Judah's foreign policy—*Isaiah 7:1–17*

"The people who walked in darkness have seen a great light . . ." (used at Christmas, midnight Mass)—*Isaiah 9:1–6*

Lucifer myth—*Isaiah 14:12–23*

Divine vindicator—*Isaiah 26*

Israel's deliverance—*Isaiah 35*

d. **Micah prophecies** (to Judea), contemporary of Isaiah      *Micah*

The glory of the remnant—*Micah 4—5* (see *Isaiah 2:2–4*)

The case against Israel—*Micah 6:1—7:20*

On religion—*Micah 6:1–8*

e. **Jonah** (Nineveh addressed)

Jonah, a prophet in a separate category, is the name of the central figure in this story that was written much later, in the fifth century.      *Jonah*

Jonah's prayer from the belly of the fish—*Jonah 2:2–9*

2. The Fall of the North

a. **Amos prophecies** (to Israel) during Jeroboam II's reign, 786–746 BC

Judgment of the nations (woes)—*Amos 1—2*      *Amos*

On religion—*Amos 5:21–27*

Against luxury and complacency—*Amos 6*

Symbolic visions: threats and promises—*Amos 7—9*

Messianic restoration ("fallen hut of David")—*Amos 9:8–15*

b. **Hosea prophecies** (to Israel), during Jeroboam II's reign, 786–746 BC

Hosea's marriage—*Hosea 1—3*      *Hosea*

On religion (insincere conversion)—*Hosea 5:15—6:6*

"When Israel was a child . . ."—*Hosea 11:1–11*

The infidelity of Israel (represented by Jacob, "corporate personality")—*Hosea 12:3–7*

c. Tobit (probably from the early second century BC)

*This book is named after its principal hero, "a devout and wealthy Israelite living among the captives deported to Nineveh from the northern kingdom of Israel in 721 BC. . . . It combines specifically Jewish piety and morality with oriental folklore . . . "the inspired author of the book used the literary form of religious novel (as in Jonah and Judith) for the purpose of instruction and edification. There may have been a historical nucleus around which the story was composed, but this possibility has nothing to do with the teaching of the book" (NAB introduction to the Book of Tobit).* **Tobit**

Prayers of Tobit, Sarah, Tobiah, and Raguel—*Tobit 3:2–6, 11–15; 8:5–7, 15–17; 13*

Raphael reveals his identity—*Tobit 12:11–22*

## Apocrypha/Deuterocanonical

Tobit is one of seven books classified as "apocrypha" in some Bibles. In the Protestant tradition, the word refers to books considered non-canonical in the Protestant tradition, including the books called "deuterocanonical" (secondary canon) in the Catholic tradition. When the word appears on the cover of a Bible published in Protestant traditions ("including apocrypha"), it's referring to the seven deuterocanonical books. For more on this topic, see Chapter 2.

Besides Tobit, the deuterocanonical books are Judith, 1 and 2 Maccabees, Wisdom, Sirach (also known as Ecclesiasticus), and Baruch (including the "Epistle of Jeremiah").

3. Pre-Exilic Judah

Discovery of Deuteronomy (622 BC) and Josiah's reform—*2 Kings 22—23*

a. **Jeremiah prophecies**, about 650–585 BC        *Jeremiah*

Call of Jeremiah—*Jeremiah 1:1–10 (see 15:16, 20:9)*

Early prophecy—*Jeremiah 2:1—3:5*

Against infidelity—*Jeremiah 2—3, 5—7*

The temple sermon—*Jeremiah 7:1–15*

Indictment of Jerusalem for idolatry—*Jeremiah 10*

Jeremiah's complaints ("jeremiads")—*Jeremiah 15:10–21, 18:18–23, 20:7–18*

Potter symbol—*Jeremiah 18:1–6*

Potter's flask symbol—*Jeremiah 19*

The two baskets of figs—*Jeremiah 24*

Promises of Israel's restoration—*Jeremiah 30—32*

The new covenant prophecy ("gospel before the Gospel") — *Jeremiah 31:31–34*

Jeremiah in Jerusalem's last days — *Jeremiah 36:1 —40:6*

b. **Zephaniah's prophecies**, Josiah's reign, 640–609 BC

The Day of the Lord (a classic description on which the Christian hymn *Dies Irae* is based) — *Zephaniah 1:2–18*　　*Zephaniah*

The remnant — *Zephaniah 3* (including the Remnant's Hymn, *3:14–20*)

c. **Nahum prophecies** (against Nineveh), about 615 BC

The fall of Jerusalem — *2 Kings 24 —25*

d. **Habakkuk prophecies**, 605–597 BC　　*Habakkuk*

A person questions God (first Jewish example?) — *Habakkuk 1*

The prayer of Habakkuk (a religious lyric) — *Habakkuk 3*

E. **The Babylonian Exile**, 587–537 BC

1. Lamentations (the following are the only two uses in the lectionary)

A weekday Mass — *Lamentations 2:2, 10–14, 18–19*　*Lamentations*

"For the Dead" and "For Any Need" — *Lamentations 3:17–26*

2. Baruch

A confession of guilt — *Baruch 1:15–22*　　*Baruch*

Praise of Wisdom (used at the Easter Vigil) — *Baruch 3:9–15, 3:32 —4:4*

Jerusalem consoled — *Baruch 5:1–9*

3. **Ezekiel prophecies**　　　　*Ezekiel*

*(the first prophet to receive the call outside the Holy Land)*

Call of Ezekiel — *Ezekiel 1 —4*

Revelation of his mission — *Ezekiel 1 —3, 5, 10*

The first vision — *Ezekiel 1:4 —3:15*

Vision of temple abominations — *Ezekiel 8:1–18*

God's glory departs Jerusalem — *Ezekiel 10*

Personal responsibility — *Ezekiel 14:12–23, 18, 33:10–20*

The faithless spouse — *Ezekiel 16, 20, 23*

The prophet as watchman — *Ezekiel 33:1–9*

The prophet's false popularity — *Ezekiel 33:30–33*

Parable of the shepherds — *Ezekiel 34*

Visions of restored community (used at the Easter Vigil) — *Ezekiel 36:16 —37:14*

Vision of the dry bones (used on Pentecost) — *Ezekiel 37:1–14*

Vision of the temple restoration — *Ezekiel 40 —43*

4. **Second Isaiah prophecies** (toward the end of the exile)    *Isaiah*
Suffering servant oracles—*Isaiah 42:1–4, 49:1–7, 50:4–11, 52:13—53:12*
Promise of salvation—*Isaiah 40*
Promises of restoration—*Isaiah 43—44*
An invitation to grace (used at the Easter Vigil)—*Isaiah 55:1–11*
The effectiveness of God's Word—*Isaiah 55:10–11*

F. **Early Post-Exilic Period**

1. Liberation and return

   a. **Third Isaiah prophecies**, 537 BC

   The nature of true fasting—*Isaiah 58*
   Sin and confession—*Isaiah 59*
   Glory of the New Jerusalem (used at the Easter Vigil)—*Isaiah 60*
   The mission to the afflicted ("The Old Testament Good News")—*Isaiah 61*
   Supplication for the Lord's bride (used at Christmas, the vigil Mass, and Mass at dawn)—*Isaiah 62—64*

2. Restoration

   a. Ezra, religious and cultic reformer    *Ezra*

   The decree of Cyrus (538–529 BC)—*Ezra 1*
   Samaritan interference—*Ezra 4:1–5, 24*
   The rebuilding of the temple—*Ezra 5—6*
   The "Ezra Memoirs"—*Ezra 7—10* (and *Nehemiah 8—9*)

   b. Nehemiah, builder and administrator    *Nehemiah*

   Nehemiah's prayer—*Nehemiah 1:5–11*
   Return to Jerusalem—*Nehemiah 2*
   The rebuilding of the temple—*Nehemiah 4—6*
   Ezra reads the Law—*Nehemiah 8:1–12*
   Confession of the people—*Nehemiah 9—10*

   c. **Haggai prophecies**, beginning in 520 BC    *Haggai*

   Exhortation to rebuild the temple—*Haggai 1*

   d. **Zechariah prophecies**, beginning in 520 BC    *Zechariah*

   Promotion of temple rebuilding—*Zechariah 6:9–15*
   Entry of the messiah (used on Palm Sunday)—*Zechariah 9:9–17*
   The apocalyptic battle for Jerusalem—*Zechariah 14*

   e. **Malachi prophecies**, about 450 BC    *Malachi*

   The messenger of the covenant—*Malachi 3:1–3*

   f. **Obadiah prophecies**, fifth century BC    *Obadiah*

g. **Joel prophecies**, about 400 BC  *Joel*

The Day of the Lord—*Joel 2—3*

Call to repentance—*Joel 2:12–17* (used on Ash Wednesday)

Spirit poured out—*Joel 2:28–29*

The last judgment—*Joel 3:1–21*

## G. Israel after the Exile

In "short story" style, this nationalistic writing treats the Jewish relationship to their Gentile neighbors. (See also the Book of Tobit, mentioned above, because of its setting in the eighth century BC.)

1. Judith, about 100 BC

    *This book is a lively story of God, using Judith as an instrument, delivering the Jewish people in a grave crisis. "Since it is no longer possible to deter-mine with any precision the underlying events which may have given rise to this narrative, it is enough to note that the author sought to strengthen the faith of his people in God's abiding presence among them. The Book of Judith is a tract for difficult times . . ." (NAB introduction to the Book of Judith).*

    Achior's speech before Bethulia—*Judith 5:5–21*  *Judith*

    Prayer of Judith—*Judith 9*

    Judith and Holoferenes—*Judith 10:20—13:10*

    Hymn in praise of Judith—*Judith 16*

2. Esther

    *This book is named after its heroine, the Jewess become queen of Persia. "It tells the story of the plot of Haman, jealous and powerful vizier of King Xerxes (Ahasuerus) of Persia (485–464 BC), to destroy in a single day all the Jews living in the Persian Empire" (NAB introduction to the Book of Esther). It is not a historical work but instructive ("didactic"), showing divine providence preserving God's people from extermination.*

    Queen Vashti, rebellious beauty—*Esther 1*  *Esther*

    Esther intercedes with Ahasuerus—*Esther 5:7*

    Prayers of Mordecai and Esther—*Esther 13:9–17, 14:3–19* (Addition C)

    The Feast of Purim—*Esther 9:20–32*

3. Daniel, about 165 BC

    *"This Book takes its name, not from the author . . . but from its hero, a young Jew taken early to Babylon, where he lived at least until 538 BC. Strictly speaking, the book does not belong to the prophetic writings" (where it is found in the NAB). "This work was composed during the bitter persecution carried on by Antiochus IV Epiphanes (167–164 BC) and was written to strengthen and comfort the Jewish people in their ordeal" (NAB introduction to the Book of Daniel).*

a. Six folk tales about Daniel—Daniel 1—6  *Daniel*

Daniel and his friends in the king's palace—*Daniel 1*

Daniel's interpretation of an unrevealed dream—*Daniel 2*

Shadrach, Meshack, and Abednego in the furnace—*Daniel 3*

Nebuchadnezzar's dream—*Daniel 4*

Belshazzar's party and the writing on the wall—*Daniel 5*

Daniel in the lions' den—*Daniel 6*

b. Four visions—Daniel 7—12

The four beasts—*Daniel 7* (see also *Daniel 2:36–45*)

The ram and the he-goat—*Daniel 8*

The "70 weeks"—*Daniel 9* (see also *Jeremiah 25:11, 29:10*)

A history of the world's kingdoms—*Daniel 10—12*

c. Appendix: two didactic short stories—Daniel 13—14

Susanna's virtue—*Daniel 13*

Bel and the dragon—*Daniel 14*

## H. Rebellion and Jewish Independence

1. 1 Maccabees, about 100 BC  *1 Maccabees*

Portrait of Judas Maccabeus—*1 Maccabees 3*

Four laments—*1 Maccabees 1:25–28, 1:36–40, 2:8–13, 3:45*

Three hymns of praise—*1 Maccabees 2:51–64* ("Our Father"), *3:3–9* (Judas), *14:4–15* (Simon)

The death of Antiochus Epiphanes—*1 Maccabees 6*

Roman alliance—*1 Maccabees 8*

The death of Judas Maccabeus—*1 Maccabees 9:1–22*

The rule and death of Simon—*1 Maccabees 14*

2. 2 Maccabees, about 100 BC  *2 Maccabees*

The author's preface—*2 Maccabees 2:19–32*

Heliodorus' attempt to profane the temple—*2 Maccabees 3*

The martyrdom of Eleazar and the seven brothers—*2 Maccabees 6—7*

## IV. Wisdom Literature

*The following seven works are in their own category of literature and not included in this overview in the above chronology according to the plot of the salvation story. "The wisdom literature of the Bible is the fruit of a movement among ancient oriental people to gather, preserve and express, usually in aphoristic style, the results of human experience as an aid toward understanding and solving the problems of life. In Israel especially, the movement concerned itself with such basic and vital problems as man's origin and destiny, his quest for happiness, the problem of suffering, of good and evil in human conduct, of death, and the state beyond the grave" (NAB introduction to the Wisdom Books).*

**A. Job**, seventh to fifth century BC                              *Job*

Core story — *Job 1 — 2, 42:7–17* (prologue and epilogue)

Dialogues with the three comforters — *Job 3 — 31*

Elihu's speeches about suffering — *Job 32 — 37*

The Lord's answer — *Job 38:1 — 40:26*

**B. Ecclesiastes**, about 300 BC                              *Ecclesiastes*

"Vanity of vanities" — *Ecclesiastes 1:2–11*

"A time to be born, a time to die" — *Ecclesiastes 3:1–15*

"Cast your bread upon the waters" — *Ecclesiastes 11*

**C. Psalms**, to fourth century BC                              *Psalms*

*See Chapter 6 for suggested readings.*

**D. Proverbs**, edited early fifth century BC                              *Proverbs*

Exhortations of the wise man to his son — *Proverbs 1 — 6*

Numerical proverbs — *Proverbs 30:7–33*

The poem of the valiant woman — *Proverbs 31:10–31*

**E. Song of Solomon**, late sixth century BC                    *Song of Solomon*

"A tryst in spring" — *Song of Solomon 2:8–17*

**F. Sirach** (or Ecclesiasticus), early second century BC                    *Sirach*

Duties toward God — *Sirach 2*

True friendship — *Sirach 6:5–17, 9:10–16*

"Happy the husband of a good wife" — *Sirach 26:1–18*

Prayer for God's people — *Sirach 36*

The introduction to the hymn of the ancestors — *Sirach 44:1–15*

**G. Wisdom**, about 100 BC                              *Wisdom*

On suffering ("The souls of the righteous are in the hand of God") — *Wisdom 3:1–12*

Solomon's prayer for wisdom — *Wisdom 9*

# A New Testament Overview

### *The Gospel*

The following principal divisions of the Gospel accounts are taken from the introductions to the Gospels in the revised NAB.

## The Gospel According to Matthew

**1.** The Infancy Narrative       *Matthew 1:1 — 2:23*
**2.** The Proclamation of the Kingdom       *Matthew 3:1 — 7:29*
**3.** Ministry and Mission in Galilee       *Matthew 8:1 — 11:1*
**4.** Opposition from Israel       *Matthew 11:2 — 13:53*
**5.** Jesus, the Kingdom, and the Church    *Matthew 13:54 — 18:35*
**6.** Ministry in Judea and Jerusalem       *Matthew 19:1 — 25:46*
**7.** The Passion and Resurrection       *Matthew 26:1 — 28:20*

## The Gospel According to Mark

**1.** The Preparation for the Public
Ministry of Jesus       *Mark 1:1–13*
**2.** The Mystery of Jesus       *Mark 1:14 — 8:26*
**3.** The Mystery Begins to be Revealed       *Mark 8:27 — 9:32*
**4.** The Full Revelation of the Mystery       *Mark 9:33 — 16:8*
The Shorter Ending
The Longer Ending       *Mark 16:9–20*
The Freer Logion (in the note on 16:9–20)

## The Gospel According to Luke

**1.** The Prologue       *Luke 1:1–4*
**2.** The Infancy Narrative       *Luke 1:5 — 2:52*
**3.** The Preparation for the Public Ministry    *Luke 3:1 — 4:13*
**4.** The Ministry in Galilee       *Luke 4:14 — 9:50*
**5.** The Journey to Jerusalem
(the Travel Narrative)       *Luke 9:51 — 19:27*
**6.** The Teaching Ministry in Jerusalem    *Luke 19:28 — 21:38*
**7.** The Passion Narrative       *Luke 22:1 — 23:56*
**8.** The Resurrection Narrative       *Luke 24:1–53*

## The Gospel According to John

**1.** Prologue       *John 1:1–18*
**2.** The Book of Signs       *John 1:19 — 12:50*
**3.** The Book of Glory       *John 13:1 — 20:31*
**4.** Epilogue: Resurrection Appearance in Galilee    *John 21:1–25*

## The Words of Jesus

### Parables

The House Built on Rock—*Matthew 7:24–27, Luke 6:47–49*

The Sower—*Matthew 13:1–23, Mark 4:1–12, Luke 8:4–10*

The Seed Grows of Itself—*Mark 4:26–29*

The Weeds—*Matthew 13:24–30, 36–43*

The Mustard Seed—*Matthew 13:31–32, Mark 4:30–32, Luke 13:18–19*

The Leaven—*Matthew 13:33, Luke 13:20–21*

The Found Treasure—*Matthew 13:44*

The Precious Pearl—*Matthew 13:45–46*

The Net—*Matthew 13:47–50*

The Unmerciful Servant—*Matthew 18:23–35*

The Laborers in the Vineyard—*Matthew 20:1–16*

The Two Sons—*Matthew 21:28–32*

The Tenants—*Matthew 21:33–46, Mark 12:1–12, Luke 20:9–19*

The Marriage Feast—*Matthew 22:1–14, Luke 14:15–24*

The Wedding Garment—*Matthew 22:11–14*

The Ten Virgins—*Matthew 25:1–13*

The Talents—*Matthew 25:14–30, Luke 19:12–27*

The Sheep and the Goats—*Matthew 25:31–46*

The Two Debtors—*Luke 7:36–50*

The Good Samaritan—*Luke 10:29–37*

The Importunate Friend—*Luke 11:5–8*

The Rich Fool—*Luke 12:16–21*

The Servants Who Waited—*Luke 12:35–48*

The Barren Fig Tree—*Luke 13:6–9*

The Last Seat—*Luke 14:7–11*

The Great Supper—*Luke 14:15–24*

Luke's Three Parables of Mercy: "The gospel within the Gospel"

The Lost Sheep—*Luke 15:3–7*
The Lost Coin—*Luke 15:8–10*
The Prodigal Son—*Luke 15:11–32*

The Dishonest Steward—*Luke 16:1–13*

The Rich Man and Lazarus—*Luke 16:19–31*

The Persistent Widow—*Luke 18:1–8*

The Pharisee and the Tax Collector —*Luke 18:9–14*

The Gold Pieces—*Luke 19:11–27*

## The Miracles of Jesus

### Nature Miracles

*The only miracle recorded by all four Evangelists is the multiplication of the loaves.*

Changing water into wine at Cana—*John 2:1–11*

Miraculous catch of fish—*Luke 5:1–11;* compare *John 21:1–14*

Calming of the storm—*Matthew 8:23–27, Mark 4:35–41, Luke 8:22–25*

Multiplication of loaves—*Matthew 14:13–21, Mark 6:32–44, Luke 9:12–17, John 6:1–13;* compare *Matthew 15:32–38, Mark 8:1–9*

Walking on water—*Matthew 14:22–33, Mark 6:45–52, John 6:16–21*

Coin in the fish's mouth—*Matthew 17:24–27*

Cursing the fig tree—*Matthew 21:18–19, Mark 11:12–14*

### Healings

*Very numerous in Jesus' ministry, and often only referred to scripturally* (Matthew 4:23–25, Luke 4:16–30, Mark 6:1–6). *Many are mentioned specifically:*

Healing of the royal official's son—*John 4:46–54*

Cleansing a leper—*Matthew 8:2–4, Mark 1:40–45, Luke 5:12–14*

Cure of the mother-in-law of Peter—*Matthew 8:14–15, Mark 1:29–31, Luke 4:38–41*

Healing a paralytic—*Matthew 9:1–8, Mark 2:3–12, Luke 5:18–26*

Healing a sick man at Bethzatha—*John 5:1–9*

Restoring a man with a withered hand—*Matthew 12:9–13, Mark 3:1–6, Luke 6:6–11*

Healing a centurion's servant—*Matthew 8:5–13, Luke 7:1–10*

Healing of a blind and mute person—*Matthew 12:22*

Healing a woman with a hemorrhage—*Matthew 9:20–22, Mark 5:25–34, Luke 8:43–48*

Opening the eyes of two blind men—*Matthew 9:27–31*

Cure of a mute man—*Matthew 9:32–34*

Healing a deaf and mute man—*Mark 7:31–37*

Opening the eyes of a blind person at Bethsaida—*Mark 8:22–26*

Opening the eyes of a person born blind—*John 9:1–41*

Restoring an infirm woman—*Luke 13:10–17*

Healing of a man with dropsy—*Luke 14:1–6*

Cleansing the lepers—*Luke 17:12–19*

Opening the eyes of the blind man—*Matthew 20:29–34, Mark 10:46–52, Luke 18:35–43*

Healing Malchus' ear—*Matthew 26:51–52, Mark 14:47, Luke 22:49–51, John 18:10–11*

**3**

**Book of Covenants**

## Exorcisms (Deliverances)

*Evidently very numerous in his ministry, given the scriptural formulas (see Mark 1) that recur. Seven are mentioned specifically:*

Demoniac at Capernaum—*Mark 1:23–28, Luke 4:33–37*

Blind and mute demoniac—*Matthew 12:22–29, Luke 11:14–15*

Gadarene/Gerasene demoniacs—*Matthew 8:28–34, Mark 5:1–15, Luke 8:26–39*

Mute demoniac—*Matthew 9:32–34*

Daughter of Syro-Phoenician woman—*Matthew 15:21–28, Mark 7:24–30*

Child with a demon—*Matthew 17:14–21, Mark 9:14–29, Luke 9:37–43*

Infirm woman—*Luke 13:10–17*

## Resuscitations

*Not truly resurrections, like Jesus' own. That is, these people were brought back to life, but they still had to die eventually.*

The daughter of Jairus—*Matthew 9:18–26, Mark 5:21–43, Luke 8:41–56*

The son of the widow of Nain—*Luke 7:11–17*

Lazarus—*John 11:1–44*

## The "Seven Signs"

These miracles, called "signs' in the Gospel according to John, are from the first part of that Gospel called "The Book of Signs."

1. Changing water to wine at Cana—*John 2:1–11*
2. Cure of royal official's son—*John 4:46–54*
3. Cure on a Sabbath feast—*John 5:1–15*
4. Multiplication of loaves at Passover—*John 6:1–15*
5. Walking on the sea—*John 6:16–21*
6. Cure of man blind from birth—*John 9:1–34*
7. Raising of Lazarus—*John 11:1–44*

## Luke's Banqueting Scenes

Jesus' table ministry shows Luke's preference for banquet scenes as a way of conveying his theological points.

1. Levi's reception for Jesus—*Luke 5:29–32*—Eating and drinking with sinners
2. Simon the Pharisee's dinner—*Luke 7:36–50*—A woman bathes Jesus' feet.
3. At Martha and Mary's house—*Luke 10:38–42*—Mary chooses the better part.
4. A Pharisee's dinner —*Luke 11:37–54*—"[W]oe to you Pharisees!"
5. A leading Pharisee's Sabbath meal—*Luke 14:1–6*—"Is it lawful to cure people on the sabbath, or not?"
6. Parable told at a Pharisee's meal: The Marriage Feast—*Luke 14:7–14*—Highest place and lowest place

7. Parable told at a Pharisee's meal: The Great Supper—*Luke 14:15–24*—"[B]ring in the poor [and] the crippled"
8. Parable of the Prodigal Son —*Luke 15:11–32*—Celebration: "[G]et the fatted calf and kill it"
9. At Zacchaeus' house—*Luke 19:1–10*—"I must stay at your house today."
10. The Last Supper—*Luke 22:14–38*—"Do this in remembrance of me."
11. The Emmaus meal—*Luke 24:13–32*—"Then their eyes were opened"

## *The Passion of Jesus*

### The Three Predictions of the Passion in Mark

These are not the only times in the Gospels that the Evangelists mention predictions of the passion. See also the "Sign of Jonah" passage in Matthew (*12:39–40*) and Jesus' saying according to Luke (*13:32–33*), ". . . Listen, I am casting out demons and performing cures today and tomorrow, and on the third day I finish my work. Yet today, tomorrow, and the next day I must be on my way, because it is impossible for a prophet to be killed outside of Jerusalem." The Evangelists also record Jesus' prediction of the Resurrection (see *Matthew 17:9* and parallels).

1. After Peter's confession—*Mark 8:31* (with parallels in *Matthew 16:21* and *Luke 9:22*)
2. While passing through Galilee—*Mark 9:30–31* (with parallels in *Matthew 17:22–23* and *Luke 9:44*)
3. Near Jerusalem—*Mark 10:32–34* (with parallels in *Matthew 20:17–19* and *Luke 18:31–33*)

### The Seven Last Words

1. "Father, forgive them; for they do not know what they are doing." —*Luke 23:34*
2. "Woman, here is your son. . . . Here is your mother." —*John 19:26, 27*
3. "I am thirsty." —*John 19:28*
4. "[T]oday you will be with me in Paradise" —*Luke 23:43*
5. "My God, my God, why have you forsaken me?" —*Matthew 27:46; Mark 15:34*
6. "It is finished." —*John 19:30*
7. "Father, into your hands I commend my spirit." —*Luke 23:46*

## *The Resurrection of Jesus*

The following overview is provided to help the reader compare the Evangelists' accounts of the Resurrection and invite the reader to go to the text.

### According to Matthew

- Mary Magdalene and the other Mary visit the tomb—*28:1*
- An angel of the Lord appears—*28:2–7*
- Jesus appears to the women—*28:9–10*
- Chief priests bribe guards—*28:11–15*
- Jesus commissions the disciples—*28:16–20*

## According to Mark

- Mary Magdalene, Mary mother of James, and Salome visit the tomb—*16:1–3*
- They encounter a young man, announcing the Resurrection—*16:5–7*
- Jesus appears to Mary Magdalene—*16:9*
- Mary tells his companions, who disbelieve—*16:10–11*
- Jesus appears to three disciples going to the country—*16:12*
- Jesus appears to the Eleven at table—*16:14–18*
- The Ascension—*16:19–20*

## According to Luke

- Mary Magdalene, Mary mother of James, Joanna visit the tomb—*24:1–2*
- Two men appear, announcing the Resurrection—*24:2–8*
- The women tell the news to the Eleven, who do not believe—*24:9–11*
- Peter runs to the tomb—*24:12*
- Jesus appears to two on the way to Emmaus (and to Peter)—*24:13–32*
- Report to the Eleven and others about Emmaus appearance—*24:33–35*
- Jesus appears to the Eleven in Jerusalem—*24:36–49*
- The Ascension—*24:50-52*

## According to John

- Mary Magdalene visits the tomb, then returns to Peter and John—*20:1–2*
- Peter and John run to the tomb and see burial clothes—*20:3–10*
- Jesus appears to Mary Magdalene—*20:11–17*
- Mary announces the Resurrection to the disciples—*20:18*
- Jesus appears to the Eleven, minus Thomas, Sunday evening—*20:19–25*
- Jesus appears to the Eleven, including Thomas, one week later—*20:26–29*
- Jesus appears to two Apostles by the Sea of Galilee later—*21:1–23*

### The Post-Resurrection Appearances of Jesus

**According to Paul** (*1 Corinthians 15:5-8*): ". . . he appeared to Cephas, then to the twelve. Then he appeared to more than five hundred brothers and sisters at one time . . . Then he appeared to James, then to all the apostles. Last of all, as to one untimely born, he appeared also to me."

**According to Luke** (*Acts 1:3 and 13:30-31*): "After his suffering he presented himself alive to them by many convincing proofs, appearing to them during forty days and speaking about the kingdom of God . . . But God raised him from the dead;

and for many days he appeared to those who came up with him from Galilee to Jerusalem . . . "

### An Overview of the Acts of the Apostles

The following list includes many of the well-known stories and passages of Acts as suggestions for the beginning reader.

Ascension—*Acts 1:1–12*

Pentecost—*Acts 2*

The ministry of deacons—*Acts 6:1–7*

Stephen, the first martyr—*Acts 6:5–15; 7*

Philip and the Ethiopian—*Acts 8:26–39*

Saul of Tarsus—*Acts 9:1–30*

Peter and Cornelius—*Acts 10*

Peter in prison—*Acts 12:1–19*

Paul's first missionary journey— *Acts 13:4—14:27*

The first council—*Acts 15:1–35*

Paul's second missionary journey —*Acts 15:36—18:22*

Paul in prison—*Acts 16:16–40*

Paul's third missionary journey— *Acts 18:23—21:16*

The riot of the Ephesus silversmiths —*Acts 19:23–41*

Paul's voyage to Rome—*Acts 27, 28*

3

Book of Covenants

## CHAPTER 4

# Journal of God's People

## The Word of God

The earliest forms of Christian chatechesis made regular use of the Old Testament and the personal witness of the apostles and disciples that would become the New Testament. Much of the catechesis in the Patristic period took the form of commentary on the word of God contained in Sacred Scripture. . . .

Catechesis should assume the thought and perspective of Sacred Scripture and make frequent, direct use of the biblical texts themselves.

—*National Directory for Catechesis*, p. 280

## Of What Went Before and What Follows

In his *History of the English People*, the historian and theologian Bede the Venerable records this story:

Thirteen hundred years ago, a band of monks journeyed to the island of Britain, a violent and savage land of warlords and tribes. A heathen king named Edwin was fascinated by the monk's stories of the Gospel of Jesus—his teachings about God's love, his miracles, and his resurrection from the dead. Edwin had become disenchanted with Woden and Thor and the other gods of his own Saxon religion and was seriously considering being baptized into this "new" religion. But the king was having a great deal of trouble making up his mind. So he called a meeting of his counselors and Saxon priests.

To Edwin's surprise, the chieftains and priests of the council expressed their own misgivings about their religion. Perhaps this Christianity was worth a try. Then, one of King Edwin's counselors addressed him: "Your majesty, in trying to understand our present life on earth and the time of which we know nothing, it seems to me that this life of ours is like that of a small sparrow on a winter's night. As we gather in the warmth of our banquet hall, protected from the snow and rain raging outside, the little sparrow flies through the hall, in one door and out through another. While it is inside, the sparrow is safe from the winter storm; but after a few moments, the sparrow vanishes from sight into the stormy night from which it came."

"It is like us, O king. We appear on earth for only a short time. But of what went before this life or what follows, our religion teaches us nothing. If this new religion brings us new understanding, it seems only right that we should follow."

# The Mission of the Church

The mission of the Church is threefold. The message is first, followed by fellowship and service. The message comes from Sacred Scripture; together with sacred Tradition, it is the heart of the Church's life and mission. Translation, interpretation, analysis, and commentary are vital parts of the Church's stewardship of Scripture. (See CCC, 849–856.)

**Message** (Greek: *Kerygma*)
The message consists of the proclamation of the Good News, the core of which is that Jesus who died is risen and now lives among us (see *Romans 16:25*).

**Fellowship** (Greek: *Koinonia*)
People are social by nature. The Catholic Church understands this and promotes a healthy sense of family and community.

**Service** (Greek: *Diakonia*)
Because we are a part of community, we are also called by the Gospel message of Jesus Christ to work for social justice.

# The Translation of Scripture

See Appendix 4, "A History of the Translation of Scripture into English."

## The Languages of Scripture

To simplify and generalize, the following four-point outline introduces this treatment of Scripture translation.

**1. Hebrew** (and closely related Aramaic)
Hebrew was the original language of the Old Testament. The following is *Genesis 1:1* in Hebrew:

את אלהים ברא בראשית
הארץ: ואת השמים

### 2. Greek

At the time of Christ, Greek was the universal language and was familiar in Jerusalem where Jews from the world over gathered. The word "Hellenistic" describes non-Greeks who had appropriated aspects of Greek language and culture. "Hellenistic Jews" were Jews who spoke Greek. "Hellenistic Jewish Christians," likewise, were Greek-speaking Jews who became Christians.

- The Jews' own Greek translation of their Scriptures, known as the Septuagint, was done before the time of Christ and was the commonly accepted Bible of the Early Church. When the authors of the New Testament quoted

## The Legend of the Septuagint

There was a time when both Jews and Christians generally believed a legend about the origin of the Greek translation of the Old Testament. The legend of the "Septuagint" originated in the fictitious, second-century BC *Letter of Aristeas to Philocrates*. This colorful narrative, especially popular with Christians, became part of the belief in the early Church about a miraculous origin of the Bible.

The story goes that the librarian of the Egyptian king, Ptolemy II Philadelphus (285-246), wanted to include a copy of the Jewish law in the famous library in Alexandria, Egypt. With the encouragement of the librarian, the king asked the high priest in Jerusalem to send a group of seventy-two elders, six from each tribe, to Alexandria to produce a translation. In 275 BC their mission was accomplished in seventy-two days and was acceptable to all, including the Jews in Alexandria.

It was called the "Septuagint," which means seventy, the rounded-off number of the translators and the days of their work according to the story. That word became traditional as the name not only for the Greek version of the Torah (the Pentateuch, the first five books of the Old Testament) but for the whole body of Old Testament translations and compositions in Greek.

The part of this story that is factual is that a Greek translation of the Torah was completed in the early third-century BC. The point of the story is that the Septuagint is trustworthy because the translation was inspired—confirmed by the identical translations.

4

Scripture, it was from what Christians today call the Old Testament and usually it was a Greek translation of it. (Behind this simple statement is much scholarship. Basically, every quote needs to be examined separately. Most appear to be from the Septuagint, but comparing a New Testament quotation in Greek to an Old Testament Hebrew text and a Greek translation of a Hebrew text is a study filled with obscurity and ambiguity.)

- Greek is the original language of the New Testament. This is *John 3:16* in Greek:

Διότι τόσον πολύ ἀγάπησε ὁ Θεὸς τὸν κόσμον, ὥστε ἔδωκε τὸν Υἱόν του

## The Pope, the Scholar, and the Vulgate

The Vulgate came about because of the request of one man, the work of one man, and a crying need in the Church. "By the close of the fourth century, there was such a confusing diversity among Latin manuscripts [handwritten copies] of the New Testament that Augustine lamented, 'Those who translated the Scriptures from Hebrew into Greek can be counted, but the Latin translators are out of all number. For in the early days of the faith, everyone who happened to gain possession of a Greek manuscript [of the New Testament] and thought he had any facility in both languages, however slight that might have been, attempted to make a translation.'"

"In these circumstances, the stage was set for the most decisive series of events in the whole history of the Latin Bible. In the year 383, Pope Damasus urged Jerome (about 342-420), the most learned Christian scholar of his day, to produce a uniform and dependable text of the Latin Scriptures; he was not to make a totally new translation but to revise a text of the Bible in use at Rome. Jerome's first inclination was to say 'No, thank you' to the pope's invitation. He wrote:

'You urge me to revise the Old Latin version, and, as it were, to sit in judgment on the copies of the Scriptures that are now scattered throughout the world; and inasmuch as they differ from one another, you would have me decide which of them agree with the original. The labor is one of love, but at the same time it is both perilous and presumptuous—for in judging others I must be content to be judged by all. . . . Is there anyone learned or unlearned, who, when he takes the volume in his hands and perceives that what he reads does not suit his settled tastes, will not break out immediately into violent language and call me a forger and a profane person for having the audacity to add anything to the ancient books, or to make any changes or corrections in them?'" (Bruce Metzger, *The Bible in Translation*, pp. 31-32).

Nevertheless, Jerome undertook the task, risking the reaction he recognized from the beginning. He agreed because, as he revealed in his letter of dedication to Damasus that declared the occasion and scope of the undertaking, it was an assignment that came from the supreme pontiff of the Church. His other reason for embarking on such a task came from his scholarly side: The need was great because of the astonishing diversity among the Old Latin manuscripts—"almost as many forms of text," he wrote, "as there are manuscripts."

## 3. Latin

The Bible commonly used in the Church for centuries was a Latin translation of both the Greek Septuagint and the Greek New Testament called "the Vulgate."

- It was translated around the year 400 by Saint Jerome.

- It was called the Vulgate, a word that means "common" in Latin; Latin was the common language of Europe until well into the Middle Ages.

- Jerome's translation prevailed for centuries, in liturgical use and as the basis for vernacular translations of the Bible.

## 4. Vernacular

Vernacular means the language of one's native people. Many people can read and speak "foreign" (learned) languages as well as their own vernacular language.

- When vernacular languages began to develop, the Bible was one of the first books to be translated (predating printing by centuries).

- Scripture has been translated throughout the world into many, many vernacular languages.

- As with Scripture's very composition, so its translation into English (as well as other languages) was at first an oral process. Caedmon, one of twelve Anglo-Saxon poets identified in medieval sources, was said to have retold Bible stories in alliterative verses. According to Saint Bede, the sole source of original information about Caedmon's life in Historia ecclesiastica, in the seventh century, Caedmon sang about the world's creation; about Israel's Exodus from Egypt and journey into the promised land; about the passion, Resurrection, and Ascension of Jesus into heaven; and of the coming of the Holy Spirit and the apostles' teaching. Bede, who died in 735, may be responsible for the earliest written translation in English of any portion of the Bible; he is said to have translated the Gospel of John into Anglo-Saxon. Alfred the Great, who reigned from 871 to 901, is credited with translating passages from Exodus as well as part of the Ten Commandments. Following this, in 950 the *Lindisfarne Gospels* were written in the Northumbrian dialect as "interlinear glosses" (between-the-line translations) on a seventh-century Latin manuscript. And then in the tenth century, the earliest existent Old English version of the gospels was written—the Wessex Gospels.

- The production of Scripture translation into English (actually "Anglo-Saxon"—Old English) stopped in 1066 with the Norman conquest of England (Normandy is part of modern-day France). "For some three centuries, Norman French largely supplanted English among educated people; Latin, of course, continued to be used by the clergy. In the fourteenth century, English translation of parts of the Scriptures began to appear again, the form of the language being what is now called Middle English" (Bruce Metzger, *The Bible in Translation*, p. 56).

- Before the flourishing of Middle English (1150–1475) and the age of Chaucer (1340–1400), there is no evidence of English translations of significant portions of the Bible. There was, in the 1300s, a metrical translation of the psalms into English done by William of Shoreham and another by Blessed Richard Rolle (1300–1349; first of the great fourteenth century English mystics).

- "These translations were not unusual. Similar efforts to translate the Bible into vernacular languages were made throughout Europe, long before the Protestant Reformation. In Germany, eighteen translations had been made in the fifty-six years before Luther's rendition (1522). Even before the discovery of America, an Italian version (1471), a Dutch version (1478), and a French version (1479) had been made. This list, of course, does not pretend to be complete" (Richard Murphy, O.P., *Background to the Bible*, p. 84).

# Alphabets

| Hebrew | | |
| --- | --- | --- |
| Letter | Name | Transliteration |
| א | aleph | - or ' |
| ב | beth | b,v |
| ג | gimel | g |
| ד | daleth | d |
| ה | he | h |
| ו | vav | v, w |
| ז | zayin | z |
| ח | cheth | ḥ |
| ט | teth | ṭ |
| י | yod | y, j, i |
| כ ך¹ | kaph | k, kh |
| ל | lamed | l |
| מ ם¹ | mem | m |
| נ ן¹ | nun | n |
| ס | samekh | s |
| ע | ayin | ' |
| פ ף¹ | pe | p, f |
| צ ץ¹ | sadi | ṣ |
| ק | koph | ḳ |
| ר | resh | r |
| שׁ | shin | sh, š |
| שׂ | śin | ś |
| ת | tav | t |

¹At end of word.

| Greek | | | |
| --- | --- | --- | --- |
| Letter | | Name | Transliteration |
| A | α | alpha | a |
| B | β | beta | b |
| Γ | γ | gamma | g |
| Δ | δ | delta | d |
| E | ε | epsilon | e |
| Z | ζ | zeta | z |
| H | η | eta | e (or ē) |
| Θ | θ | theta | th |
| I | ι | iota | i |
| K | κ | kappa | k |
| Λ | λ | lambda | l |
| M | μ | mu | m |
| N | ν | nu | n |
| Ξ | ξ | xi | x |
| O | o | omicron | o |
| Π | π | pi | p |
| P | ρ | rho | r |
| Σ | σ, ς¹ | sigma | s |
| T | τ | tau | t |
| Υ | υ | upsilon | y |
| Φ | φ | phi | ph |
| X | χ | chi | ch, kh |
| Ψ | ψ | psi | ps |
| Ω | ω | omega | o (or ō) |

¹At end of word.

## A Basic Vocabulary

The Bible in its original languages (Hebrew/Aramaic and Greek) is the authoritative one; all translations need to be measured against it. A Scripture scholar once said that reading the Bible in English is like kissing your bride through her veil. Unfortunately, those who cannot read Hebrew, Aramaic, or Greek will have to settle for this. Scripture scholarship, in resources like footnotes and commentaries, can help lift the veil. The following words are used in the study of Scripture and are all illustrated in the pages ahead.

### Translation

A translation is the change of the biblical text into another language.

### Transliteration

A transliteration is a phonetic spelling of the original words using another alphabet. Sometimes footnotes will include Greek words, transliterating them first (by using letters of the English alphabet instead of the Greek). They are then often translated too and explained.

- A few Greek words are mainly transliterated—like *hupokrita*, coming over into English as "hypocrite."

- Some Greek words need only minimal translation—like *philanthropia*, which, transliterated, is immediately recognized as "philanthropy" in English, which means "love for mankind" (and a whole lot more). It is used in *Titus 3:4–5* (a passage familiar from the Christmas Mass at dawn). The NAB translates, "But when the kindness and generous love of God our savior appeared, / not because of any righteous deeds we had done but because of his mercy, / he saved us. . . ." The NKJV renders it, "But when the kindness and the love of God our Savior toward man appeared. . . ." But what would be the risk if a translation simply read: "But when the kindness and philanthropy of God our savior appeared. . ."? God, the ultimate philanthropist.

- Most Greek words, of course, need translation—like *margarita*, which means "pearl." Without translation, the reader would think that the merchant in Jesus' parable in Matthew 13:45–46 was searching for fine margaritas. The Greek *margarita* (if not the English) is the one that should not be thrown before swine, it says in Matthew 7:6.

### Paraphrase

A paraphrase is a loose translation of the biblical text using colloquial or culturally specific language.

### Literal

A literal translation and a literal interpretation are two different things. Furthermore, the term "literal" interpretation does not have the same meaning to many today that it had in the early ages of the Church (when it was coined).

1. **A literal translation**
   The first part of this chapter is about translating, in which the

word "literal" means "word-for-word." A literal translation is a needed and noble thing. There are many examples below of the challenging balance between fidelity to the precise wording of the text (a literal translation) on the one hand and intelligibility and readability (a "freer" translation) on the other.

## 2. A literal interpretation

A later part of this chapter is about interpretation and includes the Church's teaching about the importance of historical context, literary styles, and figures of speech. The term "literal" (as it was originally used in the early centuries of the Church and is still used in the *Catechism* and in scholarly circles) is a technical term. It has a very positive connotation and serves a very helpful purpose.

• The meaning of the literal sense of Scripture for early Church writers was what the author intended to say and what the first audience understood. The "literal" sense distinguished it from "spiritual" interpretation or "typological" interpretation, for example (both of which also have their place). There is more about this later in this chapter.

• The common, secular implication of "literal interpretation" is that it's opposed to "metaphorical interpretation"— meaning, somebody is not

understanding a metaphor (a figure of speech). For example, if somebody took the phrase "she hit the roof" in a literal way, they would think that she must have gone and gotten a ladder and physically made contact with the roof. Or it would mean that somebody is not understanding a figure of speech like a hyperbole and taking *Matthew 18:8* literally, "If your hand or your foot causes you to stumble, cut it off and throw it away . . ." (A hyperbole is an intentional, obvious exaggeration; see Appendix 2, "Figures of Speech in Scripture.") Or it would mean someone did not understand King Henry II fuming about Bishop Thomas Becket, "Will no one rid me of this troublesome priest!" (Four of his knights took him literally: They went and killed Becket in his Canterbury cathedral.)

• The literalist readings of fundamentalist Churches today is explained later in this chapter (see "Fundamentalism"). This use of the word is not about interpreting metaphors literally but about maintaining that "what the Bible says" is not colored by context and is always literally factual. Inspiration is understood as dictation. Most literary forms are not recognized.

• "Literal sense" as used in the Catholic Tradition has

nothing to do with how the word "literal" is used commonly or in fundamentalist contexts.

## Principles of Translation

The following distinction is a well-known one that explains the differences among Scripture translations. Saint Jerome himself said, "For I myself not only admit but freely proclaim that in translating from the Greek (except in the case of the holy scriptures where even the order of the words is a mystery) I render sense-for-sense and not word-for-word." (In his Vulgate, however, he was not always consistent in applying this rule.)

1. **Form-centered** (also known as "formal equivalence")
   "Literal," word-form-for-word-form (word-for-word); the word order and sentence structure of the original is preserved as much as possible in translation (a verb is usually translated with a verb and a pronoun with a pronoun, even though there may be a more idiomatic English expression). Expect traditional language and complicated sentence structure.

2. **Content-centered translation** (also known as "dynamic equivalent")
   "Idiomatic," thought-for-thought (idiomatically powerful but still faithful to the inspired text); also called "functional equivalent," the form of the original is adjusted in translation to English usage, attempting to produce the same impact on readers today that the original had.

### Comparing form-centered and content-centered translations

These three examples all involve idioms and illustrate the difficult decisions translators need to make. This is how *The Oxford American Dictionary and Language Guide* defines "idioms:" "**1** a group of words established by usage and having a meaning not deductible from those of the individual words (as in *at the drop of a hat, see the light*), **2** a form of expression peculiar to a language, person, or group of people . . ." This particular dictionary adds what it calls a "Grammar Tip" from time to time for certain words. It does this for "idiom." It says, "An idiom is a phrase or expression that is peculiar to a language and that often transcends grammatical rules or literal meanings. For example, when you say that someone has 'a skeleton in the closet,' you don't literally mean that the person has human bones hidden behind a closed door. Because the meanings of idioms usually cannot be deduced from their individual words, they are among the most difficult features of the English language for a nonnative speaker."

1. *Judges 1:35*

   - Form-centered (NRSV): ". . . the hand of the house of Joseph rested heavily on them, . . ."

- Content-centered (REB): "But the Joseph tribes increased their pressure on them."

**2.** *1 Kings 20:11*

- Form-centered (KJV): "And the king of Israel answered and said, Tell him, Let not him that girdeth on his harness boast himself as he that putteth it off."

- Form-centered, somewhat modernized (DR): "And the king of Israel answering, said: Tell him: Let not the girded boast himself as the ungirded."

- Form-centered, modernized (NAB, 1970 and revised): The King of Israel replied, "Tell him, 'It is not for the man who is buckling his armor to boast as though he were taking it off.'"

- Content-centered (REB): "The time for boasting is after the battle" (trying a natural semantic equivalent for a proverbial saying)

- Content-centered (original NEB): "The lame must not think himself a match for the nimble" (bearing no resemblance to the original text)

**3.** *Matthew 20:15*
This verse comes at the end of Jesus' parable, The Workers in the Vineyard. It's the landowner's response to the disgruntled day laborers.

- The NKJV (form-centered, like its predecessor the KJV): "Or is your eye evil because I am good?" That's a word-for-word translation of *ophthalmos ponaros* (eye evil), evidently an idiom for envy.

- The revised NAB (content-centered in this instance): "Are you envious because I am generous?"

## Categories of Translations

"Any translation of a masterpiece must be a failure," observed Edgar Goodspeed (a New Testament professor at the University of Chicago whose "Chicago Bible"—a New Testament—appeared in 1923 as the earliest American modern-speech translation. See Appendix 4.) Or, according to the old Latin adage, *"Omnis traductor traditor"* ("Every translator is a traitor"). There are two important first points:

- No one translation can become the Bible for all readers.

- A new translation (or at least a major revision) is needed at least every thirty years.

Philip W. Comfort in *The Complete Guide to Bible Versions* suggests the following gradation from literal translation to idiomatic paraphrase:

**1. Strictly literal**
New American Standard Bible

**2. Literal**
New King James Version, Revised Standard Version, The Revised New American Bible

**3. Literal with freedom to be idiomatic**
New Revised Standard Version, New American Bible

**4. Thought-for-thought**
New International Version, New Jerusalem Bible, Revised English Bible

**5. Dynamic equivalent**
The Complete Bible, Phillips, Today's English Version, New English Bible

**6. Paraphrastic**
The Living Bible

## The 1986 Revision of the 1970 New American Bible

As noted above, the revision of the NAB (1970) moved it in the literal direction (from category 3 to category 2).

**1. An observation**
"Some other contemporary biblical versions have adopted, in varying degrees, a dynamic-equivalence approach, which attempts to respect the individuality of each language by expressing the meaning of the original in a linguistic structure suited to English, even though this may be very different from the corresponding Greek structure." So says the preface of the revised NAB, recognizing the benefits of dynamic-equivalence ("often fresh and brilliant renderings") but also its disadvantages, which it describes in these words:

- "more or less radically abandoning traditional biblical and liturgical terminology and phraseology"

- "expanding the text to include what more properly belongs in notes, commentaries, or preaching"

- "tending toward paraphrase"

**2. A goal**
The preface to the revised edition of the NAB says, "The primary aim of the revision is to produce a version as accurate and faithful to the meaning of the Greek original as is possible for a translation. The editors have consequently moved in the direction of a formal-equivalence approach to translation, matching the vocabulary, structure, and even word order of the original as closely as possible in the receptor language."

## The Need for New Translations/ Revisions

Over the course of the years—and even centuries, new translations of the Bible as well as revisions of existing translations have been produced. It is not only the demand for Scripture available in more of today's languages that spurs the work of translators, but also factors like those noted below.

## Comparing Translations of a Familiar Text–*1 Corinthians 13:13*

### 1. The text

- In the New American Bible (1970):
  "There are in the end three things that last: faith, hope, and love, and the greatest of these is love."

- In the revised edition of the New American Bible:
  "So faith, hope, love remain, these three; but the greatest of these is love."

### 2. A comparison

- In Greek, there is a simple, crisp, three-word phrase: "But now remains. . . ." Instead of that discipline or economy or poetry, the 1970 NAB used nine words and said it more prosaically–and not literally. The succinct revision of the NAB illustrates the virtues of a literal translation.

- The 1970 NAB twice adds the conjunction "and" where there was none ("faith, hope, <u>and</u> love"), ignoring a nice asyndeton (the omission, for effect, of a conjunction). The revised NAB restores it ("So faith, hope, love remain"). The older NAB changes the word order, putting "these three" (*ta tria tauta*) in its logical (not rhetorical) place, adds the banal "things," and loses the pleonasm (an unnecessary but effective repetition of words). The revised NAB restores it ("So faith, hope, love remain, <u>these three</u>").

"Asyndeton?!" "Pleonasm?!" If you like to know what's behind a phrase with force and flourish, see Appendix 2, "Figures of Speech in Scripture." It explains the asyndeton and the pleonasm and dozens of other figures of speech.

**4**

**Journal of God's People**

### Theology

Because spirituality and theology are reflected in translation (see "Factors in Translation" below), no *one* translation will ever satisfy all needs or pass the test of time.

### Language

Language and vocabulary are fluid by their very nature. The meaning of words is constantly evolving.

- For example, when King James II first saw St. Paul's Cathedral, the work of the great Christopher Wren, he declared it "awful, artificial, and amusing." In other words, he loved it—in *other* words, not those words as we know them today. Those words, in the seventeenth century, meant, respectively, "deserving of awe," "full of skillful artifice," and "absorbing." You've got to keep up, and so do Scripture translations. (King James II was the successor of King James I, who commissioned the "Authorized Version"—the "King James Version"—of the Bible that was published in 1611.)

- Another example is the use of the word "brothers" in the Bible. According to an Old Testament expression, as the *Catechism* observes (500), "brothers" of the Lord are in fact close relatives. The Church has never understood the Scriptures using this phrase as referring to other children of Mary (see *Mark 3:31–35, 6:3; 1 Corinthians 9:5; Galatians 1:19*). James and Joseph ("brothers of Jesus") are in fact sons of another Mary who was a disciple of Christ ("the other Mary," see *Matthew 13:55, 28:1*; see also *Matthew 27:56*).

### Joseph's Second Wife

There is one tradition that says Joseph was chosen to be Mary's protector-husband, and that he was a widower with a grown family of sons. The story appears in the apocryphal gospels, the earliest apparently being the second-century Protevangelium of James (also called the Gospel of James), quoted by the Christian teacher, writer, and theologian Origen; mentioned by the theologian and Church Father Saint Clement of Alexandria; and also by the Christian apologist Saint Justin. They (as well as by Eusebius of Caesarea) used the tradition to explain the scriptural references to the "brethren of the Lord."

### Scholarship

There is continuing progress in theology and Scripture scholarship just as in other fields of study and practice. Through the course of history, there have been discoveries of ancient manuscripts (handwritten copies) and insights about existing manuscripts that improve the fidelity of translations.

## The Needs of Readers/Hearers
### Best Bible?

There is no best Bible or best Bible translation. What makes one better than another for a particular reader is its purpose and use. The following three broad categories, each with its own unique needs, are often cited in discussions about Scripture translations.

1. **Personal reading**
   Personal enrichment can be better served by the more readable and less literal translations.

2. **Bible study**
   Study of Scripture requires a translation with a priority on fidelity to the original text, including all its difficulties.

3. **Public proclamation**
   The idiomatic, colloquial translations popular for private reading are not as suitable for public reading. The revised NAB is the translation widely used in lectionaries for Mass in the United States. As the preface to the Revised Edition of its New Testament says, "The liturgy is a formal situation that requires a level of discourse more dignified, formal, and hieratic than the world of business, sport, or informal communication." ("Hieratic" means "priestly.")

Along with the Scripture text itself, many Bibles include articles, introductions, cross references, footnotes, and maps, for example. Some advertise these features by calling themselves "study Bibles." Other features like size of print, appearance, and durability (paperback, hardcover, leather cover) also influence a person's choice of Bible.

## Familiarity

For personal reading, people have preferences that are unrelated to scholarship when choosing a Bible. Some of the factors in translation discussed below, like readability and vitality, also affect a person's preference for one Bible over another for personal reading. But simple familiarity (not a factor in translation) drives some people's choice of Bible. Some people cling to scriptural phrases that have become familiar—phrases that sometimes change in new translations or revisions of translations because of better scholarship. The following are four examples.

### 1. Good will to man

"Peace on the earth, good will to men, from heav'n's all gracious King."
When the Massachusetts minister, Edmund Sears, wrote the renowned Christmas carol, *It Came upon the Midnight Clear*, he was quoting the Bible he knew, the King James.

- The full verse from which that phrase comes, *Luke 2:14*, appeared as follows in the KJV: "Glory to God in the highest, and on earth peace, <u>good will toward men</u>."

- The Catholic CCD version didn't sound quite the same;

the phrase "good will" has moved from the greeting to the greeted: "Glory to God in the highest, and on earth peace <u>among men of good will</u>."

- The "good will" disappeared completely in the 1970 NAB and its revision: "Glory to God in the highest / and on earth <u>peace to those on whom his favor rests</u>." The revised NAB explains in a footnote that this is the word order found in the oldest and best manuscripts.

- The NKJV keeps the traditional language but admits in a footnote that "toward men of goodwill" is in the best manuscript tradition.

### 2. The good fight

This well-worn phrase from *2 Timothy 4:7* cannot be found in all translations:

- NAB (1970): "I have fought the good fight."

- NAB (revised): "I have competed well."

- The Greek text reads as follows: "*ton* (the) *kalon* (good) *agona* (fight) *agonismai* (I have fought)."

### 3. The Good Shepherd Psalm

Psalm 23 was not always identified as "the Good Shepherd Psalm" in Catholic translations:

- The Douay-Rheims Bible begins *Psalm 23*, "The Lord

ruleth me . . ." and includes a footnote on verse one: "*Ruleth me*. In Hebrew, *Is my shepherd*, viz., to feed, guide, and govern me." This is from Bishop Challoner's eighteenth-century revision, which prevailed in Catholic circles until well into the twentieth century. A fresh translation of the psalms (including "The Good Shepherd" psalm) was finally published in 1945 by the professors of the Pontifical Biblical Institute of Rome. That was two years after Pope Pius XII's encyclical *Divino Afflante Spiritu*, which allowed and encouraged translators to work from original languages instead of only from Saint Jerome's Latin translation, the Vulgate.

- Today's NAB translation begins Psalm 23 in the familiar way. To illustrate the evolution and the value of footnotes, here is the NAB's note for verse 1: "*My shepherd*: God as good shepherd is common in both the Old Testament and the New Testament (Ezekiel 34:11–16 and John 10:1–18)."

4. **Lead us not into temptation**
This well-known petition comes from the Lord's prayer—and *Matthew 6:13*. Don't look in the revised NAB for that very wording, however.

- "Lead us not into temptation" is the wording in the CCD

translation that came before today's NAB.

- The revised NAB reads instead, "Do not subject us to the final test."

(The rest of the traditional Lord's Prayer is also more or less verbatim from the CCD translation—with the exception of "trespasses" for the scriptural "debts.")

## Factors in Translation

In the following pages there are eight factors discussed, with examples, that influence the translation of Scripture from its original languages: fidelity to the intended meaning of the text, misinterpretation potential, readability, intelligibility, consistency of vocabulary, style, vitality, and punctuation.

## Fidelity to the Intended Meaning of the Text

Sometimes word-for-word translations faithfully and accurately represent the original biblical text but sound clumsy in English or are difficult to understand without commentary.

For example, *Psalm 89:18* (in the revised NAB) says, "You are the majestic strength;/ by your favor our horn is exalted."

- The idiomatic-translation school says that the Greek word for "horn" in this context means "strength" in English. Translating it literally is not "sensitive to the contextual meaning of words" (a goal of idiomatic translations).

- The literal-translation school says that translating the word "horn" as "strength" would not be faithful to the original text (and would ignore the metaphor on top of it). So the revised NAB adds a footnote explaining that "horn" is a metaphor for strength. For another occurrence of the horn metaphor (Psalm 18:3), the revised NAB footnote gets more graphic: "The horn referred to is the weapon of a bull and a symbol of fertility." The footnote also calls the reader's attention to a New Testament use of the same metaphor, "He has raised up a mighty savior for us in the house of his servant David . . ." (*Luke 1:69*).

## The Return of *Behold*

That word "behold" is interwoven very liberally in the Bible—restored in the revised NAB translation. The Greek word that's translated "behold" (*idou*) is sometimes an exclamation: See! Lo! Behold! (*Ecce* in Latin). Sometimes it is used as an imperative. In either case, the revised version of the NAB often translates it "behold." Usually, the NAB (1970) had either eliminated it as an exclamation, translated it as "suddenly" or "immediately," or translated it as "See" or "Look." In each of the following examples, the first Scripture quotation is from the 1970 NAB and the second is from the revised NAB.

1. *Matthew 1:20* (the annunciation to Joseph)
- "Such was his intention when suddenly the angel of the Lord appeared . . ."
- "Such was his intention when, behold, the angel of the Lord appeared . . ."

2. *Matthew 1:23* (the Isaiah quotation)
- "The virgin shall be with child/ and give birth to a son . . ."
- "Behold, the virgin shall be with child and bear a son . . ."

3. *John 1:29* (John the Baptist)
- "Look! There is the Lamb of God/ who takes away the sin of the world!"
- "Behold, the Lamb of God, who takes away the sin of the world."

4. *John 19:5* (Pilate to the crowds)
- "Look at the man!"
- "Behold, the man!"

5. *Matthew 28:9* (a Resurrection appearance)
- "Suddenly, without warning, Jesus stood before them and said, 'Peace!'"
- "And behold, Jesus met them on their way and greeted them."

6. *Matthew 28:20* (the great commission)
- "And know that I am with you always, until the end of the world!"
- "And behold, I am with you always, until the end of the age."

**4**

**Journal of God's People**

## Misinterpretation Potential

Sometimes, the word-for-word translation accurately represents the original, but uses a figure of speech unfamiliar to today's readers. The original audience (a different culture) would have understood it perfectly; today's audience, centuries and miles removed, might get the wrong impression. Take *Matthew 6:13*, one of the petitions of the Lord's prayer, for example: "Lead us not into temptation."

- Why would a person even need to ask God to *not* lead us into temptation? This expression in the Lord's prayer is called a "Semitic causative" and should not suggest that God sends temptation. However, to those unfamiliar with that Hebrew manner of speaking, that is what is implied. The purpose of this expression is to acknowledge God's sovereignty and power. There is nothing beyond God's power or outside of God's control.

- Most translations let this "Semitic causative" stand. The revised NAB, for example, translated it, "Do not subject us to the final test" while the NKJV and the NIV translated it, "Do not lead us into temptation."

- Some freer translations sacrifice accuracy so as not to lead the reader into misunderstanding: The CEV reads "Keep us from being tempted"; the NLT, "Don't let us yield to temptation"; and, of course, *The Message*, "Keep

us safe from ourselves and the Devil. / You're in charge! / You can do anything you want!"

In other cases, word-for-word translations do not accurately represent the original meaning or intent of the text or, worse yet, could be the source of misinterpretation of a text. An important and problematic example is the potential for anti-Semitism, particularly in the Gospel of John. The following, from the revised NAB, are but two examples.

- "My kingdom is not from this world. If my kingdom were from this world, my followers would be fighting to keep me from being handed over to the Jews" (*John 18:36*).

- "From then on Pilate tried to release him, but the Jews cried out, 'If you release this man, you are no friend of the emperor'" (*John 19:12*).

In each of these cases, the CEV translates "the Jews" as "the Jewish leaders."

In their 2002 document *The Jewish People and Their Sacred Scriptures in the Christian Bible*, the Pontifical Biblical Commission discusses problems such as these. The commission pointed out that attempting to lessen the conflict between Judaism and Christianity by translating "Jews" as "Judeans," creates a different problem in the process. So doing gives the wrong impression of the nature of the conflict: The contrast then would not be

between the Jews and Jesus' disciples, but between the inhabitants of Judea, presented as hostile to Jesus, and those of Galilee, presented as flocking to their prophet. Contempt by Judeans for Galileans is certainly expressed in the Gospel (7:52), but the evangelist did not draw the lines of demarcation between faith and refusal to believe along geographical lines . . .",
The commission continues by pointing out that when the Gospel according to John refers to "the world" it means all sinners and not merely "Jews who are hostile to Jesus."

- *John 8:23* reads (along with verse 22, for context), "So <u>the Jews</u> said, 'He is not going to kill himself, is he, because he said, Where I am going you cannot come?' He said to them, 'You belong to what is below, I belong to what is above. <u>You belong to this world</u>, but I do not belong to this world'" (revised NAB translation).

- In the revised NAB, *John 6:41* is translated, "<u>The Jews</u> murmured about him because he said, 'I am the bread that came down from heaven. . . .'" In this same verse, the CEV translates "The Jews" as "<u>The people</u>."

- In the revised NAB, *John 6:52* is translated, "<u>The Jews</u> quarreled among themselves, saying, 'How can this man give us his flesh to eat?'" In this same verse, the CEV translates "The Jews" as "<u>They</u>."

The following thoughts are gleaned from part II of the 1974 "Guidelines and Suggestions for Implementing the Conciliar Declaration *Nostra Aetate*, 4" of the Vatican Commission for Religious Relations with the Jews. (*Nostra Aetate* is the Latin name for Vatican II's *Declaration on the Relationship of the Church to Non-Christian Religions*.)

- When commissions translate for liturgy, particular attention must be paid to phrases or formulas which Christians, lacking background information, might misunderstand as being prejudicial. This must be done without altering the text of the Bible.

- So for a Bible translation to be used in liturgy, the greatest consideration should be given to the explicit meaning of the text, while accounting for the truths of scriptural studies.

- The *Guidelines* concludes the matter relating to the Christian understanding of the meanings and implications of Gospel references to the Jews, "Thus the formula 'the Jews,' in Saint John, sometimes according to the context means 'the leaders of the Jews,' or 'the adversaries of Jesus,' terms which express better the thought of the evangelist and avoid appearing to arraign the Jewish people as such."

**4**

**Journal of God's People**

## Pope John Paul II Condemning Anti-Semitism

"On October 31, 1997, Pope John Paul II received a group of scholars attending a symposium on 'The Roots of Anti-Judaism in the Christian Milieu,' sponsored by the Holy See. He told them that 'erroneous and unjust interpretations of the New Testament regarding the Jewish people and their alleged culpability have circulated (in the Christian world) for too long, engendering feelings of hostility toward this people. They contributed to the lulling of consciences, so that when the wave of persecutions swept across Europe . . . the spiritual resistance of many was not what humanity rightfully expected from the disciples of Christ. Your examination of the past, in view of a purification of memory, is particularly appropriate for clearly showing that anti-Semitism has no justification and is absolutely reprehensible'" (Introduction, *The Bible, the Jews and the Death of Jesus. A Collection of Catholic Documents*, 2004).

## Readability

How should translations of the biblical text sound? In the following example, the less literal translation does not affect the meaning but certainly does alter the sound and style of the author. It features the lowly conjunction. When authors omit conjunctions (like "and") it's called "asyndeton"; when they multiply them it's called "polysyndeton." Literary critics say that writers will prefer one or the other: Asyndetons are more common in Shakespeare, for example, and polysyndetons in Scripture.

(There's more about this in Appendix 2, "Figures of Speech in Scripture.")

- The Greek conjunction *kai* is usually translated "and" or "but." *Kai* appears no less than forty-seven times in Revelation 12 (eighteen verses), fifty-one times in Revelation 13 (eighteen verses) and fifty-five times in Revelation 14 (twenty verses). That's *poly*. In some English translations that polysyndeton is eliminated because it's not the practice of English speakers. Not in the King James Version. In this version of Revelation 12, for, example, there are sixteen sentences; fifteen of them begin with "and" (as commonly as in the original). Thirty-one of the other thirty-two are all brought into English, translated "and" in every case.

- By comparison, the NAB (1970) translated Revelation 12:1–18 into twenty-two sentences. None of them begin with the conjunction "and." And what happened to those forty-seven *kai*'s? Only twenty-two of them were translated "and." Five were translated "then," three were translated "but," one was translated "with," one was translated "as," one was translated "however," one was made into a semi-colon, and thirteen of them were left behind and not translated at all. And so, in the NAB (1970), the Book of Revelation doesn't preserve the rhetorical feel of the original text as it might. But it's easier to read.

## Intelligibility

One translation may be more readable than another, but both are readily understandable. In other cases, the very intelligibility is at stake, as in the following example. At what point does fidelity to the original text yield to the needs of the reader? How literal does a translation need to be? Below, *2 Corinthians 1:17–20* illustrates the dilemmas and decisions of translators. The first example is from the 1970 version of the NAB; the second, a more word-for-word translation, is from the revised NAB. Was the less-literal NAB (1970) less accurate or just more intelligible?

- "Do you suppose that in making those plans I was acting insincerely? Or that my plans are so determined by self-interest that I change my mind from one minute to the next? As God keeps his word, I declare that my word to you is not 'yes' one minute and 'no' the next. Jesus Christ, whom Silvanus, Timothy, and I preached to you as Son of God, was not alternately 'yes' and 'no'; he was never anything but 'yes.' Whatever promises God has made have been fulfilled in him; therefore it is through him that we address our Amen to God when we worship together."

- "So when I intended this, did I act lightly? Or do I make my plans according to human considerations, so that with me it is 'yes, yes' and 'no, no'? As God is faithful, our word to you is

not 'yes' and 'no.' For the Son of God, Jesus Christ, who was proclaimed to you by us, Silvanus and Timothy and me, was not 'yes' and 'no,' but 'yes' has been in him. For however many are the promises of God, their Yes is in him; therefore, the Amen from us also goes through him to God for glory."

Things readily understood in one generation are not in the next. Examples are endless: Meanings of words evolve and, certainly, everyday things in one culture or era are foreign in another—or are known by another name.

### Genus and species

- "Wheat and tares together sown, / Unto joy or sorrow grown. . . ." So goes the thanksgiving hymn "Come, Ye Thankful People, Come." Tares? The tare (a noxious weed) is a word made famous by the King James Bible, which used it as the translation for "weeds" in the parable of Jesus about the enemy sowing weeds in the wheat while the farmer slept (*Matthew 13:24–30*). The Douay-Rheims used "cockle." Other translations used "darnel." Most contemporary translations simply say "weeds." *The Message*, however, paraphrases the verse this way: "That night, while his hired men were asleep, his enemy sowed thistles all through the wheat. . . ." For invasiveness, the pernicious thistle might impress the modern-day reader more than the generic "weed." For likeness to wheat, darnel was a good choice, but who knows that today?

- In some cases, the text itself explains a word whose meaning might be lost on a contemporary reader. *Matthew 13:31*, for instance, says, "The kingdom of heaven is like a mustard seed that someone took and sowed in his field; it is the smallest of all the seeds, but when it has grown it is the greatest of shrubs and becomes a tree . . ."

## Weights and measures

- Text: "Now there were six stone water jars there for Jewish ceremonial washings, each holding twenty to thirty gallons" (*John 2:6* in the revised NAB).

- The revised NAB footnote explains: "Literally, 'two or three measures'; an Attic liquid measure contained 39.39 liters. The vast quantity recalls prophecies of abundance in the last days (Amos 9:13–14; Hosea 14:7; Jeremiah 31:12)."

- The Douay-Rheims translated it word-for-word: "measures," which for us is so vague that the allusion to abundance was lost.

- The King James translation used the word "firkin," a unit of volume equal to a quarter of a barrel and a British equivalent for the ancient "measure." That word was helpful in King James' day but it isn't now. The sheer volume is still lost on us. So the translations continue.

## Times and watches

- In telling time, the revised NAB sometimes moves in the direction of a literal translation. It revised, for example, the original NAB (1970) translation of *Luke 12:32–48* from "Should he happen to come at midnight, or before sunrise. . ." to "Should he come in the second or third watch. . . ."

- In other cases, the revised NAB opts for clarity over literal translation: It says that the royal official's son healed by Jesus began to get better at "about one in the afternoon" (*John 4:52*). More strictly literal translations say it happened "at the seventh hour."

## Consistency of Vocabulary

The preface to the revised NAB says, "A particular effort has been made to insure consistency of vocabulary. Always to translate a given Greek word by the same English equivalent would lead to ludicrous results and to infidelity to the meaning of the text. But in passages where a particular Greek term retains the same meaning, it has been rendered in the same way insofar as this has been feasible; this is particularly significant in the case of terms that have a specific theological meaning."

The following three terms, for example, are not always translated the same way because they do not "retain the same meaning:"

- the Greek word *episkopos* is translated both "overseer" and "bishop"

- the Greek word *presbuteros* is translated both "elder" and "presbyter"
- the Greek word *diakonos* is translated both "servant" and "deacon"

Each of these Greek terms had both a general usage and, in the later part of the first century, a specific application in Christian churches for publicly recognized roles. Translating these Greek words with the same English words in every case, regardless of context, would not accurately capture their meaning. The following illustration uses *diakonos* as an example:

- The seven chosen in Acts 6:1–7 ("The Need for Assistants"), are traditionally called the first "deacons" in the apostolic Church. However, the term *diakonos* does not appear in this passage, although the Greek verb *diakonein* does, and is translated "to serve." (These seven may simply have been table waiters.)
- Earlier, of course, that Greek word behind "to serve," "service," and "servant" is used often, without the connotations of the word "deacon" today. For example, in *Mark 10:44* Jesus said, ". . . whoever wishes to be first among you must be slave of all (*diakonos*). . . ." Even though later in the New Testament *diakonos* is translated "deacon," that's not the English translation of the same Greek word in *Mark 10:44* ("Whoever wishes to be great among you will be your

deacon"). This is a good example of the importance of literary and historical context for translation: There was no Christian Church in Jesus' day, nor any "deacons." Likewise, Paul often speaks of himself and other Apostles using the word *diakonos*, translated "ministers" of God.

- In the pastoral epistles (Timothy and Titus), thought to have been written later—approximately AD 90–100, the *diakonos* had become an established role in the local church. So the revised NAB translates *diakonos* as "deacon" in those passages where that word has the connotations familiar today, as in *1 Timothy 3:8*, "Similarly, deacons must be dignified. . . ."

## Style

There are many rhetorical flourishes in the original language that are better preserved by literal translations. These word-for-word translations are more faithful to the literary style of the original text than "thought-for-thought" translations. In many cases, the meaning isn't directly affected but the impact is. ("It's not what you said, it's how you said it.") There are many examples in Appendix 2, "Figures of Speech in Scripture."

## Vitality

Just the right word can make an idea not only better understood, but it can make it come alive. *Malachi 3:20*, for example, is explaining how an experience of the son of righteousness will "rouse the energies" of those who fear the Lord, as one commentary says. If you've seen what it is describing, you'll probably pick the fourth translation below. It makes a difference.

- "And ye shall go forth, and grow up as calves of the stall" (KJV).

- "And you shall go forth, and shall leap like calves of the herd" (DR).

- "And you will gambol like calves out of the stall" (revised NAB).

- "And you will leap like calves going out to pasture" (JB).

How do you express outrage? *2 Samuel 13:1–22* records the story of the crime of Amnon against his sister Tamar. When he accosts her, she resists and answers, "No, my brother! Do not shame me! That is an intolerable crime in Israel" (1970 NAB translation). In the next phrase, which translation best expresses Tamar's outrage for you?

- "Do not commit this insensate deed" (NAB, 1970).

- "Do not behave like a beast" (NEB).

- "Do not behave so infamously" (REB).

- "Do not do anything so vile!" (revised NAB)

- "Do not commit such an outrage" (JB).

## Punctuation

In the Sermon on the Mount, Jesus said, "You have heard that it was said, 'You shall love your neighbor <u>and hate your enemy</u>'" (*Matthew 5:43*).

- The Old Testament passage cited, *Leviticus 19:18*, does not say that, however. It only says, according to the revised NAB, "You shall love your neighbor as yourself." Mark, followed by Matthew, record Jesus quoting this passage as the second of the two most important commandments of God (see *Matthew 22:39, Mark 12:31*).

- About Matthew 5:43, *The New Jerome Biblical Commentary* says, "This is followed by the non biblical words 'you shall hate your enemy,' a negative view that would confine our love in a narrow ethnocentric framework. It is regrettable that some translations include these words in the same quotation marks with the biblical citation. Jesus is attacking a false interpretation of the Old Testament."

- The revised NAB includes the whole phrase in quotes but says in a footnote to Matthew 5:43, "There is no Old Testament commandment demanding hatred of one's enemy."

- Various other contemporary translations, including the NIV, NKJV, and CEV, also include that phrase in quotes but when cross-referencing Leviticus 19:18 put the asterisk after "love your neighbor," not "hate your enemy."

- The NLT, however, excludes "hate your enemy" from the quotes. The TM (a paraphrase, not a translation) makes it even clearer: "You're familiar with the old written law, 'Love your friend,' and its unwritten companion, 'Hate your enemy.'"

# The Interpretation of Scripture

Interpretation is about bringing out the meaning. It stands between hearing (or reading) and understanding. "The Church loves Sacred Scripture and is anxious to deepen its understanding of the truth and to nourish its own life by studying these sacred writings" (Introduction to the Lectionary of the Roman Missal).

## The Value of Interpretation

These are some examples in Scripture itself of the importance of learning to interpret and reinterpret Sacred Scripture.

### Some Pharisees

- When Pharisees objected to Jesus including sinners in table fellowship, he responded, "Go and learn what this means, 'I desire mercy, not sacrifice'" (*Matthew 9:13*).

- Against the Pharisees' concerns about ritual purity, Jesus quoted Hosea (6:6), telling them not to go and learn the words (which he recognized they already knew) but to go and learn the meaning of the words. Readers and hearers

of Scripture are constantly learning the meaning and the deeper meaning of words heard many times before.

### An Ethiopian

- "Do you understand what you are reading?" Philip asked a Bible-reading Ethiopian, who responded, "How can I, unless someone guides me?" (*Acts 8:30, 31*). He was reading Isaiah.

- Philip, sent by an angel of the Lord, explained that the passage he was reading (*Isaiah 53:7–8*: ". . . like a lamb that is led to the slaughter . . .") referred not to the servant Israel in Isaiah but to Jesus. "Then Philip began to speak, and starting with this scripture, he proclaimed to him the good news about Jesus" (*Acts 8:35*).

### John the Baptist

- Early in his ministry, John made the bold prediction, "I baptize you with water; but one who is more powerful than I is coming; I am not worthy to untie the thong of his sandals. He will baptize you with the Holy Spirit and fire. His winnowing fork is in his hand, to clear his threshing floor and to gather the wheat into his granary; but the chaff he will burn with unquenchable fire." (*Luke 3:16–17*).

- Later on, John sent disciples to Jesus to ask, "Are you the one who is to come, or are we to wait for another?" (*Luke 7:18–19*).

- In answer, Jesus paraphrased the blessings of Isaiah 61 as signs, if interpreted rightly, that John's

**4**

**Journal of God's People**

prophecy is now fulfilled: "Go and tell John what you have seen and heard: the blind receive their sight, the lame walk, the lepers are cleansed, the deaf hear, the dead are raised, the poor have good news brought to them" (*Luke 7:22*).

- Why did John doubt that Jesus was the one expected? Probably because he did not see the one "mightier than I," described in his announcement, in what was "seen and heard" in Jesus' compassion and message of love of enemies and forgiveness. John needed his own prophetic word interpreted.

## Hermeneutics

Hermeneutics (a Greek word, pronounced her-meh-*new*-tix) is the field of study that deals with the interpretation of written texts and oral communication.

### Hermes

Hermes is the name of the messenger of the Greek gods, especially Zeus, and gives us the word "hermeneutics." He is usually represented in fully human form as a herald, equipped for traveling with a broad-brimmed hat, sandals, and the herald's staff. "A herald must of course state his business plainly and on occasion plead the cause of those who sent him. Hence from a fairly early date Hermes is associated with oratory . . . [and is] a general patron of literature" (*The Oxford Classical Dictionary*, pp. 417-418).

It can refer to philosophical concerns like how things come to be known and how language makes meaning.

On a more practical level, it can refer to the principles and processes by which texts are interpreted. This second meaning of the word is usually intended in the context of the interpretation of Scripture.

## Interpreters of Scripture

Vatican II's *Constitution on Divine Revelation* declared, "sacred scripture must be read and interpreted with its divine authorship in mind" (12). The *Catechism* echoes this fundamental point in the very heading it gives to one of its five sections on Scripture: "The Holy Spirit, Interpreter of Scripture" (109–119).

"The Scriptures, as given to the Church, are the communal treasure of the entire body of believers" and "all members of the Church have a role in the interpretation of Scripture," says the Pontifical Biblical Commission in *The Interpretation of the Bible in the Church* in a section called "Roles of Various Members of the Church in Interpretation" (III.B.3).

"The Bible came into existence within believing communities. In it the faith of Israel found expression, later that of the early Christian communities. United to the living tradition that preceded it, which accompanies it and is nourished by it (see the *Constitution on Divine*

*Revelation*, 21), the Bible is the privileged means that God uses yet again in our own day to shape the building up and the growth of the Church as the people of God" (*The Interpretation of the Bible in the Church*, III.C.1).

### The reader

"The reader" is the first interpreter of Scripture mentioned by the *Catechism*, as it explains the goal of Scripture reading (paraphrasing the *Constitution on Divine Revelation*, 12): "To interpret Scripture correctly, the reader . . ." (109); "In order to discover the sacred authors' intention, the reader . . ." (110). (Actually, "the interpreter" was the term used in that passage of the *Constitution on Divine Revelation*.)

- The purpose of Scripture reading and interpretation is to benefit spiritually the individual as well as the community of faith: "The Spirit . . . is given to individual Christians, so that their hearts can 'burn within them' (see Luke 24:32) as they pray and prayerfully study the Scripture within the context of their own personal lives. This is why the Second Vatican Council insisted that access to Scripture be facilitated in every possible way (see the *Constitution on Divine Revelation*, 22, 25). This kind of reading, it should be noted, is never completely private, for the believer always reads and interprets Scripture within the faith of the Church and then brings back to the community the fruit of that reading for the enrichment of the common faith" (*The Interpretation of the Bible in the Church*, III.B.3).

- The "hearer" of Scripture is mentioned in particular in *The Interpretation of the Bible in the Church*: "[Vatican II] teaches that all the baptized, when they bring their faith in Christ to the celebration of the Eucharist, recognize the presence of Christ also in his word, 'for it is he himself who speaks when the Holy Scriptures are read in the Church' (*Constitution on the Sacred Liturgy*, 7). To this hearing of the word, they bring that 'sense of the faith' (*sensus fidei*) that characterizes the entire people [of God]. . . . For by this sense of faith, aroused and sustained by the Spirit of truth, the people of God, guided by the sacred magisterium [see below] which it faithfully follows, accepts not a human word but the very Word of God (see 1 Thessalonians 2:13). It holds fast unerringly to the faith once delivered to the saints (see Jude 3), it penetrates it more deeply with accurate insight and applies it more thoroughly to Christian life' (*Dogmatic Constitution on the Church*, 12)" (III.B.3).

### The ordained

*The Interpretation of the Bible in the Church* next moves to bishops, priests, and deacons in the Church (III.B.3):

- "In the exercise of their pastoral ministry, *bishops*, as successors of

**4**

**Journal of God's People**

the apostles, are the first witnesses and guarantors of the living tradition within which Scripture is interpreted in every age. 'Enlightened by the Spirit of truth, they have the task of guarding faithfully the word of God, of explaining it and through their preaching making it more widely known' (Vatican II's *Constitution on Divine Revelation*, 9; see also the *Dogmatic Constitution on the Church*, 25)."

- "As co-workers with the bishops, *priests* have as their primary duty the proclamation of the word (see Vatican II's *Decree on the Ministry and Life of Priests*, 4). They are gifted with a particular charism for the interpretation of Scripture, when, transmitting not their own ideas but the word of God, they apply the eternal truth of the gospel to the concrete circumstances of daily life."

- "It belongs to priests and to *deacons*, especially when they administer the sacraments, to make clear the unity constituted by word and sacrament in the ministry of the Church."

### The exegete

Exegesis (pronounced ex-eh-*jee*-sis) is the scholarly investigation of the meaning of a Scripture text ("the most fruitful part of biblical studies" according to Pope Leo XIII). Somebody trained in exegetical work is called an exegete (pronounced *ex*-eh-jeet). It is about their work that *The Interpretation of the Bible in the Church* speaks next:

"The task of Catholic exegetes embraces many aspects. It is an ecclesial task [a work 'of the Church'], for it consists in the study and explanation of Holy Scripture in a way that makes all its riches available to pastors and the faithful" (III.C. Introduction). Both the Commission and the Council emphasize the goal of exegesis:

- ". . . In their work of interpretation, Catholic exegetes must never forget that what they are interpreting is the *word of God*. Their common task is not finished when they have simply determined sources, defined forms or explained literary procedures. They arrive at the true goal of their work only when they have

### The Skills of the Exegete

The Committee on Priestly Life and Ministry of The National Conference of Catholic Bishops published a document on preaching in 1982 called *Fulfilled in Your Hearing*. It speaks about the exegete's specific skills: "For exegesis to be done at the highest professional level, the exegete must have

- knowledge of the original languages,
- access to the tools of textual criticism,
- extensive historical and archeological background,
- a comprehensive knowledge of the development of biblical faith, and
- a familiarity with the history of the theological interpretation of texts in both the synagogue and the Christian churches" (II, "Interpreting the Scriptures").

explained the meaning of the biblical text as God's word for today" (III.C.1).

- "It is the task of exegetes to work . . . towards a better understanding and explanation of the meaning of sacred scripture in order that their research may help the church's judgment to mature" (Vatican II, *Constitution on Divine Revelation*, 12).

### The magisterium

*Magisterium* (pronounced ma-jih-*stair*-ee-um) is the Latin term for what the *Constitution on Divine Revelation* calls the "living, teaching office of the Church" (10). It generally and usually refers to the pope and the bishops collectively in their teaching role. *The Interpretation of the Bible in the Church* explains the role of the magisterium like this (III.B.3):

- "[I]n the last resort, it is the magisterium that has the responsibility of guaranteeing the authenticity of interpretation and, should the occasion arise, of pointing out instances where any particular interpretation is incompatible with the authentic gospel."

- "[The magisterium] discharges this function within the *koinonia* of the body, expressing officially the faith of the Church, as a service to the Church; to this end, it consults theologians, exegetes, and other experts, whose legitimate liberty it recognizes and

with whom it remains united by reciprocal relationship in the common goal of 'preserving the people of God in the truth which sets them free' (the Congregation for the Doctrine of the Faith, *Instruction Concerning the Ecclesial Vocation of the Theologian*, 21)." ("*Koinonia*"—pronounced koy-no-nee-ah—is a Greek word meaning fellowship and, as explained at the beginning of this chapter, is one of three terms used to describe the mission of the Church; the other two are *kerygma*—message—and *diakonia*—service.)

In very pastoral language, Vatican II's *Constitution on Divine Revelation* explains the role of the magisterium in servant terms: "This magisterium is not superior to the word of God, but is rather its servant. It teaches only what has been handed on to it . . . it listens to it devoutly, guards it reverantly and expounds it faithfully" (10).

## The Senses of Scripture

"According to an ancient tradition, one can distinguish between two *senses* of Scripture: the literal and the spiritual, the latter being subdivided into the allegorical, moral, and anagogical senses. The profound concordance of the four senses guarantees all its richness to the living reading of Scripture in the Church" (*CCC*, 115). The Pontifical Biblical Commission has added a third sense (noted below).

**Literal sense of Scripture**

The term "literal" was coined in the early centuries of the Church. It has a very positive connotation and serves a very helpful purpose. Today unfortunately, "taking something literally" often has negative and simplistic connotations. (See the explanation early in this chapter of literalist reading or interpretation. See also the section on fundamentalism beginning on p. 165.)

• The literal sense is what the author intended to say and what the first audience understood. The term "literal sense" distinguishes it from "spiritual" or "typological" (both of which have their place).

• The literal sense is the answer to the question, "What does the author mean?" The literal sense is the meaning, interpreted rightly, on which all other senses are based. The literal sense may describe a historical person, place, or event. This is the starting point. Know the context and what the word meant for those for whom it was written.

**"Re-reading Texts in New Contexts":** At the end of its treatment of the literal sense of Scripture, *The Interpretation of the Bible in the Church* includes an invitation, and a caution:

• "The literal sense, is, from the start, open to further developments, which are produced through the 'rereading' of texts in new contexts" (II.B.1).

• "It does not follow from this that we can attribute to a biblical text whatever meaning we like, interpreting it in a wholly subjective way. On the contrary, one must reject as unauthentic every interpretation alien to the meaning expressed by the human authors in their written text. To admit the

## A Scholar's Case for the Literal Sense

Raymond Brown, S.J., writes in *The New Jerome Biblical Commentary* (71:22) with a broad historical perspective about the place and priority of the historical critical approach to the study of Scripture and the literal sense of the biblical text.

"In the history of biblical interpretation in the Catholic Church, each time there has been a movement that put emphasis on the primacy of literal exegesis . . . this movement has been quickly swallowed up in a more attractive movement that stressed the theological or the spiritual aspects of Scripture almost to the exclusion of literal exegesis. . . ."

"In part this history may warn us that literal exegesis must be careful to be religiously relevant and not only informative (in an academic way). But it should also warn us that it is the duty of those who teach and study Scripture not to allow themselves to be misled into easier paths which in the long run will take them away from the biblical text with all its complexities. The encyclical [*Divino Afflante Spiritu* (1943)] confirmed by Vatican II, has made a thoroughgoing quest for the literal sense a real possibility for Catholics for the first time in centuries."

possibility of such alien meanings would be equivalent to cutting off the biblical message from its root, which is the word of God in its historical communication; it would also mean opening the door to interpretations of a wildly subjective nature" (II.B.1). ("Eisegesis" is a term sometimes used for bringing meaning to—not out of—the text, imposing a meaning alien to it. "Accommodation," described below, is eisegesis.)

- "There are reasons, however, for not taking 'alien' in so strict a sense as to exclude all possibility of higher fulfillment" (*The Interpretation of the Bible in the Church*, II.B.2).

### Spiritual sense

The term "spiritual sense" is used to distinguish it from the literal sense. (Generally, the broad term "spiritual" means different things in different contexts.)

- The spiritual sense is the answer to the question, "What does a text mean to me?"

- The spiritual sense is "the meaning expressed by the biblical texts when read, under the influence of the Holy Spirit, in the context of the paschal mystery of Christ and of the new life that flows from it" (*The Interpretation of the Bible in the Church*, II.B.2).

"This very precise statement serves to rescue the spiritual sense from its being construed as anything that any reader wants it to be. Rather, following the lead of the New Testament writers and the

great patristic writers, the document takes the paschal mystery (Jesus' life, death, and resurrection) and its appropriation by believers under the Holy Spirit's influence as the key that opens up the true spiritual sense of Scripture" (Daniel Harrington, S.J., *How Do Catholics Read the Bible?*, p. 104).

The spiritual sense is a metaphorical or symbolic interpretation of the text that expresses a "more-than-literal" meaning in one or all of the following ways (in traditional terminology):

- **The "allegorical sense"**
  This sense of Scripture is about Jesus Christ and refers to the biblical text's significance recognized in Christ. "The fathers had recourse fairly frequently to the allegorical method. But they rarely abandoned the literalness and historicity of texts. . . . Recourse to allegory stems also from the conviction that the Bible, as God's book, was given by God to his people, the Church. In principle, there is nothing in it that is to be set aside as out-of-date or completely lacking meaning. God is constantly speaking to his Christian people a message that is ever relevant for their time. In their explanations of the Bible, the fathers mix and weave together typological and allegorical interpretations in a virtually inextricable way. But they do so always for a pastoral and pedagogical purpose, convinced that everything that has been written has been written for our instruction

(see 1 Corinthians 10:11)" (*The Interpretation of the Bible in the Church*, III.B.2). ("Pastoral" refers to a pastor's care of the faithful; "pedagogical" refers to the science of teaching.)

- **The "moral sense"**
  This sense of Scripture is about the moral life and refers to the biblical text's role in leading us to act justly.

- **The "anagogical sense"**
  This sense of Scripture is about out eternal destiny and refers to the biblical text's eternal significance. "Anagogy" (pronounced an-a-go-jee), probably the least familiar term in this section, refers to a kind of symbolic interpretation that seeks hidden meanings about the end of life or humanity's intended destiny.

In Appendix 1, "The Four-Fold Sense of Scripture," there is an example from the writing of Pope Saint Gregory the Great of how the fathers of the Church had recourse to allegory in the interpretation of Scripture. (The "fathers of the Church" were theologians and writers of the first eight centuries, eminent in holiness and learning. They were such authoritative witnesses to the belief and teaching of the Church that their unanimous acceptance of doctrines as divinely revealed has been regarded as evidence that such doctrines were so received by the Church consistent with apostolic tradition and Sacred Scripture. Their unanimous rejection of doctrines branded the ideas as heretical.)

**Typological Interpretation:** "One of the possible aspects of the spiritual sense is the typological," says *The Interpretation of the Bible in the Church* at the end of its section on the spiritual sense (II.B.2). Typology is an approach to the Old Testament that interprets Christian significance on the basis of figures (types) that are historical persons and events foreshadowing a future person or event, which is thereby explained in its richness and significance by the type. (See Chapter 3 for much more on this. See also *CCC*, 1094 and 128–130.)

### The fuller sense

In addition to the literal sense and the spiritual sense, the Pontifical Biblical Commission lists "the fuller sense" as a third "sense" of Scripture in a section called "The Meaning of Inspired Scripture" in its document *The Interpretation of the Bible in the Church*. In the course of its explanation, it recognizes that "one might think of the 'fuller sense' as another way of indicating the spiritual sense of a biblical text'" (II.B.3).

"The term 'fuller sense' (*sensus plenior*), which is relatively recent, . . . is defined as a deeper meaning of the text, intended by God but not clearly expressed by the human author" (II.B.3).

The Commission goes on to explain that "its existence in the biblical text comes to be known when one studies the text

- in the light of other biblical texts that utilize it or

- in its relationship with the internal development of revelation" (II.B.3). "Internal development of revelation" is what Vatican II's *Constitution on Divine Revelation* called "analogy of faith" (treated in the pages ahead), a term referring to the inner unity among the truths of faith and with Christian revelation taken as a whole.

The Commission continues to explain the "fuller sense" in greater detail: "It has its foundation in the fact that the Holy Spirit, principal author of the Bible, can guide human authors in the choice of expressions in such a way that the latter will express a truth the fullest depths of which the authors themselves do not perceive. This deeper truth will be more fully revealed in the course of time—on the one hand, through further divine interventions that clarify the meaning of texts and, on the other, through the insertion of texts into the canon [the list of inspired books] of Scripture. In these ways there is created a new context, which brings out fresh possibilities of meaning that had lain hidden in the original context" (II.B.3). The document gives three examples of the fuller sense:

- The context of Matthew 1:23 ("the virgin shall conceive") gives a fuller sense of Isaiah 7:14 ("the young woman" will conceive).

## Terminology of the Fathers

In the writings of the fathers of the Church, the three terms below were sometimes used to describe levels of meaning of Scripture. They corresponded to the Pauline three-part description of the human person: body, soul, and spirit. (In ancient philosophy, basically, "body" referred to matter, "soul" to the animating principle, and "spirit" to the mind or essence of the human being–what survived death. (In this schema, animals were thought to have body and "soul" but not "spirit.") Thus, the three levels of meaning indicated a person's point of development in the spiritual life. Also, the point of spiritual development determines one's ability to understand the meaning of Scripture.

Neither modern scholarship nor the *Catechism* refers to these three levels, matches meanings with the dimensions of the human person, or uses these terms in the same way today. As explained above, the terms "literal" and "spiritual" are still used but with somewhat different definitions to describe the "senses" of Scripture.

### 1. Somatic (literal) meaning, corresponding to the body
This is the most superficial meaning, evident even to the unbeliever.

### 2. Psychic (inner) meaning, corresponding to the soul
This is a deeper meaning, grasped by one with some spiritual maturity. (This term as used by the fathers is the most difficult to define in today's terms.)

### 3. Pneumatic (spiritual) meaning, corresponding to the spirit
The fully mature Christian is able to grasp the "spiritual" meaning, contrasted by the fathers to the somatic and psychic meanings.

- Patristic teachings and statements of early Church councils about the Trinity provide the fuller sense of the New Testament texts about God the Father, the Son, and the Holy Spirit.

- The definition of original sin by the Council of Trent expresses the fuller sense of Paul's teaching in Romans 5:12–21 about the consequences of Adam's sin for humanity.

**Accommodation:** This is a term that a person may read or hear in Scripture study. As the general definition of the word implies ("to adapt to suit a different purpose"), "accommodation" when using Scripture is the application of a text, because of a similarity or by analogy, to something not intended by the sacred author. Accommodation goes beyond, not only the literal sense, but also the spiritual sense and the fuller sense. It uses a text about a person or event in Scripture that resembles a person or event today. (When preachers, eulogizing Pope John XXIII, cited *John 1:6*, "A man named John was sent from God," they were accommodating.)

"Accommodation is inevitable with a book that is as familiar and as respected as the Bible. And, in truth, a certain tolerance can be extended to accommodation when it is done with intelligence, sobriety, and taste. . . . Preachers may find accommodation easy and may resort to it rather than taking the trouble to draw a relevant message from the literal sense of Scripture. They are then in danger of substituting their own ingenuity for God's word. If it is made clear to the audience that the writer or speaker is accommodating, some of the danger is removed" (Raymond Brown, S.J., *The New Jerome Biblical Commentary*, 71:79).

## Saint Hippolytus (170–236) on Right Interpretation of Scripture
*from a treatise against the heresy of Noetus (used in the Liturgy of the Hours, Office of Readings, for December 23)*

"There is only one God, brethren, and we learn about him only from sacred Scripture. It is therefore our duty to become acquainted with what Scripture proclaims and to investigate its teachings thoroughly. We should believe them in the sense that the Father wills, thinking of the Son in the way the Father wills, and accepting the teaching he wills to give us with regard to the Holy Spirit. Sacred Scripture is God's gift to us and it should be understood in the way that he intends: we should not do violence to it by interpreting it according to our own preconceived ideas."

## Characteristics of Catholic Interpretation
### Three criteria for interpreting Scripture within the life of the Church

In their study of Scripture, biblical scholars rely on methods and processes of biblical criticism (treated later in this chapter). Their work enhances and enlightens the readers' interpretation of Scripture and the Church's ministry of the word. When the *Catechism* speaks to the reader of Scripture regarding its interpretation, it speaks first about the sacred authors' intention (the literal sense), then about the literary form of the text and the historical conditions in which it was produced; it then explains the following three criteria (112–114, quoting Vatican II's *Constitution on Divine Revelation*, 12). These criteria assure that a particular verse or larger text will not be isolated from its larger context in Scripture and the faith of the Church.

1. *"Be especially attentive 'to the content and unity of the whole Scripture'"* (CCC, 112). This means that there cannot be any contradiction between Scripture's various parts.

2. *"Read the Scripture within 'the living Tradition of the whole Church'"* (CCC, 113). *The Interpretation of the Bible in the Church* declares that "what characterizes Catholic exegesis is that it deliberately places itself within the living tradition of the Church, whose first concern is fidelity to the revelation attested by the Bible" (III. Introduction). The *Catechism*, echoing a saying of the Fathers, teaches that "Sacred Scripture is written principally in the Church's heart rather than in documents and records, for the Church carries in her Tradition the living memorial of God's Word, and it is the Holy Spirit who gives her the spiritual interpretation of the Scripture ('according to

the spiritual meaning which the Spirit grants to the Church'[1])" (113). *The Interpretation of the Bible in the Church* too speaks of biblical interpretation that stands "in continuity with a dynamic pattern of interpretation that is found within the Bible itself and continues in the life of the Church" (III. Introduction).

3. *"Be attentive to the analogy of faith"* (see *CCC*, 114, see also 90). The *Catechism* explains this principle as "the coherence of the truths of faith among themselves and within the whole plan of Revelation" (114).

- "Analogy of faith" is one of the terms used in Catholic Scripture scholarship. The meaning of the word "analogy" in this case includes the secondary meanings found in a dictionary: agreement, comparison, kinship, correspondence. The "analogy of faith" recognizes a unity and consistency in the truths that God has revealed.

- The analogy of faith "is an understanding of the Bible which arises from an understanding of the whole of the Christian fact in its development and its completion, in virtue of which the interpreter recognizes by a habitual insight how the meaning of the Bible in a particular context is in harmony with the stages of the total revelation" (John

McKenzie, S.J., *Dictionary of the Bible*, p. 395).

## The importance of context for right interpretation

A "contextual" approach to Scripture looks at a text from an "incarnational" point of view. The contextual approach to Scripture has been not only recommended but required by the Church:

- In 1943 by Pius XII in the encyclical *Divino Afflante Spiritu*
- In 1965 by Vatican II in *Dei Verbum* (Divine Revelation)
- In 1994 by *The Catechism of the Catholic Church*

The Pontifical Biblical Commission, in its 1993 *The Interpretation of the Bible in the Church*, defined the "historical-critical method" as "particularly attentive to the historical development of texts or traditions across the passage of time" (Intro, A). The Commission expressed its desire "to indicate the paths most appropriate for arriving at an interpretation of the Bible as faithful as possible to its character, both human and divine" (Intro, B). Just like every other human word has

## "It Says in the Bible . . ."

Those five words, as a starting point, could easily lead to quoting Scripture out of context—which usually means excerpting a text and stripping it from its literary and historical context. The contextual approach to Scripture examines various contexts and is a basis for historical and literary biblical criticism. It is the official Catholic position and an alternative to a literalist reading of Scripture.

- For example, Scripture often speaks of "the world," but that term doesn't have the same meaning in every case. It depends on the context. "Do not love the world or the things in the world" it says in *1 John 2:15*. This seems to contradict what Scripture says elsewhere. The opening chapter of the Bible in Genesis says that all God made is good. Elsewhere the Gospel of John says in a celebrated phrase that ". . . God so loved the world that he gave his only Son . . ." (*John 3:16*). The next verse says the Son came that the world might be saved through him. "World" in the context of 1 John 2:15 refers to all in the world that is hostile to God and estranged from God because of sin.

- The topic of marriage is another example: Paul in 1 Corinthians 7 said it was better not to marry, but that can't be taken to mean Christians should not marry. Instead, we need to recognize that Paul (wrongly) thought the end time was coming soon.

A text "out of context" is usually taken from its original setting and used in a new context in which it does not fit and that was not intended by the author.

An "anachronism" is a kind of context violation that takes something like a concept or a tradition from today or from a later time back (*ana-*) to a former time (*kronos*). It's anachronistic, for example, to say the author of the letters of Peter was the first pope, to look for a confessional in the ministry of Jesus, or to assert that Jesus ordained priests.

a context, so do the inspired words of human authors of the Bible. Before a passage can be interpreted for its contemporary meaning, its meaning to those for whom it was originally written must be determined. (See below for examples.)

### Examples of the importance of context

Below are six examples of the significance of context, both literary and historical/cultural/religious/political contexts as well as the larger context of Christian faith: Peter, predestination, faith and works, Jesus and the Father, the rapture, and "the unforgivable sin."

### 1. Peter's Selfishness?

This is an illustration of how the literary context—the nearby verses—can help us understand the tone and even the meaning of a verse. The meaning of anything taken out of context is clouded if a person doesn't know or can't remember what was said just before.

- Text: "Peter began to say to him, 'Look, we have left everything and followed you'" (*Mark 10:28*). Matthew adds "What then will we have?" in his version (*Matthew 19:27*), perhaps making Peter's question sound self-congratulatory, even selfish.

- Context: Mark includes this episode just after one in which Jesus told a rich young man that he must give up his belongings and turn his back on life as he knew it if he wanted

to be a follower. Mark concludes the encounter: "When he heard this, he was shocked and went away grieving, for he had many possessions." (*Mark 10:22*). In this context, Peter sounds more insecure than self-congratulatory.

### 2. Predestination?

This is an illustration of the importance of taking into consideration the larger literary context, specifically literary styles and ancient figures of speech.

- Text: "To you has been given the secret of the kingdom of God, but for those outside, everything comes in parables; in order that 'they may indeed look, but not perceive,/and may indeed listen, but not understand;/so that they may not turn again and be forgiven.'" (*Mark 4:11–12*, quoting *Isaiah 6:9–10*).

- Context: This is an example of a Semitic worldview at the time, attributing to God the disciples' understanding and the crowd's non-understanding. This scriptural language of predestination and election may be offensive to some (in the Catholic Tradition) but is intended to affirm the sovereignty of God and the certainty of God's will being fulfilled. The lack of understanding by "those outside" was certainly not Jesus' intent but their own choice in response to his previous clear teaching and also a sign of their hard heartedness (which Mark had noted in 3:5–6).

This is also an example of a subtle irony. This is not the only time that Scripture makes it sound like human obstinacy would be caused (instead of merely occasioned) by the prophet's warning. This irony in Isaiah 6:9–10 is boldly brought into the Gospel by Mark. Matthew removes it, saying instead, "The reason I speak to them in parables is that 'seeing they do not perceive, and hearing they do not listen . . .'" (13:13), softening Mark's " . . . 'they may indeed look, but not perceive . . .'" (This quote is found throughout early Christian literature, used to explain why the people of the promise did not immediately and fully embrace the promised one: "God willed it.")

### 3. Faith or Works?

For many years, a label was put on the Catholic/Protestant difference: "Faith or good works." Scriptures were quoted to put the thought of Saint Paul ("justification by faith") against that of Saint James (so-called "justification by works").

- A text in Paul: "For if Abraham was justified by works, he has something to boast about, but not before God. For what does the scripture say? 'Abraham believed God, and it was reckoned to him as righteousness.' Now to one who works, wages are not reckoned as a gift but as something due. But to one who without works trusts him who justifies the ungodly, such faith is reckoned as righteousness. So also David speaks of the blessedness of those to whom God reckons righteousness apart from works . . ." (*Romans 4:1–6*; see also *Galatians 2:16 — 3:22*).

- The Context: Paul is making a complex theological point about how one is made in right relationship with God. Paul's Jewish brothers and sisters and some Jewish Christians said it was about obedience to the covenant (law). Paul said it's a gift (grace) that comes through Jesus Christ to all who believe, whether Jew or Gentile.

- A text in James: "What good is it, my brothers and sisters, if you say you have faith but do not have works? Can faith save you? . . . For just as the body without the spirit is dead, so faith without works is also dead" (*James 2:14, 26*).

- The Context: James is making a concrete pastoral point about the need to live the Christian faith day-to-day. As *The New Jerome Biblical Commentary* says, "James is not opposing faith and works, but living faith and dead faith" (58:19). *The Collegeville Bible Commentary* explains further, "The echoes of Paul's teaching on 'works vs. faith' are strong, but it is not correct to argue, as many do, that James is attacking Paul or radically disagreeing with him. They are discussing two different issues. . . . Paul opposed Jewish claims that the principle of salvation is the keeping of the law. . . (*law vs. faith*). James is dealing with a different problem; he presupposes justification through faith and treats of two kinds of faith: *active vs. dead faith*. He is consistently trying to show that true religion is not just a right confession of words, which a convert makes initially and forgets later. But true religion is covenant faith in God and covenant love of neighbor which lasts, which realizes itself in deeds of love, and which is alive and active" (*The Collegeville Bible Commentary*, pp. 1222–1223).

## 4. Jesus and the Father

Arianism, one of the heresies of the fourth century, denied the divinity of Christ, claiming that Jesus "came to be from things that were not" and that he was "from another substance" than that of the Father. Nicaea I, the Church's first ecumenical council, identified Arianism as a heresy and declared Jesus the Son of God, "begotten, not made, of the same substance as the Father" (a formulation that still echoes in the Nicene Creed at Mass).

- The Text: "If you loved me, you would rejoice that I am going to the Father, because the Father is greater than I" (*John 14:28*). This verse was used by Arians to support a "subordinationist christology" (a position professing that Christ is subordinate, not equal, to the Father).

- The Context: *The New Jerome Biblical Commentary*, "The Fourth Gospel, which is clearly able to affirm a unity of Father and Son, could hardly have had such questions (the Arian controversy) in view. The expression (in John 14:28), like the proverb in 13:16, is part of the Gospel's portrayal of Jesus as God's agent. He acts in perfect obedience to what he has seen and heard from the Father and is thus not blasphemously claiming to 'be God' as his opponents charged." (The proverb alluded to in John 13:16 is "Very truly, I tell you, servants are not greater than their master, nor are messengers greater than the one who sent them.")

## 5. Rapture

The word "rapture" is not in the Bible. It is, however, based on a word that is (in 1 Thessalonians 4:17). Its connotations in evangelical circles come from elsewhere (Matthew 24:39–40, for example).

- The Text of *1 Thessalonians 4:17*: "Then we who are alive, who are left, will be caught up in the clouds together with them to meet the Lord in the air." This is the event "the rapture" refers to. The word comes from the Latin verb *rapiemur* in the Vulgate translation of that verse—"caught up" in the English of most Bibles (including the revised NAB).

- The Context: Comfort. Saint Paul is reassuring the Thessalonians who expected the Second Coming of Christ any time, when believers would be united with the risen Christ. But with the delay came the death of some of their number and doubts about the destiny of the deceased. Paul reassures them, "For since we believe that Jesus died and rose again, even so, through Jesus, God will bring with him those who have died" (4:14). In fact, he said, they will even be first. Then the living will be "caught up in the clouds together with them." This is not a warning to the living. This is a reassurance about the dead.

- The Text of *Matthew 24:39–40*: ". . . so too will be the coming of the Son of Man. Then two will be in the field; one will be taken and one will be left"

(see also Lukan parallel). This is one of the verses that inspired the ominous connotations of "the rapture."

- The Context: Warning. Jesus is preaching vigilance for the second coming, recalling the days of Noah to drive home his point. Putting "the rapture" in this context emphasizes the risk of being "left behind."

### 6. The Unforgivable Sin
The "unforgivable sin" passage is an example of the importance of reading a text in its ultimate context, which is the faith of the Church.

- Text: ". . . but whoever blasphemes against the Holy Spirit can never have forgiveness, but is guilty of an eternal sin . . ." (*Mark 3:29*, see also *Matthew 12:32* and *Luke 12:10*). A revised NAB footnote explains, "This sin is called 'an everlasting sin' because it attributes to Satan, who is the power of evil, what is actually the work of the holy Spirit, namely, victory over the demons."

- The Context of the Church's Faith: *The Catechism of the Catholic Church* cites this verse and says, "There are no limits to the mercy of God, but anyone who deliberately refuses to accept his mercy by repenting, rejects the forgiveness of his sins and the salvation offered by the Holy Spirit. Such hardness of heart can lead to final impenitence and eternal loss[2]" (1864).

## Artistic interpretations of Scripture

In their treatment of scriptural themes, artists interpret biblical texts and rely on non-biblical traditions related to those themes. Like their counterparts in the printed word, they have their differences. Some are literalist representations, or intend to be. Some are more interpretive, even imaginative. Some reflect past misreadings or misinterpretations of scriptural texts.

### 1. The Pieta

The *pieta* of Michelangelo is the well-known sculpture of Mary holding the broken body of her Son in her lap. It was created in 1498 when the artist was only 23. It's not an artistic interpretation of any particular scriptural text, because there isn't one that describes this exact scene. Saint John, alone among the four Evangelists, records Mary's presence at the foot of the cross (see *John 19:25*) but mentions only Joseph of Arimathea and Nicodemus receiving him for burial (see *John 19:38*).

### 2. "They Reclined at Table . . ."

That's what Scripture says (see *Mark 14:18*, NAB) but that's not what most of us see. In our mind's eye and also in many Last Supper pictures, we see a seated gathering reflective of cultural practices of a much later period. Nevertheless, "they reclined at table," just as Scripture says, since formal diners in Christ's time were more likely to recline on floor cushions during meals. Chairs are part of later history. Leonardo da Vinci's "Last Supper"—with its anachronistic chairs—is a long-time favorite. It was originally painted on the dining room wall of a Milan convent (about 1495). Although the building was virtually destroyed during World War II, the wall with the unharmed painting remained.

### 3. Paul Knocked off a Horse

This is a common depiction of the conversion of Saint Paul. The text actually says, "Now as he was going along and approaching Damascus, suddenly a light from heaven flashed around him. He fell to the ground and heard a voice . . ." (*Acts 9:3–4*). The horse is in the picture by artistic license, reflective of the fact that horses were common transportation for the well-to-do in the medieval period.

### 4. Adam Eating an Apple

A delicious apple is a typical element of another common picture of the salvation story. The account of the Fall in Genesis 3:1–6 makes several references to "the fruit of the tree in the middle of the garden." The biblical text does not include the kind of fruit. However, in art and literature the fruit came to be identified with the apple, possibly because of a word play in Latin: *malus* means evil and *malum* means apple.

## 5. Ox and Ass (or Donkey) at the Manger

Contemporary art often includes these particular animals at the nativity. Don't look for them in Matthew or Luke (the only Gospel versions that include the Christmas story). They had to come a long way to get to Bethlehem. They may have come to this serene scene from *Isaiah 1:3* ("The ox knows its owner, / and the donkey its master's crib"), a verse in an Isaiahan prophecy drawing an unfavorable comparison between Israel and the ox and the ass (donkey), two animals proverbial for their stubbornness and stupidity.

## 6. Three Wise Men Visiting Bethlehem

Of the mysterious magi, there is little more than mention in the Gospel. "Magi" (*magoi*) is all Matthew calls them when he tells of the three gifts they brought (see *Matthew 2:1*, NAB). This has given rise to the tradition that there were three visitors. Originally, they were often pictured as astrologers, but since the early Middle Ages, kings became the more common image.

Because the Venerable Bede (672–735) considered the magi representatives of the three continents of Europe, Asia, and Africa, we often see them racially as white, yellow, and black. He gives these colorful details: "The first was called Melchior; he was an old man, with white hair and long beard; he offered gold to the Lord as to his king. The second, Gaspar by name, young, beardless, of ruddy hue, offered to Jesus his gift of incense, the homage due divinity. The third, of black complexion, with heavy beard, was called Baltasar; the myrrh he held in his hands prefigured the death of the Son of Man."

## 7. Veronica Wiping the Face of Jesus

Tradition, not Scripture, says that a woman with this name wiped the face of Jesus on his way to Calvary (the sixth station of the cross). "Veronica" is actually a composite of the two Latin words, *vera* and *icon*, "true image," referring to Jesus' face. The word "veronica" is used not only as a personal name but also for the veil that tradition says was used. No mention of an actual person with that name can be found earlier than the fifth century.

## 8. "They Have Pierced My Hands and My Feet"

Although crucifixion was a common form of execution for some crimes in Jesus' day, later generations were left with only scant scriptural evidence—and their own imagination—to determine details of how his feet, for example, were affixed. Michelangelo's "Crucifixion," showing the feet of the crucified Jesus separated with a nail through each, has influenced images more than Scripture or recent contemporary archeological or literary evidence.

**9. A Horned Moses**

Michelangelo's statue of Moses, following earlier paintings, includes horns because of a mistranslation of the Hebrew word for "radiant" in *Exodus 34:29*. That verse in the revised NAB reads: "As Moses came down from Mount Sinai with the two tablets of the commandments in his hands, he did not know that the skin of his face had become radiant while he conversed with the LORD." The Old Testament of the Douay-Rheims Bible, first published in 1609, used the English word "horned" instead of "radiant." The Bible commonly read in the Catholic Tradition until the NAB of 1970 included the Douay Old Testament (with explanatory notes of Bishop Challoner). It added a footnote to Exodus 34:29: "*Horned*: that is, shining, and sending forth rays of light like horns."

## Famous Faces

Two of the twelve face cards in a deck of cards are scriptural. W. Gurney Benham, in his book *Playing Cards, The History and Secrets of the Pack*, says that the following twelve (beginning with the two from the Bible) were the inspirations for the court cards.

1. The king of spades is David. (On French cards, he holds a harp, alluding to the psalms. On English cards, he carries the sword of Goliath whom he slew.)

2. The queen of diamonds is Rachel, wife of Jacob whose twelve sons founded the twelve tribes of Israel.

3. The king of hearts is Charlemagne.

4. The king of diamonds is Julius Caesar.

5. The king of clubs is Alexander the Great.

6. The queen of hearts is Judith of Bavaria, a daughter of Charlemagne.

7. The queen of spades is Pallas, Greek goddess of war and wisdom (the Latin Minerva).

8. The queen of clubs is Marie d'Anjou (at least according to tradition), wife of the dauphin, Charles VII.

9. The jack of hearts is La Hire, a 15th-century French warrior.

10. The jack of spades is Hogier, one of Charlemagne's paladins (one of the twelve peers or knight champions of legend attending Charlemagne).

11. The jack of diamonds is Hector, or Roland, or possibly half-brother to Lancelot of the Round Table.

12. The jack of clubs is Lancelot, a knight of King Arthur's Round Table.

## 10. Healing in His Wings

Every year, a misreading of Malachi 3:20 is repeated a million times. *Hark, the Herald Angels Sing* is one of the world-class Christmas songs. Charles Wesley, its author, took that line *"Ris'n with healing in his wings"* from Malachi 3:20, except "wings" is not the correct translation of the word. The KJV is noble literature—but it didn't get it right every time. (Every translation needs revisions.) Today, in the NAB, *Malachi 3:20* is translated "But for you who fear my name, there will arise/ the sun of justice with its healing rays." Not wings, rays. Like sunrays. Like ". . . the dawn from on high will break upon us,/ to give light to those who sit in darkness and in the shadow of death,/ to guide our feet into the way of peace." That's *Luke 1:78*, in the Canticle of Zechariah, a flower that came from the seed of that promise in Malachi 3:20.

## 11. Mary Treading on a Snake

This familiar image is based on *Genesis 3:15*, God's curse of the serpent after the Fall. The Bible commonly read in the Catholic Tradition, including the Douay Old Testament (first published in 1609) reads, "I will put enmities between thee and the woman, and thy seed and her seed: *she shall crush* thy head, and thou shalt lie in wait for *her* heel." In modern translations, like the revised NAB, it reads:

"I will put enmity between you and the woman,/ and between your offspring and hers;/ <u>He</u> will strike at your head,/ while you strike at <u>his</u> heel." (The antecedent for "he" and "his" is the offspring, not the woman.)

# Biblical Criticism

"Biblical criticism" is one of the technical terms in the glossary of a serious Scripture student. It will certainly appear in articles and discussions about Scripture.

## Definition

"Biblical criticism" means analyzing Scripture using scientific methods like, in other fields, a literary critic does, or a historian, anthropologist, or archeologist. A critical analysis is not necessarily positive or negative. (Many "critical" reviews of books and movies, for example, are favorable.) A critical analysis is more than just another opinion. It is a professional judgment—limited as all human knowledge is, but based on the best scholarship on all things related to the biblical text and its historical, cultural, and literary contexts.

## Origins

Historical and literary critical methods used today have gradually developed since the eighteenth century, but biblical analysis has been done in various forms from the time that people first revered the text as sacred. The questions were different because their social-scientific worldview was different. Today's approaches to biblical study are deeply impacted by the post-age-of-enlightenment in which we live.

- The first generation Christians didn't need to practice biblical criticism of the inspired New Testament texts. They produced them. They did, however, analyze what we call today the Old Testament.

- There were already commentaries of New Testament texts by the third century, even though the early generations of Christians were still close to the authoring community, its culture, and its worldview.

- Through the centuries many of God's children could not read, so reading Scripture—much less "criticizing" it—wasn't an option. But there were scholars and theologians who could, and did, just as those trained in these fields today do this professional work that the untrained person is not equipped to do.

- It took the intellectual ferment of the Enlightenment, raising questions about the science and history and geography treated in the Bible, for the Church to think about Scripture in a new way.

## The Place of Biblical Criticism in the Church Today

The third of the four parts of the document *The Interpretation of the Bible in the Church* is called "Characteristics of Catholic Interpretation." It begins by saying,

- "Catholic exegesis does not claim any particular scientific method as its own."

- "It recognizes that one of the aspects of biblical texts is that they are the work of human authors, who employed both their own capacities for expression and the means which their age and social context put at their disposal."

- "Consequently, Catholic exegesis freely makes use of the scientific methods and approaches that allow a better grasp of the meaning of texts in their linguistic, literary, sociocultural, religious, and historical contexts, while explaining them as well through studying their sources and attending to the personality of each author."

## Kinds

There are various and specific kinds of biblical criticism, specializing in some aspect of the analysis of Scripture (see below).

## Goal

As noted earlier, *The Interpretation of the Bible in the Church* includes the reminder that the goal of biblical critics is not scientific but spiritual: "Their common task is not finished when they have simply determined sources, defined forms or explained literary procedures. They arrive at the true goal of their work only when they have explained the meaning of the biblical text as God's word for today" (III.C.1).

## The Place of Biblical Criticism in Fundamentalism

The literalist and the fundamentalist ask very different questions because their starting points are different. They don't embrace modern approaches like redaction criticism, for example (see below), but, recently at least, do analyze historical context and cultural practices. (See "Fundamentalism," beginning on p. 165.)

## The Value of Biblical Criticism for the Faithful

Biblical criticism is an important part of Scripture scholarship. An informed Catholic reader of Scripture is interested in knowing about biblical criticism in general and in using Bibles with introductions and footnotes and other resources for personal reading or Bible study that reflect its insights.

### Kinds of Biblical Criticism

There are six kinds of biblical criticism described below. Actually, the second, third, fourth, and fifth (form criticism, textual criticism, source criticism, and redaction criticism) could technically all be considered sub-headings under "historical criticism."

In its comments on "the tasks of the exegete," the Pontifical Biblical Commission says about research, "The exegetical task is far too large to be successfully pursued by individual scholars working alone. It calls for a division of labor, especially in *research*, which demands specialists in different fields. Interdisciplinary collaboration will help overcome any limitations that specialization may tend to produce. It is very important for the good of the entire church . . . that a sufficient number of well-prepared persons be committed to research in the various fields of exegetical study" (*The Interpretation of the Bible in the Church*, III.C.2).

## Historical Criticism

Historical criticism is a general term addressing the questions "What did the author intend to say?" and "What did his original audience understand him to say?" Historical criticism is the kind usually meant when the term "biblical criticism" is used with no other adjective to define it. It gives due regard to the human person inspired by God to write. God speaks to people in a way they can understand, as they are at a given point. Historical criticism takes this seriously and contributes greatly, with its own skills, to the reconstruction of the circumstances in which the text was written and to the search for meaning. Historical criticism commonly combines with literary criticism (see below) to provide contemporary readers with the best possible interpretation of biblical texts.

The Pontifical Biblical Commission spoke most forcefully about the value of the historical critical method in its document *The Interpretation of the Bible in the Church*: "The historical critical method is the indispensable method for the scientific study of the meaning of ancient texts. Holy Scripture, inasmuch as it is the 'word of God in human language,' has been composed by human authors in all its various parts and in all the sources that lie behind them. Because of this, its proper understanding not only admits the use of this method but actually requires it" (I.A).

The following, usually called "questions of introduction," is typically the kind of information behind a text that is sought by historical criticism:

- The author (background, purpose, personal situation)
- The context or situation in which the writer wrote (as an understanding parent does who interprets a daughter's word, "She said that when she was angry")
- The audience or readership for whom the material was written

Historical critics also ask about the kind of literature, rhetorical features used by historical authors, and the history of composition of the biblical text.

### Examples of historical criticism

Like Jesus, Scripture was fully incarnated in history and culture. It is in the world and of the world. The historical and cultural conditions of the biblical authors influenced what was recorded, which then evolved through the course of time. Values and beliefs like the three examples cited below—the dignity of the human person, monogamy, and eternal blessedness, so core to Christian life today—are not taught in a consistent way in the Scriptures because ancient peoples did not have the same awareness about these social issues as we have today.

### Slavery

As noted in Chapter 1, there are many "casual" references to slavery in Scripture and a seeming neutrality and tolerance that is troublesome for the modern reader. Social and moral views on slavery changed only gradually. Both pro-slavery and abolitionist positions used Scripture to prove their position. It is not likely that people on either side would have recognized points like the following:

- Biblical authors, writing in their own words and out of their own social setting, never questioned the morality of slavery, which was so thoroughly part of the socio-economic fabric of their day.

- Scripture is the word of God in the words of human authors, inerrant as a guide to salvation, but not verbally inerrant on all matters like social structures and science, for example.

## Polygamy

Scholars of Middle East history say that marriage among the ancient Hebrews was basically polygamous—as it was among all their neighbors. In Scripture there is, however, a tradition that describes monogamy as instituted in creation (see *Genesis 2:18–25*).

- So what emerges in the Old Testament is monogamy as an ideal with polygamy accepted and practiced through the course of Israel's history (see *Deuteronomy 21:15*). There isn't certainty about the extent because the sources are mainly from the nation's elite and ruling classes (among whom multiple wives were status symbols): The patriarchs had more than one wife and kings of Israel and Judah had harems, of which Solomon's was the most notorious (see *1 Kings 11:1–8*).

- There is a mild protest in *Deuteronomy 17:17* ("And he must not acquire many wives for himself, or else his heart will turn away . . .") But even here, Scripture is more moderating excess than imposing monogamy.

- By the Roman period, there is evidence that monogamy was the common practice. In reading Scripture passages on the wedding at Cana (see *John 2:1–12*) and on divorce (see *Matthew 5:31–32, Mark 10:2–12,* and *Luke 16:18*), it is evident that Jesus viewed marriage positively, with monogamy as the ideal.

## The Afterlife

The study of the afterlife in the view of ancient Middle East cultures is complex. Greeks and Egyptians, for example, believed in the immortality of the soul, though expressed differently. Israelites' concept of the human person was somewhat different in that the essence of the person (*nefesh*) included one's physical existence. Therefore, there was no conscious existence after death—at least before Hellenization (see point two below).

- *Early Judaism*
  Before the exile (587–537 BC), the Israelites, like other cultures in the ancient Middle East, believed that people continued to exist after death but not that there was reward or punishment. The spirits of the dead, righteous and wicked alike, went down to a land below the earth, most often called Sheol (or the netherworld), a kind of Jewish counterpart to the Greek Hades.

- *A Breakthrough*
  After the exile (587–537 BC), especially with Greek influences in the wake of the conquest of Alexander the Great in 332, there was a major shift in Jewish thought about death and the afterlife. By the second century BC, Jewish Scripture, particularly in the books of Daniel and Wisdom, began to speak positively of life with God at judgment/the end of time.

- *The Good News*
  The New Testament "repeatedly affirms that each will be rewarded immediately after death in accordance with his works and faith" (*CCC*, 1021). Citing *1 John 3:2, 1 Corinthians 13:12*, and *Revelation 22:4*, the *Catechism* says, "Those who die in God's grace and friendship and are perfectly purified live for ever with Christ. They are like God for ever, for they 'see him as he is,' face to face" (1023). Also, "Jesus often speaks of 'Gehenna,' of 'the unquenchable fire' reserved for those who to the end of their lives refuse to believe and be converted, where both soul and body can be lost (see *Matthew 5:22, 29; 10:28; 13:42, 50; Mark 9:43–48*). Jesus solemnly proclaims that he 'will send his angels, and they will collect . . . all evildoers, and . . . throw them into the furnace of fire,' (*Matthew 13:41–42*) and that he will pronounce the condemnation: 'You that are accursed, depart from me into the eternal fire!' [*Matthew 25:41*]."

## Form Criticism

Form criticism was a twentieth-century development of biblical criticism that developed alongside source criticism (see p. 163), which by definition worked with the written sources at hand. Form criticism searches out and analyzes the origin and history of the oral ("preliterate") traditions behind the written texts.

- The basic premise of New Testament form criticism is that the Gospels were not written as the Pauline letters were but were composed of many smaller, independent units of written material that circulated in the early Christian community. It studies the patterns ("forms") of these component stories and sayings and the reasons they were preserved in the community and incorporated into the written work.

- Form criticism distinguishes three levels in the formation and preservation of the Gospel material that have become traditional in Scripture study: the situation in the life of Jesus, the situation in the life of the Church, and the situation in the Gospel. (See "The Formation of the Gospels" in Chapter 2.)

## Textual Criticism

There are no originals (called "autographs") of any of the books of the Bible. They were lost long ago, primarily because the original materials disintegrated or they were destroyed in times of persecution, natural disaster, or war. Textual criticism is the study of the scriptural text to determine, as much as possible, what had been originally recorded by the sacred author. It works with manuscripts (handwritten copies) that have come down to us, their preservation, and comparison of texts.

- Because the wording varies within the manuscripts of the

**4**

**Journal of God's People**

## New Testament Manuscripts

The following numbers will give the reader a sense of the amount, nature, and age of the materials used by the text critic.

"At last count, more than 5,700 Greek manuscripts have been discovered and catalogued ... [including] everything from the smallest fragments of manuscripts—the size of a credit card—to very large and magnificent productions, preserved in their entirety. Some of them contain only one book of the New Testament; others contain a small collection (for example, the four Gospels or the letter of Paul); a very few contain the entire New Testament. There are, in addition, many manuscripts of the various early versions (= translations) of the New Testament. ... In addition to these Greek manuscripts, we know of about 10,000 manuscripts of the Latin Vulgate, not to mention the manuscripts of other versions, such as the Syriac, Coptic, Armenian, Old Georgian, Church Slavonic, and the like. ... In addition, we have the writings of church fathers such as Clement of Alexandria, Origen, and Athanasius among the Greeks and Tertullian, Jerome, and Augustine among the Latins—all of them quoting the texts of the New Testament in places, making it possible to reconstruct what their manuscripts (now lost, for the most part) must have looked like" (Bart Ehrman, *Misquoting Jesus* [2005], pp. 88-89).

This vast array of "witnesses" led one scholar to say, "The New Testament is the best established ancient literature by so great a margin that no comparison with Greek and Latin literature is possible. ... The problems of New Testament textual criticism arise from an embarrassment of riches, not from poverty of material" (John McKenzie, S.J., *Dictionary of the Bible*).

According to the *Oxford Companion to the Bible*, in terms of antiquity, the oldest known New Testament manuscript contains five verses from John 18 and was written on a fragment of papyrus. It is dated to AD 100-150. The oldest substantial portions of the New Testament (dated about AD 200) are the Bodmer papyrus of John and the Chester Beatty papyrus, which contains ten Pauline letters. The oldest parchment New Testament copies are from the fourth century. About 300 manuscripts remain from around AD 300-1000. And from about 1000-1500, approximately 2,000 copies have survived. Only 59 of all of these known copies contain the entire New Testament. So it is safe to say that prior to the invention of printing (around 1450), relatively few individuals or congregations possessed a complete New Testament.

A word about writing materials: "papyri," the oldest manuscripts that have come down to us are written on paper made from the papyrus plant. Parchment is a high-quality writing material made from animal skins. Torah scrolls intended for public reading were usually made of parchment and/or leather. During the first two centuries AD, parchment gradually replaced papyrus for most purposes. It remained the standard writing material in Europe until mechanical printing came along. Therefore, the great majority of biblical manuscripts are written on parchment.

Hebrew Bible and the Greek New Testament to various degrees, the study of scriptural texts, or textual criticism, is necessary to attempt to determine, as much as possible, the real intent of the original author's text before alterations were made, which resulted in the existent copy. Scholars who perform textual criticisms of biblical texts use as their sources: Hebrew or Greek manuscripts, ancient translations in other languages, and quotes from rabbis and Church fathers.

- Sometimes textual criticism enables a scholar to determine why or how a scribe introduced textual variations. Examples of what they find include unintentional errors as well as cases of intentional change. Deliberate changes include making corrections to spelling and grammar, purposely conforming a reading to a parallel passage, polishing the text by adding a more familiar word or a phrase where one seemed to be called for, and correcting historical and/or geographical inaccuracies.

## Source Criticism

The source critic is engaged in a kind of historical criticism that investigates how a text came to be—the source or sources of a text.

- It was Old Testament source criticism, for example, that called into question the long-held assump

tion of Moses' authorship of the first five books of the Bible. In accounting for the great variety of styles and interests, the repetition and unevenness in the Pentateuch, source critics proposed what is called the Documentary Theory. "According to this view, the Pentateuch is made up of four strands of tradition which emanated from different times and places. It was argued that all of these documents were late compositions, written in the fifth century BC, long after Moses" (Richard Murphy, *Background to the Bible*, p. 32). The Documentary Theory was a major contribution of source criticism in the history of biblical criticism, although it has been modified through continuing study of Scripture and the ancient Middle East (giving us new information, for example, about extra-biblical counterparts for some of the Pentateuch's laws and institutions). The Yahwist, Elohist, Deuteronomist, and Priestly sources (or "traditions" as scholars commonly refer to them today), as explained in Chapter 2, are now part of our understanding of the composition of the Old Testament.

- Source criticism was the crowning achievement of nineteenth-century New Testament study. Vatican II's *Constitution on Divine Revelation*, in its treatment of the Gospels, incorporated one of its fruits when it explained the three stages in the development of the Gospels: the life and teaching of Jesus, the oral tradition (in the apostolic Church), and the written Gospels (the Evangelists). One of source criticism's most important contributions (described in Chapter 2) was the establishment of the historical priority of the Gospel of Mark and the identification of Q (*quelle*, the German word for "source"). "According to the Two-Source Theory of Synoptic Gospel Relationships, both Matthew and Luke used Q independently to produce their revised and expanded versions of Mark's Gospel around AD 85 or 90" (Daniel Harrington, S.J., *How Do Catholics Read the Bible?*, pp. 60–61).

## Redaction Criticism

"Redaction" is a technical word from literature and publishing; it means to edit for publication. Redaction criticism studies the way in which a Scripture text was edited to produce its final form.

- In New Testament study, it recognizes the creative work that makes each Evangelist unique in the way he shaped the material that was preserved in the community or gathered by the author.

- In comparing one Evangelist with another, redaction criticism studies what each "redactor" did with the sources in editing and combining them and then suggests conclusions about the purposes of each Evangelist and the nature of the particular community addressed.

## Literary Criticism

This term usually refers to contemporary approaches like narrative criticism. These methods developed in reaction to historical criticism and so literary critics tend to set aside historical questions, considering these studies futile. They would say that what we know is the text that survives today and the contemporary reader—these should be the subject of our analysis.

- Studies in literary genre and literary form as well as rhetorical criticism analyze the literary form, its words and style, of a whole book of Scripture. Whereas form criticism is mainly concerned with the components that make up a book of Scripture, literary criticism looks at the book as a whole.

- "This library [the Bible] has all the diversity we would expect in the literary output of an articulate culture that spanned nearly 2,000 years. In the Bible the library books have been bound together into one, without the advantage of dust jackets. There must be a serious endeavor to classify them according to the type of literature they represent. This is what is meant by determining the literary form . . . which the author has employed. The encyclical [*Divino Afflante Spiritu* (1943)] and Vatican

II have made this approach imperative for all serious Catholic students of the Bible" (Raymond Brown, S.J., "Hermeneutics," *The New Jerome Biblical Commentary*, 71:23).

## A Word of Caution

At the end of his article on "Canonicity" in *The New Jerome Biblical Commentary*, Raymond Brown, S.J., said, "Perhaps a word of caution is called for here." At the end of this section on biblical criticism, his caution bears repeating.

"The realization that there is much in Scripture that reflects the time-conditioned mentality of its authors should not lead readers to assume that they can quickly or easily recognize this mentality. Often there is the tendency to think that whatever in the Bible does not agree with the spirit of modern times can be dismissed as time-conditioned and irrelevant. For instance, some would do away with all divine moral imperatives on the principle that God's ethical commands in the Bible reflect the customs of the times. Such generalizations are more often based on inclination than on careful exegesis and have the effect of stripping Scripture of its corrective value. A good practical rule for avoiding self-deception in this matter is to pay more attention to Scripture when it disagrees with what we want to hear than when it agrees. When the Bible disagrees with the spirit of our times, it is not always because the biblical authors are giving voice to a limited, out-of-date religious view; frequently it is because God's ways are not our ways."

# Fundamentalism

## The Term

The term "fundamentalist" originated in the American Biblical Congress held at Niagara, New York, in 1895 at which conservative Protestant exegetes defined "five points of fundamentalism":

1. The total inerrancy of the Bible (in its literalist sense)

2. The divinity of Christ

3. The virgin birth

4. The atonement

5. The Resurrection and future return of Jesus

## A Definition

"Fundamentalist interpretation starts from the principle that the Bible, being the word of God, inspired and free from error, should be read and interpreted literally in all its details. But by 'literal interpretation' it understands a naively literalist interpretation, one, that is to say, which excludes every effort at understanding the Bible that takes account of its historical origins and development. It is opposed, therefore, to the use of the historical-critical method, as indeed to the use of any other scientific method for the interpretation of Scripture" (*The Interpretation of the Bible in the Church*, I.F).

## Origins

The fundamentalist approach to biblical interpretation originated in the sixteenth century, at the time of the Protestant Reformation, arising out of concern for fidelity to the literal meaning of Scripture. By the end of the 1800s, it emerged in Protestantism as a bulwark against liberal biblical interpretation and the historical and literary critical methods developed especially since the eighteenth century.

It's been said that one powerful movement provokes another. Nineteenth-century liberalism was one powerful movement. Fundamentalism was another one, provoked by it. With enthusiasm, liberalism explained away many long-cherished beliefs, all in the name of common sense and reason. The reaction among conservative Protestant evangelicals, who organized and took their stand on five fundamentals, came to be known as fundamentalism.

## Characteristics

In its document *The Interpretation of the Bible in the Church*, the Pontifical Biblical Commission taught forcefully about the dangers of fundamentalism (I.F).

### The incarnation

"The basic problem with fundamentalist interpretation . . . is that, refusing to take into account the historical character of biblical revelation, it makes itself incapable of accepting the full truth of the incarnation itself. As regards relationships with God, fundamentalism seeks to escape any closeness of the divine and the human."

### Scripture and inspiration

"It refuses to admit that the inspired word of God has been expressed in human language and that this word has been expressed, under divine inspiration, by human authors possessed of limited

## The Enlightenment

The Age of Enlightenment was a philosophical movement of the seventeenth and eighteenth centuries. It was a time of intellectual tumult and glorification of reason that generated a tension between orthodoxy (the truth of faith) and rationalism, between tradition and "enlightenment." In terms of Scripture, for example, it was fashionable for people who embraced the Enlightenment to deny that Moses ever existed.

Besides this philosophical ferment, there were advances in the natural sciences in the early seventeenth century. This raised questions about Scripture's version of the origin and structure of the universe. This brought challenges about the inerrancy of Scripture. Also, historians were learning about sources other than the Old Testament for the chronology of world history. This brought skepticism about the historicity of Scripture. Besides all this, possibly the most significant result of rationalism for religion and theology was the rise of deism which emphasized natural religion, rejected the supernatural, and denied revelation.

For biblical study, all this clearly created an atmosphere hostile to the traditional interpretation of Scripture. This powerful movement of the Enlightenment created a context for the counter movement of fundamentalism among certain Protestant churches.

capacities and resources. For this reason, it tends to treat the biblical text as if it had been dictated word-for-word by the Spirit. . . ."

## History

Fundamentalism often considers material historical, which never claimed to be historical. "It considers historical everything that is told with verbs in the past tense, failing to take the necessary account of the possibility of symbolic or figurative meaning."

## Science and culture

Fundamentalism accepts "the literal reality of an ancient, out-of-date cosmology simply because it is found expressed in the Bible; this blocks any dialogue with a broader way of seeing the relationship between culture and faith. Its relying upon a non-critical reading of certain texts of the Bible serves to reinforce political ideas and social attitudes that are marked by prejudices—racism, for example—quite contrary to the Christian gospel."

## Tradition and church

"In its attachment to the principle 'Scripture alone,' fundamentalism separates the interpretation of the Bible from the tradition, which, guided by the Spirit, has authentically developed in union with Scripture in the heart of the community of faith. It fails to recognize that the New Testament took form within the Christian church and that it is the Holy Scripture of this church, the existence of which preceded the composition of the texts. Because of this, fundamentalism is often anti-church. . . . [I]t presents itself as a form of private interpretation which does not acknowledge that the church is founded on the Bible and draws its life and inspiration from Scripture."

## Appeal and danger of fundamentalism

Especially because of fundamentalists' massive use of radio and television, millions have been influenced (not only Protestants but Catholics and Jews too) with this pre-critical line of thinking, "The fundamentalist approach is dangerous, for it is attractive to people who look at the Bible for ready answers to the problems of life. It can deceive these people, offering them interpretations that are pious but illusory, instead of telling them that the Bible does not necessarily contain an immediate answer to each and every problem. Without saying as much in so many words, fundamentalism actually invites people to a kind of intellectual suicide. It injects into life a false certitude for it unwittingly confuses the divine substance of the biblical message with what are its human limitations." Engaging fundamentalism, as one Scripture scholar has observed, falls under apologetics more than Scripture studies.

# Biblical Commentary

Even in a vernacular, contemporary translation of the Bible, there are Scripture passages that are unclear or misleading or plain unintelligible. While the inspired text alone can be inspiring, there are passages that are obscure to the modern reader because they are so rooted in the context of their own culture and history. The average reader wouldn't usually have knowledge of that context. A good translation doesn't make every passage clear and intelligible, nor should it. Don't expect the translation to do all the work. In particular, footnotes and commentaries are especially helpful.

Commentary on Scripture is part of the work of the Scripture scholar. The magisterium of the Church (treated earlier in this chapter) is a servant of the word of God and shepherd of its interpretation for the life of the Church. The expertise of the biblical scholar is intended to contribute to the right understanding of Scripture. It is not uncommon to find words and phrases like "perhaps," "seems to indicate," "suggests," "some commentators argue that," and "many scripture scholars see this as," because biblical scholars have limited evidence on which to build a case. Often there is no evidence external to the biblical text to verify particular claims, so a responsible scholar will acknowledge a certain degree of speculation. A commentary published by a reputable academic press will be clear about its authority: It may declare the meaning of a certain word or idiom or allusion but would not declare a single absolute meaning of a passage.

## Footnotes

Footnotes are the quickest and easiest accessed points of reference. In many Bibles, there they are, right on the page. And if the reader's in luck, there's one with a word of explanation about the very verse that may be puzzling.

- Footnotes are only a first step in Scripture study. They are very brief and so tend to oversimplify some issues. They may be a reader's invitation to go to a commentary (see p. 170).

- There are more footnotes in the revised NAB than in the 1970 version. For example, in Matthew 13:4–58 (two pages that face one another in one publication of the 1970 NAB), there are two footnotes. For the same verses in the revised NAB, there are twenty-six.

Below are some examples of the value of footnotes and the variety of ways they can enrich the reading of Scripture.

### Cultural-religious background

The phrase about "swallowing the camel" is familiar, having become a figure of speech, and its conventional meaning well known.

However, a footnote like the one in the revised NAB brings out a deeper significance in the phrase.

- The text: *Matthew 23:24*
  "You blind guides! You strain out a gnat but swallow a camel!"

- A footnote (revised NAB)
  "Cf Lev 11:41–45 that forbids the eating of any 'swarming creature.' The Pharisees' scrupulosity about minor matters and neglect of greater ones (Matthew 23:23) is further brought out by this contrast between straining liquids that might contain a tiny 'swarming creature' and yet swallowing *the camel*. The latter was one of the unclean animals forbidden by the law (Lev 11:4), but it is hardly possible that the scribes and Pharisees are being denounced as guilty of so gross a violation of the food laws. To *swallow the camel* is only a hyperbolic way of speaking of their neglect of what is important." ("Hyperbolic" means exaggerated.)

### Cultural context

- The text: *Sirach 50:25–26*
  "Two nations my soul detests, / the third is not even a people: / Those who live in Seir, and the Philistines, / and the foolish people that live in Shechem."

- A footnote (revised NAB)
  "The author's abhorrence of the pagan Edomites (Idumeans), Philistines and Samaritans can be understood in the light of Old Testament thinking, which does not always distinguish between hatred of evildoers and hatred of the evil they do." This particular footnote instructs the reader not only about a foreign way of speaking but also the need for reading Scripture in context (the context of a culture in this case).

### Vocabulary

- The text: *Romans 1:18*
  Just after expressing the principal theme of the letter, salvation through faith, Paul says, "For the wrath of God is revealed from heaven against all ungodliness and wickedness of those who by their wickedness suppress the truth."

- A footnote (revised NAB)
  "*The wrath of God:* God's reaction to human sinfulness, an Old Testament phrase that expresses the irreconcilable opposition between God and evil (see *Isaiah 9:11, 16, 18, 20; 10:4; 30:27*). It is not contrary to God's universal love for his creatures, but condemns Israel's turning aside from the covenant obligations. Hosea depicts Yahweh as suffering intensely at the thought of having to punish Israel (Hosea 11:8–9). God's wrath was to be poured forth especially on the 'Day of Yahweh'. . . ."

### Interpretation

- The text: *Matthew 22:1–14*
  The Parable of the Wedding Feast, ending on an especially harsh note (one of the invited who did respond was thrown out for not wearing a wedding garment).

- A footnote (revised NAB) "22:11: *A wedding garment*: the repentance, change of heart and mind, that is the condition for entrance into the kingdom (Matthew 3:2; 4:17) must be continued in a life of good deeds (Matthew 7:21–23)."

### Cross reference

- The text: *Matthew 26:24*
  At the last supper, Jesus said, "The Son of Man goes as it is written of him . . ." Written where? As is often the case, the text of Matthew doesn't say. In some Bibles, a footnote does.

- The cross reference (in the revised NAB): *Isaiah 53:8–10*
  The reader now has the opportunity to find the Scripture Matthew's Jesus had in mind ("By a perversion of justice he was taken away./ Who could have imagined his future? . . . "), to discover that it's from the last of the four servant oracles, and to learn that Matthew saw Jesus as that mysterious figure foretold so many centuries before.

## Commentaries

A Bible commentary is not so much a book about the Bible or its specific books. A "commentary" is on the text itself (word-for-word and verse-for-verse in scholarly commentaries). Bible commentaries are an especially important and very specific response to the call of Vatican II, "Access to sacred scripture ought to be widely available to the christian faithful" (*Constitution on Divine Revelation*, 22).

The *Constitution* went on to encourage exegetes (Scripture scholars investigating the meaning of a Scripture text): "Catholic exegetes and other workers in the field of sacred theology should work diligently together and under the watchful eye of the magesterium . . ." (23). The "exposition" of a biblical text and its meaning is the fruit of the "exploration" of a scholar that is written in a commentary.

The purpose of the commentary— as well as a purpose of Scripture itself—is explained in the next sentence of the *Constitution*: "they should together set about examining and explaining the sacred texts in such a way that as many . . . ministers of God's word may be able to dispense fruitfully the nourishment of the scriptures to the people of God. This nourishment enlightens the mind, strengthens the will and fires the hearts of men and women with the love of God" (23). (While a good commentary is a helpful resource for any reader of Scripture, the *Constitution* envisions the scholarly commentary to be a tool first of all for the "minister" of the word—the one entrusted with preaching and teaching in the community of faith.)

The nature and purpose and value of a commentary is well expressed in the preface of a contemporary commentary itself: The general editors of *The Collegeville Bible Commentary* recognized an increased interest in Scripture as they explained the purpose of the commentary they edited: "Prayer groups look for leaders who can guide them beyond private interpretation into the spiritual depths of the tradition. People are searching for new insights and are turning to biblical scholars to provide them. Non-specialists are no longer satisfied with a merely devotional understanding of the Bible. They are asking literary, historical, and theological questions that require learned answers." (A commentary is not an intermediary between the Scripture and the reader but a reader's resource.)

### Kinds of commentaries

The following three terms are ways of categorizing the range of commentaries available today. Each level increases not only in size but in depth, from the devotional to the scholarly (which always includes a verse-by-verse analysis). A person with a high school or college level education today will probably ask questions of certain passages that require a Scripture resource—a commentary in particular—at a comparable level. Throughout this book are examples of the kind of assistance, insight, and background a commentary can provide.

1. **Pamphlet style**
   Some of these are published monthly or seasonally as accompaniments to the lectionary.

2. **Single/double-volume book**
   Some are modest in size and written on a more popular, "layperson's" level. Others are

more sizeable and written on a more scholarly level; *The New Jerome Biblical Commentary* and *The Collegeville Bible Commentary* are two well-respected Catholic commentaries at this level.

3. **Multi-volume works**
   This category includes book-length commentaries on a single book of the Bible.

### Examples of commentary

More than footnotes, commentaries can provide scriptural background that the average reader would not have.

1. This example is from *The Collegeville Bible Commentary* (p. 982).

   • Text: "And the Word became flesh / and made his dwelling among us, / and we saw his glory, / the glory as of the Father's only Son, / full of grace and truth" (*John 1:14*).

   • Commentary: "The Greek text tells us that the Word 'pitched his tent' among us, a striking reference to God's Old Testament presence in the tent-tabernacle during Moses' wanderings with Israel in the desert" (p. 982).

2. This example is from *The New Jerome Biblical Commentary* (43:184).

   • Text: Luke ends his account of Jesus' agony in the garden by saying, "When [Jesus] rose from prayer and returned to his disciples, he found them sleeping from grief. He said to them, 'Why are you sleeping? Get up and pray that you may not undergo the test'" (*Luke 22:45–46*).

- Commentary (including a quotation from another commentary): "There is a conscious play on the word for resurrection here (see 24:7). 'Only by the power of the risen Jesus will his followers be able to throw off their lethargy and despondency in the trials they will have to face and so obtain strength to pray *continually* to avoid the *temptation* that would lead inevitably to apostasy . . . 'Now he has risen, and they are to rise with him to face in the constant spirit of his prayer all that lies before them'"

## Compassion

The following short study is an example of how Scripture reading can be enriched by the use of a concordance.

The word "compassion," coming from a Greek word for "bowels" (*esplagchnistha*), refers to being moved to the depths of one's being. In the New Testament, the word is used almost exclusively of Jesus. There are three exceptions (noted below). Looking up the word compassion in a concordance is a way to appreciate the Evangelists' treatment of this core Christian value.

### The Compassion of Jesus

1. Matthew 9:32 says Jesus' heart was moved with compassion at an exhausted crowd.

2. Matthew 14:14 describes Jesus as moved with compassion by the pain of the sick.

3. Matthew 15:32 quotes Jesus, faced with the hunger of the crowds, "I have compassion for the crowd . . ."

4. Matthew 20:34 says Jesus was moved with compassion at the plight of the blind.

5. Mark 1:41 tells of Jesus' compassion at the lepers' exclusion from the community.

6. Luke 7:13 says Jesus was moved with compassion at the widow's grief.

### The Compassion of Others

Those three exceptions? All three involve characters in parables, two of them describing the compassion of God and one the compassion required of the disciple.

1. A king forgave a huge debt because he was filled with compassion—a metaphor for God's forgiveness (see *Matthew 18: 23-35*).

2. The father of the prodigal son, when he saw his son a long way off, returning, was filled with compassion—a metaphor for God's forgiveness (see *Luke 15:11-32*).

3. The "Good Samaritan," coming upon a man beaten and robbed, was moved with compassion at the sight—an example of what it means to "love your neighbor as yourself" (see *Luke 10:29-37*).

(a quotation from D. M. Stanley, *Jesus in Gethsemane* [NY, 1980], 220). (The Greek word for "rose" is *anastas*, a word Luke used in a slightly different form—*anastanai*, meaning "rise"—in 24:7, describing Jesus' Resurrection.) Incidentally, the revised NAB brings this allusion to the Resurrection into English as does the NKJV, NAS, and NIV. The NRSV, CEV, NLT, and NCV, for example, do not, but instead simply say something like he "got up."

## Other Resources
### Concordances

A Scripture concordance is a book that lists alphabetically the important words used in Scripture along with the citation of the passages in which they are used, sometimes even printing their immediate context. This is a great source if you are looking for a Scripture quote to fit a specific topic.

### Handbooks

Scripture handbooks vary widely in the material they include but usually give an overview of the Bible and perhaps an outline and synopsis of each book in the Bible.

A good current example is *The Catholic Bible Study Handbook* by Jerome Kodell, O.S.B. (2001). It includes bibliographies for those seeking more resources: "Aids for Private Bible Study" (pp. 241–244), "Aids for Group Bible Study" (pp. 255–257), "Aids for Praying the Bible" (pp. 268–271), "Bibles with Considerable Study Help for Catholics" (pp. 273–274), and "Other Resources for Reading the Bible" (including Bible dictionaries, atlases, and other Bible handbooks, pp. 274–277).

### Dictionaries

A Bible dictionary defines and discusses important scriptural words and themes. See the bibliography mentioned above in *The Catholic Bible Study Handbook* by Jerome Kodell for examples of some that are available.

## CHAPTER 5

# Word of the Liturgy

## Liturgical
## Catechesis

While all Liturgy has a catechetical dimension, liturgical catechesis is most explicit in the form of the homily received during the celebration of the sacraments. As such, liturgical catechesis within the context of a sacred action is an integral part of that action.[1] Its function is "the immediate preparation for reception of the different sacraments, the celebration of sacramentals and above all of the participation of the faithful in the Eucharist, as a primary means of education in the faith."[2]

—*National Directory for Catechesis*, p. 50

## Quasimodo

"One fine morning—it happened to be Quasimodo Sunday—a living creature was laid after Mass in the church of Notre-Dame in the wooden bed walled into the porch on the left hand. . . . On this wooden bed it was customary to expose foundlings to the public charity. Anyone took them who felt so disposed. Before the wooden bed was a copper basin to receive the alms of the charitable. The living creature which lay upon this hard couch on the morning of Quasimodo Sunday, 1467, appeared to excite a high degree of curiosity."

Those are the opening lines of Victor Hugo's *The Hunchback of Notre Dame*. Quasimodo Sunday? Once upon a time, Sundays had nicknames, some of which became very well known. Two of them are still used in some parts: Gaudete Sunday and Laetare Sunday (pronounced gouw-*day*-tay and lay-*tah*-ray). These Latin words are the first words of what used to be called the "introit" of that Mass: *Gaudete*, on the third Sunday of Advent, and *Laetare*, on the fourth Sunday of Lent. Both words mean "Rejoice." (The introit, meaning "a going in," is now called the entrance antiphon and is omitted if there is a hymn.)

The entrance antiphon for the Sunday after Easter (the "Second Sunday of Easter") is from *1 Peter 2:2*: "Like newborn infants, long for the pure, spiritual milk, so that by it you may grow into salvation—if indeed you have tasted that the Lord is good." Those first words—"Like newborn infants . . ."—in Latin are: "*Quasimodo geniti infantes*." From this we get Quasimodo Sunday, the setting for the story of the hunchback of Notre Dame.

# Liturgy in the Church

"For the liturgy through which 'the work of our redemption takes place,' especially in the divine sacrifice of the Eucharist, is supremely effective in enabling the faithful to express in their lives and portray to others the mystery of Christ and the real nature of the true church" (Vatican II, *Constitution on the Sacred Liturgy*, 2).

## Scripture in the Liturgy

"In principle, the liturgy and especially the sacramental liturgy, the high point of which is the Eucharistic celebration, brings about the most perfect actualization of the biblical texts, for the liturgy places the proclamation in the midst of the community of believers, gathered around Christ so as to draw near to God. Christ is then 'present in his word, because it is he himself who speaks when Sacred Scripture is read in the church' (Vatican II, *Constitution on the Sacred Liturgy*, 7). Written text thus becomes living word" (*The Interpretation of the Bible in the Church*, IV.C.1).

Sacred Scripture is of "paramount importance" in the celebration of the liturgy (*Constitution on the Sacred Liturgy*, 24), not only in the Liturgy of the Word (1 and 2 below) but also throughout the Mass (3 and 4 below). Throughout this chapter there are examples of both. The Catholic Church is most clearly the Church of the Word of God at Mass.

1. Lessons from Scripture are read and explained in the homily.
2. Psalms from Scripture are sung.
3. The prayers and liturgical songs are scriptural in their inspiration.
4. Actions and signs derive their meaning from Scripture.

## The Jewish Heritage of Christianity

The *Catechism* can't teach about "The Celebration of the Christian Mystery" (the second of the *Catechism*'s four parts) without reference to God's covenant with Israel and the Jewish heritage of Christianity (*CCC*, 1093–1096).

"Since Christ's Church was 'prepared in marvelous fashion in the history of the people of Israel and in the Old Covenant,'[3] the Church's liturgy has retained certain elements of the worship of the Old Covenant as integral and irreplaceable, adopting them as her own. . . ." (*CCC*, 1093) It then cites examples:

- reading the Old Testament

- praying the Psalms

- recalling "the saving events and significant realities" that are fulfilled in the mystery of Christ "(promise and covenant, Exodus and Passover, kingdom and temple, exile and return)"

"A better knowledge of the Jewish people's faith and religious life as professed and lived even now can help our better understanding of certain aspects of Christian liturgy" (*CCC*, 1096). The *Catechism* teaches that Christian liturgy has parallels with Jewish prayer (while noting that there are differences in content). The following Christian worship practices have ties to Jewish practice:

### As It Was in the Beginning, Is Now, and Ever Shall Be

The following is a description of early Eucharistic celebrations by the apologist Saint Justin, martyr, from his *First Apology*, 67. Note especially his mention of "the memoirs of the apostles" and "the writings of the prophets."

"On the day called Sunday there is a meeting in one place of those who live in cities or the country, and the memoirs of the apostles or the writings of the prophets are read as long as time permits. When the reader has finished, the president in a discourse urges and invites us to the imitation of these noble things. Then we all stand up together and offer prayers. And, as said before, when we have finished the prayer, bread is brought, and wine and water, and the president similarly sends up prayers and thanksgivings to the best of his ability, and the congregation assents, saying the Amen; the distribution, and reception of the consecrated elements by each one, takes place and they are sent to the absent by the deacons. Those who prosper, and who so wish, contribute, each one as much as he chooses to. What is collected is deposited with the president, and he takes care of orphans and widows, and those who are in want on account of sickness or any other cause, and those who are in bonds, and the strangers who are sojourners among us, and, briefly, he is the protector of all those in need."

- the Liturgy of the word (in structure and proclamation)
- the response to this word (in praise, intercession, petition for mercy)
- the Liturgy of the Hours
- various liturgical texts and formularies
- venerable prayers like the Lord's Prayer
- the Eucharistic prayers
- some of the great feasts of the liturgical year (Passover, first of all)

### Jewish-Christian Relationship

The Vatican Commission for Religious Relations with the Jews issued a statement in 1974 called "Guidelines and Suggestions for Implementing the Conciliar Declaration *Nostra Aetate*, 4." (*Nostra Aetate* is Vatican II's *Declaration on the Relationship of the Church to Non-Christian Religions*.) It included the following reminder and exhortation:

- The connection between the Christian and Jewish liturgies is clear. Both have a "community in the service of God, and in the service of men for the love of God" and this is featured in the liturgies of both (II. Liturgy).

- An important key to strengthening Jewish-Christian relations, is to recognize their "common elements of the liturgical life (formulas, feasts, rites, etc.)" many of which originate with the shared Old Testament (II. Liturgy).

## The Liturgy of the Word

"From the earliest days of the Church, the reading of Scripture has been an integral part of the Christian liturgy, an inheritance to some extent from the liturgy of the synagogue" (*The Interpretation of the Bible in the Church*, IV.C.1). It is in the Jewish synagogue service that people gather to hear and meditate on the word of God.

- Ezra proclaims a liturgical reading of the law to the assembly from a wooden platform "that had been made for the purpose," with an open scroll "in the sight of all the people" and a greeting to which the people responded aloud (*Nehemiah 8:2–10*).

- Jesus served as lector in the Nazareth synagogue: "When he came to Nazareth, where he had been brought up, he went to the synagogue on the sabbath day, as was his custom. He stood up to read, and the scroll of the prophet Isaiah was given to him. He unrolled the scroll and found the place where it was written . . ." (*Luke 4:16–21*).

## Jesus the Lector

Many people of Jesus' day could not read. His public reading in the Nazareth synagogue (see *Luke 4:16-21*) is the only suggestion in the Gospel that Jesus was literate. There is no doubt that he knew the Scriptures, whether he could read or not.

The author of 2 Timothy says, "But as for you, continue in what you have learned and firmly believed, knowing from whom you learned it, and how from childhood you have known the sacred writings . . ." (2 *Timothy 3:14-15*). From infancy, and from Mary and Joseph, Jesus would have known the Sacred Scriptures.

Most in Jesus' day would have known the Scriptures not because they read them, but because they heard them and memorized them. Because they breathed the air in which they were spoken and shared, believed, and willed to the next generation. Jesus likewise would have known the Jewish Scriptures first from an oral tradition and not from a book.

Luke describes the beginning of Jesus' public ministry with his reading that day in the Nazareth synagogue in which he presented himself as the prophet par excellence: "The Spirit of the Lord is upon me,/ because he has anointed me/ to bring good news to the poor./ He has sent me to proclaim release to the captives/ and recovery of sight to the blind,/ to let the oppressed go free,/ to proclaim the year of the Lord's favor."

His "homily" was brief: "Today this scripture has been fulfilled in your hearing." This is all Luke records. Every homily ever since in some way is the same.

# The Lectionary

The Lectionary is the "collection of readings" (Scripture) assigned for liturgical proclamation. The current Lectionary was introduced in 1970 and revised in 1981. It has five parts.

1. A three-year cycle of readings for Sundays
2. A two-year cycle of readings for weekdays
3. A one-year cycle of readings for saints' days
4. A variety of other readings for various occasions
5. Responsorial psalms and alleluia verses

## Cycles

Spreading out Scripture readings over three years, allowing for "a more varied and richer reading of Sacred Scripture," means that the same texts are read only every fourth year (Introduction of the *Order of Readings for Mass*, 66, 2). Each year of the Order of Reading for Sundays is designated "Year A," "Year B," or "Year C." (These years don't correspond exactly with the calendar year because the lectionary begins with the First Week of Advent, which comes in the preceding year of the civil calendar.) "The years in each cycle are marked in a sense by the principal characteristic of the Synoptic Gospel used for the semi continuous reading of

## Reading the Bible in Public

The *General Instruction of the Liturgy of the Hours* (1970) provides the following catechesis about the nature of public proclamation of Scripture in the Catholic tradition.

"The reading of Sacred Scripture, which, following an ancient tradition, takes place publicly in the liturgy, is to be held in the highest respect by all Christians, not only in the celebration of the Eucharist but also in the Divine Office."

"This reading is not the result of individual choice or devotion but is the planned decision of the Church itself, in order that in the course of the year the bride of Christ may unfold the mystery of Christ 'from incarnation and nativity to ascension, Pentecost and expectation of the blessed hope and coming of the Lord'."

"In addition, in liturgical celebration the reading of Sacred Scripture is always accompanied by prayer in order that the reading may yield great fruit, and prayer—especially prayer of the psalms—may in its turn gain fuller understanding and become more fervent and devout" (140).

Ordinary Time. Thus the first Year of the cycle is the Year for the reading of the Gospel of Matthew and is so named; the second and third Years are the Year of Mark and the Year of Luke" (Introduction of the *Order of Readings for Mass*, footnote 102). (Matthew, Mark, and Luke are called "synoptics," from the Greek "to see together," because the outline of their Gospels is very similar and they agree substantially in their content.)

## General Principles

1. The Council directed that in the revision of liturgical celebrations "more ample, more varied, and more suitable selection of readings from sacred scripture should be restored" (*Constitution on the Sacred Liturgy*, 35) so that at Mass "the treasures of the bible [can be] opened up more lavishly so that a richer fare may be provided for the faithful at the table of God's word" (*Constitution on the Sacred Liturgy*, 51).

2. "In this way the more significant part of the sacred scriptures will be read to the people over a fixed number of years" (*Constitution on the Sacred Liturgy*, 51).

3. Even though a "more ample" reading of Scripture is included in the Lectionary than in the past (point 1 above) and a "more representative portion" of the Bible is made available (point 2 above), there are still passages of Scripture not included in the Lectionary.

   • The *General Instruction of the Roman Missal* explains that, in the three readings assigned for Sundays and solemnities, "the Christian people are brought to know the continuity of the work of salvation according to God's wonderful plan" (357).

- The Introduction of the *Order of Readings* for Mass goes on to explain, "In this way the more significant parts of God's revealed word can be read to the assembled faithful within an appropriate period of time. Weekdays present a second series of texts from Sacred Scripture and in a sense these complement the message of salvation explained on festive days" (65).

## The Arrangement of the Lectionary

Readings and psalmody (psalms used for singing or reciting in a time of prayer) are arranged in keeping with the traditional rule that the Old Testament is read first, then the writings of the Apostles, and finally the Gospel. The basic purpose of the Lectionary is twofold:

- to provide for a comprehensive reading of the Scriptures (see "organic" on p. 182)

### Vatican II

Vatican II was the most recent of 21 ecumenical—worldwide—councils in the history of the Catholic Church. Convened by Pope John XXIII (who died before it was over), it was presided over by Pope Paul VI who called its documents "the greatest catechism of our times." About 2,500 bishops attended its sessions, held from 1962 until 1965. Also present were leading Catholic theologians and teachers, and religious and lay people, to contribute to the discussions, as well as non-Catholic observers and delegates who were given the opportunity to speak. It produced 16 documents (the most well known often referred to by their first words in Latin). They are, in three categories of solemnity of conciliar statements:

#### Four Constitutions

Dogmatic Constitution on Divine Revelation (*Dei Verbum*)

Dogmatic Constitution on the Church (*Lumen Gentium*)

Pastoral Constitution on the Church in the Modern World (*Gaudium et Spes*)

Constitution on the Liturgy (*Sacrosanctum Concilium*)

#### Eight Decrees

| | |
|---|---|
| Decree on Communications | Decree on Religious Formation |
| Decree on Ecumenism | Decree on Laity |
| Decree on Eastern Churches | Decree on Priests |
| Decree on Bishops | Decree on Missions |

#### Three Declarations

Declaration on Education

Declaration on Non-Christians

Declaration on Religious Freedom

5

Word of the Liturgy

- to ensure that the Scripture texts appropriate to a feast or season are read at that time (see "thematic" below)

## Ordinary Time

This bland word in English is from the Latin word *ordinare*, meaning *"to set in order or in relation to each other."* When not celebrating the sacred seasons of Advent and Christmas or Lent and Easter, the Church simply sets our Sundays in order. These are the 33 or 34 numbered (ordered, "Ordinary") Sundays in each liturgical cycle "that do not celebrate a specific aspect of the mystery of Christ but are devoted to the mystery of Christ in all its aspects" (*General Norms for the Liturgical Year and Calendar,* 43).

### Organic

This is a term for a continuous or semi-continuous reading of a text (picking up the biblical text where the previous week ended). A particular book or letter is treated as a whole (organically), and not "as related to something else."

- In Ordinary Time, the first reading at daily Mass is organic, like the second reading on Sunday, although more selective than on Sundays, since both Testaments are used (Old Testament, organic in a limited way; New, organic in an extensive way). Sundays provide a semi-continuous reading of Paul and James. The Letters of Peter and John are read during the Easter and Christmas seasons.

- In Ordinary Time, the Gospel reading is also organic: On Sundays, Matthew is read during years designated Year A, Mark during Year B, and Luke during Year C; on weekdays, Mark is read during weeks 1–9, Matthew during weeks 10–21, and Luke during weeks 22–34.

### Thematic

This is a term for a passage chosen because of its relationship to a theme chosen beforehand or suggested by another reading or by a feast.

- The first reading on Sunday during the Ordinary Time of the year is thematic. (There is no table of these readings provided here, since there is no pattern from week to week regarding the source of these readings.) The choices according to themes show clearly the unity of and relationship between the Old and New Testaments.

- For special seasons (Advent, Christmas, Lent, and Easter) and feasts (like saints days and feast days like Trinity Sunday, for example) both Sunday and weekday readings are thematic.

### Both organic and thematic

Sometimes Scripture reading is both organic and thematic, as when Daniel and Revelation are read at the end of the liturgical year because of their eschatological (end times) themes.

## Criteria for the Choice/ Arrangement of Readings

### 1. Certain Books, Certain Seasons

Certain books of Scripture are reserved for specific liturgical seasons.

#### Isaiah

The reading of the book of the prophet Isaiah, especially the first part, is traditionally assigned to Advent. Parts of Isaiah's writings, along with 1 John, are also read during the Christmas season.

#### John

There is also a tradition in the Lectionary of reading the Gospel of John during the last weeks of Lent—specifically, "a semicontinuous reading . . . made up of texts that correspond more closely to the themes proper to Lent" (Introduction, *Order of Readings for Mass*, 98). Similarly, on the weekdays of the Easter season, "there is a semicontinuous reading of the Gospel of John, but with texts that have a paschal character, in order to complete the reading from John during Lent. This paschal reading is made up in large part of the Lord's discourse and prayer at the end of the Last Supper" (Introduction, *Order of Readings for Mass*, 101).

#### The Acts of the Apostles

There is a tradition in the Lectionary of reading the Acts of the Apostles during the Easter season. These readings "beautifully illustrate how the total life of the Church springs from the paschal mystery" (*Introduction to the Lectionary* [1969], VI. a). (The term "paschal mystery" refers to the redemptive work of Christ, especially the events of the Last Supper, the suffering, death, and Resurrection of Christ.)

### 2. Lengthy Texts

"A *middle way* is followed in regard to the length of texts. A distinction has been made between narratives, which require reading a fairly long passage but which usually hold the attention of the faithful, and texts that should not be lengthy because of the profundity of their doctrine" (Introduction, *Order of Readings for Mass*, 75).

### 3. Difficult Texts

"[T]exts that present real difficulties are avoided for pastoral reasons. The difficulties may be objective, in that the texts themselves raise profound literary, critical, or exegetical problems; or the difficulties may lie, at least to a certain extent, in the ability of the faithful to understand the texts. But there could be no justification for concealing from the faithful the spiritual riches of certain texts on the grounds of difficulty if the problem arises from the inadequacy either of the religious education that every Christian should have or of the biblical formation that every pastor of souls should have" (Introduction, *Order of Readings for Mass*, 76).

## Ordinary Time Readings

### Sundays

| Sun. | Second reading | | | Sun. | Gospel reading | | |
|------|---------|---------|---------|------|--------|--------|--------|
| | Year A | Year B | Year C | | Year A | Year B | Year C |
| 2 | 1 Cor 1 | 1 Cor 6 | 1 Cor 12 | 2 | John 1 | John 1 | John 2 |
| 3 | 1 Cor 1 | 1 Cor 7 | 1 Cor 12 | 3 | Mt 4 | Mk 1 | Lk 1, 4 |
| 4 | 1 Cor 1 | 1 Cor 7 | 1 Cor 12–13 | 4 | Mt 5 | Mk 1 | Lk 4 |
| 5 | 1 Cor 2 | 1 Cor 9 | 1 Cor 15 | 5 | Mt 5 | Mk 1 | Lk 5 |
| 6 | 1 Cor 2 | 1 Cor 10–11 | 1 Cor 15 | 6 | Mt 5 | Mk 1 | Lk 6 |
| 7 | 1 Cor 3 | 2 Cor 1 | 1 Cor 15 | 7 | Mt 5 | Mk 2 | Lk 6 |
| 8 | 1 Cor 4 | 2 Cor 3 | 1 Cor 15 | 8 | Mt 6 | Mk 2 | Lk 6 |
| 9 | Rom 3 | 2 Cor 4 | Gal 1 | 9 | Mt 7 | Mk 2—3 | Lk 7 |
| 10 | Rom 4 | 2 Cor 4–5 | Gal 1 | 10 | Mt 9 | Mk 3 | Lk 7 |
| 11 | Rom 5 | 2 Cor 5 | Gal 2 | 11 | Mt 9—10 | Mk 4 | Lk 7 |
| 12 | Rom 5 | 2 Cor 5 | Gal 3 | 12 | Mt 10 | Mk 4 | Lk 9 |
| 13 | Rom 6 | 2 Cor 8 | Gal 5 | 13 | Mt 10 | Mk 5 | Lk 9 |
| 14 | Rom 8 | 2 Cor 12 | Gal 6 | 14 | Mt 11 | Mk 6 | Lk 10 |
| 15 | Rom 8 | Eph 1 | Col 1 | 15 | Mt 13 | Mk 6 | Lk 10 |
| 16 | Rom 8 | Eph 2 | Col 1 | 16 | Mt 13 | Mk 6 | Lk 10 |
| 17 | Rom 8 | Eph 4 | Col 2 | 17 | Mt 13 | John 6 | Lk 11 |
| 18 | Rom 8 | Eph 4 | Col 3 | 18 | Mt 14 | John 6 | Lk 12 |
| 19 | Rom 9 | Eph 4—5 | Heb 11 | 19 | Mt 14 | John 6 | Lk 12 |
| 20 | Rom 11 | Eph 5 | Heb 12 | 20 | Mt 15 | John 6 | Lk 12 |
| 21 | Rom 11 | Eph 5 | Heb 12 | 21 | Mt 16 | John 6 | Lk 13 |
| 22 | Rom 12 | Jas 1 | Heb 12 | 22 | Mt 16 | Mk 7 | Lk 14 |
| 23 | Rom 13 | Jas 2 | Philemon | 23 | Mt 18 | Mk 7 | Lk 14 |
| 24 | Rom 14 | Jas 2 | 1 Tim 1 | 24 | Mt 18 | Mk 8 | Lk 15 |
| 25 | Phil 1 | Jas 3 | 1 Tim 2 | 25 | Mt 20 | Mk 9 | Lk 16 |
| 26 | Phil 2 | Jas 5 | 1 Tim 6 | 26 | Mt 21 | Mk 9 | Lk 16 |
| 27 | Phil 4 | Heb 2 | 2 Tim 1 | 27 | Mt 21 | Mk 10 | Lk 17 |
| 28 | Phil 4 | Heb 4 | 2 Tim 2 | 28 | Mt 22 | Mk 10 | Lk 17 |
| 29 | 1 Thes 1 | Heb 4 | 2 Tim 3–4 | 29 | Mt 22 | Mk 10 | Lk 18 |
| 30 | 1 Thes 1 | Heb 5 | 2 Tim 4 | 30 | Mt 22 | Mk 10 | Lk 18 |
| 31 | 1 Thes 2 | Heb 7 | 2 Thes 1–2 | 31 | Mt 23 | Mk 12 | Lk 19 |
| 32 | 1 Thes 4 | Heb 9 | 2 Thes 2–3 | 32 | Mt 25 | Mk 12 | Lk 20 |
| 33 | 1 Thes 5 | Heb 10 | 2 Thes 3 | 33 | Mt 25 | Mk 13 | Lk 21 |
| 34 | 1 Cor 15 | Rev 1 | Col 1 | 34 | Mt 25 | John 18 | Lk 23 |

## Ordinary Time Readings (*continued*)

### Weekdays

| First reading | | | Gospel | |
|---|---|---|---|---|
| Week | Year 1 | Year 2 | Week | |
| 1 | Heb | 1 Sm | 1 | |
| 2 | Heb | 1 Sm | 2 | |
| 3 | Heb | 1 Sm | 3 | |
| 4 | Heb | 2 Sm; 1 Kgs 1–16 | 4 | |
| 5 | Gn 1—11 | 1 Kgs 1–16 | 5 | Mark |
| 6 | Gn 1—11 | Jas | 6 | |
| 7 | Sir | Jas | 7 | |
| 8 | Sir | 1 Pt; Jude | 8 | |
| 9 | Tb | 2 Pt; 2 Tim | 9 | |
| 10 | 2 Cor | 1 Kgs 17–22 | 10 | |
| 11 | 2 Cor | 1 Kgs 17–22; 2 Kgs | 11 | |
| 12 | Gn 12–50 | 2 Kgs; Lam | 12 | |
| 13 | Gn 12–50 | Am | 13 | |
| 14 | Gn 12–50 | Hos; Is | 14 | |
| 15 | Ex | Is; Mi | 15 | |
| 16 | Ex | Mi; Jer | 16 | Matthew |
| 17 | Ex; Lv | Jer | 17 | |
| 18 | Nm; Dt | Jer; Na; Hb | 18 | |
| 19 | Dt; Jos | Ez | 19 | |
| 20 | Jgs; Ru | Ez | 20 | |
| 21 | 1 Thes | 2 Thes; 1 Cor | 21 | |
| 22 | 1 Thes; Col | 1 Cor | 22 | |
| 23 | Col; 1 Tim | 1 Cor | 23 | |
| 24 | 1 Tim | 1 Cor | 24 | |
| 25 | Ezr; Hg; Zec | Prv; Eccl | 25 | |
| 26 | Zec; Neh; Bar | Jb | 26 | |
| 27 | Jon; Mal; Jl | Gal | 27 | |
| 28 | Rom | Gal; Eph | 28 | Luke |
| 29 | Rom | Eph | 29 | |
| 30 | Rom | Eph; Phil | 30 | |
| 31 | Rom | Phil | 31 | |
| 32 | Wis | Ti; Phlm; 2, 3 Jn | 32 | |
| 33 | 1, 2 Mc | Rv | 33 | |
| 34 | Dn | Rv | 34 | |

## Behold an Illustration

The psalm response is chosen because of what the first reading of the liturgy proclaimed. It matches. Sometimes the choice is particularly striking. Even when it isn't, the relationship is always there, however subtle or hidden. It always helps to approach the psalm with expectation, and even appreciation, for the care given its choice. The following example, from a daily Mass (Tuesday of the fifth week of the year), illustrates.

Psalm 8 is used from time to time in the liturgy. It includes the verses, "When I look at your heavens,/ the work of your fingers,/ the moon and the stars that/ you have established;/ what are human beings that you/ are mindful of them,/ . . . that you care for them?/ Yet you have made them a little/ lower than a God, . . . " (verses 3-5).

One of its appearances in the Lectionary is on Tuesday of the fifth week of the year (Year I). The first reading for that day (see *Genesis 1:20-2:4*) is a portion of the story of creation from Genesis (days five and six), which culminate in the creation of human life. Psalm 8 is a psalm of praise and thanks for God's creation. It's an invitation to "behold." And to praise.

## 4. Omitted Verses

Sometimes "one or two verses of little pastoral worth or involving truly difficult questions" (*Introduction to the Lectionary* [1969], VI.d) are omitted in a reading so that an entire passage with good spiritual merit won't be lost because of great length or problem passages.

## The Advent Sunday Lectionary
(See chart on pp. 188-189)

Notice in the chart on pp. 188–189 how the Gospel readings are arranged so that on the first Sunday of Advent the Lord's final coming is featured; on the second and third Sundays, the readings are on the ministry of John the Baptist; and, finally, on the fourth Sunday, we have the nativity stories (Christ's coming in "history, mystery, and majesty," but in reverse order). The Old Testament readings, all taken from the prophets (including the oracle of Nathan, from 2 Samuel), are about the Messiah and the Messianic age. The reading of Isaiah, in particular, is assigned to Advent (for seven of the 12 first readings). In the second reading during the Sundays of Advent, "[t]he readings from an Apostle contain exhortations and proclamations, in keeping with the different themes of Advent" (Introduction, *Order of Readings for Mass*, 93).

## The Advent Daily Lectionary

There are two series of readings for the weekdays of Advent: one for the beginning of Advent until December 16; the other for December 17–24, the eight days before Christmas. During the days before the celebration of Christ's nativity, these are the sacred stories brought before the faithful at liturgy. The first biblical text is the first reading, the second is the Gospel. For each day, the two relate to one another.

The former is sometimes a pre-figuration of the latter. At other times the latter includes a quotation from or reference to the former. The Lectionary recalls for us the whole of the salvation story in all its richness.

### The Octave days before Christmas
1. December 17
   - Jacob's blessing of Judah (see *Genesis 49:2, 8–10*)
   - Matthew's genealogy of Jesus (see *Matthew 1:1–17*)

2. December 18
   - "... I will raise up for David a righteous Branch, ..." (*Jeremiah 23:5–8*)
   - The announcement of the birth of Christ to Joseph (see *Matthew 1:18–24*)

3. December 19
   - The announcement and birth of Samson (see *Judges 13:2–7, 24–25*)
   - The announcement of the birth of John to Zechariah (see *Luke 1:5–25*)

4. December 20
   - The Lord's word to Ahaz, "Look, the young woman is with child and shall bear a son ..." (*Isaiah 7:10–14*)
   - The annunciation of Jesus' conception and birth to Mary (see *Luke 1:26–38*)

5. December 21
   - "The voice of my beloved! / Look, he comes, / ..." (*Song of Solomon 2:8–14*)
   - The visitation (see *Luke 1:39–45*)

6. December 22
   - Hannah's prayer at the presentation of Samuel (see *1 Samuel 1:24–28*)
   - Mary's prayer during the visitation, the *Magnificat* (see *Luke 1:46–56*)

7. December 23
   - The Old Testament's last words: "I will send you the prophet Elijah ..." (see *Malachi 3:1–4, 4:5*)
   - The birth of John (see *Luke 1:57–66*)

8. December 24
   - The Oracle of Nathan "Your house and your kingdom shall be made sure forever before me; ..." (*2 Samuel 7:16*)
   - Zechariah's prayer at the birth of John, the *Benedictus* (see *Luke 1:67–79*)

## The Christmas Scriptures
The Christmas feast, also called the Solemnity of the Nativity, offers 16 Scripture texts, spread like a banquet before the community of the faithful. Why not read the Bible with the Church? The person who goes to Mass does. Those who can't can still pray with the Church by using the Lectionary. The Lectionary alone is a Scripture course and a guided reading of the Bible.

1. Christmas Vigil
   - *Isaiah 62:1–5* ("Jerusalem the Lord's Bride")

## THE SUNDAYS OF ADVENT

| | | YEAR A |
|---|---|---|
| **1** | 1st Reading | *Isaiah 2:1-5*<br>"... the mountain of the Lord's house/ shall be established ..." |
| | 2nd Reading | *Romans 13:11-14*<br>"... it is now the moment for you to wake from sleep." |
| | Gospel | *Matthew 24:37-44*<br>Jesus citing Noah and announcing the Day of the Lord |
| **2** | 1st Reading | *Isaiah 11:1-10*<br>"A shoot shall come out from the stump of Jesse, ..." |
| | 2nd Reading | *Romans 15:4-9*<br>Christ is the salvation of all. |
| | Gospel | *Matthew 3:1-12*<br>"... John the Baptist appeared in the wilderness of Judea, proclaiming, ..." |
| **3** | 1st Reading | *Isaiah 35:1-6, 10*<br>"The wilderness and the dry land shall be glad, ..." |
| | 2nd Reading | *James 5:7-10*<br>"Strengthen your hearts, for the coming of the Lord is near." |
| | Gospel | *Matthew 11:2-11*<br>"When John heard in prison what the Messiah was doing, ..." |
| **4** | 1st Reading | *Isaiah 7:10-14*<br>"... the Lord spoke to Ahaz, saying Ask a sign of the Lord your God; ..." |
| | 2nd Reading | *Romans 1:1-7*<br>Jesus Christ is the descendant of David and the Son of God. |
| | Gospel | *Matthew 1:18-24*<br>"Now the birth of Jesus the Messiah took place in this way." |

| YEAR B | YEAR C |
|---|---|
| *Isaiah 63:16b-17; 64:1, 3b-8*<br>"O that you would tear open the heavens and come down, . . ." | *Jeremiah 33:14-16*<br>". . . I will cause a righteous Branch to spring up for David; . . ." |
| *1 Corinthians 1:3-9*<br>". . . as you wait for the revealing of our Lord Jesus Christ." | *1 Thessalonians 3:12–4:2*<br>". . . may the Lord . . . strengthen your hearts . . . at the coming of our Lord . . ." |
| *Mark 13:33-37*<br>"Beware, keep alert; for you do not know when the time will come." | *Luke 21:25-28, 34-36*<br>"There will be signs in the sun, the moon, and the stars . . ." |
| *Isaiah 40:1-5, 9-11*<br>". . . make straight in the desert a highway for our God." | *Baruch 5:1-9*<br>Jerusalem, "Take off the garment of your sorrow and affliction, . . ." |
| *2 Peter 3:8-14*<br>". . . we wait for new heavens and a new earth, . . ." | *Philippians 1:4-6, 8-11*<br>". . . so that in the day of Christ you may be pure and blameless, . . ." |
| *Mark 1:1-8*<br>The opening words of Mark, quoting Isaiah, ". . . Prepare the way . . ." | *Luke 3:1-6*<br>John "went into all the region around the Jordan, proclaiming . . ." |
| *Isaiah 61:1-2, 10-11*<br>". . . he has sent me to bring good news to the oppressed, . . ." | *Zephaniah 3:14-18*<br>"Sing aloud, O daughter Zion;/ shout, O Israel!" |
| *1 Thessalonians 5:16-24*<br>". . . may you . . . be kept sound and blameless at the coming of our Lord . . ." | *Philippians 4:4-7*<br>"The Lord is near. Do not worry about anything, . . ." |
| *John 1:6-8, 19-28*<br>"There was a man sent from God, whose name was John." | *Luke 3:10-18*<br>The crowds asked John the Baptist, "What then should we do?" |
| *2 Samuel 7:1-5, 8b-12, 14a, 16*<br>The oracle of Nathan, promising David an heir and an eternal kingdom | *Micah 5:1-4*<br>"But you, O Bethlehem of Ephrathah,/ . . . shall come forth for me/ one who is to rule in Israel, . . ." |
| *Romans 16:25-27*<br>". . . the mystery . . . kept secret for long ages . . . is now disclosed, . . ." | *Hebrews 10:5-10*<br>"when Christ came into the world, he said: '. . . I have come to do your will . . .'" |
| *Luke 1:26-38*<br>The account of the annunciation | *Luke 1:39-45*<br>The account of the visitation |

"For as a young man marries a young woman, / so shall your builder marry you . . ."

- *Psalm 89:4–5, 16–17, 27, 29* (about David's dynasty) "I have made a covenant with my chosen one, . . ."

- *Acts 13:16–17, 22–25* (from Paul's sermon in the Antioch synagogue) "The God of [David's] people . . . has brought to Israel a Savior, Jesus, . . ."

- *Matthew 1:1–25* ("The Genealogy of Jesus the Messiah") "An account of the genealogy of Jesus the Messiah, the son of David, the son of Abraham. . . ."

2. Mass at Midnight
- *Isaiah 9:1–6* ("The Righteous Reign of the Coming King") "The people who walked in darkness have seen a great light; . . ."

- *Psalm 96:1–2, 2–3, 11–12, 13* ("Praise to God Who Comes in Judgment") "For great is the LORD, and greatly to be praised; / . . . to judge the earth."

- *Titus 2:11–14* ("Teach Sound Doctrine") "For the grace of God has appeared, bringing salvation to all, . . ."

- *Luke 2:1–14* ("The Birth of Jesus") "In those days a decree went

out from Emperor Augustus . . ."

3. Mass at Dawn
- *Isaiah 62:11–12* ("The Vindication and Salvation of Zion") "Say to daughter Zion, / 'See, your salvation comes;' . . ."

- *Psalm 97:1, 6, 11–12* ("The Glory of God's Reign") ". . . all the peoples behold his glory. / Light dawns for the righteous, . . ."

- *Titus 3:4–7* (continuing the passage begun at Midnight Mass) "But when the goodness and loving kindness of God our Savior appeared, . . ."

- *Luke 2:15–20* (the visit of the shepherds) "Let us go now to Bethlehem and see this thing that has taken place, . . ."

4. Mass during the Day
- *Isaiah 52:7–10* ("Let Zion Rejoice") ". . . for in plain sight they see / the return of the LORD to Zion."

- *Psalm 98:1, 2–3, 3–4, 5–6* ("Praise the Judge of the World" like Psalm 96) "The LORD has made known his victory; . . ."

- *Hebrews 1:1–6* (introduction and Messianic enthronement) "Long ago God spoke to our ancestors in many and various ways by the prophets, . . ."

- *John 1:1–18* (the prologue of the Gospel of John)
  "And the Word became flesh and lived among us, . . ."

## The Lenten Lectionary
### The Gospel Readings of Lent

Because cycle A is the year of Matthew, B of Mark, and C of Luke, each one predominates in its own cycle, with the exception of passages from Saint John that replace them on some of the Sundays. The Gospel for the first Sunday in each of the three cycles, the temptation of Christ, is a natural choice (see "40" symbolism on pp. 238–239 about the roots of Lent in Jesus' 40 days in the desert). The Gospel for the second Sunday in each of the three cycles is the account of the transfiguration. It is understood theologically as prefiguring the Resurrection; in the Gospels it is accompanied by a prediction of Jesus' death, hence the connection with Easter and Good Friday.

### Passion Sunday

The sixth Sunday of Lent is Passion Sunday. Also known as Palm Sunday, it is the beginning of Holy Week. The first reading and second readings are the same for all three cycles. The responsorial psalm is always Psalm 22, a lament unusual for its intensity of feeling ("My God, my God, why have you forsaken me?") and important in the New Testament (quoted or alluded to by the Evangelists in the story of Jesus' passion).

### The Week of the Servant

The Servant Poems of Isaiah are read during Holy Week (on Monday, Tuesday, Wednesday, and Friday).

### The Servant of the Lord

In Isaiah 40-55, the mysterious figure of the Servant of the Lord appears. "The Servant suffers and dies, possibly by execution but certainly with an evil reputation. His death is mysterious because of his innocence; the mystery is revealed as the vicarious atoning merit of his death, vindicated by his resurrection" (John McKenzie, *Dictionary of the Bible*, p. 791).

The identity of the Servant has been much debated. "Many identifications have been proposed, for example, historical Israel, ideal Israel, an Old Testament historical character before or during the lifetime of the prophet, the prophet himself. The New Testament and Christian tradition, however, have seen a fulfillment of these prophecies in Jesus Christ" (NAB footnote to Isaiah 42:1-4).

There are four Servant-of-the-Lord Oracles or poems in these chapters of Isaiah: 42:1-4, 49:1-6, 50:4-11, and 52:13–53:12.

1. Monday, *Isaiah 42:1–4*
   "Here is my servant, whom I uphold, . . ./ a bruised reed he will not break, . . ."
2. Tuesday, *Isaiah 49:1–6*
   "The LORD called me before I was born,/ while I was in my mother's womb he named me."
3. Wednesday, *Isaiah 50:4–11* (also used on Passion Sunday)
   "The Lord GOD has given me the

## THE SUNDAYS OF LENT

| | | YEAR A |
|---|---|---|
| **1** | 1st **Reading** | *Genesis 2:7–9, 3:1–7*<br>Creation and the fall of man |
| | 2nd **Reading** | *Romans 5:12–19*<br>Sin and death came through Adam; in Christ has come acquittal and life. |
| | Gospel | *Matthew 4:1–11*<br>The temptation of Jesus |
| **2** | 1st **Reading** | *Genesis 12:1–4*<br>The call of Abraham |
| | 2nd **Reading** | *2 Timothy 1:8b–10*<br>God "saved us and called us with a holy calling, ..." |
| | Gospel | *Matthew 17:1–9*<br>The transfiguration |
| **3** | 1st **Reading** | *Exodus 17:3–7*<br>Grumbling; water from the rock |
| | 2nd **Reading** | *Romans 5:1–2, 5–8*<br>"... since we are justified by faith, we have peace with God ..." |
| | Gospel | *John 4:5–42*<br>The woman at the well |
| **4** | 1st **Reading** | *1 Samuel 16:1b, 6–7, 10–13a*<br>The anointing of David as king |
| | 2nd **Reading** | *Ephesians 5:8–14*<br>"... awake!/ Rise from the dead,/ and Christ will shine on you." |
| | Gospel | *John 9:1–41*<br>The healing of the man blind from birth |
| **5** | 1st **Reading** | *Ezekiel 37:12–14*<br>From the dry bones prophecy |
| | 2nd **Reading** | *Romans 8:8–11*<br>"... the Spirit of him who raised Jesus from the dead dwells in you, ..." |
| | Gospel | *John 11:1–45*<br>The restoration of Lazarus |
| **6** | 1st **Reading** (all three cycles) | *Isaiah 50:4–7 (The Third Servant Song: "The Lord GOD has* |
| | 2nd **Reading** (all three cycles) | *Philippians 2:6–11 (Christ was in the form of God but* |
| | Gospel | *Matthew 26:14–27:66*<br>The passion of Christ |

| YEAR B | YEAR C |
|---|---|
| *Genesis 9:8-15* <br> The covenant with Noah after the flood | *Deuteronomy 6:4-10* <br> The confession of faith, and first fruits |
| *1 Peter 3:18-22* <br> The flood "and baptism, which this prefigured, now saves you . . ." | *Romans 10:8-13* <br> The confession of faith of all who believe in Christ |
| *Mark 1:12-15* <br> The temptation of Jesus | *Luke 4:1-13* <br> The temptation of Jesus |
| *Genesis 22:1-2, 9, 10-13, 15-18* <br> The test of Abraham, sacrificing Isaac | *Genesis 15:5-12, 17-18* <br> God's covenant with Abraham |
| *Romans 8:31b-34* <br> "He who did not withhold his own Son . . . will . . . give us everything else . . ." | *Philippians 3:17–4:1* <br> Christ will change our lowly body to be like his glorified body. |
| *Mark 9:2-10* <br> The transfiguration | *Luke 9:28-36* <br> The transfiguration |
| *Exodus 20:1-17* <br> The Ten Commandments | *Exodus 3:1-8, 13-15* <br> Moses' call, the burning bush, "I AM" |
| *1 Corinthians 1:22-25* <br> ". . . but we proclaim Christ crucified . . . the power . . . and the wisdom of God." | *1 Corinthians 10:1-6, 10-12* <br> The life of the people with Moses in the desert is a warning to us. |
| *John 2:13-25* <br> The cleansing of the temple | *Luke 13:1-9* <br> The falling tower; the barren fig tree |
| *2 Chronicles 36:14-17, 19-29* <br> The temple destruction and the exile | *Joshua 5:9, 10-12* <br> Passover before the siege of Jericho |
| *Ephesians 2:4-10* <br> Even when dead in our transgressions, by grace we have been saved. | *2 Corinthians 5:17-21* <br> "God . . . reconciled us to himself through Christ, . . ." |
| *John 3:14-21* <br> To Nicodemus: Christ lifted up | *Luke 15:1-3, 11-32* <br> The Prodigal Son parable |
| *Jeremiah 31:31-34* <br> The new covenant prophecy | *Isaiah 43:16-21* <br> Isaiah's prophecy of something new |
| *Hebrews 5:7-9* <br> Christ learned obedience and became the source of eternal salvation. | *Philippians 3:8-14* <br> "I regard everything as loss . . . that I may gain Christ . . ." |
| *John 12:20-33* <br> The grain of wheat; "Glorify your Son" | *John 8:1-11* <br> The woman caught in adultery |
| given me the tongue of a teacher, . . .") | |
| humbled himself even to death and God greatly exalted him.) | |
| *Mark 14:1–15:47* <br> The passion of Christ | *Luke 22:14–23:56 (or 23:1-49)* <br> The passion of Christ |

5

Word of the Liturgy

tongue of a teacher, . . . / I did not hide my face from insult and spitting."

4. Friday, *Isaiah 52:13—53:12* (the most familiar, reserved for Good Friday)

"See, my servant shall prosper; . . . Just as there were many who were astonished at him / —so marred was his appearance, beyond human semblance, . . ."

On Holy Thursday the Church presents a picture of the servant to go with the songs: the account of Jesus washing his disciples' feet (see *John 13:1–17*). It's easy to see how the early Christian community saw Jesus fulfilling the words of Isaiah.

## The Scriptures of the Sacred Triduum

### The first day

(nightfall Thursday to nightfall Friday)

*Evening Mass of the Lord's Supper ("Holy Thursday")*

"[T]he remembrance of the meal preceding the Exodus casts its own special light because of Christ's example in washing the feet of his disciples and Paul's account of the institution of the Christian Passover in the Eucharist" (Introduction, *Order of Readings for Mass*, 99).

- *Exodus 12:1–8, 11–14*
  The law about the Passover meal

- *1 Corinthians 11:23–26*
  "For I received from the Lord what I also handed on to you . . ."

- *John 13:1–15*
  The washing of the feet

*Good Friday of the Lord's Passion*

"[T]he liturgical service has as its center John's narrative of the Passion of him who was proclaimed in Isaiah as the Servant of the Lord and who became the one High Priest by offering himself to the Father" (Introduction, *Order of Readings for Mass*, 99).

- *Isaiah 52:13—53:12*
  "See, my servant shall prosper; / he shall be exalted and lifted up, . . ."

- *Hebrews 4:14–16, 5:7–9*
  ". . . he learned obedience from what he suffered; . . . he became the source of eternal salvation for all who obey him, . . ."

- *John 18:1—19:42*
  The passion of Christ

### The second day

(nightfall Friday to nightfall Saturday)

"On Holy Saturday the Church waits at the Lord's tomb, meditating on his suffering and death. The altar is left bare, and the sacrifice of the Mass is not celebrated. Only after the solemn vigil during the night, held in anticipation of the Resurrection, does the Easter celebration begin, with a spirit of joy that overflows into the following period of fifty days" (from the *Sacramentary*).

### The third day

(nightfall Saturday to nightfall Sunday)

*The Easter Vigil*

"[T]here are seven Old Testament readings which recall the wonderful works of God in the history of salvation. There are two New Testament readings, the announcement of the Resurrection according to [Matthew, Mark, or Luke] and a reading from Saint Paul on Christian baptism as the sacrament of Christ's Resurrection" (Introduction, *Order of Readings for Mass*, 99). While the number of these readings may be reduced, at least three Old Testament selections should be read (always including the account of the Exodus).

- *Genesis 1:1–22*
  The Creation

- *Genesis 22:1–18*
  Abraham put to the test: the sacrifice of his son Isaac

- *Exodus 14:15 — 15:1*
  The Exodus

- *Isaiah 54:5–14*
  ". . . but with great compassion I will gather you. . . ."

- *Isaiah 55:1–11*
  "Ho, everyone who thirsts,/ come to the waters;/ . . . I will make with you an everlasting covenant, . . ."

- *Baruch 3:9–15, 32 — 4:4*
  "You have forsaken the fountain of wisdom./ . . . Turn, O Jacob, and take her;/ walk toward the shining of her light."

- *Ezekiel 36:16–17a, 18–28*
  "I will sprinkle clean water upon you, and you shall be clean from all your uncleannesses, . . ."

- *Romans 6:3–11*
  "Do you not know that all of us who have been baptized into Christ Jesus were baptized into his death? . . . For if we have been united with him in a death like

his, we will certainly be united with him in a resurrection like his."

- *Luke 24:1–12*
  "They found the stone rolled away from the tomb, but when they went in, they did not find the body . . . suddenly two men in dazzling clothes stood beside them. 'Why do you look for the living among the dead?'"

### Easter Sunday Morning

- *Acts 10:34, 37–43*
  (From Peter's sermon leading to Cornelius' baptism)
  "[We] ate and drank with him after he rose from the dead."

- Either *Colossians 3:1–3*
  "So if you have been raised with Christ, seek the things that are above, . . ."

- Or *1 Corinthians 5:6–8*
  "Clean out the old yeast so that you may be a new batch, as you really are unleavened."

- *John 20:1–9*
  Mary of Magdala discovers the empty tomb; summons Peter and John

## The Easter Season Lectionary

Easter Sunday is the first Sunday of Easter and Pentecost is the 50th day of Easter. The Easter Season is considered as a whole on the Church's liturgical calendar. All seven Sundays from Easter to Pentecost belong to the Easter season, Easter Sunday being the first. The next Sunday is not the first Sunday *after* Easter but the second Sunday *of* Easter.

## THE SUNDAYS OF EASTER

| | | YEAR A |
|---|---|---|
| 1 | **Easter Sunday** (see "The Scriptures of the Sacred Triduum" for the readings of Easter Sunday) | |
| 2 | 1st **Reading** | *Acts 2:42-47*<br>Summary description of the early Church |
| | 2nd **Reading** | *1 Peter 1:3-9*<br>God gave "us a new birth into a living hope through the resurrection of Jesus . . ." |
| | **Gospel** (resurrection appearances) | *John 20:19-31* (Sunday evening; Jesus appears in locked |
| 3 | 1st **Reading** | *Acts 2:14, 22-28*<br>Peter's Pentecost discourse (middle part) |
| | 2nd **Reading** | *1 Peter 1:17-21*<br>"He was destined before the foundation of the world, but was revealed . . . for your sake." |
| | **Gospel** (resurrection appearances) | *Luke 24:13-35*<br>On the way to Emmaus |
| 4 | 1st **Reading** | *Acts 2:14, 36-41*<br>Peter's Pentecost discourse (ending) |
| | 2nd **Reading** | *1 Peter 2:20-25*<br>". . . but now you have returned to the shepherd and guardian of your souls." |
| | **Gospel** (The Good Shepherd) | *John 10:1-10*<br>". . . I am the gate for the sheep. . . ." |
| 5 | 1st **Reading** | *Acts 6:1-7*<br>Seven assistants for the Church |
| | 2nd **Reading** | *1 Peter 2:4-9*<br>"Come to him, a living stone . . . chosen and precious in God's sight, . . . a holy priesthood, . . ." |
| | **Gospel** | *John 14:1-12* (From The Last Discourse)<br>"Do not let your hearts be troubled." |
| 6 | 1st **Reading** | *Acts 8:5-8, 14-17*<br>Philip in Samaria; Samaritans receive the Holy Spirit |
| | 2nd **Reading** | *1 Peter 3:15-18*<br>". . . put to death in the flesh, but made alive in the spirit, . . ." |
| | **Gospel** (from The Last Discourse) | *John 14:15-21*<br>About the Advocate |

| YEAR B | YEAR C |
|---|---|
| *Acts 4:32-35* <br> Second description of the early Church | *Acts 5:12-16* <br> Third description of the early Church |
| *1 John 5:1-6* <br> "... whatever is born of God conquers the world." | *Revelation 1:9-13, 17-19* <br> "I was dead, and see, I am alive forever and ever; ..." (From the first vision of John) |
| room, gives the Holy Spirit; reappears one week later, greeting Thomas) | |
| *Acts 3:13-15, 17-19* <br> Peter's second discourse, after a healing | *Acts 5:27-32, 40-41* <br> Peter before Sanhedrin, fourth discourse |
| *1 John 2:1-5* <br> "... he is the atoning sacrifice for our sins, and ... for the sins of the whole world." | *Revelation 5:11-14* <br> "Worthy is the Lamb that was slaughtered/ to receive power and wealth ..." |
| *Luke 24:35-48* <br> In Jerusalem, after Emmaus appearance | *John 21:1-19 (or 21:1-14)* <br> At the Sea of Tiberias |
| *Acts 4:8-12* <br> Peter's discourse before the Sanhedrin | *Acts 13:14, 43-52* <br> Paul and Barnabas in Antioch, to Gentiles |
| *1 John 3:1-2* <br> "... we are God's children now; ..." <br> (also read on All Saints Day) | *Revelation 7:9, 14-17* <br> "... for the Lamb ... will be their shepherd,/ and he will guide them to springs of the water of life, ..." |
| *John 10:11-18* <br> "I am the good shepherd." | *John 10:27-30* <br> "I know them, and they follow me." |
| *Acts 9:26-31* <br> Paul, new convert, visits Jerusalem. The Church at peace. | *Acts 14:21-27* <br> "... they called the church together and related all that God had done with them, ..." |
| *1 John 3:18-24* <br> "And this is his commandment, that we should believe ... and love one another, ..." | *Revelation 21:1-5* <br> The new heaven and the new earth |
| *John 15:1-8* (From The Last Discourse) <br> The vine and the branches | *John 13:31-35* <br> "I give you a new commandment, ..." |
| *Acts 10:25-26, 34-35, 44-48* <br> The beginning of the Gentile mission; Peter's preaching; Cornelius' baptism | *Acts 15:1-2, 22-29* <br> The Jerusalem Council; about the Jewish law applying to Gentile converts |
| *1 John 4:7-10* <br> "Beloved, let us love one another, ... God is love." | *Revelation 21:10-14, 22-23* <br> The new Jerusalem |
| *John 15:9-17* <br> "No one has greater love than this, ..." | *John 14:23-29* <br> "... the Holy Spirit ... will teach you ..." |

5

Word of the Liturgy

| | | YEAR A |
|---|---|---|
| **7** | **1ˢᵗ Reading** | *Acts 1:12-14*<br>After the Ascension, to the upper room |
| | **2ⁿᵈ Reading** | *1 Peter 4:13-16*<br>". . . rejoice insofar as you are sharing Christ's sufferings, . . ." |
| | **Gospel** (From Jesus' High Priestly Prayer) | *John 17:1-11*<br>"Father, the hour has come; . . ." |

### The first reading

During the Easter season, Old Testament readings are omitted, replaced by readings from the Acts of the Apostles, which stress the impact of the Resurrection on the early Church.

### The second reading

On Easter Sunday, there is an option for the second reading and it's the same in each of the three years of the lectionary cycle. On the other Sundays of the season, 1 Peter is the source in Year A, 1 John in Year B, and the Book of Revelation in Year C.

### The Gospel

There are seven Sundays in the Easter season ("1" in the chart beginning on p. 196 is Easter Sunday). The Gospel readings are mainly from the Gospel of John and contain memorable expressions of Jesus' care for and presence in the community: the Good Shepherd, the Vine and the Branches, the Love Command. The fourth Sunday is a kind of Good Shepherd Sunday because in each of the three years of the Lectionary cycle, part of the Good Shepherd passage in John 10 is read. On the fifth and sixth Sundays every year (with one exception), the Lectionary uses passages from the Last Discourse of Jesus.

### The Ascension of the Lord

When the Ascension of the Lord is celebrated the following Sunday, the second reading and Gospel from the seventh Sunday of Easter may be read on the sixth Sunday of Easter.

- 1ˢᵗ Reading
  *Acts 1:1–11* (an account of the Ascension)

- 2ⁿᵈ Reading (there is an option)
  *Ephesians 1:17–23* ("Christ . . . seated . . . in the heavenly places")
  *Hebrews 9:24–28; 10:19–23* ("Christ . . . entered heaven itself.")

- Gospel (the concluding verses of Matthew, Mark, and Luke)
  Year A: *Matthew 28:16–20*
  Year B: *Mark 16:15–20* (including an account of the Ascension)
  Year C: *Luke 24:46–53* (including an account of the Ascension)

| YEAR B | YEAR C |
|---|---|
| *Acts 1:15-17, 20-26*<br>Choosing Matthias to replace Judas | *Acts 7:55-60*<br>The martyrdom of Stephen |
| *1 John 4:11-16*<br>"God is love, and those who abide in love abide in God, and God abides in them." | *Revelation 22:12-14, 16-17, 20*<br>The Alpha and the Omega; "Come . . ." |
| *John 17:11-19*<br>"Holy Father, protect them in your name . . ." | *John 17:20-26*<br>"I ask . . . that they may all be one. . . ." |

# The Homily

"It is the first task of priests . . . to preach the Gospel of God to all" (*Decree on the Ministry and Life of Priests*, 4). "Proclamation" happens in many ways, including simply living the Christian life in a way that speaks—and even proclaims— the good news of Christ. But still "a key moment in the proclamation of the Gospel is preaching, preaching which is characterized by 'proclamation of God's wonderful works in the history of salvation, that is, the mystery of Christ, which is ever made present and active within us, especially in the celebration of the liturgy'" (*Fulfilled in Your Hearing*, "Introduction," quoting Vatican II, *Constitution of the Sacred Liturgy*, 35, 2. *Fulfilled in Your Hearing* is a document published in 1982 by The Bishops' Committee on Priestly Life and Ministry of The National Conference of Catholic Bishops.)

The document *Fulfilled in Your Hearing* cites a statement of Saint Paul's about the primacy of preaching: "But how can they call on one in whom they have not believed? And how are they to believe in one of whom they have never heard? And how are they to hear without someone to proclaim him?" (*Romans 10:14*).

## Preaching in the New Testament

The word "to proclaim" (*keryssein* in Greek) is the word most commonly used in the New Testament for preaching. The word "presupposes that the preachers are heralds who announce simply that which they are commissioned to announce, not in their own name, but by the authority of the one who sent them" (John McKenzie, *Dictionary of the Bible*, p. 689).

## The "Homily" in the New Testament

In the New Testament, there is not a specific technical word to describe the preaching understood today as a "homily." "The word *homileo* does appear in the New Testament, and its usage there can provide a way to understand a homiletic approach to preaching as distinguished from preaching addressed to unbelievers (*kerygma*)" (*Fulfilled in Your Hearing*, endnote 8). These are two such examples:

**5**

**Word of the Liturgy**

- "Now on that same day two of them were going to a village called Emmaus, about seven miles from Jerusalem, and talking with each other about all these things that had happened" (*Luke 24:13–14*; from the beginning of the story of the appearance of the risen Christ on the road to Emmaus).

- "[Felix] used to send for [Paul] very often and converse with him" (*Acts 24:26*). Paul was in prison in Caesaria while M. Antonius Felix was procurator of Judea. Felix "sent for Paul and heard him speak concerning faith in Jesus Christ" (*Acts 24:24*).

This use of the word *homileo* in the New Testament "suggests that a homily should sound more like a personal conversation, albeit a conversation on matters of utmost importance, than like a speech or a classroom lecture" (*Fulfilled in Your Hearing*, III. "Homiletic Style").

## The Homily Today

The homily is a specific kind of preaching. (A "sermon" is a talk on a religious or moral topic. It's a broad term, as its Latin root suggests—*sermo*, discourse, talk. It often takes the form of instruction and / or exhortation.) The following three descriptions of a homily come from three different documents of the Church.

- The homily should draw its content mainly from "scripture and liturgy, for in them is found the proclamation of God's wonderful works in the history of salvation, the mystery of Christ, ever made present and active in us, especially in the celebration of the liturgy" (Vatican II, *Constitution on the Sacred Liturgy*, 35).

- The homily in liturgy "should be an exposition of some aspect of the readings from Sacred Scripture . . . and should take into account both the mystery being celebrated and the particular needs of the listeners" (*General Instruction of the Roman Missal*, 65).

- "The homily points to the presence of God in people's lives and then leads a congregation into the Eucharist, providing, as it were, the motive for celebrating the Eucharist in this time and place"[4] (*Fulfilled in Your Hearing*, III. "The Homily and the Liturgy of the Eucharist").

Homilies are not meant to be lessons from a Scripture course or a Bible study group. This "does not exclude doctrinal instruction and moral exhortation. Such instruction and exhortation, however, are here situated in a broader context, namely, in the recognition of God's active presence in the lives of the people and the praise and thanksgiving that this response elicits"[5] (*Fulfilled in Your Hearing*, III. "The Limits and Possibilities of Liturgical Preaching").

## The Preparation of a Homily

The document *Fulfilled in Your Hearing* teaches that the preacher goes to the Scriptures asking these four questions (in this order):

- "What is the human situation to which these texts were originally addressed?"
- "To what human concerns and questions might these same texts have spoken through the Church's history?"
- "What is the human situation to which they can speak today?"
- "How can they help us to understand, to interpret our lives in such a way that we can turn to God with praise and thanksgiving?" (III. "The Homily and the Lectionary")

## The Preparation of the Preacher

"*Dabitur vobis*" is an old piety that a preacher need not prepare because "it will be given to you" in the pulpit. This is not helpful. This ignores the cultivation of Scripture, which is an absolute requirement of those ordained as preachers of the word.

- "Therefore, all [the clergy] should immerse themselves in the scriptures by constant spiritual reading and diligent study. For it must not happen that any of them become 'empty preachers of the word of God to others, not being hearers of the word in their own hearts,' (Saint Augustine) when they ought to be sharing the boundless riches of the divine word with the faithful committed to their care, especially

in the sacred liturgy" (Vatican II, *Constitution on Divine Revelation*, 25).

- "Want of preparation . . . leads to the temptation to avoid plumbing the depths of the biblical readings and to being content simply to moralize or to speak of contemporary issues in a way that fails to shed upon them the light of God's word" (*The Interpretation of the Bible in the Church*, IV.C.3).

## The Structure of a Homily

The following three-part structure of a homily is suggested in *Fulfilled in Your Hearing* as an approach "in keeping with its function of enabling people to celebrate the liturgy with deepened faith."

- It could "begin with a description of a contemporary human situation which is evoked by the scriptural texts, rather than with an interpretation or reiteration of the text."
- "After the human situation has been addressed, the homilist can turn to the Scriptures to interpret this situation, showing how the God described therein is also present and active in our lives today."
- "The conclusion of the homily can then be an invitation to praise this God who wills to be lovingly and powerfully present in the lives of his people" (*Fulfilled in Your Hearing*, III. "Homiletic Style").

## Some Professional Advice

The most common advice to preachers is probably about the length of the homily. The best advice is about something much deeper, as the following three points illustrate.

- "Many homilies seem to fall into the same three-part pattern: "In today's readings . . . This reminds us . . . Therefore let us . . ." The very structure of such homilies gives the impression that the preacher's principal purpose is to interpret scriptural texts rather than communicate with real people, and that he interprets these texts primarily to extract ethical demands to impose on a congregation. Such preachers may offer good advice, but they are rarely heard as preachers of good news, and this very fact tends to distance them from their listeners" (*Fulfilled in Your Hearing*, III. "Homiletic Style").

- "Preachers should certainly avoid insisting, in a one-sided way, on the obligations incumbent upon believers. The biblical message must preserve its principal characteristic of being the good news of salvation freely offered by God. Preaching will perform a task more useful and more conformed to the Bible if it helps the faithful above all to 'know the gift of God' (*John 4:10*) as it has been revealed in Scripture; they will then understand in a positive light the obligations that flow

from it" (*The Interpretation of the Bible in the Church*, IV.C.3).

- The Vatican Commission for Religious Relations with the Jews called special attention in 1974 to the image of Jews in preaching: "With respect to liturgical readings, care will be taken to see that homilies based on them will not distort their meaning, especially when it is a question of passages which seem to show the Jewish people as such in an unfavorable light. Efforts will be made so to instruct the Christian people that they will understand the true interpretation of all the texts and their meaning for the contemporary believer" (from part II of "Guidelines and Suggestions for Implementing the Conciliar Declaration *Nostra Aetate*, 4").

## Resources of the Preacher

These are basic tools of the preacher of the word.

1. Current and scholarly commentaries help with the exegesis of the text. (Exegesis is the scholarly investigation of the meaning of a Scripture text. See Chapter 4 for more on this and various kinds of commentaries.) "Exegetes have [also] helped produce publications designed to assist pastors in their responsibility to interpret correctly the biblical texts of the liturgy and make them properly meaningful for today" (*The Interpretation of the Bible in the Church*, IV.C.3).

2. A concordance helps in locating related passages.
3. A good Bible dictionary helps with an understanding of the background of a passage.
4. A theological dictionary of Scripture helps explain ideas and themes common in the Old and New Testaments.
5. A book of Gospel parallels helps by aligning similar texts found in more than one Gospel.

# Served from One Table

The *Catechism of the Catholic Church* teaches that the Church's twofold treasure of the word of God and the Body of Christ is served from one table (103, 1346).

## The View of the Early Church

In the third century, the great Scripture scholar Origen put side by side the word of God and the Body of Christ: "You who are accustomed to take part in the divine mysteries know, when you receive the body of the Lord, how you protect it with all caution and veneration lest any small part fall from it, lest anything of the consecrated gift be lost. For you believe, and correctly, that you are answerable if anything falls from there by neglect. But if you are so careful to preserve His body, and rightly so, how do you think that there is less guilt to have neglected God's word than to have neglected His body?" (From *The Lamb's Supper*, Hahn, p. 48, "Origen, *On Exodus*, 13.3)

## The View of Today's Church

In the twentieth century, Vatican II spoke in similar terms: "The Church has always venerated the divine scriptures as it has venerated the Body of the Lord, in that it never ceases, above all sacred liturgy, to partake of the bread of life and to offer it to the faithful from one table of the word of God and the Body of Christ" (*Constitution on Divine Revelation*, 21). In 1998, the Introduction of the *Order of Readings for Mass* spelled this out ever further: "The Church is nourished spiritually at the twofold table of God's word and of the Eucharist: from the one it grows in wisdom and from the other in holiness. In the word of God the divine covenant is announced; in the Eucharist the new and everlasting covenant is renewed. On the one hand the history of salvation is brought to mind by means of human sounds; on the other it is made manifest in the sacramental signs of the Liturgy" (10).

# Scriptural Threads

The Liturgy of the Word has Scripture as its focus but the Liturgy of the Eucharist is scriptural too. There are biblical quotations and allusions at every turn. There are scriptural threads throughout the whole fabric of the Mass.

## Prayer in Common

"On the day called Sunday there is a meeting in one place of those who live in cities or the country." So begins a description of the Eucharistic celebration of the Church in AD 150 by Justin, martyr. From the beginning, Christians have valued prayer in common.

- The Gospels suggest that Jesus participated in the common prayer of his Jewish contemporaries. Jesus modeled the value of common prayer. "When he came to Nazareth, where he had been brought up, he went to the synagogue on the sabbath day, as was his custom." (*Luke 4:16*).

- Likewise, Christians imitate the early Church, which Luke describes in the first of three summary passages: "They devoted themselves to the apostles' teaching and fellowship, to the breaking of bread and the prayers" (*Acts 2:42*).

- In his first letter to the Corinthians, Paul devotes a large section (1 Corinthians 11:2—14:40) to regulation of conduct in liturgical assemblies. At one point he writes, "For, to begin with, when you come together as a church, I hear that there are divisions . . . When you come together, it is not really to eat the Lord's supper. For when the time comes to eat, each of you goes ahead with your own supper, and one goes hungry and another becomes drunk" (*1 Corinthians 11:18–21*). He then recounts the tradition of the Eucharist (1 Corinthians 11:23–25—believed to be the earliest written account of the institution of the Lord's Supper in the New Testament).

## Mass on Sunday

The first day of the week, the day after the Sabbath, had special meaning for Christians from the very beginning because it was a commemoration of the Resurrection of Jesus, which the Gospels say took place on the first day of the week.

- In *Revelation 1:10* the prophet John says, "I was in the spirit on the Lord's day . . ." The term "the Lord's day" indicates liturgical significance (that is, his readers knew that it referred to a day set aside for worship).

- In *1 Corinthians 16:2* Saint Paul mentions the liturgical assembly "[o]n the first day of every week" when he called for this fellowship to express itself in generosity to others. The First Letter to the Corinthians was written in the middle 50s of the first century.

- In *Acts 20:7* Saint Luke comments, "[o]n the first day of the week, when we met to break bread . . .", probably reflecting the custom of Sunday evening (not eve) Eucharist in his own time. The Acts of the Apostles was written in approximately AD 85.

## Prayer in Christ

When commenting on the prayers and other parts of the Mass pertaining to the priest, the *General Instruction of the Roman Missal* says, "The foremost is the Eucharistic Prayer, which is the high point of the entire celebration. Next are the orations [the opening prayer, the prayer of the gifts, and the prayer after communion]. These prayers are addressed to God in the name of the entire holy people and all present, by the priest who presides over the assembly in the person of Christ" (30). About the opening prayer in particular, it says, "In accordance with the ancient tradition of the Church, the [opening prayer] is usually addressed to God the Father, through Christ, in the Holy Spirit . . ." (54).

- This brings to mind the teaching of our Lord, "I will do whatever you ask in my name, so that the Father may be glorified in the Son. If in my name you ask me for anything, I will do it" (*John 14:13–14*).

- In teaching about the high priesthood of Jesus, the Letter to the Hebrews says, "Consequently [Jesus] is able for all time to save those who approach God through him, since he always lives to make intercession for them" (*Hebrews 7:25*).

## Scriptural Foundation of Gestures and Postures Commonly Used in Liturgy

### Genuflecting

This gesture (bending the right knee to touch the floor), common in Scripture, was an act of respect and homage given to kings and deities. When used in the Eucharistic celebration, it acknowledges the real presence of Christ in the consecrated bread and wine. The following are examples from Scripture of homage given to God and to Jesus.

- "To me every knee shall bow, / every tongue shall swear" (*Isaiah 45:23*).

- "The Father judges no one but has given all judgment to the Son, so that all may honor the Son just as they honor the Father" (*John 5:22–23*).

- "As I live, says the Lord, every knee shall bow to me, / and every tongue shall give praise to God" (*Romans 14:11*).

- "Therefore God also highly exalted him / and gave him the name / that is above every name, / so that at the name of Jesus / every knee should bend, / in heaven and on earth and under the earth, . . ." (*Philippians 2:9–10*).

### Kneeling

Kneeling is a common posture for prayer, private adoration, and repentance. Lying face down is an even more profound posture, used during the liturgy of Good Friday

5

**Word of the Liturgy**

and the Rite of Ordination. The following are examples of figures in Scripture who included the posture of kneeling in their prayer.

- Moses and Aaron "fell prostrate" in intercessory prayer numerous times during the Hebrews' journey from slavery to freedom (see *Numbers 14:5, 16:22, 17:10, 20:6*).

- Solomon, at the dedication of the temple, "knelt on his knees in the presence of the whole assembly of Israel, and spread out his hands toward heaven" (*2 Chronicles 6:13*).

- The psalmist: "O come, let us worship and bow down, / let us kneel before the LORD our Maker!" (*Psalm 95:6*).

- Daniel: "Although Daniel knew that the document had been signed, he continued to go to his house, which had windows in its upper room open toward Jerusalem, and to get down on his knees three times a day to pray to his God and praise him, . . ." (*Daniel 6:10*).

- Ezra: "At the evening sacrifice I got up from my fasting, with my garments and my mantle torn, and fell on my knees, spread out my hands to the LORD my God, . . ." (*Ezra 9:5*).

- Jesus, during the agony in the garden: "Then he withdrew from them about a stone's throw, knelt down, and prayed, . . ." (*Luke 22:41*).

- A leper seeking the ministry of Jesus: "A leper came to him begging him, and kneeling he said to him, . . ." (*Mark 1:40*).

- Peter, when he restored Tabitha to life: "Peter put all of them outside, and then he knelt down and prayed" (*Acts 9:40*).

- Paul, with the elders of Ephesus: "When he had finished speaking, he knelt down with them all and prayed" (*Acts 20:36*). (This is one of the few scriptural illustrations of the community kneeling for common prayer.)

- Paul, on his way to Jerusalem: "When our days there were ended, we left and proceeded on our journey; and all of them, with wives and children, escorted us outside the city. There we knelt down on the beach and prayed and said farewell to one another" (*Acts 21:5–6*).

- In the heavenly liturgy of Revelation, "And all the angels stood around the throne and around the elders and the four living creatures, and they fell on their faces before the throne . . ." (*Revelation 7:11*)

## Uplifted Hands

Uplifted hands, called "orans" (Latin for praying), were common in the ancient world among Jews and Gentiles as an expression of supplication. Some scholars think it was the only generally accepted prayer position at least into the second century. (In addition to the following examples, see also *Psalms 63:5, 88:10, 119:48, 134:2,* and *143:6.*)

- "Hear the voice of my supplication,/ as I cry to you for help,/ as I lift up my hands/ toward your most holy sanctuary" (*Psalm 28:2*).

- "Let my prayer be counted as incense before you,/ and the lifting up of my hands as an evening sacrifice" (*Psalm 141:2*).

- In the introduction to the text of a prayer of Ezra, his uplifted hands are mentioned: "At the evening sacrifice I got up from my fasting, with my garments and my mantle torn, and fell on my knees, spread out my hands to the LORD my God, and said . . ." (*Ezra 9:5*).

### Dorothy Day on Her Knees

The *New York Times* called Dorothy Day "the most influential person in the history of American Catholicism" when she died. That was in November of 1980, when she was 84. She describes her conversion to Christ and reception into the Catholic Church in her book *From Union Square to Rome.*

It was as a child that she first felt an attraction to the faith when she came upon the mother of one of her friends kneeling in prayer. She was moved at the sight of this woman kneeling and she never forgot it. When she tells her own story, she relates how, during the time before her conversion, she often would spend the whole night in a bar. From there she would go to an early morning Mass at St. Joseph's Church on 6th Avenue. It was the people kneeling in prayer that attracted her to the Mass: "I longed for their faith. . . . So I used to go in and kneel in a back pew."

### The Church at Prayer

"In the catacombs the Church is often represented as a woman in prayer, arms outstretched in the praying position. Like Christ who stretched out his arms on the cross, through him, with him, and in him, she offers herself and intercedes for all men" (*CCC*, 1368).

## Laying on of Hands

The gesture of laying on of hands is common in liturgy and Christian prayer. Deacons, priests, and bishops are ordained by a bishop through the laying on of hands in the Sacrament of Holy Orders. It is also used in the Sacraments of Confirmation, Penance, and Anointing of the Sick as well as in various blessings. In both the Old and New Testaments, the laying on of hands is often mentioned. Its significance varies but usually involves designating persons for a task and calling upon them divine favor and power to do it.

- It was used by Israel, giving his parental blessing to Ephraim and Manasseh (see *Genesis 48:17–18*).

- Aaron and his sons laid hands on the bullock in an ordination sacrifice (see *Exodus 29:10*).

- Moses laid hands on Joshua in conferring his authority to his successor (see *Numbers 27:18; Deuteronomy 34:9*).

- An official asked Jesus to lay his hand on his daughter who had died, to make her live again (see *Matthew 9:18*).

**5**

**Word of the Liturgy**

- Jesus laid hands on children when he blessed them (see *Matthew 19:15*).

- The Twelve laid hands on the seven chosen "to serve at table" (see *Acts 6:6*).

- Peter and John laid hands on some Samaritans who had only been baptized "and they received the Holy Spirit" (see *Acts 8:17*).

- Leaders in the Church at Antioch laid hands on Barnabas and Saul before they began the first mission (see *Acts 13:3*).

### Scripture in the Elements of the Mass

### The Sign of the Cross

The familiar words spoken in the sign of the cross go back to *Matthew 28:19*, "Go therefore and make disciples of all nations, baptizing them in the name of the Father and of the Son and of the Holy Spirit." Quoting those words—"In the name of the Father . . . "—while tracing the cross of Christ on one's body is a simple prayer involving words and actions that originated in the second century, expressing the core of the Christian creed—the

### A Sign within the Sign of the Cross

It's a tradition in the eastern Churches to make the Sign of the Cross with the thumb, index, and middle fingers touching one another, apart from the other two digits: the three representing the Trinity of persons in God, the two fingers representing the two natures, divine and human, in Christ.

Trinity, the incarnation, and redemption. Making the sign of the cross with holy water increases its baptismal significance and makes it a conscious commitment to renew the baptismal covenant in the Eucharist.

### The Greeting

The priest "signifies the presence of the Lord to the community gathered there by means of the Greeting. By this Greeting and the people's response, the mystery of the Church gathered together is made manifest" (*General Instruction of the Roman Missal*, 50). There are many religious greetings in the New Testament letters (Romans 16:20, 1 Thessalonians 5:28, Philemon 25, Philippians 4:23, 1 Corinthians 16:23, 1 Corinthians 16:24, Galatians 6:18, Ephesians 6:23, Ephesians 6:24, Colossians 1:2, 1 Timothy 1:2, 2 Timothy 1:2, 2 Thessalonians 3:18, 2 Timothy 4:22, 2 Peter 1:2, Jude 2). There are three options for the greeting provided in the Introductory Rites of The Order of Mass:

- A: "The grace of our Lord Jesus Christ and the love of God and the fellowship of the Holy Spirit be with you all," from *2 Corinthians 13:13* ("The grace of the Lord Jesus Christ, the love of God, and the communion of the Holy Spirit be with all of you").

- B: "The grace and peace of God our Father and the Lord Jesus Christ be with you," from *Romans 1:7, 1 Corinthians 1:3, 2 Corinthians*

1:2, *Ephesians 1:2, Philippians 1:2, 2 Thessalonians 1:2, Philemon 3* ("Grace to you and peace from God our Father and the Lord Jesus Christ").

- C: "The Lord be with you," from *2 Thessalonians 3:16* and parallels ("The Lord be with all of you").

## The Penitential Rite

After the introduction to the Mass, "the priest invites the assembly to recall their sins and to repent of them in silence" (from the *Order of Readings for Mass*). After the Act of Penitence, the invocation "Lord, have mercy" begins (unless it was already part of the Act of Penitence). "It is a chant by which the faithful acclaim the Lord and implore his mercy . . ." (*General Instruction of the Roman Missal*, 52). (The ancient Greek form of "Lord, have mercy," *Kyrie, eleison*, is not uncommon in the liturgy of the Latin west.) "Lord, have mercy" is a familiar prayer in both the Old and the New Testaments. God's mercy is one of the most repeated themes of Scripture.

- In his conversation with God on Mt. Sinai, Moses declares, "The LORD, the LORD, a God merciful and gracious, slow to anger, and abounding in steadfast love . . ." (*Exodus 34:6*).

- In *Psalm 51:1*, for example, like other penitential psalms, the psalmist prays, "Have mercy on me, O God, according to your steadfast love; . . . "

- In *Matthew 15:22* a Canaanite woman prays for mercy.

- In *Matthew 17:15* the father of a boy with a demon prays for mercy.

- In *Matthew 20:30* two blind men by the roadside near Jericho pray for mercy.

- *James 5:16* says, "Therefore confess your sins to one another, and pray for one another, so that you may be healed." The words of the *Confiteor*, one of the options in the penitential rite, are based on this: "I confess to almighty God and to you, my brothers and sisters . . . , and I ask blessed Mary, ever virgin, all the angels and saints and you, my brothers and sisters, to pray for me to the Lord our God."

## The *Gloria*

"The *Gloria* is a very ancient and venerable hymn in which the Church, gathered together in the Holy Spirit, glorifies and entreats God the Father and the Lamb" (*General Instruction of the Roman Missal*, 53). It's also known as the Greater Doxology (Greek: *doxa*, glory), the Lesser Doxology being the "Glory to the Father" prayer.

- This prayer begins with an acclamation that recalls the song the angels sang when they went to inform the shepherds of Jesus' birth (see *Luke 2:14*)—hence, "the Angelic Hymn."

- Other sections of the *Gloria* paraphrase the angelic praises of God's power in the Book of Revelation (see especially *Revelation 15:3–4*).

## The Proclaimer's Prayer before the Gospel

"Almighty God, cleanse my heart and my lips that I may worthily proclaim your gospel." That's what the priest prays, if there's no deacon, before proclaiming the Gospel at Mass.

• This allusion to the prophet Isaiah was even clearer in the Latin version of this prayer that began "*Munda cor meum:*" "Cleanse my heart and my lips, almighty God, as you cleansed the lips of the prophet Isaiah with a burning coal. In your mercy so cleanse me that I may worthily proclaim your holy gospel, through Christ our Lord. Bless me, O Lord. The Lord be in my heart and on my lips, that I may worthily and fittingly proclaim his gospel. Amen."

• Today the sacramentary only calls for a simplified version of the last sentence of that prayer. It refers to the call of Isaiah in Chapter 6. (The "*munda cor meum*" prayer is still usable—not only for priest-proclaimers.)

## The Creed

Creeds crystallize the Church's faith. The Nicene Creed was formulated by the ancient ecumenical councils of Nicaea (325) and Constantinople (381), using lines that already were woven by common use in the Church's Scripture and liturgy. The *Catechism* explains, "From the beginning, the apostolic Church expressed and handed on her faith in brief formulae for all[6]" (*CCC*, 186). For examples, it then cites Saint Paul:

• *Romans 1:1–4*
"Paul, a servant of Jesus Christ, called to be an apostle, set apart for the gospel of God, which he promised beforehand through his prophets in the holy scriptures, the gospel concerning his Son, who was descended from David according to the flesh and was declared to be Son of the God with power according to the spirit of holiness by resurrection from the dead, Jesus Christ our Lord . . ." A revised NAB footnote comments: "Paul here cites an early confession that proclaims Jesus' sonship as messianic descendant of David (see *Matthew 22:42, 2 Timothy 2:8, Revelation 22:16*) and as Son of God by the resurrection."

• *1 Corinthians 15:3–5*
"For I handed on to you as of first importance what I in turn had received: that Christ died for our sins in accordance with the scriptures, and that he was buried, and that he was raised on the third day in accordance with the scriptures, and that he appeared to Cephas, then to the twelve." A revised NAB footnote comments: "The language by which Paul expresses the essence of the 'gospel' (1) is not his own but is drawn from older creedal formulas. This

credo highlights Jesus' death for our sins (confirmed by his burial) and Jesus' resurrection (confirmed by his appearances) and presents both of them as fulfillment of prophecy. *In accordance with the Scriptures*: conformity of Jesus' passion with the Scriptures is asserted in Matthew 16:1; Luke 24:25–27, 32, 44–46. Application of some Old Testament texts (Psalms 2:7, 16:8–11) to his Resurrection is illustrated by Acts 2:27–31; 13:29–39; and Isaiah 52:13—53:12 and Hosea 6:2 may also have been envisaged."

The *Catechism* explains further, "But already early on, the Church also wanted to gather the essential elements of its faith into organic and articulated summaries, intended especially for candidates for Baptism:

- 'This synthesis of faith was not made to accord with human opinions, but rather what was of the greatest importance was gathered from all the Scriptures, to present the one teaching of the faith in its entirety. And just as the mustard seed contains a great number of branches in a tiny grain, so too this summary of faith encompassed in a few words the whole knowledge of the true religion contained in the Old and New Testaments'" (CCC, 186, quoting Saint Cyril of Jerusalem, 315–386[7]).

- The *Catechism* goes on to say: "Such syntheses are called 'professions of faith' since they

summarize the faith that Christians profess . . . The first 'profession of faith' is made during Baptism. The symbol of faith is first and foremost the *baptismal* creed. Since Baptism is given 'in the name of the Father and of the Son and of the Holy Spirit,' (*Matthew 28:19*) the truths of faith professed during Baptism are articulated in terms of their reference to the three persons of the Holy Trinity" (CCC, 187, 189).

## The Preparation of the Altar and the Gifts

As the priest washes his fingers he prays, "Lord, wash away my iniquity; cleanse me from my sin."

- That's verse two from the great penitential psalm, Psalm 51, called the *Miserere*. Those in fact are the very words from the CCD edition of the Bible "with a new translation of the psalms from the new Latin version"; today's NAB has restored the exact word order—and the chiasmus—of the original. A chiasmus is an "inverted parallelism:"

See Appendix 2 for more about the chiasmus.

- Before the reform, *Psalm 26:6* was prayed, "*Lavabo inter innocentes . . .*" ("I wash my hands in innocence,/ and go around your altar, O Lord"). This is another

## The Eucharistic Prayer

This central proclamation of the liturgy of the Eucharist is a prayer of thanksgiving and sanctification. It consists of these parts:

**1. Thanksgiving,** expressed especially in the preface, for salvation or some specific aspect of it

**2. An acclamation,** in the "holy, holy" all, united with the angels, proclaim the holiness of God

**3. An epiclesis,** invoking the Holy Spirit, asking that the gifts of bread and wine be consecrated—become Christ's Body and Blood—and become a source of salvation for those who receive them

**4. The institution and consecration narrative,** "in which, by means of words and actions of Christ, the Sacrifice is carried out which Christ himself instituted at the Last Supper, when he offered his Body and Blood under the species of bread and wine, gave them to his Apostles to eat and drink, and left them the command to perpetuate this same mystery" (*General Instruction of the Roman Missal*, 79)

**5. An anamnesis,** acclaiming, at Christ's command, his presence: passion, Resurrection, and Ascension

**6. The offering,** of the victim in memorial, whom the Church becomes in Eucharist, to the Father in the Spirit

**7. Intercessions,** expressive of the Eucharist as the assembly's celebration with the whole Church of heaven and earth and for the Church and all her members living and dead

**8. A doxology,** expressing praise of God, confirmed and concluded by the acclamation of the people

example of the incorporation of Scripture into the liturgy.

• The liturgical act of washing is another part of the Christian liturgy's Jewish heritage (see *Exodus 30:19, 21; 40:31–32*). It represents an inner cleanness in preparation for worship (see also *Isaiah 1:16*).

### "Lift up your hearts"

After the greeting "The Lord be with you," this invitation to prayer begins the Eucharistic Prayer. In Scripture, "the heart is the source of thoughts, desires, and deeds" (John McKenzie, *Dictionary of the*

*Bible*, p. 343). It's a commonly used term, especially in the prophets when exposing ritualism and insincerity in religious practice. "Soul" is a related term in Scripture, usually used to translate the Hebrew term *nepes*—to lift up the soul to something is to desire it (John McKenzie, *Dictionary of the Bible*, pp. 836–837).

• "Then Joshua said to the people, 'You are witnesses against yourselves that you have chosen the LORD, to serve him.' And they said, 'We are witnesses.' He said, 'Then put away the foreign gods that are among you, and incline your hearts to the LORD, the God of Israel'" (*Joshua 24:22–23*).

- "Because these people draw near with their mouths and honor me with their lips, while their hearts are far from me, . . ." (*Isaiah 29:13*, cited in *Matthew 15:8* in a discussion between Jesus and some Pharisees and scribes about the tradition of the elders).

- "To you, O LORD, / I lift up my soul" (*Psalm 25:1–2*).

- "Gladden the soul of your servant, / for to you, O Lord, I lift up my soul" (*Psalm 86:4*).

- "Let us lift up our hearts as well as our hands / to God in heaven" (*Lamentations 3:41*).

## The "Holy, Holy"

This acclamation, called the "*sanctus*" in Latin, glorifies the Father and gives thanks for the whole work of salvation. Its text is scriptural.

- Seraphim ("burning ones," celestial beings) sing in Isaiah's vision of the heavenly throne, "Holy, holy, holy is the LORD of hosts; the whole earth is full of his glory" (*Isaiah 6:3*). This angelic origin has given this acclamation the name Seraphic Hymn.

- To this is added the acclamation of the crowds (quoting *Psalm 118:26*) as Jesus entered Jerusalem, ". . . 'Blessed is the one who comes in the name of the Lord! / Hosanna in the highest heaven!'" (*Matthew 21:9*).

- Jesus ends his lament over Jerusalem by saying, "For I tell you, you will not see me again until you say, 'Blessed is the one who comes in the name of the Lord'" (*Matthew 23:39*), a reference to his end-time return in glory.

## The Consecration

Consecration refers to the words of Christ, spoken at the Last Supper in the institution of the Eucharist, that are pronounced at Mass through which the bread and wine become the Real Presence of the Body and Blood of Christ.

- The institution of the Eucharist at the last supper is recorded in *Matthew 26:26–28* (with parallels in *Mark 14:22–24* and *Luke 22:19–20*): "While they were eating, Jesus took a loaf of bread, and after blessing it he broke it, gave it to the disciples, and said, 'Take, eat; this is my body.' Then he took a cup, and after giving thanks he gave it to them, saying, 'Drink from it, all of you; for this is my blood of the covenant, which is poured out for many for the forgiveness of sins.'"

- Scholars think the oldest consecration prayer, already traditional in Paul's time, is in *1 Corinthians 11:23–26*: "For I received from the Lord what I also handed on to you, that the Lord Jesus on the night when he was betrayed took a loaf of bread, and when he had given thanks, he broke it and said, 'This is my body that is for you. Do this in remembrance of me.' In the same way he took the cup also, after supper, saying, 'This cup is the new covenant in my blood. Do this, as often as you drink it, in remembrance of me.' For as often as you eat this bread and drink the cup, you proclaim the Lord's death until he comes."

- The scriptural foundation for the belief in the "real" presence of Jesus' Body and Blood in the consecrated bread and wine includes the Bread of Life passage in *John 6* (see especially verses 52–56): "The Jews then disputed among themselves, saying, 'How can this man give us his flesh to eat?' So Jesus said to them, 'Very truly, I tell you, unless you eat the flesh of the Son of Man and drink his blood, you have no life in you. Those who eat my flesh and drink my blood have eternal life, and I will raise them up on the last day; for my flesh is true food and my blood is true drink. Those who eat my flesh and drink my blood abide in me, and I in them.'"

## Memorial Acclamation

The following are the four optional responses to the invitation "Let us proclaim the mystery of faith." All are typical of the credal statements incorporated in the New Testament letters.

1. "Christ has died, Christ is risen, Christ will come again."
    - "It is Christ Jesus, who died, yes, who was raised, who is at the right hand of God,

who indeed intercedes for us" (*Romans 8:34*).

- "Grace to you and peace from him who is and who was and who is to come, . . ." (*Revelation 1:4*).

- "The one who testifies to these things says, 'Surely I am coming soon.' Amen. Come, Lord Jesus!" (*Revelation 22:20*)

2. "Dying you destroyed our death, rising you restored our life. Lord Jesus, come in glory."
    - ". . . [Jesus] . . . abolished death and brought life and immortality to light through the gospel" (*2 Timothy 1:10*).

    - "[W]e have been buried with him by baptism into death, so that, just as Christ was raised from the dead by the glory of the Father, so we too might walk in newness of life" (*Romans 6:4*).

    - "The one who testifies to these things says, 'Surely I am coming soon.' Amen. Come, Lord Jesus!" (*Revelation 22:20*)

3. "When we eat this bread and drink this cup, we proclaim your death, Lord Jesus, until you come in glory."
    - "For as often as you eat this bread and drink the cup, you proclaim the Lord's death until he comes" (*1 Corinthians 11:26*).

4. "Lord, by your cross and resurrection you have set us free. You are the Savior of the world."

- See *Romans 6:4-23*, especially "For if we have been united with him in a death like his, we shall certainly be united with him in a resurrection like his" (verse 5) and "set free from sin, [you] have become slaves of righteousness" (verse 18) and "But now that you have been freed from sin and enslaved to God, the advantage you get is sanctification. The end is eternal life" (verse 22).

- "It is no longer because of what you said that we believe, for we have heard for ourselves, and we know that this is truly the Savior of the world" (*John 4:42*, words spoken by the Samaritans to the Samaritan woman who met Jesus at the well).

- "And we have seen and do testify that the Father has sent his Son as the Savior of the world" (*1 John 4:14*).

## The Lord's Prayer

"[Jesus] was praying in a certain place, and after he had finished, one of his disciples said to him, 'Lord, teach us to pray, as John taught his disciples'" (*Luke 11:1*). The prayer known as the Lord's Prayer—the "Our Father"—was given in response to this request. It appears in the Gospel of Luke as well as in the Gospel of Matthew.

- Saint Luke's version is shorter, made up of five petitions:

"Father, hallowed be your name. / Your kingdom come. / Give us each day our daily bread. / And forgive us our sins, / for we ourselves forgive everyone indebted to us. / And do not bring us to the time of trial." (*Luke 11:2–4*).

- Saint Matthew's version, the one used in the Church's liturgical tradition, is more developed, consisting of seven petitions: "Our Father in heaven, / hallowed be your name. / Your kingdom come. / Your will be done, / on earth as it is in heaven. / Give us this day our daily bread. / And forgive us our debts, / as we also have forgiven our debtors. / And do not bring us to the time of

### "For thine is the kingdom and the power and the glory ..."

"Very early on, liturgical usage concluded the Lord's Prayer with a doxology. In the *Didache*, we find, 'For yours are the power and the glory for ever.'[8] The *Apostolic Constitutions* add to the beginning: 'the kingdom,' and this is the formula retained to our day in ecumenical prayer[9]. . . . The *Roman Missal* develops the last petition in the explicit perspective of 'awaiting our blessed hope' and of the Second Coming of our Lord Jesus Christ.[10] Then comes the assembly's acclamation or the repetition of the doxology from the *Apostolic Constitutions*" (*CCC*, 2760).

The doxology "for thine is the kingdom . . ." was added in the sixteenth century. Originally a liturgical ending, it was used during Mass with the insertion "Deliver us, O Lord . . ."

trial, / but rescue us from the evil one." (*Matthew 6:9–13*).

- The third-century Christian writer Tertullian called the Lord's Prayer "truly the summary of the whole gospel."

- "After showing how the psalms are the principal food of Christian prayer and flow together in the petitions of the Our Father, St. Augustine concludes: 'Run through all the words of the holy prayers [in Scripture], and I do not think that you will find anything in them that is not contained and included in the Lord's Prayer'" (*CCC*, 2762).

- "All the Scriptures—the Law, the Prophets, and the Psalms—are fulfilled in Christ (see *Luke 24:44*). The Gospel is this 'Good News.' Its first proclamation is summarized by St. Matthew in the Sermon on the Mount (see *Matthew 5—7*); the prayer to our Father is at the center of this proclamation" (*CCC*, 2763).

## The Sign of Peace

This ritual, coming just before communion, recalls the words of Christ recorded in *Matthew 5:23–24*: "So when you are offering your gift at the altar, if you remember that your brother or sister has something against you, leave your gift there before the altar and go; first be reconciled to your brother or sister, and then come and offer your gift."

The priest begins the Sign of Peace with a prayer: "Lord Jesus Christ,

you said to your apostles: / I leave you peace, my peace I give you. / Look not on our sins, but on the faith of your Church, / and grant us the peace and unity of your kingdom / where you live for ever and ever." The words of Jesus that are cited are from *John 14:27*.

Then the priest greets the assembly, "The peace of the Lord be with you always." This recalls a Resurrection appearance of Jesus: "When it was evening on that day, the first day of the week, and the doors of the house where the disciples had met were locked for fear of the Jews, Jesus came and stood among them and said, 'Peace be with you.'" (*John 20:19*).

Then the deacon (or priest) invites the assembly, "Let us offer each other the sign of peace." This recalls the "holy kiss" mentioned at the end of several New Testament letters. At the end of 1 Thessalonians, for example, is the verse, "Greet all the brothers and sisters with a holy kiss" (*1 Thessalonians 5:26*; see also *Romans 16:16, 1 Corinthians 16:20, 2 Corinthians 13:12*, and *1 Peter 5:14*). Scholars are unsure about exactly what this meant or how it was practiced but they agree it was liturgical in nature. The revised NAB footnote to *1 Thessalonians 5:26*, for example, says, "*Kiss*: the holy embrace was a greeting of respect and affection, perhaps given during a liturgy at which Paul's letter would have been read."

## The Breaking of the Bread

The priest breaks the Eucharistic Bread as the supplication "Lamb of God" is sung.

- Christ's action of breaking bread at the Last Supper is recalled in this rite (*see Matthew 26:26–28, Mark 14:22–24, Luke 22:19–20, 1 Corinthians 11:23–26*).

- The breaking of bread—in fact, the whole fourfold liturgical action of taking, blessing, breaking, and giving—is included in post-Resurrection episode "The Walk to Emmaus" (*Luke 24:13–35*): "When he was at the table with them, he took bread, blessed and broke it, and gave it to them. Then their eyes were opened, and they recognized him; and he vanished from their sight." (*Luke 24:30–31*).

- This ritual action "gave the entire Eucharistic Action its name in apostolic times" (*General Instruction of the Roman Missal*, 83): "They devoted themselves to the apostles' teaching and fellowship, to the breaking of bread and the prayers" (*Acts 2:42*).

- The breaking of the bread "signifies that the many faithful are made one body by receiving Communion from the one Bread of Life which is Christ, who died and rose for the salvation of the world" (*General Instruction of the Roman Missal*, 83). This is in direct reference to *1 Corinthians 10:17* which says, "Because there is one bread, we who are many are one body, for we all partake of the one bread."

The supplication, preferably sung, that accompanies the breaking of the bread is: "Lamb of God, you take away the sins of the world: have mercy on us." It is repeated at least three times, the final time ending with "Grant us peace." The communion rite follows, beginning with the presentation of the Eucharistic Bread, "This is the Lamb of God / who takes away the sins of the world. / Happy are those who are called to his supper." And then, with the assembly these words are spoken, "Lord, I am not worthy to receive you, / but only say the word and I shall be healed." The repetition of Christ's title "Lamb of God" at this point in the Mass indicates the importance of this imagery for understanding the Eucharistic celebration.

- This prayer repeats the words of John the Baptist, "Here is the Lamb of God who takes away the sin of the world!" (*John 1:29*).

- The beatitude paraphrases *Revelation 19:9*: "Blessed are those who are invited to the marriage supper of the Lamb."

- This title of Christ recalls the Passover sacrifice made in commemoration of God's liberation of the Israelites from slavery in Egypt (see *Exodus 12*) and the Yom Kippur lamb that is offered as a sin offering on the Day of Atonement.

- "Lamb of God" also echoes the Suffering Servant Song in which the servant is described as a lamb silent before the slaughter (see *Isaiah 53:7, 10*).

- The Lamb of God title also alludes to the victorious song of the lamb who destroys the world's evil by his triumph over death (see *Revelation 5—7, 17:14*).

- The assembly's response paraphrases the words of the Roman centurion who came to Jesus to ask for healing for his servant. Jesus told him he would come to his house, but the centurion responded, "Lord, I am not worthy to have you come under my roof; but only speak the word, and my servant will be healed" (*Matthew 8:8*). It's a prayer of humility before receiving the gift of Christ presenting the Eucharist.

## Communion

The petition of the Lord's Prayer "Give us this day our daily bread. . . ." finds an answer in the bread of the Eucharist, as Rev. Raymond Brown explains in his essay on the Our Father in *New Testament Essays*: "There is good reason, then, for connecting the Old Testament manna and the New Testament Eucharistic bread with the petition. . . . Thus, in asking the Father 'Give us our bread,' the community was employing words directly connected with the Eucharist. And so our Roman Liturgy may not be too far from the original sense of the petition in having the [Our Father] introduce the Communion of the Mass." (From Rev. Raymond

Brown's essay on the Our Father in *New Testament Essays*, New York: Doubleday, 1968, p. 307.)

# The Sacraments

"Since [the] sacraments are sacraments of faith, and since 'faith is born of the Word and nourished by it', the preaching of the Word is an essential part of the celebration of the sacraments" (*Fulfilled in Your Hearing*, Introduction, quoting Vatican II, *Decree on the Ministry and Life of Priests*, 4). The same document explains the purpose of this "essential part" of sacraments: "The goal of the liturgical preacher is not to interpret a text of the Bible (as would be the case in teaching a Scripture class) as much as to draw on the texts of the Bible as they are presented in the Lectionary to interpret peoples' lives. To be even more precise, the preacher's purpose will be to turn to these Scriptures to interpret peoples' lives in such a way that they will be able to celebrate Eucharist—or be reconciled with God and one another, or be baptized into the Body of Christ, depending on the particular liturgy that is being celebrated" (*Fulfilled in Your Hearing*, III. "The Homily and the Lectionary").

## Baptism

Baptism shares the Liturgy of the Word of the Mass in which it is celebrated; if celebrated apart from Mass, it has its own liturgy of the Word.

• The Baptism of adults ("catechumens") is part of their initiation through the Sacraments of Baptism, Confirmation, and the Eucharist. The "Easter Vigil should be regarded as the proper time for the sacraments of initiation" (*The Rites of the Catholic Church*, Christian Initiation of Adults, 8). Scripture—the liturgy of the word of the Easter Vigil, precedes the baptism of adults, in this way.

• The Baptism of children is normally part of the Sunday celebration: "To bring out the paschal character of baptism, it is recommended that the sacrament be celebrated during the Easter Vigil or on Sunday, when the Church commemorates the Lord's resurrection. On Sunday, baptism may be celebrated even during Mass, so that the entire community may be present and the relationship between baptism and eucharist may be clearly seen . . ." (*The Rites of the Catholic Church*, Baptism for Children, 9). When children are baptized apart from Mass, the rite calls for a liturgy of the word "directed toward stirring up the faith of the parents, godparents, and congregation, and toward praying in common for the fruits of baptism before the sacrament itself" (*The Rites of the Catholic Church*, Baptism for Children, 17).

## Confirmation

"Ordinarily confirmation takes place within Mass in order to express more clearly the fundamental connection of this sacrament with the entirety of Christian initiation. The latter reaches its culmination in the communion of the body and blood of Christ. The newly confirmed should therefore participate in the eucharist which completes their Christian initiation" (*The Rites of the Catholic Church*, Rite of Confirmation, 13).

"If the candidates for confirmation are children who have not received the eucharist and are not admitted to first communion at this liturgical celebration or if there are other special circumstances, confirmation should be celebrated outside Mass. When this occurs, there is first to be a celebration of the word of God" (*The Rites of the Catholic Church*, Rite of Confirmation, 13).

## Reconciliation

After commenting on the preparation of priest and penitent and the welcome of the penitent, the rite says, "Next, . . . the priest, or even the penitent, [may] read a text of holy Scripture, or this may be done as part of the preparation for the sacrament. For through the word of God Christians receive light to recognize their sins and are called to conversion and to confidence in God's mercy" (*The Rites of the Catholic Church*, Penance, 17).

In the "Rite for Reconciliation of Several Penitents with Individual Confession and Absolution," an opening directive says, "It is fitting that they be prepared for the sacrament by a celebration of the

## Sacraments

| Signs | Words |
|---|---|
| **Baptism**<br>Pouring of water (Baptism, Chrismation, and Eucharist are celebrated together, in the Eastern Rites.) | "N., I baptize you in the name of the Father, and of the Son, and of the Holy Spirit." |
| **Confirmation**<br>Laying on of hands, anointing with oil | "N., be sealed with the, Gift of the Holy Spirit." |
| **Eucharist**<br>Bread and wine | The Eucharistic Prayer within the liturgy, with its institution narrative: "This is my body . . . this is my blood . . . " |
| **Reconciliation**<br>Contrition, confession, and satisfaction | "God the Father of mercies, through the death and resurrection of his Son, has reconciled the world to himself and sent the Holy Spirit among us for the forgiveness of sins; through the ministry of the Church, may God give you pardon and peace; and I absolve you from your sins in the name of the Father, and of the Son, and of the Holy Spirit." |
| **Anointing of the Sick**<br>Anointing with oil and laying on of hands | "Through this holy anointing may the Lord in his love and mercy help you with the grace of the Holy Spirit." "Amen." "May the Lord who frees you from sin save you and raise you up." "Amen." |
| **Marriage**<br>Mutual consent to live together as husband and wife (In Eastern Rites, priest is the minister.) | In the West, the external expression of this is through the interchange of the couple with the Church witness (priest, deacon), as he elicits their intention (questions preceding the vows) and their consent (wedding vows). |
| **Holy Orders**<br>Laying on of hands | The Prayer of Consecration that follows the laying on of hands. |

## Scriptures

Necessity of rebirth–*John 3:5*
Institution by Christ–*Matthew 28:18-20*
In the early Christian community:
 • *Acts 8:26-39* (the Ethiopian eunuch)
 • *Acts 16:16f* (the jailer of Paul and Silas)
 • *Acts 19:1-7* (the disciples in Ephesus)
Paul's theology of Baptism:
 • *Romans 6:3-11*
 • Meaning and effect: *Galatians 2:19-20; 3:14, 26-29; Ephesians 1:3-5, 2:4-10; Colossians 1:14, 2:9-13, 3:1-3; 1 Peter 1:3-5*

*Acts 8:14-17, 9:17-19, 10:5, 19:5; Titus 3:4-8*

Roots in Jewish Passover–*Exodus 12:1-28*
Melchizedek's offering–*Genesis 14:18*
The priesthood of David–*Psalm 110*
The priesthood of Jesus–*Hebrews 8-10*
Multiplication of loaves–*John 6:1-15*
The Bread of Life–*John 6:25-71*
The Last Supper–*Matthew 26:26-28; Mark 14:22-25; Luke 22:7-20*
The Emmaus event–*Luke 24:13-53*
Apostolic Church–*Acts 2:42-47, 20:7*
The meaning and effect of the Eucharist–*1 Corinthians 10:16-17*

Sin lists: *1 Corinthians 5:3-5, 6:9-10; Galatians 5:19-20; Ephesians 5:5; 1 Timothy 1:19-21*
Jesus' mission
 • *Mark 2:16-17* ("I have come to call sinners . . .")
 • *Luke 7:47-50* (Mary Magdalene)
 • *Luke 19:7-10* (Zacchaeus)
Christ's continued ministry in the Church
 • *John 16:1-8* (coming of the Paraclete)
 • *Matthew 16:13-19* (keys of the kingdom)
 • *John 20:19-23* (commissioning the Church)
 • *Acts 9:1-5* (Saul's conversion)
Early Church ministry regarding post-baptismal sin
 • *Matthew 18:15-18* (fraternal correction, Church authority)
 • *2 Thessalonians 2:6, 14-15* (excommunication)
 • *1 Timothy 1:19-20* (ostracization)
Reconciliation before Communion
 • *Mark 11:25* ("When you pray, forgive . . .")
 • *Mark 5:23-24* ("If you bring your gift . . .")
Scandal: *Matthew 18:5-7*

Institution–*James 5:13-16*
The ministry of the community to the sick–*Isaiah 52:13–53:12; 1 Corinthians 12:12-22, 24b-27; Matthew 25:31-40*
Suffering–*2 Corinthians 12:9-10*
Anointing the sick–*Isaiah 61:1-3a; John 9:1-7*
Healing–*1 Kings 19:1-8; Acts 4:8-12 (3:1-10); Matthew 8:1-4 (5-17)*
Healing and forgiveness–*Job 7:12-21; Mark 2:1-12*
Faith–*Job 3:1-3, 11-17, 20-23; Isaiah 35:1-10*
Hope and confidence–*Job 19:23-27a (7:1-4, 6-11); Romans 8:18-27; 1 Corinthians 1:18-25; Matthew 8:1-4; 25:31-40*
The power of prayer–*Job 7:12-21; James 5:13-18; Luke 11:5-13*

The question of divorce–*Matthew 19:3-12 (Mark 10:2-12)*
Christian wives and husbands–*Ephesians 5:25-32*
A believing spouse consecrates a partner–*1 Corinthians 7:12-16*

Presbyters installed in the early Church–*Acts 14:22-23*
The priestly role–*Hebrews 5:1-10*
Counsel to Timothy–*1 Timothy 4:12-16*
Exhortation to faithfulness–*2 Timothy 1:6-8*
Apostolic charge–*2 Timothy 4:2, 5:7-8*
Qualities of a presbyter–*Titus 1:5-9*

word of God" (*The Rites of the Catholic Church*, Penance, 22).

It says further that "the sacrament of penance should begin with a hearing of God's word, because through his word God calls his people to repentance and leads them to a true conversion of heart. One or more readings may be chosen. If more than one are read, a psalm, another suitable song, or a period of silence should be inserted between them, so that the word of God may be more deeply understood and heartfelt assent may be given to it. If there is only one reading, it is preferable that it be from the gospel. Readings should be chosen that will:

a) let God's voice be heard, calling his people back to conversion and ever closer conformity with Christ;

b) call to mind the mystery of our reconciliation through the death and resurrection of Christ and through the gift of the Holy Spirit;

c) bring to bear . . . God's judgment of good and evil as a light for the examination of conscience" (*The Rites of the Catholic Church*, Penance, 24)

### Anointing of the Sick

In the "Rite of Anointing a Sick Person" the instruction is given, Before he anoints a sick person, "the priest should inquire about [his] condition [in order] to plan the celebration by choosing the readings and prayers" (*The Rites of the Catholic Church*, Rite of Anointing and Pastoral Care of the Sick, 64).

### Matrimony

About the importance of Scripture at a wedding, the "Rite of Marriage" says, "The liturgy of the word . . . is a highly effective means for the catechesis on the sacrament of marriage and its duties" (*The Rites of the Catholic Church*, Rite of Marriage, 11).

The Rite includes specific suggestions about the kind of preaching expected as well as its purposes: "After the gospel, the priest gives a homily drawn from the sacred text. He speaks about the mystery of Christian marriage, the dignity of wedded love, the grace of the sacrament and the responsibilities of married people . . ." (22).

In the Rite for Celebrating Marriage Outside Mass, the rite calls for a liturgy of the word (41).

### Holy Orders

The ordination of deacons, priests, and bishops takes place within the Mass.

## Scripture and Sacramentals

Sacramentals are "sacred signs by which, somewhat after the manner of the sacraments, effects of a spiritual nature, especially, are symbolised and are obtained through the church's intercession. By them, people are made ready to receive the much greater effect of the sacraments, and various occasions in life are rendered holy" (Vatican II, *Constitution on the Sacred Liturgy*, 60).

The *Catechism* explains further that the purpose of sacramentals is "the sanctification of certain ministries of the Church, certain states of life, a great variety of circumstances in Christian life, and the use of many things helpful to man" (1668).

The elements of a sacramental are always a prayer and often a specific external sign or object like the laying on of hands, the Sign of the Cross, or the sprinkling of holy water.

The following are some examples, with their foundation in Scripture explained.

## Anointing

Anointing (literally) is the pouring of blessed oil on someone or something in a religious ceremony. In Scripture, the purpose of anointing is to make holy the person or object anointed.

Anoint, anointing, and anointed are common terms in the Old Testament. *Psalm 2:2*, for example, prays, "The kings of the earth set themselves,/ and the rulers take counsel together,/ against the Lord and his anointed, . . ." In Israel, the power of office was given through anointing to kings (see *Judges 9:8, 1 Samuel 9:16, 16:12–13*) and to high priests (see *Leviticus

*8:12, Numbers 3:3*). "Anointed" in Hebrew is *mashijah* and in Greek *christos*. Those very words, Messiah and Christ, are brought right into English—capitalized because of the person of Jesus for whom they have become titles.

Anointing is used in the Sacraments of Initiation (Baptism and Confirmation), in the Anointing of the Sick (in which both the forehead and the palms of the hands are anointed), and in Holy Orders (in which the hands of the newly ordained are anointed).

The Church also recognizes the use of blessed oil by a layperson, as it does the use of other sacramentals like holy water and candles. The purpose normally is for healing and protection, and the method, a simple signing of the forehead (or appropriate part of the body) with a cross using the oil.

Here are a few New Testament texts that mention anointing:

- ". . . God anointed Jesus of Nazareth with the Holy Spirit and with power . . ." (*Acts 10:38*).

- "But it is God who establishes us with you in Christ and has anointed us, by putting his seal on us and giving us his Spirit in our hearts as a first installment" (*2 Corinthians 1:21–22*).

- "Are any among you sick? They should call for the elders of the church and have them pray over them, anointing them with oil in the name of the Lord . . ." (*James 5:14*).

5

Word of the Liturgy

## Ashes

Ashes are a sign of repentance. Their most well known use is for Ash Wednesday markings. They are also used during altar consecrations and church dedications. Here are some examples of the scriptural foundation for the use of ashes as a sign of repentance:

- The familiar Ash Wednesday exhortation that is given to people who come forward to receive ashes is, "Remember that you are dust and to dust you shall return." It's an old translation of *Genesis 3:19*, from the last sentence of God's statement to Adam and Eve after the fall and alludes to the creation of human beings out of clay (see *Genesis 2:7*). Its revised NAB translation is "For you are dirt, / and to dirt you shall return." (In today's revised liturgy, the person distributing ashes may also use the exhortation, "Repent, and believe in the gospel." In the Gospel of Mark, these are the words that inaugurate Jesus' preaching ministry [*Mark 1:15*].)

- In *Jonah 3:6* it says, "When the news reached the king of Nineveh, he rose from his throne, removed his robe, covered himself with sackcloth, and sat in ashes."

- In *Matthew 11:21* it says, "Woe to you, Chorazin! Woe to you, Bethsaida! For if the deeds of power done in you had been done in Tyre and Sidon, they would have repented long ago in sackcloth and ashes."

## Candles

Light—fire, candles—is an important symbol in Scripture and so too in the liturgical life of the Church.

### The Christ candle

Also known as the Easter candle and Paschal Candle, the Christ candle is an important symbol of the risen Savior, the Light of the World. It has a prominent place in the solemn beginning of the Easter Vigil, the Service of Light. It is lit from the new fire as the vigil service begins. In an optional rite, grains of incense are embedded in the candle as symbols of Christ's wounds.

The Easter proclamation ends with the words, "May the Morning Star which never sets find this flame still burning: / Christ that Morning Star, who came back from the dead, / and shed his peaceful light on all mankind." During the blessing of water of the Liturgy of Baptism, the Easter candle is lowered, once or three times, into the water, an allusion to Saint Paul's teaching on Baptism, "Do you not know that all of us who have been baptized into Christ Jesus were baptized into his death? Therefore we have been buried with him by baptism into death, so that, just as Christ was raised from the dead by the glory of the Father, so we too might walk in newness of life" (*Romans 6:3–4*).

### The Baptism candle

At every Baptism the newly baptized—or, if an infant, the parents —are presented with a candle, lit from the Christ candle:

*Receive the light of Christ.*
*This child of yours*
*may he/she walk always*
*as a child of the light…*
*reflecting the word of the Lord,*
*"I am the light of the world.*
*Whoever follows me*
*will never walk in darkness but will*
*have the light of life" (John 8:12)*

### The sanctuary candle

Also referred to as the sanctuary lamp, it signals the presence of the Blessed Sacrament and is reminiscent of the pillar of fire and cloud of the Exodus: "The LORD went in front of them in a pillar of cloud by day, to lead them along the way, and in a pillar of fire by night, to give them light, . . . Neither the pillar of cloud by day nor the pillar of fire by night left its place in front of the people" (*Exodus 13:21–22*). It eventually came to rest before the Ark of the Covenant. It signified God's presence in the dwelling: "For the cloud of the LORD was on the tabernacle by day, and fire was in the cloud by night, before the eyes of all the house of Israel at each stage of their journey" (*Exodus 40:38*). See also *Numbers 9:15–22, Deuteronomy 1:33, Nehemiah 9:19, Psalms 78:14, 105:39,* and *Wisdom 10:17*.

### Altar candles

Candles on or around the altar express "devotion or the degree of festivity" (*General Instruction of the Roman Missal*). Candles ("vigil lights") are common in church, representing the prayerful vigilance of expectant faith. Candles for home use (traditionally blessed on Candlemas Day) borrow symbolism from all the candle uses in church and liturgy and bring it into the domestic Church of the home.

Here are some examples from Scripture concerning the symbolism of light:

- "No one after lighting a lamp puts it in a cellar, but on the lampstand so that those who enter may see the light. . . . Therefore consider whether the light in you is not darkness. If then your whole body is full of light, with no part of it in darkness, it will be as full of light as when a lamp gives you light with its rays" (*Luke 11:33–36*).

- "You are the light of the world" (*Matthew 5:14*).

- "So we have the prophetic message more fully confirmed. You will do well to be attentive to this as to a lamp shining in a dark place, until the day dawns and the morning star rises in your hearts" (*2 Peter 1:19*).

## Incense

The practice of using incense was common throughout the ancient world. Incense has a rich prayer and purification symbolism with an ancient heritage in the Old Testament where its spicy scent was a sign of a pure offering, pleasing to God. Christian use is based on the notion that incense was offered up to honor God and that it was a symbolic way of sending prayers from the earthly realm to the heavenly realm.

5

Word of the Liturgy

Incensing, as in the incensation of the altar, the book of the Gospel, the gifts of bread and wine, the assembly, and the body of the deceased during a funeral shows veneration.

- From earliest Christian days, incense has been associated with Christ, beginning with the magi gift (see *Matthew 2:10–11*).

- Prayer is the most common meaning of incense: "Let my prayer be counted as incense before you, and the lifting up of my hands as an evening sacrifice" (*Psalm 141:2*).

- There are many references to incense in the liturgy of the Book of Revelation: ". . . each [of the elders] holding a harp and golden bowls full of incense, which are the prayers of the saints" (*Revelation 5:8*). "Another angel with a golden censer came and stood at the altar; he was given a great quantity of incense to offer with the prayers of all the saints . . . the smoke of the incense, with the prayers of the saints, rose before God from the hand of the angel" (*Revelation 8:3–4*).

## Palms

Palm branches are a symbol of victory, common in the ancient world for greeting conquerors or soldiers returning from battle. As with so many symbols, palms were appropriated in Scripture and later in liturgy and so have been given a spiritual significance. The battle is against evil and the victor is Christ

and those faithful to him—hence, the association of palms with the martyrs. At Mass they are used on Palm Sunday as a prayerful reminder of Christ's triumphant entry into Jerusalem, which will culminate in his death and Resurrection.

- The use of palms is mentioned in *John 12:12–13*: "The next day the great crowd that had come to the festival heard that Jesus was coming to Jerusalem. So they took branches of palm trees and went out to meet him . . ."

- The author of the Gospel of John (referencing *Zechariah 9:9)* "Jesus found a young donkey and sat on it; as it is written: / 'Do not be afraid, daughter of Zion. / Look, your king is coming, / sitting on a donkey's colt!'" (*John 12:14–15*). (The donkey's colt, unlike the war-horse, was a symbol of peace. The *New Jerome Biblical Commentary* suggests, "Introduction of palm branches may have been symbolic victory. . . . The crowd going out to meet Jesus may have been copying the welcome accorded a visiting king or dignitary. The real truth of Jesus' kingship will not be evident until the crucifixion" (61:160).

- There is mention of palm branches in 1 Maccabees 13:51 and 2 Maccabees 10:7 for welcoming great conquerors.

- In the heavenly liturgy described in the Book of Revelation it says, ". . . there was a great multitude . . . standing before the throne and before the Lamb, robed in white, with palm branches in their hands" (*Revelation 7:9*).

## Water

The use of water is another symbol inherited by the Christian Church from her Jewish ancestors and widely used in the ancient world. Water is a symbol of grace and divine life and is used for baptizing (and recalling it). Also symbolizing exterior and interior purity, water is blessed in solemn ritual during the Easter Vigil and is used in fonts (like miniature baptisteries) at church doorways and in homes to recall Baptism and invite recommitment to living it out. It is sometimes sprinkled on individuals and assemblies and objects as part of a blessing. It is part of the revised penitential rite. (The *"asperges"* is the old Latin name used for the ceremony of holy water sprinkling at Mass, from the first words of the psalm used in the rite, "You will sprinkle me with hyssop . . ." The *asperges* is replaced in the Easter season by the hymn *Vidi Aquam*, "I Beheld Water" from *Ezekiel 47:1–12*.) The following are examples from Scripture of the ritual of sprinkling and references to the symbolism of water.

- "Moses took the blood and dashed it on the people, and said, 'See the blood of the covenant that the LORD has made with you in accordance with all these words'" (*Exodus 24:8*, from the account called "The Blood of the Covenant").

- "[T]hen a clean person shall take hyssop, dip it in the water, and sprinkle it on the tent, on all the furnishings, on the persons who were there . . ." (*Numbers 19:18*).

- "Purge me with hyssop, and I shall be clean;/ wash me, and I shall be whiter than snow" (*Psalm 51:7*, mentioning the hyssop bush whose branch was a natural sprinkler).

- See the "Water Flowing from the Temple" prophecy of *Ezekiel 47:1–12*.

- ". . . a fountain shall come forth from the house of the LORD . . ." (*Joel 3:18*).

- ". . . those who drink of the water that I will give them will never be thirsty. The water that I will give will become in them a spring of water gushing up to eternal life" (*John 4:14*, from the account of the woman at the well).

- "Let anyone who is thirsty come to me, and let the one who believes in me drink. As the scripture has said, 'Out of the believer's heart shall flow rivers of living water'" (*John 7:37–38*).

- ". . . one of the soldiers pierced his side with a spear, and at once blood and water came out" (*John 19:34*).

# Jewish and Christian Calendars

Sirach sings of David the liturgist: "In all that he did he gave thanks to the Holy One, the Most High, proclaiming his glory; / he sang praise with all his heart, and he loved his Maker. / He placed singers before the altar, / to make sweet melody with their voices" (*Sirach 47:8–9*). Like David, the Church daily sings the praises of God and like David, the Church adds beauty to the feasts and solemnizes the seasons each year and provides sweet melody for the psalms. It's a tradition. The Church has inherited an ancient tradition of festival making and calendar keeping with it's roots in the Sacred Scriptures.

## The Jewish Liturgical Calendar

From the time of the Law of Moses, the People of God have observed fixed feasts, starting with Passover. The *Catechism* notes four purposes of keeping feasts (CCC, 1164).

1. To commemorate the Savior God's wondrous actions
2. To give thanks to God for them
3. To insure remembrance of them
4. To teach new generations to lead life according to them

## The Day

In the Jewish tradition, a day is not counted from midnight to midnight but from sunset to sunset. The day ends, naturally, when the sun goes down; thus, a new day's beginning is in the womb of the night—its birth, in the rising sun.

- This is the origin of the Christian tradition of beginning the celebration of solemnities with a "vigil" (the Easter Vigil being the best example). Likewise, every Sunday, the Church's prayer in the Liturgy of the Hours (see Chapter 6) begins with "Evening Prayer I"—"Saturday night," which is the vigil of Sunday liturgically. (Sunday evening's Evening Prayer is called "Evening Prayer II.")

- Christmas Eve and the Easter Vigil are the two most well known examples of the Church's celebrations of feasts beginning on "the night before"—from their conception, the Church would say, not waiting until dawn.

## Sabbaths and Jubilees

The sacred number seven is central in the celebration of Jewish holy days.

1. **Every seven days**—the Sabbath/Shabbat (the seventh day)
2. **After seven weeks**—the jubilee day (the fiftieth day)
3. **In the seventh month**—Rosh Hashanah (feast of Trumpets, the first day of the Jewish new year)
4. **In the seventh year**—the sabbatical year (commemorating the Exodus)
5. **After seven times seven years**—the jubilee year (the fiftieth year), the "Sabbath of the Sabbatical Years" or "the Holy Year," commemorating the Exodus
   - Fields are left fallow for this one year (see *Exodus 23:10–12, Leviticus 25:3–7, Deuteronomy 15:1–11*).

- Land is restored to those from whom it had been dispossessed (see *Leviticus 25:13*).

- Release is given to those obliged into hired service (see *Leviticus 25:1–34, 39–54, 27:16–24*).

(We don't know if these jubilees were kept in fact—there is no Old Testament evidence of that. "Although we cannot exclude the possibility of its being observed in the early years of the land's occupation, its presence here is best explained as a social blueprint, founded on the deeply religious concepts of justice and equality, which strove to apply the simple sabbatical principle to a society that had become more economically complex. . . . [I]ts spirit of appreciation for personal rights and human dignity synthesizes much of [Old Testament] teaching." NJBC 4:53)

## The Seven Set Feasts

The Jews have three tiers of holy days: three Great Festivals (pilgrimage feasts), two Festivals of Awe, and two Lesser Festivals. The Jewish months in which these holy days occur are mentioned in the following list. In the Jewish calendar, the year was based on the lunar cycle and consisted of twelve months of twenty-nine or thirty days each (see *1 Chronicles 27:15, Revelation 22:2*). A "lunar" month is measured by the revolutions of the moon: The month begins with the new moon and ends with the

following new moon. The use of an intercalary month is disputed but may have occurred (see *1 Kings 12:33*). An "intercalary" month is "inserted."

1. **Passover (*Pesach*) or Festival of Unleavened Bread**
   - see Leviticus 23:4–14
   - begun on the eve of the 14th day of *Nisan* (March–April)
   - the festival of redemption and deliverance

2. **Pentecost (*Shovuos*) or Festival of Weeks (or Harvest, or First Fruits)**
   - see Exodus 23:16, Leviticus 23:15–21, Numbers 28:26, Deuteronomy 16:9
   - celebrated on the sixth day of *Sivan* (50th day after Passover; May–June)
   - Spring feast of thanks; ends the weeks of the grain harvest; involves a covenant renewal

3. **Tabernacles (*Sukkot*) or Feast of Ingathering (or Booths)**
   - see Leviticus 23:33–43
   - begun on the eve of the 15th day of *Tishri* (September–October)
   - celebrates the autumn harvest with thankfulness and merrymaking

5 Word of the Liturgy

**4. Trumpets (*Rosh Hashanah*) or Day of Awe**

- see Numbers 29:1, Leviticus 23:23–25

- the first and second days of *Tishri* (September–October)

- Jewish New Year, contrition; begins the most solemn month on the Jewish calendar

**5. Atonement (*Yom Kippur*) or Day of Awe**

- see Leviticus 23:26–32; also Leviticus 10:1–2; 16

- the 10th day of *Tishri* (September–October)

- great feast of the year, fast day, repentance; the day the scapegoat was sent into the wilderness to die for the people's sins; the high priest enters the holy of holies

---

**"A Great Miracle Happened Here"**

There is a popular *Hanukkah* game of chance that uses a dreidel, a four-sided top. Each side of the top bears the initial letters of the words in the saying *Nas gadol hayah shom* ("a great miracle happened here").

Part of the Hanukkah story concerns a small jar of oil found in the destroyed Temple in 165 BC. The oil, which should have been consumed in one day, miraculously burned for eight, allowing time for new sacred oil to be produced. The dreidel game, like the lighting of the Hanukkah candles, memorializes that miracle.

---

**6. Feast of Lights (*Hanukkah*) or Dedication**

- see 1 Maccabees 4:36

- the 25th day of *Chislev* (November–December)

- Hanukkah is the first day of an eight-day celebration of Judas Maccabeus' victory, in 167 BC over the Syrian-Greek king who had an altar to Zeus built in the Jewish temple in Jerusalem. This desecration of the temple triggered a rebellion by Jewish nationalists. After their victory, the temple was cleansed and rededicated. Hanukkah celebrates the rededication, religious liberty, and the survival of Judaism.

**7. Purim or Mordecai Day**

- see the Book of Esther

- the 14th day of *Adar* (February–March)

- celebrating Jewish deliverance; celebrates with pageantry and satire the deliverance of the Jews from death by the bravery of the Persian queen, Esther

## The Christian Liturgical Calendar

The events, truths, and saints celebrated on the liturgical calendar all have their foundations in Scripture.

## The Choice of Scriptures

The solemnities on the calendar all have their own readings assigned, as described below.

## The Hierarchy of Eucharistic Liturgies

The term "feast day" is sometimes used in a generic way, referring to any of the liturgical observances that are actually ranked according to the following three levels of importance.

### 1. Solemnities

Solemnities celebrate events, beliefs, and personages of greatest importance and universal significance in salvation history. (Their observance begins with Evening Prayer I of the preceding day.)

### 2. Feasts

Feasts are of lesser significance.

### 3. Memorials

Memorials are of the least significance. They are either "obligatory" or "optional" (those important only to a local country, church, or religious community).

- These readings are all chosen "thematically." This is a term, described earlier in this chapter, for a Scripture passage chosen because of its relationship to a theme chosen beforehand or suggested by another reading or by a feast.

- This means, in some cases, they interrupt the "organic" reading of Scripture. This is a term, described earlier in this chapter, for a continuous or semi-continuous reading of a text (one picking up the biblical text where the previous week ended). A particular book or letter is treated as a whole (organically), and not "as related to something else."

## The Integrity of the Lectionary

On the liturgical calendar, there are many other observances ("feasts and memorials"). A lot of them honor saints in the history of the Church. While the Church fosters and provides opportunities litur-gically for the legitimate honor of saints, she is careful about priorities:

- Saints' days should not take precedence over feast days or seasons commemorating the mysteries of salvation (whose foundation is scriptural).

- Saints' days should not continually disrupt the ordinary sequence of Scripture at Mass (see the charts on the Lectionary earlier in this chapter) and psalms in the Liturgy of the Hours (see Chapter 6 in this book).

## The Solemnities of the Church Year

Of the 17 solemnities, nine commemorate events or celebrate truths of the Lord, four are for Mary, and four are for other saints (John the Baptizer, Joseph, Peter and Paul, and All Saints). The lectionary includes Scriptures for all these solemnities that feature the person being celebrated and/or describe the event or truth and its significance. (These are listed from first to last on the liturgical calendar, which begins on the First Sunday of Advent, four Sundays before Christmas.)

1. **Immaculate Conception (December 8)**

5

Word of the Liturgy

Celebrating Mary and the incarnation of the Son of God

- *Genesis 3:9–15, 20* ("I will put enmity between you and the woman, and between your offspring and hers")

- *Psalm 98:1, 2–3, 4* ("O sing to the LORD a new song, / for he has done marvelous things.")

- *Ephesians 1:3–6, 11–12* (God chose us in Christ before the foundation of the world.)

- *Luke 1:26–38* ("Greetings, favored one! The Lord is with you.")

2. **Christmas (December 25)**
   Celebrating the incarnation of the Son of God
   See "Christmas Lectionary," earlier in this chapter.

3. **Mary, Mother of God (January 1)**
   Celebrating the divine motherhood of Mary and the divinity of Christ

   - *Numbers 6:22–27* ("So they shall put my name on the Israelites, and I will bless them.)

   - *Psalm 67:2–3, 5, 6, 8* ("May God be gracious to us and bless us . . .")

   - *Galatians 4:4–7* (When his appointed time came, God sent his Son, born of a woman.)

   - *Luke 2:16–21* (The shepherds found Mary and Joseph and the infant lying in the manger. . . . When the eighth day came they gave him the name of Jesus.)

4. **Epiphany (the Sunday after January 1)**
   Celebrating the incarnation and the mission of Christ as Savior of the world

   - *Isaiah 60:1–6* (". . . the glory of the LORD has risen upon you")

   - *Psalm 72:1–2, 7–8, 10–11, 12–13* (Every nation on earth will adore him.)

   - *Ephesians 3:2–3, 5–6* (The revelation means that pagans now share the same inheritance, that they are parts of the same body.)

   - *Matthew 2:1–12* (We have come from the East to worship the king.)

5. **Joseph (March 19)**
   Celebrating the husband of Mary

   - *2 Samuel 7:4–5, 12–14, 16* (The Lord will give to him the throne of his father, David.)

   - *Psalm 89:2–3, 4–5, 27, 29* ("I will establish [David's] line forever . . .")

   - *Romans 4:13, 16–18, 22* (Against all hope he believed in hope.)

   - *Matthew 1:16, 18–21, 24* (Joseph did as the angel of the Lord commanded him.)

   - *Luke 2:41–51* (See how your father and I have been in sorrow seeking you.)

6. **Annunciation (March 25)**
   Celebrating Mary and the incarnation of the Son of God

- *Isaiah 7:10–14* (The virgin will conceive.)

- *Psalm 40:7–8, 9, 10, 11* ("Here I am; . . . I delight to do your will, . . .")

- *Hebrews 10:4–10* (In the scroll of the book it was written of me that I should obey your will, O God.)

- *Luke 1:26–38* (You are to conceive and bear a son.)

7. **Easter (first Sunday in Spring)**
Celebrating the Resurrection of Christ
See "Easter Lectionary," earlier in this chapter.

8. **Ascension (forty days after Easter; seventh Sunday of Easter)**
Celebrating the Ascension of Christ into heaven
See "Easter Lectionary," earlier in this chapter.

9. **Pentecost (fifty days after Easter)**
Celebrating the gift of the Holy Spirit

*Vigil of Pentecost*
- *Genesis 11:1–9* (It was named Babel because there the Lord confused the language of the whole earth.)

- *Exodus 19:3–8, 16–20* (The Lord God appeared before all the people on Mount Sinai.)

- *Ezekiel 37:1–14* (Dry bones of Israel, I shall put my spirit in you, and you will live.)

- *Joel 3:1–5* (I will pour out my spirit on all mankind.)

- *Psalm 104:1–2, 24, 25, 27–28, 29, 30* ("[Lord,] When you send forth your spirit, . . ./ . . . you renew the face of the ground.")

- *Romans 8:22–27* (The Spirit himself pleads for us in a way that could never be put into words.)

- *John 7:37–39* (From his breast shall flow fountains of living waters.)

*Pentecost Sunday*
- *Acts 2:1–11* (They were all filled with the Holy Spirit, and began to speak in different languages.)

- *Psalm 104:1, 24, 29–30, 31, 34* ("[Lord,] When you send forth your spirit, . . ./ . . . you renew the face of the ground.")

- *1 Corinthians 12:3–7, 12–13* (In one Spirit we were all baptized, making one body.)

- *John 20:19–23* (As the Father sent me, so I send you: Receive the Holy Spirit.)

10. **Trinity (the Sunday after Pentecost)**
Celebrating the Blessed Trinity

*Year A*
- *Exodus 34:4–6, 8–9* (The Lord, God, ruler of all, merciful and loving.)

- *Daniel 3:52, 53, 54, 55, 56* ("Blessed are you, O Lord, God of our ancestors, and to be praised and highly exalted forever;")

- *2 Corinthians 13:11–13* ("The grace of the Lord Jesus Christ, the love of God, and the communion of the Holy Spirit be with all of you.")

- *John 3:16–18* (God sent his Son to save the world through him.)

*Year B*
- *Deuteronomy 4:32–34, 39–40* ("... the LORD is God in heaven above and on the earth beneath; there is no other.)

- *Psalm 33:4–5, 6, 9, 12, 18–19, 20, 22* ("Happy is the nation whose God is the LORD, / the people whom he has chosen as his heritage.")

- *Romans 8:14–17* (You have received the Spirit that makes you God's own children, and in that Spirit we call God: Father, our Father!)

- *Matthew 28:16–20* (Baptize them in the name of the Father, and of the Son, and of the Holy Spirit.)

*Year C*
- *Proverbs 8:22–31* (Wisdom was born before the earth was made.)

- *Psalm 8:4–5, 6–7, 8–9* ("O LORD, our Sovereign, / how majestic is your name in all the earth!")

- *Romans 5:1–5* (To God through Christ in the love which is poured out through the Spirit.)

- *John 16:12–15* (Whatever the Father has is mine. The Spirit will receive what I give and tell you about it.)

11. **Body and Blood of Christ (the Sunday after Trinity Sunday)**
Celebrating the Holy Eucharist

*Year A*
- *Deuteronomy 8:2–3, 14–16* (He gave you food which you and your fathers did not know.)

- *Psalm 147:12–13, 14–15, 19–20* ("Praise the LORD, O Jerusalem!")

- *1 Corinthians 10:16–17* (Though we are many, we form a single body because we share this one loaf.)

- *John 6:51–58* (My flesh is real food and my blood is real drink.)

*Year B*
- *Exodus 24:3–8* (This is the blood of the covenant that the Lord has made with you.)

- *Psalm 116:12–13, 15–16, 17–18* ("I will lift up the cup of salvation and call on the name of the LORD,")

- *Hebrews 9:11–15* (The blood of Christ will purify our inner selves.)

- *Mark 14:12–16, 22–26* (This is my body. This is my blood.)

*Year C*
- *Genesis 14:18–20* (Melchizedek brought bread and wine.)

- *Psalm 110:1, 2, 3, 4* ("You are a priest forever according to the order of Melchizedek.")

- *1 Corinthians 11:23–26* (Every time you eat this bread and drink this cup, you are proclaiming the death of the Lord.)

- *Luke 9:11–17* (They all ate and were filled.)

12. **Sacred Heart (the Friday after the second Sunday after Pentecost)**
Celebrating the loving kindness of Christ

*Year A*
- *Deuteronomy 7:6–11* (The Lord loves you and has chosen you.)

- *Psalm 103:1–2, 3–4, 6–7, 8, 10, 11* (". . . so great is his steadfast love toward those who fear him;")

- *1 John 4:7–16* (God loved us first.)

- *Matthew 11:25–30* (I am gentle and humble of heart.)

*Year B*
- *Hosea 11:1, 3–4, 8–9* (Israel, how could I give you up? My heart turns against it.)

- *Isaiah 12:2–3, 4, 5–6* ("With joy you will draw water from the wells of salvation.")

- *Ephesians 3:8–12, 14–19* (To know the love of Christ is better than all knowledge.)

- *John 19:31–37* (One of the soldiers pierced his side with a lance, and immediately there came out blood and water.)

*Year C*
- *Ezekiel 34:11–16* (I will watch over my sheep and tend them.)

- *Psalm 23:1–2, 3–4, 5, 6* ("The LORD is my shepherd, / I shall not want.")

- *Romans 5:5–11* (God has entrusted his love to us.)

- *Luke 15:3–7* (Share my joy; I have found my lost sheep!)

13. **Birth of John the Baptist (June 24)**
Celebrating the forerunner of Christ

*Vigil*
- *Jeremiah 1:4–10* (Before I formed you in the womb, I knew you.)

- *Psalm 71:1–2, 3–4, 5–6, 15, 16* (Since my mother's womb, you have been my strength.)

- *1 Peter 1:8–12* (The prophets searched and inquired for this salvation.)

- *Luke 1:5–17* (A son is born to you and you will name him John.)

*Mass during the day*
- *Isaiah 49:1–6* (Behold I will make you a light to the nations.)

- *Psalm 139:1–3, 13–14, 15* ("I praise you, for I am fearfully and wonderfully made.")

5

Word of the Liturgy

- *Acts 13:22–26* (Christ's coming was announced beforehand by the preaching of John.)

- *Luke 1:57–66, 80* (John is his name.)

## 14. Peter and Paul (June 29)
Celebrating the Apostles and the beginning of the Church

*Vigil*
- *Acts 3:1–10* (What I have, I give to you; in the name of Jesus stand up and walk.)

- *Psalm 19:2–3, 4–5* (". . . their voice goes out through all the earth,")

- *Galatians 1:11–20* (God chose me while I was still in my mother's womb.)

- *John 21:15–19* (Feed my lambs, feed my sheep.)

*Mass during the day*
- *Acts 12:1–11* (Now I know it is indeed true: the Lord has saved me from the power of Herod.)

- *Psalm 34:2–3, 4–5, 6–7, 8–9* ("The angel of the LORD encamps around those who fear him, and delivers them.")

- *2 Timothy 4:6–8, 17–18* (All that remains now is the crown of righteousness.)

- *Matthew 16:13–19* (You are Peter; and I will give you the keys of the Kingdom of heaven.)

## 15. Assumption (August 15)
Celebrating Mary and the destiny of the Church

*Vigil*
- *1 Chronicles 15:3–4, 15, 16; 16:1–2* (They brought in the ark of God and set it inside the tent which David had pitched for it.)

- *Psalm 132:6–7, 8, 9–10, 13–14* ("Rise up, O LORD, and go to your resting place, you and the ark of your might.")

- *1 Corinthians 15:54–57* (He gives us victory through Jesus Christ.)

- *Luke 11:27–28* (Blessed is the womb that bore you.)

*Mass during the day*
- *Revelation 11:19, 12:1–6, 10* (I saw a woman clothed with the sun and with the moon beneath her feet.)

- *Psalm 45:9, 10, 11, 12, 16* (". . . at your right hand stands the queen in gold of Ophir.")

- *1 Corinthians 15:20–26* (As members of Christ all men will be raised, Christ first, and after him all who belong to him.)

- *Luke 1:39–56* (He who is mighty has done great things for me; he has exalted the humble.)

## 16. All Saints (November 1)
Celebrating with the heavenly liturgy described in the Book of Revelation

- *Revelation 7:2–4, 9–14* (I saw an immense crowd, beyond hope of counting, of people from every nation, race, tribe and language.)

- *Psalm 24:1–2, 3–4, 5–6* (Lord, this is the people that longs to see your face.)

- *1 John 3:1–3* (We shall see God as he really is.)

- *Matthew 5:1–12* ("Rejoice and be glad, for your reward is great in heaven,")

17. **Christ the King (the last Sunday in Ordinary Time)** Celebrating Christ and the Kingdom of God

    *Year A*
    - *Ezekiel 34:11–12, 15–17* (You, my flock, I judge between sheep and sheep, between rams and he-goats.)

- *Psalm 23:1–2, 3–4, 5–6* ("The LORD is my shepherd, I shall not want.")

- *1 Corinthians 15:20–26, 28* (He will hand over the kingdom to God the Father, so that God may be all in all.)

- *Matthew 25:31–46* (He will sit upon his seat of glory and he will separate men one from another.)

*Year B*
- *Daniel 7:13–14* (His sovereignty is eternal.)

- *Psalm 93:1–2, 5* ("The LORD is king, he is robed in majesty;")

- *Revelation 1:5–8* (The ruler of the kings of the earth made us a line of kings, priests to serve his God.)

- *John 18:33–37* (You say that I am a king.)

## Holy Days of Obligation

This is a term more familiar to Catholics than "solemnities." The Church has designated 10 of the solemnities as "holy days of obligation." The number varies from country to country because conferences of bishops are free to set their own, with the Vatican's approval. Current practice is to retain at least two: Christmas and one feast honoring Mary. In the United States there are six besides Sundays. (Epiphany, The Body and Blood of Christ, and Ascension are transferred to the nearest Sunday; and the obligation is removed from the feasts of Saint Joseph and Saints Peter and Paul.)

| | |
|---|---|
| 1. Christmas | 6. Immaculate Conception |
| 2. Epiphany | 7. Assumption |
| 3. Ascension | 8. Saint Joseph |
| 4. The Body and Blood of Christ | 9. Saints Peter and Paul |
| 5. Mary, Mother of God | 10. All Saints |

*Year C*

- *2 Samuel 5:1–3* (They anointed David king of Israel.)

- *Psalm 122:1–2, 3–4, 5* ("I was glad when they said to me, 'Let us go to the house of the LORD!'")

- *Colossians 1:12–20* (He has taken us into the kingdom of his beloved Son.)

- *Luke 23:35–43* ("Jesus, remember me when you come into your kingdom.")

## Forties

Forty-day and 40-year periods in Scripture are periods of transition. Life begins at 40.

### In the Scriptural Tradition

1. The Hebrews spent 40 years on their journey from slavery to freedom. God freed them in the Exodus. Despite the many signs and wonders they had witnessed, however, they persisted in thinking like slaves and proved unable to live in freedom (see *Numbers 14*). And so God allowed that generation of former slaves to die off in their 40-year desert wandering. It was their children, a freeborn generation, who inherited the Promised Land.

2. Moses prayed on Mt. Sinai for 40 days and 40 nights before receiving the covenant and the Decalogue from God (see *Exodus 24:18*). This 40-day period symbolized a transition to a new way God chose to be present on the journey. (During this time Moses received "instructions on building and maintaining the dwelling, the means of God's presence for the journey to the promised land," a "mode of divine presence" the people rejected [NJBC 3:67].)

3. Elijah, after being revived by food brought by an angel, walked for 40 days and 40 nights to that same place (also known as Mt. Horeb) where he met the Living God (see *1 Kings 19:8*).

4. King David ruled Israel for 40 years before his son Solomon began his reign (see *2 Kings 2:11*).

5. Jesus retreated to the desert for 40 days between his so-called hidden life and his public ministry (see *Matthew 4:1–11* and parallels).

6. The risen Christ remained with his Apostles for 40 days before his Ascension after which he would no longer be seen in the body or in post-Resurrection appearances (see *Acts 1:3*).

### On the Catholic Liturgical Calendar

It is 40 days from Ash Wednesday to Easter (not including Sundays and the Triduum). This is the Church's annual season of Lent, the 40-day retreat for catechumens in final preparation for initiation at Easter. This annual transition in the spiritual life for those coming to faith is scheduled to culminate at Easter.

- For many years, before the renewal of the liturgical calendar, 40 was the literal number of Lenten days. Holy Saturday (noon) was considered the official end of Lent. Six full weeks multiplied by seven days each week equals 42 plus Ash Wednesday through Saturday before the first Sunday equals 46 minus the six Sundays equals 40 days.

- Today, with the restoration of The Great Three Days, Lent ends on Holy Thursday at nightfall—three days shy of 40.

5

Word of the Liturgy

## CHAPTER 6

# Prayer Book of the Church

## Integration of
## **Daily Prayer**

All dioceses and parishes . . . should pursue the following fundamental objectives: . . . To call their people to a more effective integration of daily prayer in their lives, especially the ancient practice of praying the Psalms and the Church's Liturgy of the Hours, contemplation of the mysteries of the life of Christ through the Rosary, and a greater reverence of the Eucharist through adoration of the Blessed Sacrament.

—*National Directory for Catechesis*, p. 52

# Public Prayer of the Church

This chapter is about a unique treasure of the Catholic Church: the Liturgy of the Hours. Unlike personal prayer and devotional prayer, the Liturgy of the Hours is part of the public prayer of the Church; it is steeped in Scripture. Although the ordained as well as certain religious communities have been obliged, historically, to celebrate this liturgy, the mandate to pray the Liturgy of the Hours belongs to the whole Church. This is the reason for giving the Liturgy of the Hours a chapter of its own in this *Scripture Source Book for Catholics,* calling it the "Prayer Book of the Church." The purpose is to enable Catholics to be more consciously and confidently scriptural in their life and prayer.

Below is a ranking of how you might try to incorporate the Liturgy of the Hours in your prayer life:

1. Fair: Know about this liturgy, what it is, and that it is prayed daily.
2. Good: Model your own daily prayer on the Liturgy of the Hours.
3. Better: Pray an abbreviated form of the Liturgy of the Hours.
4. Best: Pray the Liturgy of the Hours.

# The Liturgy of the Hours

The Liturgy of the Hours is an established form and order of prayer consisting of psalms, hymns, prayers, and scriptural and spiritual readings composed by the Church for chant or recitation at stated times every day. The Liturgy of the Hours is unique in the liturgical life of the Church because "it consecrates to God the whole cycle of day and night, as it has done from early Christian times" (*General Instruction of the Liturgy of the Hours,* 10). It is designed for celebration in common but is also regularly prayed by individuals.

- The Liturgy of the Hours is also known as the Divine Office, which means sacred duty. In the Benedictine tradition it's also been known as the *Opus Dei* (Latin for "Work of God"). The book used for its celebration was called the breviary.

- The Apostolic Constitution *Laudis Canticum* (Canticle of Praise) of Pope Paul VI approved the Liturgy of the Hours revised by decree of the Second Vatican Ecumenical Council (1970) for use by the Roman Catholic Church. *The General Instruction of the Liturgy of the Hours* is often quoted throughout this chapter. (In this Constitution, Pope Paul VI said that Vatican II "treated the liturgy as a whole, and the Hours in particular, with such thoroughness and skill, such spirituality and power, that there is scarcely a parallel to it in the entire history of the Church" (VI).

## The General Structure

### Elements of the Liturgy of the Hours

| Morning Prayer | Daytime Prayer | Evening Prayer | Night Prayer |
|---|---|---|---|
| Introduction (Invitatory) | Introduction | Introduction | Introduction |
| Verse | Verse | Verse | Verse |
| Antiphon | Doxology | Doxology | Doxology |
| Psalm 95 | Alleluia | Alleluia | Alleluia |
| | | | Examination of Conscience |
| | | | −Penitential Prayer |
| Hymn | Hymn | Hymn | Hymn |
| Psalmody | Psalmody | Psalmody | Psalmody |
| Psalm | Psalm | Psalm | Psalm |
| Old Testament | Psalm | Psalm | |
| Canticle | Psalm | Psalm | |
| Psalm | | New Testament | |
| | | Canticle | |
| Reading | Reading | Reading | Reading |
| −pause for reflection | −pause for reflection | −pause for reflection | −pause for reflection |
| Responsory | Responsory | Responsory | Responsory |
| Gospel Canticle | | Gospel Canticle | Gospel Canticle |
| −of Zechariah | | −of Mary | −of Simeon |
| Intercessions | | Intercessions | |
| Lord's Prayer | | Lord's Prayer | |
| Final Prayer | Final Prayer | Final Prayer | Final Prayer |
| −Trinitarian ending | −simple ending | −Trinitarian ending | −simple ending |
| Conclusion | Conclusion | Conclusion | Conclusion |
| | | | Marian Antiphon |

6

Prayer Book of the Church

# The Times

In the early Church, there is evidence of individual Christians devoting themselves to prayer at fixed times. The tradition grew in various places of assigning special times to common prayer, especially at the beginning of the day when night draws to a close "with the rising of the daystar" and at the end of the day when "the lamp is lighted." Over time, other hours came to be sanctified by common prayer. These are foreshadowed in the Acts of the Apostles.

- The disciples gathered together at 9:00 AM (see *Acts 2:1–15*).

- Peter prayed at about noon (see *Acts 10:9*).

- Peter and John went to the temple "at the hour of prayer, at three o'clock in the afternoon" (*Acts 3:1*).

- Paul and Silas were praying and singing hymns at about midnight (see *Acts 16:25*).

## The Nature of an Hour
### Chronological hour

Sixty minutes is a chronological hour. It's a measurement of time. The chronological hour tells us if we're early or late or right on time. *Chronos* is a Greek word for time that gives us words like "chronology." It also gives us calendars and late fees.

### Figurative hour

A figurative hour is the opportune moment, the right time, a unique and defining event. Jesus spoke of the culmination of his ministry as his "hour":

- From the beginning (in *John 2:4*, to his mother at Cana, "My hour has not yet come")

- Through the course of his public life (see *John 7:30, 8:20*, for example)

- To the end (*John 17:1*, "Father, the hour has come")

It was his finest hour, to use Churchill's version when he called forth England's courage in the dark days of World War II. The Greek word for this kind of time is *kairos*. It tells us not what time it is but if our action is timely or not, if it's opportune.

### Canonical hour

The hours of the Liturgy of the Hours are canonical hours. Morning Prayer, for example, is one the hours. It's not 60 minutes long necessarily and not scheduled for the 6:00 o'clock hour, or the 7:00 or 8:00 o'clock—but close. The "hours" of the Liturgy of the Hours do not refer to hours of the clock but times of the day. (The canonical hour of Morning Prayer is not to be prayed in the afternoon). One of the reasons Vatican II called for a revision of the Liturgy of the Hours was so that "the canonical hours could be more easily related to the chronological hours of the day in the circumstances of contemporary life" (Apostolic Constitution of Pope Paul VI promulgating the revision of the Liturgy of the Hours, 2), since the Hours is the means of sanctifying the day.

## The Names of the Hours
### Pre-Vatican II terminology

Traditionally, there were seven canonical hours chanted in monastic communities. This tradition recalls the psalmist's declaration, "Seven times a day I praise you" (*Psalm 119:164*). With much variation, the pattern was seven daytime offices and the night office of *Matins* (French for morning), which was prayed in the early hours of the morning, after midnight.

1. Lauds (Latin: praise, from Psalms 148–150)
2. Prime (first: 6 AM)
3. Terce (third: 9 AM)
4. Sext (sixth: noon)
5. None (ninth: 3 PM)
6. Vespers (evening, hence the medieval English term "evensong")
7. Compline (from *completorium*, "completing" the day's services)

### Post-Vatican II terminology

Morning Prayer and Evening Prayer have been restored as the most important "hinges" of each day's prayer. The Office of Readings is not a time of the day in the sense the other hours are but a prayer with two more extended readings: one biblical and one patristic (from the fathers) or hagiographical (of the saints). Daytime Prayer consolidates the little hours of Prime, Terce, Sext, and None for those not saying the Office in choir (depending upon the time one has, the choice of midmorning, midday, or mid-afternoon).

1st Hour: Office of Readings (corresponding to ancient Matins)

2nd Hour: Morning Prayer (Lauds)

3rd Hour: Daytime Prayer (Middle Hour)

4th Hour: Evening Prayer (Vespers)

5th Hour: Night Prayer (Compline)

## The Character of Particular Hours

One of the purposes of the revision of the Hours after Vatican II was to relate the canonical hours to the actual time of the day when they are used. Now Morning Prayer and Evening Prayer really are morning and evening prayers with elements that express their character—specifically in one of the psalms, the intercessions, and the concluding prayer. (In the pages ahead there are examples for each of those three elements.)

### The significance of Morning Prayer

1. A sanctification of the day
   - Morning Prayer is intended and arranged for the sanctification of the day.

   - Saint Basil the Great gives an excellent description of its character: "It is said in the morning in order that the first stirrings of our mind and will may be consecrated to God, and that we may take nothing in hand until we have been gladdened by the thought of God, as it is written: 'I was mindful of God and was glad' (Psalm 77:4), or set our bodies to any task before we do what has been said: 'I will pray to you, Lord, you will hear my voice in the morning; I will stand before you in the morning and gaze on you' (Psalm 5:4–5)" (*General Instruction of the Liturgy of the Hours*, 38).

2. A commemoration of the Resurrection of the Lord
   • As the light of a new day dawns, Morning Prayer recalls the Resurrection of Jesus, the true light enlightening everyone (see *John 1:9*) and the sun of justice (see *Malachi 4:2*), "the dawn from on high" (*Luke 1:78*).

   • The *Instruction* cites Saint Cyprian: "There should be prayer in the morning, so that the resurrection of the Lord may be celebrated by morning prayer" (*General Instruction of The Liturgy of the Hours*, 35).

**The purpose of Evening Prayer** (*General Instruction of the Liturgy of the Hours*, 39)
   1. Giving thanks "for what has been given us, or what we have done well during the day" (Saint Basil the Great)
   2. Recalling redemption in this evening prayer, which we send up "like incense in the Lord's sight" and in which "the raising up of

our hands" becomes "an evening sacrifice" (see *Psalm 141:2*)
   3. Uniting the offering of our prayer with "that true evening sacrifice which . . . was offered in the evening by the Lord and Savior, at supper with the apostles, when he instituted the most holy mysteries of the Church" (Cassian)
   4. Requesting the grace of eternal life, fixing "our hope on the light that knows no setting" (Saint Cyprian)
   5. Praising in joy "now that we have come to the setting of the sun and seen the evening star" (from a prayer of the Churches of the East)

**The place of Night Prayer**
Vatican II's *Constitution on the Sacred Liturgy* (translation by Abbot) directed that "Compline" (now known as Night Prayer) "is to be drawn up so that it will be a suitable prayer for the end of the day" (89b). Its psalmody (arranged on a one-week schedule instead of four like the other Hours), antiphons, reading, responsory, Gospel canticle, concluding prayer, and final blessing all make this Hour "suitable" for the end of the day.

**The place of prayer during the night**
Through the course of the Church's life, the Fathers and spiritual writers have often urged the faithful, especially those living the contemplative life, to pray at night. Such prayer expresses and increases the Church's hope for the Lord's return, as the following Scriptures teach.

- "But at midnight there was a shout, 'Look! Here is the bridegroom! Come out to meet him.'"(*Matthew 25:6*).

- "Therefore, keep awake—for you do not know when the master of the house will come, in the evening, or at midnight, or at cockcrow, or at dawn, or else he may find you asleep when he comes suddenly." (*Mark 13:35–36*).

Matins, as noted earlier in this chapter, was a "night hour," historically. It was chanted in the early hours after midnight by cloistered monks and nuns who, in some cases, continue the tradition today. In the revised Liturgy of the Hours, it has been replaced by the Office of Readings, which is not an "hour" in the sense of a time of the day as the other Hours are, but a prayer with two more extended readings.

Vatican II's *Constitution on the Sacred Liturgy* directed that "Matins, although it should retain the character of nocturnal praise when celebrated in choir, should be adapted so that it may be recited at any hour of the day . . ." (89c). ("Choir" here refers to the monastic chanting of the Hours in common.) The *General Instruction of the Liturgy of the Hours* recognizes the goodness of the tradition of prayer during the night and includes directives to "those obliged by their own particular law, and others laudably desiring to retain the character of this Office as a night office of praise, either by saying [the Office of Readings] at night or very early

in the morning and before Morning Prayer . . ." (58).

## The Special Character of Particular Days

The Liturgy of the Hours has many ways of helping a person experience what it calls "the special character of particular days." The Liturgy of the Hours can help make every week a holy week: Every Sunday is a little Easter Sunday, giving each week its own commemoration of the Resurrection; every Friday is a little Good Friday, giving each week its own memorial of the passion. Besides Sunday and Friday, all days of the week take on a special character during the liturgical seasons of Advent, Christmas, Lent, and Easter, as do feast days (solemnities, feasts, and memorials) throughout the year.

### The special character of Sunday

The day of the Resurrection, the third day of Holy Week's sacred Triduum, begins Saturday at nightfall and ends Sunday at nightfall. In the Liturgy of the Hours of these days, the signs of the empty tomb and the Resurrection of Christ are unmistakable each week.

Evening Prayer I? Why "I"? Isn't Evening Prayer simply Evening Prayer? Not when it comes to Sunday, the primary feast day. Not when it comes to any of the Church's solemnities (feast days of the greatest significance).

- The Church has an ancient history, rooted in its Jewish ancestry,

**6**

**Prayer Book of the Church**

of starting the celebrating of her great feasts with a vigil—"the night before," some would say today.

- In fact, the nighttime after midnight and the nighttime before midnight are both one night and belongs to the day it births. In our oldest tradition, inherited from our Jewish brothers and sisters, the day ends not midway through the night but at nightfall. And at nightfall a new day begins, like a child in the darkness of the mother's womb. Daybreak is the birth of the day.

- Christmas Eve and the Easter Vigil are the two most well-known examples of the Church starting to celebrate feasts on "the night before"—from their conception, the Church would say, not waiting until dawn.

- Every Sunday the Church does the same, starting its celebrating on Saturday evening: "Saturday evening Mass" is actually a Sunday Mass. "Evening Prayer I" is what it's called in the Liturgy of the Hours; "Evening Prayer II" is the prayer of the feast's evening (not "eve").

### The special character of Friday

The day of the passion, the first day of the sacred Triduum, is from Thursday nightfall to Friday nightfall. There are clear signs of the Last Supper and the Agony in the Garden in Thursday's Evening Prayer. Friday's Morning Prayer and Daytime Prayer too are marked with signs of the passion.

# The Psalms

"The Psalter is the book in which The Word of God becomes man's prayer. In other books of the Old Testament, 'the words proclaim [God's] works and bring to light the mystery they contain.' The words of the Psalmist, sung for God, both express and acclaim the Lord's saving works; the same Spirit inspires both God's work and man's response. Christ will unite the two. In him, the psalms continue to teach us how to pray" (*CCC*, 2587, citing Vatican II's *Constitution on Divine Revelation*, 2).

The psalms, in a sense, are timeless and universal. Although they "originated very many centuries ago in the East they express accurately the pain and hope, the unhappiness and trust, of people of every age and country, and celebrate especially faith in God, revelation, and redemption" (*General Instruction of the Liturgy of the Hours*, 107).

Although the psalms are not without their difficulties, they also bring rewards: They have the power "to raise minds to God, to inspire devotion, to evoke gratitude in favorable times and to bring consolation and fortitude in times of trial" (*General Instruction of the Liturgy of the Hours*, 100).

## The Prayer Book of Jesus

The psalms were prayers that had been written, memorized, and recited by the Jewish people over the course of many years, in response to the covenant God had made with them. They were used by prophets and kings, as well as by poor and pious people to fit numerous life situations. Sometimes they were sung to the accompaniment of musical instruments and elaborate dancing within the temple. These same psalms, given by God to his people and inspired by his Holy Spirit, were prayed by his Son, Jesus who was, as Saint Augustine put it, "this marvelous singer of the psalms."

When Jesus approached the temple in Jerusalem, at the age of twelve, to celebrate the great Jewish festivals, like other Jews he would have sung the Songs of Ascents (Psalms 120–134). And each year at Passover, he would have joined in the Great Hallel (Psalm 136), which tells of God's wondrous deeds in rescuing his people from Egypt.

At the Last Supper, in reference to the betrayal he knew was coming, Jesus said, "Even my . . . friend . . . who ate of my bread, has lifted the heel against me" (Psalm 41:9), another example of his use of the psalms in his teachings and prayers. After supper, the gospels say that Jesus and his companions sang a hymn; this was most likely the Egyptian Hallel (Psalms 113–118), the traditional conclusion to the Passover meal.

When leaving the upper room, Jesus and his disciples were probably singing psalms about God's greatness and his total faithfulness. But this time of joyfulness is soon followed by much anguish, and in the agony of dying, Jesus turns to the psalms yet again: "My God, my God, why have you forsaken me?" (Psalm 22). Although like other psalms of lament, it began with a cry of distress, it ended on a note of complete trust and triumph. According to Luke, Jesus' final words from the cross, again came from a psalm (31:5): "Father, into your hands I commend my spirit."

## The Prayer of the Assembly

In the fourth of the four parts of the *Catechism*, "Christian Prayer," there's a section on prayer in the Old Testament. It includes four paragraphs (2585–2589) called "The Psalms, the prayer of the assembly." It explains that the prayer of the psalms "is inseparably personal and communal" (2586). Reading and praying the psalms on schedule, as the Church does in the Liturgy of the Hours, requires a person to pray in the name of the Church.

Many people are more accustomed to praying in a purely personal way, including finding their own words—and, possibly, Scripture, according to their own purposes, needs, and mood. The Liturgy of the Hours, like all liturgy, is the prayer of the Church and not the same as personal prayer. The established, scheduled cycle of psalms in the Liturgy of the Hours is used, regardless of the mood of the psalm or the person praying. What would be a dissonance in private prayer is not in liturgical prayer, in which one prays in the name of the Church:

- "The person who prays the psalms in the Liturgy of the Hours prays not so much in his own person as in the name of the Church, and, in fact, in the person of Christ himself" (*General Instruction of the Liturgy of the Hours*, 108).

- "If one bears this in mind difficulties disappear when one notices in prayer that the feelings of the heart in prayer are different from the emotions expressed in the psalm, for example, when a psalm of joy confronts a person who is sad and overcome with grief, or a psalm of sorrow confronts a person full of joy . . ." (*General Instruction of the Liturgy of the Hours*, 108).

- "The person who prays the psalms in the name of the Church can always find a reason for joy or sadness, for the saying of the Apostle applies in this case also:

'Rejoice with the joyful and weep with those who weep' (Romans 12:15)" (*General Instruction of the Liturgy of the Hours*, 108).

## The "Spiritual" Sense of the Psalms

Catholic scholarship makes a distinction between what it calls the "senses" of the biblical text. The following definitions are the wording of the Pontifical Biblical Commission's document *The Interpretation of the Bible in the Church* (see Chapter 4 for more):

- The "literal sense" is "the precise meaning of texts as produced by their authors" (II.B.1).

- The "spiritual sense" is "the meaning expressed by the biblical texts when read, under the influence of the Holy Spirit, in the context of the paschal mystery of Christ, and of the new life that flows from it" (II.B.1).

"The New Testament recognizes the fulfillment of the Scriptures," the document goes on to say. "It is therefore quite acceptable to reread the Scriptures in the light of this new context, which is that of life in the Spirit. . . . [T]he death and resurrection of Jesus has established a radically new historical context, which sheds fresh light upon the ancient texts and causes them to undergo a change in meaning" (II.B.2).

Christians do typically "reread" the psalms in light of Christ and his death and Resurrection. This does not require—or even allow—that the sense of a text expressed directly by the original author be ignored.

The document explains, "One should be especially attentive to the dynamic aspect of many texts. The meaning of the royal psalms, for example, should not be limited strictly to the historical circumstances of their production. In speaking of the king, the psalmist evokes at one and the same time both the institution as it actually was and an idealized vision of kingship as God intended it to be; in this way, the text carries the reader beyond the institution of kingship in its actual historical manifestation" (II.B.1).

There are many authors today who base their commentaries on the psalms on this theological foundation while writing in a more pastoral vein. In *Praying the Psalms in the Liturgy of the Hours,* Richard Atherton explains that the advent of Christ has given the psalms "a freshness of meaning"—it has "transposed [them] into a new

## The Voice of Christ in the Psalms
(from the *General Instruction of the Liturgy of the Hours,* 109)

"The Fathers of the Church saw the whole psalter as a prophecy of Christ and the Church and explained it in this sense; for the same reason the psalms have been chosen for use in the sacred liturgy. Though somewhat tortuous interpretations were at times proposed, yet, in general, the Fathers, and the liturgy itself, could legitimately hear in the singing of the psalms the voice of Christ crying out to the Father, or of the Father conversing with the Son; indeed, they also recognized in the psalms the voice of the Church, the apostles and the martyrs."

"This method of interpretation also flourished in the middle ages; in many manuscripts of the period the Christological meaning of each psalm is set out at its head. A Christological meaning is by no means confined to the recognized messianic psalms but is given also to many others. Some of these interpretations are doubtless Christological only in an accommodated sense, but they have the traditional approval of the Church. On feast days especially, the choice of psalms is often based on their Christological meaning, and antiphons taken from these psalms are frequently used to throw light on this meaning."

The *Catechism of the Catholic Church* tempers and balances this Christological use of the Old Testament. (See especially *CCC*, 121-123, 128-130. See also Chapter 3 in this book.) Christians read the Old Testament "in the light of Christ crucified and risen. Such typological reading discloses the inexhaustible content of the Old Testament; but it must not make us forget that the Old Testament retains its own intrinsic value as Revelation reaffirmed by our Lord himself"[1] (*CCC*, 129). The *Catechism* then cites *Mark 12:29-31* in which Christ, asked for the greatest commandment, cites *Deuteronomy 6:4-5* and *Leviticus 19:18*: "The first is this: 'Hear, O Israel! The Lord our God is Lord alone! You shall love the Lord your God with all your heart, with all your soul, with all your mind, and with all your strength.' The second is this: 'You shall love your neighbor as yourself.' There is no other commandment greater than these."

key" that fits just as much with New Testament and current issues as Old Testament occurrences. He compares the triumph of the Exodus sung about in the psalms to the triumph of the Paschal Mystery. Instead of marching toward the promised land as mentioned in some psalms, God's new pilgrim people are marching toward heaven.

Atherton also uses the Songs of Zion as an example for a new way to perceive the psalms; where they once celebrated the city of Jerusalem, they now celebrate the Church on earth, as well as the new Jerusalem of heaven. Just as Jesus opened the minds of his friends on the road to Emmaus, he has opened our minds to the fuller meaning of the psalms as they still apply to us today.

## Song
### The place of singing in liturgy
The Liturgy of the Hours is not merely a personal devotional exercise; it is the prayer of the Church, a liturgical celebration. The *General Instruction of the Liturgy of the Hours* treats the place of song in paragraphs 267–284. In a commentary on the *Instruction* (*The Liturgy of the Hours, The General Instruction with Commentary*), A.M. Roguet, O.P., explains how liturgy engages the whole person—body, breath,

movement. The place of singing is central:

- "It is in the nature of the liturgy that it should be worship by a community, and this explains the importance attributed to singing: It is not a superfluous trimming but an almost essential need" (p. 121).

- "This is still more true of the Liturgy of the Hours, in which the overriding theme . . . is praise and thanksgiving. Its most important parts are therefore the psalms, canticles and hymns, namely the emotive and lyrical elements. These find their natural expression in song" (p. 121).

### The musical character of the psalms
The psalms are not "readings" (although they can sometimes be recited or "proclaimed" as such) or prose prayers but "songs of praise" (*tehillim* in Hebrew), "songs to be sung to the lyre" (*psalmoi* in Greek). The following points are from the *General Instruction of the Liturgy of the Hours*, 103 (see also 278).

- "All the psalms have a musical quality which determines the correct way of delivering them."

- "When a psalm is recited and not sung, its delivery must still be governed by its musical character."

- "A psalm presents a text to the minds of the faithful, but it aims rather at moving the hearts of those singing it or listening to it, and also of those accompanying it 'on the lyre and harp.'"

# The Poetry of the Psalms

The psalms are poetry, not prose. There are various literary techniques and devices, like rhyme and meter, that set poetry apart. (Meter is a form of rhythm in poetry that is determined by the number and length of "feet" in a particular line.) The Hebrew poetry of the psalms is characterized by "thought rhythm" not sound rhythm. Its rhythm doesn't come from an obvious meter, as in many other kinds of poetry. The smallest units of psalms are often composed of two-line couplets that are related through some kind of parallelism. Richard Atherton explains in *Praying the Psalms in the Liturgy of the Hours* that the parallelism gives "a lilt and rhythm to the words" that can be compared to the basic step of a ballroom dance (There are certainly other poetic devices used in the psalms, but parallelism is most pervasive.) These are the three most common forms of parallelism in the psalms:

### Synonymous parallelism (repetition)

The thought of one line is repeated with a slight variation in the next— as in *Psalm 103:16*: ". . . for the wind passes over it, and it is gone, / and its place knows it no more."

### Antithetical parallelism (contrast)

The thought in one line is repeated by means of a contrasting thought in the next—as in *Psalm 1:6*, for example: "for the LORD watches over the way of the righteous, / but the way of the wicked will perish."

### Synthetic parallelism (completion)

The thought of one line is completed or developed in the next line—as in *Psalm 27:1*, for example: "The LORD is my light and my salvation; / whom shall I fear? / The LORD is the stronghold of my life; / of whom shall I be afraid?"

## The Address of the Psalms

Psalms are not necessarily prayers addressed to God, as we are accustomed to finding in other prayers of the Church, but sometimes are songs sung in God's presence.

1. The psalms address God directly, as is common in traditional Judeo-Christian prayers.
2. The psalms address God's people, recalling the history of Israel.
3. The psalms address others.
4. The psalms address inanimate creation.
5. The psalmist "even introduces dialogue between God and men, even (as in psalm 2) between God and his enemies" (*General Instruction of the Liturgy of the Hours*, 105).

## The Difficulty of the Psalms

The Christian faithful recognize the "supreme value" of psalms but still can find them difficult. The person coming to the Old Testament needs to "take steps to improve their understanding of the liturgy and of the bible, especially of the psalms" in order to understand how to pray them effectively (Vatican II, *Constitution on the Sacred Liturgy*, 90).

6
**Prayer Book of the Church**

# In the Life of the Church

## The Place of the Liturgy of the Hours in the Liturgy of the Church

The Liturgy of the Hours is a "necessary complement to the fullness of divine worship" of the Mass (Apostolic Constitution of Pope Paul VI promulgating the revision of the Liturgy of the Hours). No part of the Church's prayer stands alone but always in wonderful unity with the whole prayer of the universal Church.

### Relationship to the liturgical year

- The four-week cycle of the Psalter is structured to harmonize with the liturgical year. In the first week of Advent, the first Sunday of Ordinary Time, the first Sunday of Lent and on Easter Sunday, the first week of the four-week Psalter of the Liturgy of the Hours also begins.

- The Office of Readings (explained below) is faithful to the ancient tradition of reading particular books during the liturgical seasons.

### Relationship to the Mass

- The two-year cycle of readings for the Liturgy of the Hours is so arranged that each year nearly all books of Scripture may be read, in addition to longer and more difficult texts only rarely suitable for use at Mass.

- In both the Lectionary of Mass and the revised Liturgy of the Hours, there is a fuller range of Scripture provided which "will enable the history of salvation to be constantly recalled and its continuation in the life of mankind effectively proclaimed" (Apostolic Constitution of Pope Paul VI promulgating the revision of the Liturgy of the Hours, 8).

- The New Testament as a whole is read each year, partly at Mass, partly in the Liturgy of the Hours.

- A selection has been made of those parts of the Old Testament that are of greater importance for the understanding of the history of salvation and for deepening devotion (*General Instruction of the Liturgy of the Hours*, 146).

- There are no readings from the Gospels in the Liturgy of the Hours, since they are read as a whole each year at Mass (*General Instruction of the Liturgy of the Hours*, 144).

- Deferring to the Lectionary for Mass, the Liturgy of the Hours allows for exceptions to the assigned reading, especially in a communal setting, so a longer Scripture can be read, either from the Office of Readings or from the Lectionary.

- In many cases, the Prayer of the Day that concludes each Hour as well as the Office of Readings is the same as the Prayer after Communion of the day's Mass:
  —in every day's Office of Readings
  —in Sunday's Morning Prayer,

Evening Prayer, and Daytime Prayer

—in Morning Prayer, Evening Prayer, and Daytime Prayer on all days in Advent, Christmas, Lent, and Easter

—in Morning Prayer, Evening Prayer, and Daytime Prayer on feast days (solemnities, feasts, and memorials)

## The Place of the Liturgy of the Hours in the Life of the Church

- The Liturgy of the Hours is not "the exclusive possession of clerics and monks either in its origin or by its nature, but belongs to the whole Christian community . . ." (*General Instruction of the Liturgy of the Hours*, 270). The *Catechism* teaches (1175) that it's intended to become the prayer of the whole people of God and encourages the common celebration of the principal hours, like Evening Prayer, in common on Sundays and the more solemn feasts. This prayer ministry is to include all the baptized, either with priests, among themselves, or even individually.

- "The Church commissions [sacred ministers] to celebrate the Liturgy of the Hours in order that, at least in their persons, the duty of the whole community may be carried out regularly and reliably, and the prayer of Christ continue unceasingly in the Church" (*General Instruction of the Liturgy of the Hours*, 28, citing Vatican II's *Decree on the Ministry and Life of Priests*, 13).

- "We have, therefore, every confidence that an appreciation of that 'unceasing' prayer (see Luke 18:1; Luke 21:36; 1 Thessalonians 5:17; Ephesians 6:18) which our Lord Jesus Christ entrusted to his Church will take on new life, since the Liturgy of the Hours, distributed as it is over suitable intervals of time, continually strengthens and supports that prayer" (Apostolic Constitution of Pope Paul VI promulgating the revision of the Liturgy of the Hours, 8).

- "The Liturgy of the Hours is [to be] seen, not as an artistic relic of the past, arousing our admiration only if it is preserved without change, but on the contrary as capable of living and growing in a new environment, and of becoming once again an unmistakable testimony to a community full of vigorous life" (*General Instruction of the Liturgy of the Hours*, 273).

## The Place of Scripture in the Liturgy of the Hours

The whole of the Hours is scriptural, either using, paraphrasing, or alluding to its very words.

- Those taking part in the Liturgy of the Hours have access to holiness of the richest kind through the life-giving word of God, to which it gives such great importance.

- "The readings are drawn from Sacred Scripture, God's words in the psalms are sung in his presence, and the intercessions,

**255**

prayers, and hymns are steeped in the inspired language of Scripture" (*General Instruction of the Liturgy of the Hours*, 14).

- Just as in the Liturgy of the Word at Mass, so in the Liturgy of the Hours, the desire of the Church is realized, namely, "that, within a fixed cycle of years, the more important parts of the Sacred Scriptures may be read to the people" (Vatican II, *Constitution on the Sacred Liturgy*, 51).

## The Integration of Scripture and Prayer in the Liturgy of the Hours

The Liturgy of the Hours is a school for learning to integrate Scripture reading and praying as well as a tool for those already schooled in its ways. For example, between the psalmody and the readings in the Office of Readings there is regularly a verse, "forming a transition of prayer from psalmody to listening" (*General Instruction of the Liturgy of the Hours*, 63). ("Psalmody" refers to the psalms used for singing or reciting in a time of prayer.)

- Prayer should accompany "the reading of Sacred Scripture so that there may be a conversation between God and man: 'we talk with God when we pray, we listen to him when we read God's words'" (*General Instruction of the Liturgy of the Hours*, 56, quoting the *Constitution on Divine Revelation*, 25, quoting Saint Ambrose).

- "We must recognize, therefore, as we celebrate the Office, our own voices echoing in Christ, his voice echoing in ours (Saint Augustine). To manifest this quality of our prayer more clearly, 'the warm and living love for holy Scripture' (*Constitution on the Sacred Liturgy*, 24) which is the atmosphere of the Liturgy of the Hours must come to life in all of us, so that Scripture may indeed become the chief source of all Christian prayer" (Apostolic Constitution of Pope Paul VI promulgating the revision of the Liturgy of the Hours, 8).

- "In particular, the praying of the psalms, which continually ponders and proclaims the action of God in the history of salvation, must be embraced with new warmth by the people of God. This will be achieved more easily if a deeper understanding of the psalms, in the meaning in which they are used in the liturgy, is more diligently promoted among the clergy and communicated to all the faithful by means of appropriate catechesis" (Apostolic Constitution of Pope Paul VI promulgating the revision of the Liturgy of the Hours, 8).

## Silence in the Liturgy of the Hours

"Sacred silence" is a term from Vatican II's *Constitution on the Sacred Liturgy* (30) that is repeated in the *Instruction*.

**The purpose** (*General Instruction of the Liturgy of the Hours*, 202)

- To "receive in our hearts the full resonance of the voice of the Holy Spirit"

- To "unite our personal prayer more closely with the word of God and the public voice of the Church"

- To meditate "on some text that moves the spirit" (*General Instruction of the Liturgy of the Hours*, 203)

### The opportunities

- After the psalm and before the psalm-prayer

- After the antiphon at the end of the psalm

- After the reading (before or after the responsory)

(It adds a note for those who need things spelled out: "Care must be taken to avoid the kind of silence that would disturb the structure of the Office, or embarrass and weary those taking part" [202].)

## The Purpose of the Liturgy of the Hours

This is how the *Code of Canon Law* explains the purpose of the Hours: "The Church, fulfilling the priestly function of Christ, celebrates the liturgy of the hours, whereby hearing God speaking to His people and memorializing the mystery of salvation, the Church praises Him in song and prayer without interruption and intercedes for the salvation of the whole world" (1173).

Pope Paul VI (1963–1978), putting the Liturgy of the Hours in the context of the whole Christian life, proclaimed its powerful potential: "If the prayer of the Divine Office becomes genuine personal prayer, the relation between the liturgy and the whole Christian life also becomes clearer. The whole life of the faithful, hour by hour during day and night, is a kind of *leitourgia* or public service, in which the faithful give themselves over to the ministry of love toward God and men, identifying themselves with the action of Christ, who by his life and self-offering sanctified the life of all mankind" (Apostolic Constitution of Pope Paul VI promulgating the revision of the Liturgy of the Hours, 8).

Repeatedly in the *General Instruction of the Liturgy of the Hours*, both the language and the directives themselves signal a pastoral and flexible approach (that has not always been evident in the Church's liturgy) that could help fulfill this potential. The following quotations are only examples.

- "There is great hope that new ways and expressions of public worship may be found for our own age, as has always happened in the life of the Church" (273).

- "The overriding consideration is to ensure that the celebration is not too inflexible or overelaborate or concerned only with merely formal observance but matches the reality of what is celebrated. One must strive above all to inspire hearts with a desire for genuine prayer and to show that the celebration of God's praise is a thing of joy" (279).

- Regarding hymns (175) and intercessions (183), for example,

**6**

**Prayer Book of the Church**

the *Instruction's* suggestions are "in the interests of variety."

- "Introduce fresh compositions," the *Instruction* suggests, speaking of non-biblical song (178).

- The *Instruction* also suggests substituting other readings.

## The Benefits of Praying the Hours

Citing Saint Benedict, the *General Instruction of the Liturgy of the Hours* (19) counsels that "mind and voice must be in harmony" for one to realize the following benefits:

1. The Liturgy of the Hours is a source of devotion.
2. The Liturgy of the Hours is a means of gaining God's grace.
3. The Liturgy of the Hours is a deepening of personal prayer.
4. The Liturgy of the Hours is an incentive to the work of the apostolate.

# The Elements

In the following pages, the various elements of the Liturgy of the Hours are treated, in the general order in which they appear.

## The Hymn

Non-biblical song has had a part in the Office from early times. It is the main poetic contribution of the Church. The *Instruction* (173) explains its purpose.

- Praising God
- Enabling people's participation

- Creating an atmosphere for the Hour or feast
- Inspiring devotion in the mind and heart

## Psalmody

"Psalmody" refers to the psalms used for singing or reciting in a time of prayer.

- The Liturgy of the Hours is made up mainly of the psalms, "the words of those great hymns composed under the inspiration of the Holy Spirit by sacred writers of the Old Testament" (*General Instruction of the Liturgy of the Hours*, 100). Athanasius says: "The Psalms seem to me to be like a mirror, in which the person using them can see himself, he can recite them against the background of his own emotions."

- There are 35 periods of prayer each week (five each day), at which the 150 psalms (or parts of them) are used 79 times. There are 140 periods of prayer in the four-week cycle; during which most of the 150 psalms (or parts of them) are used 316 times. As explained below, a few are used repeatedly and some, because of their length, are used in installments.

- Each psalm is prayed as a single unit, without interruption, or by alternating strophes between individuals or groups (a strophe is a separate section of a psalm, not following a regularly repeated pattern like a stanza), or responsorially (the assembly responding with the antiphon between each verse or strophe of the psalm that is spoken or sung by a leader or cantor or choir).

- Each psalm is followed by the Glory to the Father prayer (which culminates these Old Testament prayers with praise in terms of Christ and the Trinity of the New Testament).

### Which psalms when

The choice of psalms in the Psalter (like the choice of readings in the Lectionary and in the Liturgy of the Hours) "is not the result of individual choice or devotion but is the planned decision of the Church itself" (*General Instruction of the Liturgy of the Hours,* 140). (The "Psalter" is the collection of the psalms for liturgical or devotional use.) The purpose of this decision is that "in the course of the year the bride of Christ may unfold the mystery of Christ" (which means all of it, not only a particular priest's favorite parts).

1. **The whole of the Psalter**
   The Church has an interest in praying the whole Psalter regularly. The psalms are scheduled in a four-week cycle so that very few are omitted while a few traditionally more important ones are repeated. Early in the twentieth century, a new breviary had been prepared at the request of Pope Pius X (1903–1914) and promulgated by him. It restored the ancient custom of praying the 150 psalms each week. (See "The Psalter of

Mary" in Chapter 7.) The value of a regular, comprehensive use of the Psalter was kept in the 1970 revision by replacing the weekly cycle of the Psalter with an arrangement of the psalms over a period of four weeks. (The Night Prayer, arranged on a one-week schedule, is an exception.)

2. **The character of particular hours**
   Psalms are also chosen that are appropriate to certain hours; in particular, those of Morning Prayer, Evening Prayer, and Night Prayer (examples are given later in the chapter).

3. **The character of particular days**
   For Sundays, the psalms chosen are those that are traditionally important as expressions of the Paschal Mystery (this term refers to the redemptive work of Christ, especially the events of the Last Supper, the suffering, death, and Resurrection of Christ). Certain psalms of a penitential character or connected with the passion are assigned to Friday. (There is more detail about "the character of particular days" in a section earlier in this chapter, see p. 247.)

4. **The special character of seasons**
   Three psalms (78, 105, and 106) are reserved for Advent, Christmas, Lent, and Easter, as they shed special light on the history of salvation in the Old Testament as the forerunner of its fulfillment in the New.

# THE PSALMS IN THE OFFICE

*Roman numerals following psalm numbers indicate sections of the psalms*

|  | WEEK 1 | WEEK 2 | WEEK 3 | WEEK 4 |
|---|---|---|---|---|
| **SUNDAY** | | | | |
| **Evening Prayer I** | 141:1-9<br>142<br>Phil 2:6-11 | 119:105-112<br>16<br>Phil 2:6-11 | 113<br>116:10-19<br>Phil 2:6-11 | 122<br>130<br>Phil 2:6-11 |
| **Night Prayer** | 4<br>134 | 4<br>134 | 4<br>134 | 4<br>134 |
| **Office of Readings** | 1<br>2<br>3 | 104 I<br>104 II<br>104 III | 145 I<br>145 II<br>145 III | 24<br>66 I<br>66 II |
| **Morning Prayer** | 63:2-9<br>Dan 3:57-88, 56<br>149 | 118<br>Dan 3:52-57<br>150 | 93<br>Dan 3:57-88, 56<br>148 | 118<br>Dan 3:52-57<br>150 |
| **Daytime Prayer** | 118 I<br>118 II<br>118 III | 23<br>76 I<br>76 II | 118 I<br>118 II<br>118 III | 23<br>76 I<br>76 II |
| **Evening Prayer II** | 110:1-5, 7<br>114<br>Rev 19:1-7 | 110:1-5, 7<br>115<br>Rev 19:1-7 | 110:1-5, 7<br>111<br>Rev 19:1-7 | 110:1-5, 7<br>112<br>Rev 19:1-7 |
| **Night Prayer** | 91 | 91 | 91 | 91 |
| **MONDAY** | | | | |
| **Office of Readings** | 6<br>9A I<br>9A II | 31:1-7, 20-25 I<br>31:1-7, 20-25 II<br>31:1-7, 20-25 III | 50 I<br>50 II<br>50 III | 73 I<br>73 II<br>73 III |
| **Morning Prayer** | 5:2-10, 12-13<br>1 Chr 29:10-13<br>29 | 42<br>Sir 36:1-5, 10-13<br>19A | 84<br>Isa 2:2-5<br>96 | 90<br>Isa 42:10-16<br>135:1-12 |
| **Daytime Prayer** | 19B<br>7 I<br>7 II | 119:41-48 VI<br>40:2-14, 17-18 I<br>40:2-14, 17-18 II | 119:89-96 XII<br>71 I<br>71 II | 119:129-136 XVII<br>82<br>120 |
| **Evening Prayer** | 11<br>15<br>Eph 1:3-10 | 45 I<br>45 II<br>Eph 1:3-10 | 123<br>124<br>Eph 1:3-10 | 136 I<br>136 II<br>Eph 1:3-10 |
| **Night Prayer** | 86 | 86 | 86 | 86 |
| **TUESDAY** | | | | |
| **Office of Readings** | 10 I<br>10 II<br>12 | 37 I<br>37 II<br>37 III | 68 I<br>68 II<br>68 III | 102 I<br>102 II<br>102 III |
| **Morning Prayer** | 24<br>Tob 13:1-8<br>33 | 43<br>Isa 38:10-14, 17-20<br>65 | 85<br>Isa 26:1-4, 7-9, 12<br>67 | 101<br>Dan 3:26, 27, 29, 34-41<br>144.1-10 |

| | WEEK 1 | WEEK 2 | WEEK 3 | WEEK 4 |
|---|---|---|---|---|
| Daytime Prayer | 119:1-8<br>13<br>14 | 119:49-56 VII<br>53<br>54:1-6, 8-9 | 119:97-104 XIII<br>74 I<br>74 II | 119:137-144 XVIII<br>88 I<br>88 II |
| **Evening Prayer** | **20**<br>**21:2-8, 14**<br>**Rev 4:11, 5:9,**<br>**10, 12** | **49 I**<br>**49 II**<br>**Rev 4:11, 5:9,**<br>**10, 12** | **125**<br>**131**<br>**Rev 4:11, 5:9,**<br>**10, 12** | **137:1-6**<br>**138**<br>**Rev 4:11, 5:9,**<br>**10, 12** |
| Night Prayer | 143:1-11 | 143:1-11 | 143:1-11 | 143:1-11 |

## WEDNESDAY

| | WEEK 1 | WEEK 2 | WEEK 3 | WEEK 4 |
|---|---|---|---|---|
| Office of Readings | 18:2-30 I<br>18:2-30 II<br>18:2-30 III | 39 I<br>39 II<br>52 | 89:2-38 I<br>89:2-38 II<br>89:2-38 III | 103 I<br>103 II<br>103 III |
| **Morning Prayer** | **36**<br>**Jdt 16:2-3a,**<br>**13-15**<br>**47** | **77**<br>**I Sam 2:1-10**<br><br>**97** | **86**<br>**Isa 33:13-16**<br><br>**98** | **108**<br>**Isa 61:10-62:5**<br><br>**146** |
| Daytime Prayer | 119:9-16 II<br>17 I<br>17 II | 119:57-64 VIII<br>55:2-15, 17-24 I<br>55:2-15, 17-24 II | 119:105-112 XIV<br>70<br>75 | 119:145-152 XIX<br>94 I<br>94 II |
| **Evening Prayer** | **27 I**<br>**27 II**<br>**Col 1:12-20** | **62**<br>**67**<br>**Col 1:12-20** | **126**<br>**127**<br>**Col 1:12-20** | **139:1-18, 23-24 I**<br>**139:1-18, 23-24 II**<br>**Col 1:12-20** |
| Night Prayer | 31.1-6<br>130 | 31.1-6<br>130 | 31.1-6<br>130 | 31.1-6<br>130 |

## THURSDAY

| | WEEK 1 | WEEK 2 | WEEK 3 | WEEK 4 |
|---|---|---|---|---|
| Office of Readings | 18:31-35 IV<br>18:36-46 V<br>18:47-51 VI | 44 I<br>44 II<br>44 III | 89:39-53 IV<br>89:39-53 V<br>90 | 44 I<br>44 II<br>44 III |
| **Morning Prayer** | **57**<br>**Jer 31:10-14**<br>**48** | **80**<br>**Isa 12:1-6**<br>**81** | **87**<br>**Isa 40:10-17**<br>**99** | **143:1-11**<br>**Isa 66:10-14a**<br>**147:1-11** |
| Daytime Prayer | 119:17-24 III<br>25 I<br>25 II | 119:65-72 IX<br>56:2-7b, 9-14<br>57 | 119:113-120 XV<br>79:1-5, 8-11, 13<br>80 | 119:153-160 XX<br>128<br>129 |
| **Evening Prayer** | **30**<br>**32**<br>**Rev 11:17-18,**<br>**12:10b-12a** | **72 I**<br>**72 II**<br>**Rev 11:17-18,**<br>**12:10b-12a** | **132 I**<br>**132 II**<br>**Rev 11:17-18,**<br>**12:10b-12a** | **144 I**<br>**144 II**<br>**Rev 11:17-18,**<br>**12:10b-12a** |
| Night Prayer | 16 | 16 | 16 | 16 |

6
Prayer Book
of the Church

# THE PSALMS IN THE OFFICE (*CONTINUED*)

| | WEEK 1 | WEEK 2 | WEEK 3 | WEEK 4 |
|---|---|---|---|---|
| **FRIDAY** | | | | |
| Office of Readings | 35:1-2, 3c, 9-19, 22-23, 27-28 I; II; III | 38 I<br>38 II<br>38 III | 69:2-22, 30-37 I<br>69:2-22, 30-37 II<br>69:2-22, 30-37 III | 55:2-15, 17-24 I<br>55:2-15, 17-24 II<br>55:2-15, 17-24 III |
| **Morning Prayer** | **51**<br>**Isa 45:15-25**<br><br>**100** | **51**<br>**Hab 3:2-4, 13a, 15-19**<br>**147.12-20** | **51**<br>**Jer 14:17-21**<br><br>**100** | **51**<br>**Tob 13:8-11, 13-15**<br><br>**147:12-20** |
| **Daytime Prayer** | 119:25-32 IV<br>26<br>28:1-3, 6-9 | 119:73-80 X<br>59:2-5, 10-11, 17-18<br>60 | 22 I<br>22 II<br>22 III | 119:161-168 XXI<br>133<br>140:1-9, 13-14 |
| **Evening Prayer** | **41**<br>**46**<br>**Rev 15:3-4** | **116.1-9**<br>**121**<br>**Rev 15:3-4** | **135 I**<br>**135 II**<br>**Rev 15:3-4** | **145 I**<br>**145 II**<br>**Rev 15:3-4** |
| Night Prayer | 88 | 88 | 88 | 88 |
| **SATURDAY** | | | | |
| Office of Readings | 131<br>132 I<br>132 II | 136 I<br>136 II<br>136 III | 107 I<br>107 II<br>107 III | 50 I<br>50 II<br>50 III |
| **Morning Prayer** | **119:145-152**<br>**Ex 15:1-4a, 8-13, 17-18**<br>**117** | **92**<br>**Deut 32:1-12**<br><br>**8** | **119:145-152 XIX**<br>**Wis 9:1-6, 9-11**<br><br>**117** | **92**<br>**Ezek 36:24-28**<br><br>**8** |
| Daytime Prayer | 119:33-40 V<br>34 I<br>34 II | 119:81-88 XI<br>61<br>64 | 119:121-128 XVI<br>34 I<br>34 II | 119:169-176 XXII<br>45 I<br>45 II |

### 5. Solemnities

On solemnities both psalms at Evening Prayer I are taken from the *Laudete* (Praise) psalms (113, 117, 135, 146, 147A, 147B), following an ancient custom. (Evening Prayer "I," discussed later in this chapter, is prayed on the vigil of Sundays and certain feast days; Evening Prayer "II" is prayed in the evening of the day itself.) At Daytime Prayer on solemnities (except those mentioned above and those falling on Sunday) the psalms are taken from the gradual psalms.

#### The repetition of psalms

Psalm 95—The *Venite Exsultemus*, its first words in Latin, "Come, let us exalt," is part of the invitatory that opens the whole Office each day. (In its place Psalm 100, 67, or 24 may be used.)

Only two of the 150 psalms are used four times—weekly—in the major Hours (Morning Prayer and Evening Prayer) of the four-week cycle:

- Psalm 110:1–5, 7 every Sunday Evening Prayer II, because of "the special character of Sunday." An NAB footnote summarizes this familiar psalm as "a royal psalm in which a court singer recites three oracles in which God assures the king that his enemies are conquered (1–2), makes the king 'son' in traditional adoption language (3), gives priestly status to the king and promises to be with him in future military ventures (4–7)." Its first verse ("The Lord says to you, my Lord:/ 'Take your throne at my right hand . . .'") is the most often quoted Old Testament verse in the New Testament.

- Psalm 51, the most famous of the penitential psalms, every Friday Morning Prayer, because of "the special character of Friday."

Ten other psalms are used twice in the major Hours in the course of the four-week cycle (most during the weekly three-day, Friday-to-Sunday period):

- Psalm 118, every other Sunday morning (weeks 2 and 4)

- Psalm 150, every other Sunday morning (weeks 2 and 4)

---

### "Gradual" Psalms?

The term "gradual" refers to the "Psalms of the Steps" (see *Psalms 120-134*).

Some of the psalms have headings, often obscure, written above them ("superscriptions"). The old Latin Vulgate translated these "superscriptions" of Psalms 120-134 "*canticum graduum*," literally "song of the steps." Old translations of the palms translated that phrase "gradual" psalms. These 15 now have a term like "Song of Ascent" above them.

Various explanations have been offered through the years; today, the most convincing one is that they may have once formed a collection of psalms used by pilgrims going up (ascending) to Jerusalem for the great annual feasts. The Fathers of the Church, typically, interpreted the steps to be the gradual ascent by which Christians progress in virtue and perfection.

- Psalm 100, every other Friday morning (weeks 1 and 3)
- Psalm 147:12–20, on alternating Friday mornings (weeks 2 and 4)
- Psalm 119:145–152, every other Saturday morning (weeks 1 and 3)
- Psalm 92, on alternating Saturday mornings (weeks 2 and 4)
- Psalm 117, every other Saturday morning (weeks 1 and 3)
- Psalm 8, on alternating Saturday mornings (weeks 2 and 4)
- Psalm 67, Morning Prayer, Tuesday, week 3; Evening Prayer, Wednesday, week 2
- Psalm 135:1–12, Morning Prayer, Monday, week 4; Evening Prayer, Friday, week 3

### The division of psalms

Because of the length of some psalms, they're separated into sections.

1. **Principle**

   Psalms too long to be included in one Hour of the Office are assigned to the same Hour on different days so that they may be recited in full by those who do not usually pray other Hours.

2. **Example**

   The 176 verses of Psalm 119, by far the longest in the Psalter, are divided up in keeping with its own internal structure and spread over 22 days during Daytime Prayer. (In the history of the Liturgy of the Hours, Psalm 119 was not used at the morning or evening Hour, but became associated with

the times of prayer during the day, today known as Daytime Prayer.)

### The exclusion of psalms or verses of psalms

In some cases it may appear that part of a psalm has been omitted when it hasn't been. The following example is from Morning Prayer, Monday of week 1.

- The opening psalm is Psalm 5. When the psalm is identified at the top it says 5:2–10, 12–13.
- Verse one is not omitted. It's not uncommon in the Psalter for psalms to have a "directive to the choirmaster" at the beginning. Psalm 5 is one such case. Although verse 1 is part of the original psalm, it was never intended to be prayed—evidence that the psalms were intended to be sung. (The omission of verse 11 is explained below.)

Three psalms (58, 83, and 109) are not included in the Psalter cycle because they are "heavily imprecatory" in character. (The word "imprecation" is a euphemism for a curse.) Likewise, some verses of some psalms are omitted (as indicated at the head of each) because of "the difficulty they can cause because of their psychology, even though the psalms of imprecation are used as prayer in the New Testament, for example, Revelation 6:10, and their purpose is in no sense to encourage cursing" (*General Instruction of the Liturgy of the Hours*, 131). Curses need to be understood not so much as prayers for revenge as cries for vindication. They spring not from hatred but from a desire to see God's justice appear on earth. Not surprisingly, these "imprecations" often come in the midst of laments, which are often used on Friday with its echo of the passion. And with laments sometimes come curses.

- For example, *Psalm 55:2–15, 17–24*, entitled "Against a false friend," is prayed in the Office of Reading on Friday of week 4—not all of it, but most of it. Not verse 16.

- First, verse 15: "You, whose company I enjoyed, / at whose side I walked / in procession in the house of God."

- The omitted verse is: "Let death take them by surprise; / let them go down alive to Sheol, / for evil is in their homes and hearts."

### The titles of psalms

In the Roman Catholic tradition of praying the psalms, the addition of titles (along with antiphons and the "psalm-prayer" that follows a psalm) has helped Christians understand the psalms and their place in Christian prayer. Titles help explain the meaning and value of the psalm for living in faith. After the title there is often an introductory sentence from the New Testament or the Church Fathers "to foster prayer in the light of Christ's new revelation; it invites one to pray the psalms in their Christological meaning" (*General Instruction of the Liturgy of the Hours*, 111).

- For example, the title "The happiness of the just man" is given to *Psalm 112*, which begins, "Happy the man who fears the Lord," and proceeds to specifics.

- The New Testament subtitle introducing *Psalm 112* is *Ephesians 5:8–9*: "Live as children born of the light. Light produces every kind of goodness and justice and truth," which anticipates a verse in the psalm: "(The one who fears the Lord) is a light in the darkness for the upright . . ."

- The title sometimes highlights the special character of a day, like Sunday: At Sunday Evening Prayer I in week 2, Psalm 16 is used (including the verse, "And so my heart rejoices, my soul is glad; / even my body shall rest in safety. / For you will not leave my soul among the dead, / nor let your beloved know decay"). After the title is the phrase, "The Father raised up Jesus, freeing him from the grip of death" (*Acts 2:24*).

### The "psalm-prayers" following psalms

Like the titles of the psalms in the Liturgy of the Hours, the prayers after the psalm have helped Christians understand the psalms and their place in Christian prayer. Psalm-prayers help one understand the use of the psalms "in a predominantly Christian way." After a moment of silence, they "gather up and round off the thoughts and aspirations" of the prayer (*General Instruction of the Liturgy of the Hours*, 112).

- *Psalm 112* is used at Evening Prayer II on Sunday of week 4; it begins, "Happy the man who fears the Lord" and includes the verse, "He is a light in the darkness for the upright." The prayer that follows says, "Lord God, you are the eternal light which illumines the hearts of good people. . . . May we come to see the light of your countenance."

- *Psalm 116:10–19* is used at Evening Prayer I on Sunday of week 3; it includes the verses, "I trusted, even when I said: / 'I am sorely afflicted'" and "O precious in the eyes of the Lord / is the death of his faithful." The prayer that follows says, "Father, precious in your sight is the death of the saints, but precious above all is the love with which Christ suffered to redeem us."

- The prayer after the psalm sometimes reflects the character of a particular day, like Thursday evening, for example: In week 1, *Psalm 30* is used, including the verses, "I will praise you, Lord, you have rescued me / and have not let my enemies rejoice over me. / . . . O Lord, you have raised my soul from the dead, / restored me to life from those who sink into the grave. / . . . At night there are tears, but joy comes with dawn." Its psalm-prayer says, "God our Father, glorious in giving life, and even more glorious in restoring it, when his last night on earth came, your Son shed tears of blood, but dawn brought incomparable gladness. Do not turn away from us, or we shall fall back into dust, but rather turn our mourning into joy by raising us up with Christ."

### The psalms of Morning Prayer

In Morning Prayer, following the tradition of the Church, there is a "morning psalm," then a canticle from the Old Testament, and finally a second psalm of praise. These are examples of the morning psalm of Morning Prayer.

1. Morning Prayer, Thursday of week 1 includes *Psalm 57:8–9*: "My heart is ready, O God, / my heart is ready. / I will sing, I will sing your praise. / Awake, my soul, / awake, lyre and harp, / I will awake the dawn."

2. In Morning Prayer, Saturday of week 1, the antiphon for the first psalm sings, "Dawn finds me ready to welcome you, my God." The psalm itself (*Psalm 119:145–152*) includes the verses, "I rise before dawn and cry for help, / I hope in your word. / My eyes watch through the night / to ponder your promise."

3. Morning Prayer, Monday of week 1 includes this verse from *Psalm 5*: "In the morning you hear me; / in the morning I offer you my prayer, / watching and waiting."

4. Morning Prayer, Thursday of week 1 includes *Psalm 57*, which uses the bold image of song waking the new day, "Awake, my soul, / awake, lyre and harp, / I will awake the dawn." (Psalm 108, compiled partly

from Psalm 57, used at Morning Prayer on Wednesday of week 4, also uses this image.)

5. Morning Prayer, Saturday of week 4 includes *Psalm 92*, whose opening verses are: "It is good to give thanks to the Lord, / to make music to your name, O Most High, / to proclaim your love in the morning . . ."

6. Morning Prayer, Monday of week 4 includes *Psalm 90*, "In the morning, fill us with your love; / we shall exult and rejoice all our days."

### The psalms of Evening Prayer

In Evening Prayer, following the tradition of the Church, there are two psalms (or two parts of a longer psalm) appropriate to the Hour and public prayer, then a canticle from the New Testament (from the letters of the Apostles or from the Book of Revelation). The care shown in the choice of the evening psalms is clear, especially for Sunday Evening Prayer I (Saturday evening). The following, for example, are the opening lines of the Psalter in each of the weeks of the four-week cycle.

Week 1—"I have called to you, Lord; hasten to help me! / Hear my voice when I cry to you. / Let my prayer arise before you like incense, / the raising of my hands like an evening oblation" (*Psalm 141:1–2*).

Week 2—"Your word is a lamp for my steps / and a light for my path" (*Psalm 119:105*).

Week 3—"Praise, O servants of the Lord, / praise the name of the Lord! / May the name of the Lord be blessed / both now and for evermore! / From the rising of the sun to its setting / praised be the name of the Lord!" (*Psalm 113:1–3*).

Week 4—"I rejoiced when I heard them say: / 'Let us go to God's house.' / And now our feet are standing / within your gates, O Jerusalem" (*Psalm 122:1–2*).

### The psalms of Night Prayer

For Night Prayer, psalms are used that express full confidence in the Lord. This is especially evident on Sunday, as the following examples show. (For convenience, Sunday's psalms may be used through the week—especially by those who may wish to pray Night Prayer from memory.)

1. After Evening Prayer I of Sunday (Saturday evening), the psalmody consists of Psalms 4 (a prayer of trust in God) and 134 ("Exhortation to the Night Watch to Bless God").

2. After Evening Prayer II of Sunday, *Psalm 91* is used—which includes the phrase, "You shall not fear the terror of the night . . .". *Psalm 91:11–12* is cited in the Gospel accounts of the temptation of Christ in the desert (*Matthew 4:6* and *Luke 4:10–11*): "For God commands the angels / to guard you in all your ways. / With their hands they shall support you, / lest you strike your foot against a stone."

6

Prayer Book of the Church

### Psalms celebrating the special character of Sunday

#### Evening Prayer I

- In week 1, verses of *Psalm 142* include: "On the way where I shall walk/ they have hidden a snare to entrap me" and "I have no means of escape,/ not one who cares for my soul./ I cry to you, O Lord./ I have said: 'You are my refuge,/ all I have left in the land of the living'" and "Bring my soul out of this prison."

- In week 2, verses of *Psalm 16* include: "And so my heart rejoices, my soul is glad;/ even my body shall rest in safety./ For you will not leave my soul among the dead,/ nor let your beloved know decay."

- In week 3, verses from *Psalm 116:10–19* include: "I trusted, even when I said:/ 'I am sorely afflicted'" and "O precious in the eyes of the Lord/ is the death of his faithful."

- In week 4, verses from *Psalm 130* (the *"De Profundis"* after its opening words in Latin, "Out of the depths I cry to you, O Lord") include: "My soul is waiting for the Lord,/ I count on his word./ My soul is longing for the Lord/ more than watchman for daybreak."

#### Morning Prayer

Through the four-week cycle, Psalm 150 alternates with Psalms 148 and 149—praise worthy of the Lord's Day.

- Psalm 150 (used in week 2 and week 4) is the closing doxology for the fifth book of the Psalms (107–149) and for the Psalter as a whole. (There are five sections in the Psalter, each ending with a simple doxology—three of them actually not part of the psalm proper: Psalm 41:14, Psalm 72:18–19, Psalm 89:53, Psalm 106:48.) A revised NAB footnote to Psalm 150 says, "Temple musicians and dancers are called to lead all beings on earth and in heaven in praise of God. The psalm proclaims to whom praise shall be given, and where (verse 1); what praise shall be given, and why (verse 2); how praise shall be given (verses 3–5) and by whom (verse 6)." (A "doxology" is a formula or hymn of praise to God—*doxa* in Greek meaning glory; the *Gloria* of the Mass has been called the "greater doxology" and the Glory to the Father prayer, the "lesser doxology.")

- *Psalm 149* (used in week 1) includes the verse, "Sing a new song to the Lord,/ his praise in the assembly of the faithful"

- *Psalm 148* (used in week 3) includes the verse, "Praise the Lord from the heavens;/ praise him in the heights"

#### Evening Prayer II

- *Psalm 110:1–5, 7* begins, "The Lord's revelation to my Master:/ 'Sit on my right:/ your foes I will put beneath your feet'." It is used every Sunday at Evening Prayer II—one of only two instances in which a psalm is repeated every week (Psalm 51 at Friday

Morning Prayer is the other). The Church from its earliest days understood Psalm 110 as referring to the exaltation of the risen Jesus and "my Master" (or "my lord" in some translations) as referring to the Messiah.

- In *Psalm 114* God's wonders at the Exodus ("When Israel came forth from Egypt, / Jacob's sons from an alien people . . ."). It is traditionally used in Sunday's Office because the Exodus is a "type" or foreshadowing of the Paschal Mystery of Jesus crossing from death to life and the promised land is a type of heaven. (With the title, a quote from Saint Augustine is added, "You too left Egypt when, at baptism, you renounced that world which is at enmity with God.")

## Psalms celebrating the special character of Friday
### Thursday Evening Prayer

- In week 1, *Psalm 30* (with the title added, "Thanksgiving for deliverance from death") is prayed. Its verses include "I will praise you, Lord, you have rescued me / and have not let my enemies rejoice over me. / . . . O Lord, you have raised my soul from the dead, / restored me to life from those who sink into the grave. / . . . At night there are tears, but joy comes with dawn."

- In week 2, *Psalm 72* (with the title added, "The Messiah's royal power") is prayed. Its verses, conjuring up the INRI on the cross, include "O God, give your judgment to the king, to a king's son your justice, / . . . May he defend the poor of the people / and save the children of the needy / and crush the oppressor. / . . . Before him his enemies shall fall, / his foes lick the dust."

- In week 3, *Psalm 132* (with the title added, "God's promises to the house of David") is prayed. This psalm is a song for the liturgical ceremony of carrying the ark (the throne of God's glory) in procession to the temple. It refers to David's determination to build the temple and the oracle of Nathan. It includes the verses "O Lord, remember David / and all the many hardships he endured, / . . . The Lord swore an oath to David; / he will not go back on his word: / 'A son, the fruit of your body, / will I set upon your throne.' / . . . For the Lord has chosen Zion; / he has desired it for his dwelling: / 'This is my resting-place for ever, / here have I chosen to live. / I will greatly bless her produce, / I will fill her poor with bread. / I will clothe her priests with salvation / and her faithful shall ring out their joy.'"

- In week 4, *Psalm 144* is prayed. A title is added ("Prayer for victory and peace") as well as a quotation from Saint Hilary ("Christ learned the art of warfare when he overcame the world, as he said, 'I have overcome the world'"). Its verses include "Blessed be the Lord, my rock / who trains my arms for battle, / who prepares my hands for war. /

... Lord, what is man that you care for him, / mortal man, that you keep him in mind; / man, who is merely a breath, / whose life fades like a shadow? / ... Reach down from heaven and save me; / draw me out from the mighty waters, / from the hands of alien foes. . . ."

- Its psalm-prayer says "Lord, God of strength, you gave your Son victory over death. Direct your Church's fight against evil in the world. Clothe us with the weapons of light and unite us under the one banner of love, that we may receive our eternal reward after the battle of earthly life."

### Friday Morning Prayer

One of the psalms of Friday morning is always *Psalm 51*, the most famous of the seven penitential psalms and one of only two psalms repeated four times—weekly—in the four-week cycle. It begins, "Have mercy on me, God, in your kindness. / In your compassion blot out my offense. / O wash me more and more from my guilt / and cleanse me from my sin." (Although Psalm 51 is used each week, its antiphon each week varies, each time paraphrasing a different line in the psalm.)

## The Canticles

Canticles are hymns or poems (like the psalms) found outside the Book of Psalms. The 1970 revision of the Liturgy of the Hours incorporated a greater use of canticles: To increase the "spiritual richness" of Morning Prayer, some new Old Testament canticles were added and to increase "the beauty" of Evening Prayer, New Testament canticles were added. An Old Testament canticle and a New Testament (non-Gospel) canticle are always included as part of the psalmody.

### Gospel canticles

A canticle from the Gospel—an "evangelical canticle"—always follows the reading. Canticles, at the point at which they are found in the Liturgy of the Hours, are discussed below.

### The place of canticles

The revision of the Office included the introduction of some new Old Testament canticles for Morning Prayer and New Testament canticles for Evening Prayer. Their sequence is governed by tradition: "Both psalmody and readings are arranged in keeping with the traditional rule that the Old Testament is read first, then the writings of the apostles, and finally the gospel" (*General Instruction of the Liturgy of the Hours*, 139).

1. **Monthly**
   - Most of the Old Testament canticles are used only once in the four-week cycle.
   - They are prayed in Morning Prayer.

2. **Weekly**
   - Most of the New Testament canticles are used every week.
   - Every day has its own canticle.

- They are prayed in Evening Prayer.

**3. Daily**

- The Gospel canticles are used every day.

- Every hour has its own canticle.

- They are prayed in Morning Prayer, Evening Prayer, and Night Prayer.

**The canticles of Morning Prayer**

Morning Prayer includes a canticle from the Old Testament between the first and the second psalm "in accordance with custom." In the recent revision more of these were added to the Psalter so each weekday of the four-week cycle has its own proper canticle, and each Sunday includes one of the two sections of the Canticle of the Three Children, used alternately.

|  | Week One | Week Two |
|---|---|---|
| Sunday | Daniel 3:57-88, 56 | Daniel 3:52-57 |
| Monday | 1 Chronicles 29:10-13 | Sirach 36:1-5, 10-13 |
| Tuesday | Tobit 13:1-8 | Isaiah 38:10-14, 17-20 |
| Wednesday | Judith 16:2-3a, 13-15 | 1 Samuel 2:1-10 |
| Thursday | Jeremiah 31:10-14 | Isaiah 12:1-6 |
| Friday | Isaiah 45:15-25 | Habakkuk 3:2-4, 13, 15-19 |
| Saturday | Exodus 15:1-4a, 8-13, 17-18 | Deuteronomy 32:1-12 |

|  | Week Three | Week Four |
|---|---|---|
| Sunday | Daniel 3:57-88, 56 | Daniel 3:52-57 |
| Monday | Isaiah 2:2-5 | Isaiah 42:10-16 |
| Tuesday | Isaiah 26:1-4, 7-9, 12 | Daniel 3:26, 27, 29, 34-41 |
| Wednesday | Isaiah 33:13-16 | Isaiah 61:10-62:5 |
| Thursday | Isaiah 40:10-17 | Isaiah 66:10-14a |
| Friday | Jeremiah 14:17-21 | Tobit 13:8-11, 13-15 |
| Saturday | Wisdom 9:1-6, 9-11 | Ezekiel 36:24-28 |

## The canticles of Evening Prayer

Evening Prayer includes a canticle from the New Testament (but not from the Gospel) after the two psalms. There are seven canticles provided for all four weeks of the Psalter, one for each day. (On Lenten Sundays, 1 Peter 2:21–24 replaces the Alleluia Canticle from the Book of Revelation.)

| | |
|---|---|
| Saturday | Philippians 2:6–11 |
| Sunday | Revelation 19:1–7 |
| Monday | Ephesians 1:3–10 |
| Tuesday | Revelation 4:11; 5:9–10, 12 |
| Wednesday | Colossians 1:12–20 |
| Thursday | Revelation 11:17–18, 12:10–12 |
| Friday | Revelation 15:3–4 |

## Canticles celebrating the special character of Sunday

• Every Saturday evening, Sunday's Evening Prayer I features the glorious hymn from the letter to the Philippians (2:6–11), which outlines the Paschal Mystery (the redemptive work of Christ, especially the events of the Last Supper, the suffering, death, and Resurrection of Christ): the Incarnation ("Though he was in the form of God,/ Jesus did not deem equality with God/ something to be grasped at./ Rather, he emptied himself/ and took the form of a slave,/ being born in the likeness of men"); the passion ("He was known to be of human estate,/ and it was thus that he humbled himself,/ obediently accepting even death,/ death on a cross!"), and the Resurrection ("Because of this,/ God highly exalted him").

• Each Sunday morning, one of the two sections of the Canticle of the Three Children (Daniel 3:52–88) is prayed, used alternately.

• Every Sunday's Evening Prayer II features the canticle "The Wedding of the Lamb" from the Book of Revelation (19:1–7). It culminates "For the wedding day of the Lamb has come,/ his bride has made herself ready." (The four alleluias of this hymn are the only New Testament appearances of this acclamation, which is so frequent in the psalms and so central in Jewish liturgy.)

## A canticle celebrating the special character of Friday

Every Thursday evening, Evening Prayer is a kind of "Evening Prayer I" for Friday (see "Evening Prayer I" above). The New Testament canticle is *Revelation 11:17–18, 12:10b–12a*, which includes the following verses: "Now have salvation and power come,/ the reign of our God and the authority/ of his Anointed One./ For the accuser of our brothers is cast out,/ who night and day accused them before God./ They defeated him by the blood of the Lamb/ and by the word of their testimony; love for life did not deter them from death."

## The Antiphons

Along with titles and the "psalm-prayer" that follows a psalm, antiphons ("first of all") have greatly helped Christians understand the psalms and their place in Christian prayer. An antiphon is a short verse sung or spoken before and after a psalm or canticle. Antiphons may be made up of a quotation or paraphrase from or an allusion to the psalm that follows, the readings of the Mass of the day or the feast being celebrated, or a combination of both.

### The purpose and value of antiphons

This is how the *General Instruction of the Liturgy of the Hours* describes the antiphons' purpose and value (113):

1. They help bring out the psalm's character.

2. They feature a "sentence which may otherwise not attract the attention it deserves."

3. They suggest a typological meaning for the psalm—which the *Instruction* considers appropriate "as long as extravagant accommodated meanings are avoided" (about typology, see Chapter 3; about accommodation, see Chapter 4).

4. They help provide an understanding of its significance for a particular feast or season.

5. They add "pleasure and variety" to praying the psalms. For example, one of the psalms of Friday morning is always Psalm 51 (one of only two psalms repeated every week in the four-week cycle). Although the psalm is the same each week, its antiphon varies, each week paraphrasing a different line in the psalm.

   - Week 1: "Lord, you will accept the true sacrifice offered on your altar."

   - Week 2: "A humble, contrite heart, O God, you will not spurn."

   - Week 3: "You alone I have grieved by my sin; have pity on me, O Lord."

   - Week 4: "Create a clean heart in me, O God; renew in me a steadfast spirit."

6. They can be used when the psalm is sung or spoken responsorially (as explained earlier in the section on psalmody in "The Elements of the Liturgy of the Hours").

### Psalm antiphon examples

The antiphon for Psalm 112 (prayed during Evening Prayer II on Sunday, week 4) is varied according to the liturgical season, highlighting either some part of the psalm or the significance of the season:

- During Ordinary Time: "Blessed are they who hunger and thirst for holiness; they will be satisfied" (one of the Beatitudes).

- During Advent: "Crooked paths will be straightened and rough ways made smooth. Come, O Lord, do not delay, alleluia."

- During Epiphany: "A light has shone through the darkness for the upright of heart; the Lord is gracious, merciful and just."
- During Lent: "Happy the man who shows mercy for the Lord's sake; he will stand firm for ever."
- During Easter: "In the darkness he dawns: a light for upright hearts, alleluia."

**Gospel canticle antiphon examples**

After the reading and its response, a Gospel canticle is prayed. There is an explanation in the pages ahead, including more examples of the use of antiphons.

## The Reading

The readings of Scripture in the Liturgy of the Hours are linked with and complement the readings at Mass (*General Instruction of the Liturgy of the Hours*, 143). In the compiling of the Lectionary for the Liturgy of the Hours, there was an effort to avoid repeating a reading that was being used in the Lectionary for Mass on the same day or on a day near to the same day. The series of readings in the Lectionary for the Liturgy of the Hours is independent of both the Sunday and weekday Mass lectionaries and "in itself it aims at giving a fuller picture of the history of salvation and at including readings from almost every book of the Bible except the Gospels which have been traditionally reserved for the Mass" (Michael Maher, M.S.C., "The Scripture Readings of the Divine Office," *Companion to the New*

*Breviary*, edited by Austin Flannery, O.P., p. 120). The Lectionary for the Liturgy of the Hours is two-fold:

1. One is a one-year cycle. For practical reasons (the size and cost of the book), it is the cycle incorporated in the Liturgy of the Hours. The readings in the one-year cycle are shorter, "setting out some passage of Sacred Scripture in a striking way, or highlighting some shorter sentences that may receive less attention in the continuous cycle of Scripture readings" in the two-year cycle or in the Lectionary for Mass (*General Instruction of the Liturgy of the Hours*, 45).

2. The other is a two-year cycle and is provided in a supplement as an option. The two-year cycle of readings is arranged so that each year almost all Scripture books are read, including longer and more difficult passages only rarely suitable for Mass. Between the Liturgy of the Hours and the Mass, all of the New Testament as a whole is read each year. However, only those parts of the Old Testament are read that are judged to be most important for understanding the history of salvation and for deepening devotion. "All agree that the two-year course of readings satisfies in a much more perfect way the aim of the reform of the readings which was to offer us those passages which in themselves show a unity or argument, and which during the course of the year present the

principal chapters in the history of salvation" (Michael Maher, M.S.C., citing the Apostolic Constitution of Pope Paul VI promulgating the revision of the Liturgy of the Hours, in "The Scripture Readings of the Divine Office," *Companion to the New Breviary*, edited by Austin Flannery, O.P., p. 121).

### General principles of selection

1. There are no readings from the Gospels in the Liturgy of the Hours since they are read as a whole annually at Mass.

2. The special character of Friday, of Sunday, and of the individual Hours has been respected when possible. In this way Scriptures are provided that relate to the passion and Resurrection of Christ and to the morning and evening of the day.

3. At Evening Prayer the reading is chosen only from the New Testament because it follows a New Testament canticle (thereby respecting the traditional order of reading Scripture from the Old Testament before the New).

### Examples

These are examples of readings from the Easter Season, beginning with Thursday Evening Prayer, which opens the weekly Friday-to-Sunday part of the week that in some ways echoes the annual Holy Week Triduum from Holy Thursday evening to Easter Sunday evening. Each Hour has its own reading, which is different each day of the week. The assignments for each week are repeated every week (unlike during the Ordinary Time of the year).

1. Thursday Evening Prayer: *1 Peter 3:18, 22* "He was put to death insofar as fleshly existence goes . . ."

2. Friday Morning Prayer: *Acts 5:30–32* "The God of our fathers raised up Jesus whom you put to death."

3. Friday Evening Prayer: *Hebrews 5:8–10* "Son though he was, Jesus learned obedience from what he suffered . . ."

4. Saturday Morning Prayer: *Romans 14:7–9* "None of us lives as his own master and none of us dies as his own master . . . That is why Christ died and came to life again . . ."

5. Saturday Evening Prayer: *1 Peter 2:9–10* "You are 'a chosen race, a royal priesthood, a holy nation, a people he claims for his own to proclaim the glorious works' of the One who called you from darkness into his marvelous light."

6. Sunday Morning Prayer: *Acts 10:40–43* "God raised up Jesus on the third day . . ."

7. Sunday Evening Prayer: *Hebrews 10:12–14* "Jesus offered one sacrifice for sins and took his seat forever at the right hand of God . . ."

8. Monday Morning Prayer: *Romans 10:8b–10*

6

**Prayer Book of the Church**

"If you confess with your lips that Jesus is Lord, and believe in your heart . . ."

9. Monday Evening Prayer: *Hebrews 8:1b–3a*
"We have such a high priest, who has taken his seat . . ."

10. Tuesday Morning Prayer: *Acts 13:30–33*
"God raised Jesus from the dead, and for many days thereafter . . ."

11. Tuesday Evening Prayer: *1 Peter 2:4–5*
"Come to the Lord, a living stone . . ."

12. Wednesday Morning Prayer: *Romans 6:8–11*
"We know that Christ, once raised from the dead, will never die again."

13. Wednesday Evening Prayer: *Hebrews 7:24–27*
"Unlike other priests, he has no need to offer sacrifice day after day . . . He did that once for all when he offered himself."

14. Thursday Morning Prayer: *Romans 8:10–11*
"He who raised Jesus from the dead will bring your mortal bodies to life also . . ."

In the examples cited above, the theme of the Paschal Mystery is clear, as is appropriate for the Easter season. Note that the account of the passion and Resurrection is not revisited, not only because the Gospels are not used for readings in the Liturgy of the Hours (in accordance with tradition; principle 1 above), but because these readings can better teach about the meaning and significance of the Paschal Mystery. This is especially clear in the following examples.

1. **Thursday Evening Prayer**
"The reason why Christ died for sins once for all . . . was that he might lead you to God" (*1 Peter 3:18*).

2. **Friday Morning Prayer**
"He whom God has exalted at his right hand as ruler and savior is to bring repentance to Israel and forgiveness of sins . . ." (*Acts 5:31*).

3. **Friday Evening Prayer**
"He became the source of eternal salvation for all who obey him" (*Hebrews 5:9*).

4. **Saturday Morning Prayer**
"That is why Christ died and came to life again, that he might be Lord of both the dead and the living" (*Romans 14:9*).

5. **Saturday Evening Prayer**
"Once you were no people, but now you are God's people . . ." (*1 Peter 2:10*).

6. **Sunday Morning Prayer**
"He commissioned us to preach to the people and to bear witness that he is the one set apart by God as judge of the living and the dead" (*Acts 10:42*).

7. **Sunday Evening Prayer**
"By one offering he has forever perfected those who are being sanctified" (*Hebrews 10:14*).

### Optional readings

As mentioned earlier, there is flexibility built into the Hours. In this case there is a freedom in the choice of readings, especially when the Hours are prayed in common.

- The reading could be a longer one from the Office of Readings.
- The reading could be a longer one from the Lectionary for Mass.
- Other biblical readings could be chosen "on the occasion of retreats or pastoral gatherings or prayers for Christian unity or other such events" that would be more suitable (*General Instruction of the Liturgy of the Hours*, 248).

## The Responsory
### The purpose

The responsories in the Divine Office are "drawn from traditional sources or freshly composed" (*General Instruction of the Liturgy of the Hours*, 169) and flow from the reading "as a kind of acclamation, enabling God's word to sink deeper into the mind and heart" (*General Instruction of the Liturgy of the Hours*, 172).

1. To shine new light on the passage
2. To put it in the context of salvation history
3. To lead from the Old Testament to the New Testament
4. To transform what has been read into prayer and contemplation
5. To "provide pleasant variety by its poetic beauty"

In *The Liturgy of the Hours, The General Instruction with Commentary*, A.M. Roguet, O.P. makes the following comments about the response in the Office of Readings: "In order to help the reader or listener to turn his reading into prayer, the biblical passage from the Office [of Readings] is followed by a response. . . . This response takes a particularly rich and striking phrase which has just been read. It then juxtaposes to this an extract from another biblical book, often from the other Testament, which brings out the implications and nuances of the first text. The [second, non-scriptural reading] is likewise followed by a response, but a response less tied to the text just read. The short readings at [Morning Prayer and Evening Prayer] are followed by a short response which, while having the same structure, consists of much shorter phrases."

### The structure of the responsory prayer

This is the responsory for Night Prayer (responsories are designed to be prayed antiphonally, the leader taking the first line and another or others taking the part following the dash).

| | |
|---|---|
| Leader: | Into your hands, Lord, I commend my spirit. |
| All: | —Into your hands, Lord, I commend my spirit. |
| Leader: | You have redeemed us, Lord God of truth. |
| All: | —I commend my spirit. |
| Leader: | Glory to the Father and to the Son and to the Holy Spirit. |
| All: | —Into your hands, Lord, I commend my spirit. |

If the parts of the responsory are designated with letters, the pattern becomes clear. (The 1 indicates the leader; 2, another or others.)

1. A B (an acclamation or petition in two parts)
2. A B (a repetition)

1. C (a complement or completion of the initial acclamation or petition)
2. B (a repetition of the second part of the initial acclamation or petition)

1. D (a doxology)
2. A B (a repetition of the whole initial acclamation or petition)

## The Gospel Canticle

Made familiar by age-old common use in the Roman Catholic Church, the Gospel canticles are expressions of praise and thanksgiving for our redemption. Like the psalms and non-Gospel canticles, the Gospel canticles are fitted with antiphons appropriate to the day, the season, or the feast.

1. Zechariah's *Benedictus* is the Gospel canticle for Morning Prayer. It is from *Luke 1:68–79* and begins, "Blessed be the Lord, the God of Israel;/ he has come to his people and set them free./ He has raised up for us a mighty savior,/ born of the house of his servant David."
2. Mary's *Magnificat* is the Gospel canticle for Evening Prayer. It is from *Luke 1:46–55* and begins, "My soul proclaims the greatness of the Lord,/ my spirit rejoices in God my Savior/ for he has looked with favor on his lowly servant."

3. Simeon's *Nunc Dimittis* is the Gospel canticle for Night Prayer. It is from *Luke 2:29–32*, culminates the Hour, and begins, "Lord, now you let your servant go in peace. . . ."

### The Gospel canticle antiphons

The nature and purpose of antiphons are described above in a separate section. Below are some examples of the use of antiphons for the Gospel canticles.

1. **Sundays in Ordinary Time**
   Sunday takes priority. Every Sunday's Gospel canticle has its own antiphon, taken from the Gospel of the day:
   • Evening Prayer I—taken from the Gospel of Year A.

   • Morning Prayer—taken from Gospel of Year B.

   • Evening Prayer II—taken from Gospel of Year C.

("Evening Prayer I" is "the eve of Sunday"—Saturday evening; "Evening Prayer II" is Sunday evening. The designation of each year as A, B, or C is from the Lectionary and is described in Chapter 5 of this book.)

2. **Sundays in Advent, Christmas, Lent, and Easter**
   • Usually the antiphon is taken from the Scriptures of the day (usually the Gospel), sometimes (as in the Easter Season) following a pattern: Evening Prayer I's is from the lectionary readings of Year A, Morning Prayer's from Year

B, and Evening Prayer II's from Year C.

- Sometimes, the antiphon is seasonal; for example, at Morning Prayer on the first Sunday of Advent, the antiphon is "The Holy Spirit will come upon you, Mary; you have no need to be afraid. You will carry in your womb the Son of God, alleluia."

- Occasionally, the antiphon is a prayer that alludes to Scripture. For example, at Evening Prayer II on the first Sunday of Lent, when the Gospel reading is Matthew 4:1–11, Mark 1:12–15, or Luke 4:1–13 (the story of Jesus' temptation by Satan in the wilderness at the beginning of his public ministry), the antiphon is "Watch over us, eternal Savior; do not let the cunning tempter seize us. We place all our trust in your unfailing help."

3. **Weekdays in Advent, Christmas, Lent, and Easter**
The antiphon is taken from the Gospel of the day, which means that during Morning Prayer and Evening Prayer there is an echo of the Mass itself. For example, at Morning Prayer on Friday of the First Week of Lent the antiphon for the Canticle of Zechariah is, "If your virtue does not surpass that of the scribes and Pharisees . . ." That verse is from the Gospel reading for Mass that day, Matthew 5:20–26.

4. **Feast Days**
On all solemnities and some other lesser feast days the antiphon reflects the observation.

- Often the antiphon for the Gospel canticle is a Scripture quotation from the Mass of the day, as on the Annunciation, March 25: "The Holy Spirit will come upon you, Mary; and the power of the Most High will overshadow you."

- Sometimes it is a Scripture paraphrase memorializing the saint, as on December 26, the feast of Saint Stephen: "The gates of heaven opened out to blessed Stephen, and he was crowned first of martyrs."

- Sometimes it is a comment on the saint of the day, as on June 29, the feast of Saint Irenaeus: "Irenaeus, true to his name, made peace the aim and object of his life, and he labored strenuously for the peace of the Church."

5. **Weekdays in Ordinary Time**
The antiphon for the Gospel canticle, when prayed on weekdays, is simply a phrase from the canticle itself, like the refrain of the responsorial psalm at Mass. Day by day a different phrase is featured.

### Gospel canticle antiphons for Evening Prayer December 17-23

These are the ancient O Antiphons, so called because each begins with the interjection "O" in some translations. These ancient Advent

6
Prayer Book
of the Church

prayers are the antiphons for the *Magnificat* on the last seven days before Christmas (and also the alleluia verses at Mass for the same seven days).

Each O Antiphon begins with a title inspired by the Old Testament, is followed by attributes and actions of God that develop the title, and concludes with a petition commencing with the invitation "Come." The O Antiphons have been traced to an anonymous cantor of the late seventh or early eighth century. The titles of Christ that are incorporated in them originate in prayers written by Pope Saint Damasus (305?–384).

1. December 17, alluding to the responsorial psalm of the Mass (Psalm 72:3–4, 7–8, 17): "O Wisdom, O holy Word of God, you govern all creation with your strong yet tender care. Come and show your people the way to salvation."

2. December 18, alluding to the first reading of Mass, Jeremiah 23:5–8: "O Sacred Lord of ancient Israel, who showed yourself to Moses in the burning bush, who gave him the holy law on Sinai mountain: come, stretch out your mighty hand to set us free."

3. December 19, alluding to the *Benedictus* of Zechariah (1:68–79), who receives the news of the birth of his son John in the Gospel of this day's Mass (Luke 1:5–25): "O Flower of Jesse's stem, you have been raised up

as a sign for all peoples; kings stand silent in your presence; the nations bow down in worship before you. Come, let nothing keep you from coming to our aid."

4. December 20, alluding to this day's Gospel of the annunciation (Luke 1:26–38): "O Key of David, O royal power of Israel controlling at your will the gate of heaven: come, break down the prison walls of death for those who dwell in darkness and the shadow of death; and lead your captive people into freedom."

5. December 21, alluding to Malachi 3:1–4, 23–24 (first reading of December 23): "O Radiant Dawn, splendor of eternal light, sun of justice: come, shine on those who dwell in darkness and the shadow of death."

6. December 22, alluding to Hannah's prayer in the responsorial psalm of the day (1 Samuel 2:1, 4–8) and Mary's *Magnificat* in the Gospel (Luke 1:46–55): "O King of all the nations, the only joy of every human heart; O Keystone of the mighty arch of man, come and save the creature you fashioned from the dust."

7. December 23, alluding to Isaiah's Emmanuel prophecy (Isaiah 7:14): "O Emmanuel, king and lawgiver, desire of the nations, Savior of all people, come and set us free, Lord our God."(From the Liturgy of the Hours)

It has been pointed out that the initial letter of each invocation in Latin (*Sapientia*, *Adonai*, *Radix*, *Clavis*, *Oriens*, *Rex*, *Emmanuel*), in reverse order, form the acronym *"ero cras,"* Latin for "Tomorrow I shall be there." Some say this could be interpreted as Christ's response to the faithful who have daily called out "Come."

## The Intercessions

This part of the Liturgy of the Hours is similar to the familiar Prayers of the Faithful at Mass (see no. 1 below). There are also differences, as A.M. Roguet, O.P. explains in *The Liturgy of the Hours, The General Instruction with Commentary*: "The Prayer of the Faithful is a pure prayer of intercession, while the Prayers at [Morning Prayer and Evening Prayer], and above all at [Morning Prayer], have an important element of 'confession', namely the acknowledgement of the glory of God and the proclamation of our faith, on which we base our hope of being heard." There are different formulas of these intercessions provided for each of the days of the week, the liturgical seasons of the year, and feasts, not only for variety but also to more fully express the various needs of the Church, world, groups, individuals, and situations.

### 1. General Intentions

Since the Liturgy of the Hours is first of all the prayer of the whole Church for the whole Church, indeed for the salvation of the whole world, universal intentions should have priority over all others (as in the Prayers of the Faithful at Mass):

- The Church and its ministers

- The world's authorities

- The poor, the sick, and the sorrowful

- The whole world's needs (peace as well as other concerns)

### 2. Consecration

The special purpose of Morning Prayer's invocations is commending or consecrating the day and its work to God.

### 3. Adoration

The petitions, like those in the Lord's Prayer, should in some way praise and glorify God or refer to salvation history. ("Jewish and Christian tradition does not separate prayer of petition from praise of God; often enough, praise turns somehow to petition" *General Instruction of the Liturgy of the Hours*, 179.)

## The Lord's Prayer

The 1970 revision of the Liturgy of the Hours restored the Lord's Prayer in Morning Prayer and Evening Prayer. Since it's also prayed at Mass, this restoration returned the Church to the early Christian practice of saying this prayer three times daily, a tradition already testified by the Christian writer Tertullian in the third century.

1. Once every morning, at Morning Prayer
2. Once every day, at Mass
3. Once every evening, at Evening Prayer

## The Concluding Prayer

1. Sometimes the concluding prayer belongs to the day. This means that it's also used in the liturgy of the Eucharist. It will sound familiar from Mass, from which it is taken. It is called "proper" (which refers to those parts of the Mass and the Hours, which vary according to the feast or liturgical season). The following concluding prayers are typically proper: the concluding prayer of Morning Prayer, Daytime Prayer, and Evening Prayer on Sundays, on all days in Advent, Christmas, Lent, and Easter, and on feast days (solemnities, feasts, and memorials); the concluding prayer in the Office of Readings.

2. Sometimes the concluding prayer belongs to the hour. This means that it's unique to the hour (reflecting the time of the day at which it's prayed) and not taken from the Mass of the day.

   - The prayer at Morning Prayer of Monday, week 4, for example, says "God our creator, / you gave us the earth to culti-vate / and the sun to serve our needs. / Help us to spend this day / for your glory and our neighbor's good."

   - The prayer at Evening Prayer of Monday, week 4, for example, shows how the con-cluding prayer that belongs to the Hour "rounds it off," as the *Instruction* says: "Stay with us, Lord Jesus, / for eve-ning draws near, / and be our companion on our way / to set our hearts on fire with new hope. / Help us to recognize your presence among us / in the Scriptures we read, / and in the breaking of bread . . ." (This example includes language from the story of the appearance of Christ to dis-ciples on the road to Emmaus [Luke 24:13–32], illustrating the concluding prayers' com-mon allusion to Scripture.)

   - The prayer of Thursday's Night Prayer, for example, says, "Lord God, / send peaceful sleep / to refresh our tired bodies. / May your help always renew us / and keep us strong in your service."

## The Conclusion of the Hour

1. Morning Prayer and Evening Prayer end (if they are not prayed alone) as Mass does: with a greeting, a blessing, and a dismissal.

2. Night Prayer ends, after the con-cluding prayer, with the simple blessing (even when prayed privately): "May the all-power-ful Lord grant us a restful night and a peaceful death."

# The Office of Readings

The Office of Readings is not a time of the day in the sense the other hours are, but a prayer with two more extended readings. The Office of Readings provides the faithful, especially those consecrated in religious life, a greater share in the treasures of revelation and tradition.

## Psalmody

The psalms have been amended with titles, introductory sentences, antiphons, and psalm-prayers, as in the Liturgy of the Hours.

## A Verse

Between the psalmody and the readings in the Office of Readings there is regularly a verse, "forming a transition of prayer from psalmody to listening" (*General Instruction of the Liturgy of the Hours*, 63). It typically quotes or paraphrases or alludes to Scripture. During Advent, Christmas, Lent, and Easter, it reflects the character of the liturgical season. ("A voice is heard, crying in the wilderness: Prepare the way of the Lord. —Make straight the path of our God." "Christ is the true light. —He gives light to all people." "Turn back to the Lord your God. —He is kind and merciful." "My heart and my flesh, alleluia. —Rejoice in the living God, alleluia.")

## First Reading (Scripture)

The Liturgy of the Hours gives a special place to the reading of Scripture. This place is "the essential characteristic of the Office of Readings. Even if the entire Bible is not read at this Hour, at least its main passages are read in a carefully arranged order, taking into account both the chronological order of the texts and the traditional affinity of certain books to particular liturgical seasons" (A.M. Roguet, *The Liturgy of the Hours, The General Instruction with Commentary*, p. 117). Because of revisions called for by Vatican II, the Office of Readings today provides an ampler selection of Scripture than it did formerly (as does the cycle of readings at daily Mass), contributing to the spiritual life of the Church. For more on the Lectionary of the Liturgy of the Hours, see the section "The Reading" in The Elements of the Liturgy of the Hours on p. 274.

## Responsory

The responsory is like those of Morning Prayer, Evening Prayer, and the verse at Daytime Prayer, although sometimes more developed.

## Second Reading (Non-scriptural)

The Office of Readings includes, besides Scripture, "the best of the writings of Christian authors, especially of the Fathers." These are called "hagiographical" (in honor of the saints). In the choice of these readings, the first concern of the Church is that "the spiritual image of the saint and his significance for the life of the Church emerge and are placed in their true context." The purpose of the second reading is mainly to provide a meditation on Scripture that the Church has received in her tradition. The Church has always been committed to authentically teaching the word of God to the faithful, so that "the line of interpretation in regard to the prophets and apostles may follow the norm of ecclesiastical and catholic understanding" (*General Instruction of the Liturgy of the Hours*, 163, quoting Saint Vincent Lerins).

- Criteria (*General Instruction of the Liturgy of the Hours*, 166)
  1. A reading may be a text from a saint's own writings.
  2. A reading may be an account of a saint's life.
  3. A reading may refer specifically to the saint who is being commemorated.
  4. A reading may rightly be applied to the saint.

- Cautions (*General Instruction of the Liturgy of the Hours*, 167)
  1. Readings should be historically accurate.
  2. Readings should avoid anything that merely feeds the imagination.
  3. Readings should emphasize specific spiritual characteristics of the saints.
  5. Readings should be suited to modern conditions.

6. Readings should emphasize the saint's contribution to the spiritual life of the Church

## Responsory

Compared to the Scripture's responsory above, this one is connected less closely to the reading, allowing greater latitude for meditation.

## Closing Prayer

The closing prayer is taken from Morning Prayer.

# The Atmosphere

"We must recognize . . . as we celebrate the Office, our own voices echoing in Christ, his voice echoing in ours (Saint Augustine). To manifest this quality of our prayer more clearly, 'the warm and living love for holy Scripture' (*Constitution on the Sacred Liturgy*, 24) which is the atmosphere of the Liturgy of the Hours must come to life in all of us, so that Scripture may indeed become the chief source of all Christian prayer. In particular, the praying of the psalms, which continually ponders and proclaims the action of God in the history of salvation, must be embraced with new warmth by the people of God" (Apostolic Constitution of Pope Paul VI promulgating the revision of the Liturgy of the Hours, 8).

## CHAPTER 7

# Light of the Faithful

## Personal Prayer Life
### of the
## Faithful

God draws every human being toward himself, and every human being desires communion with God. Prayer is the basis and expression of the vital and personal relationship of a human person with the living and true God. . . . In prayer, the Holy Spirit not only reveals the identity of the Triune God to human persons, but also reveals the identity of the human persons to themselves.

—*National Directory for Catechesis*, p. 111

## Saint Augustine's Light

According to his *Confessions*, when he was a young man, Augustine was facing the greatest crisis in his life. After experimenting with various religious systems, he didn't know where to turn to solve his problems. One day, as he prayed even with tears, he heard a mysterious voice say, "Pick it up and read it" (*Tolle, lege*). He picked up a nearby copy of the Scriptures and it opened to Romans 13. Verses 12-14 were the first words his eyes fell on: "Let us then throw off the works of darkness and put on the armor of light; let us conduct ourselves properly as in the day, not in orgies and drunkenness, not in promiscuity and licentiousness, not in rivalry and jealously. But put on the Lord Jesus Christ, and make no provision for the desires of the flesh."

Augustine said later, "Suddenly my heart became flooded with light . . . leaving me with a profound peace." That moment became the turning point in Augustine's life. Since he had been enrolled from birth as a catechumen, he thought he'd already explored Christianity. But that day, the mysterious voice and the personal word of Scripture inspired him to complete his catechumenate and be baptized.

Augustine had already read the Scriptures in younger years, during his first exploration of Christianity, and had rejected them as not interesting or inspirational and therefore not worthwhile as the kind of guide to life for which he was searching. But this time, when he read again—for the first time, he experienced something deeper and found the real meaning of the writing.

# Scripture in the Life of the Church

"Sacred Scripture in the Life of the Church" is the title of the fifth of five points in the *Catechism* in its article on Scripture. It consists of three paragraphs (131–133) and is largely made up of quotations from Vatican II's *Constitution on Divine Revelation*. It begins with the foundational statement, "And such is the force and power of the Word of God that it can serve the Church as her support and vigor . . .[1]" (CCC, 131). The *Catechism* proceeds to specify the place of the word of God:

- In theological study: "Therefore, the 'study of the sacred page' should be the very soul of sacred theology" (CCC, 132, quoting the *Constitution on Divine Revelation*, 24).

- In pastoral ministry: "The ministry of the Word, too—pastoral preaching, catechetics, and all forms of Christian instruction, among which the liturgical homily should hold pride of place—is healthily nourished and thrives in holiness through the Word of Scripture" (CCC, 132, quoting the *Constitution on Divine Revelation*, 24).

- In personal spirituality: "The Church 'forcefully and specifically exhorts all the Christian faithful . . . to learn the surpassing knowledge of Jesus Christ (see *Philippians 3:8*), by frequent reading of the divine Scriptures" (*CCC*, 133, quoting the *Constitution on Divine Revelation*, 25).

## Scripture Source Book for Catholics

This book finds inspiration in the documents cited above for its last three chapters and their titles:

- Chapter 5, "Word of the Liturgy," which is about Scripture in the Mass and sacraments

- Chapter 6, "Prayer Book of the Church," which is about Scripture in the Liturgy of the Hours

- this chapter, "Light of the Faithful," which is about Scripture in the devotional and personal prayer life of the faithful

## "Light of the Faithful"

The title of this last chapter in the *Scripture Source Book for Catholics* uses an image common in Scripture itself. In the Gospel of John, Jesus (the Word become flesh) proclaims, "The light is with you only a little longer. Walk while you have the light, so that the darkness may not overtake you. . . . I have come as light into the world, so that everyone who believes in me should not remain in darkness" (*John 12:35, 46*). The metaphor of light for the Word of God is especially vivid in the following two examples:

1. "So we have the prophetic message more fully confirmed. You

will do well to be attentive to this as to a lamp shining in a dark place, until the day dawns and the morning star rises in your hearts" (*2 Peter 1:19*).

- Saint Augustine refers to this verse when he writes, "Learn to fix the eye of faith on the divine word of the Holy Scriptures as on a light shining in a dark place until the day dawns and the daystar arises in our hearts."

- *The New Jerome Biblical Commentary* explains further about the significance of light and dark and how the Word of God "can function as a light in darkness for those waiting for the final light, 'the morning star' (see *Revelation 2:28*), to rise with Christ's [second coming] (see *1 Thessalonians 5:4*)" (64:14).

2. "Thy word is a lamp unto my feet, and a light unto my path" (*Psalm 119:105*, King James Version). Light is an important metaphor for Scripture.

- The *Catechism* chose to use Psalm 119:105 to conclude its 41-paragraph teaching on Sacred Scripture: "'The Church has always venerated the divine Scriptures as she venerated the Body of the Lord' (Vatican II, *Constitution on Divine Revelation*, 21): both nourish and govern the whole Christian life. 'Your word is a lamp to my feet and a light to my path'[2]" (141).

- Psalm 119:105 is also used as the opening verse of the Psalter for Saturday night of Week II in the four-week Liturgy of the Hours: After that portion of Psalm 119, the psalm-prayer concludes, "Let your Word, Father, be a lamp for our feet and a light to our path, so that we may understand what you wish to teach us and follow the path your light marks out for us."

# Why Pray with Scripture

Even in infancy, when reading Scripture is impossible, knowing Scripture is not, according to *2 Timothy 3:14–15*: "But as for you, continue in what you have learned and firmly believed, knowing from whom you learned it, and how from childhood you have known the sacred writings . . ."

Vatican II in its *Constitution on Divine Revelation* spoke strong words of encouragement that the faithful be a people of the word: "Access to sacred scripture ought to be widely available to the christian faithful. . . . since the word of God must be readily available at all times, the church with motherly concern, sees to it that suitable and correct translations are made into various languages, especially from the original texts of the sacred books" (22).

In a footnote in his translation of *The Documents of Vatican II*, Fr.

Walter Abbott comments that not since the early centuries of Christianity has an official Church document urged that Scripture be available for all.

The purpose and goal of Scripture reading is declared in the last line of Vatican II's *Constitution on Divine Revelation* (26): "So may it come that, by the reading and study of the sacred books, 'the word of God may speed on and triumph' (*2 Thessalonians 3:1*) and the treasure of revelation entrusted to the church may more and more fill people's hearts. Just as from constant attendance at the eucharistic mystery the life of the church draws increase, so a new impulse of spiritual life may be expected from increased veneration of the word of God, which stands forever'" (*Isaiah 40:8*; see *1 Peter 1:23–25*). The following five points make more specific the "new surge of spiritual vitality" that the Council hoped to see in the Church.

## 1. To know Christ

The Church "forcefully and specifically exhorts all the christian faithful . . . to learn 'the surpassing knowledge of Jesus Christ,' by frequent reading of the divine scriptures. 'Ignorance of the scriptures is ignorance of Christ'" (*Constitution on Divine Revelation*, 25; referring to Philippians 3:8 and quoting Saint Jerome, repeated in CCC, 133, teaching about Scripture, and in 2653, teaching about prayer).

The first words of the widely read, fifteenth-century work, *The Imita-*

*tion of Christ* (attributed to Thomas A. Kempis), may be its most important and are certainly as central as ever to living the Christian life: "'He who follows me can never walk in darkness,' says the Lord. By these words Christ urges us to mold our lives and characters in the image of his . . . Let us therefore see that we endeavor beyond all else to meditate on the life of Jesus Christ."

### 2. To stay faithful

"For whatever was written in former days was written for our instruction, so that by steadfastness and by the encouragement of the scriptures we might have hope" (*Romans 15:4*). "[The] nourishment [of Scripture] enlightens the mind, strengthens the will and fires the hearts of men and women with the love of God" (Vatican II, *Constitution on Divine Revelation*, 14 and 23). Illustrating the power of the word, the New Testament describes Jesus' recourse to Scripture at critical times in his life:

• In the temptation (Matthew 4:1–11 and parallels), the Evangelists portray Jesus quoting Deuteronomy: ". . . one does not live by bread alone . . ." (8:3), Do not put the LORD, your God to the test . . ." (6:16), and "The LORD your God you shall fear; him you shall serve, . . ." (6:13).

• In the passion, Jesus is presented crying out in the words of *Psalm 22:2a*: "My God, my God, why have you forsaken me?" (*Matthew 27:46; Mark 15:34*) and *Psalm 31:6*:

"Father, into your hands I commend my spirit" (*Luke 23:46*).

### 3. To be saved

"[T]he sacred writings . . . are able to instruct you for salvation through faith in Christ Jesus" (*2 Timothy 3:15*).

### 4. To be equipped for good work

This phrase is from 2 Timothy, which speaks of Scripture being inspired by God and "useful." It mentions four "uses" in particular: "All scripture is inspired by God and is useful for teaching, for reproof, for correction, and for training in righteousness, so that everyone who belongs to God may be proficient, equipped for every good work" (*2 Timothy 3:16–17*).

God speaks in similar terms through Isaiah about the word and "the end for which I sent it": "For as the rain and the snow come down from heaven, / and do not return there until they have watered the earth, / making it bring forth and sprout, / giving seed to the sower and bread to the eater, / so shall my word be that goes out from my mouth; / it shall not return to me empty, / but it shall accomplish that which I purpose, / and succeed in the thing for which I sent it" (*Isaiah 55:10–11*). *The New Jerome Biblical Commentary* on this text explains, "The word comes gently from God, never intended to remain suspended like clouds in midair, but to soak the earth and to be drawn back toward God like plants and trees. God's spirit is infused within human beings where it brings forth divine fruits."

## 5. To pray

The *Catechism* cites three sources of prayer:

- first the Word of God,
- then the Liturgy of the Church,
- then the virtues of faith, hope, and charity (2653–2658)

The fourteenth-century masterpiece of Christian contemplation and mysticism, *The Cloud of Unknowing*, calls Scripture reading essential. Writing about *The Cloud of Unknowing* in his book *Catholic Spiritual Classics*, Mitch Finley says, "The three habits that are essential to the contemplative life, says the author, are reading Scripture, thinking, and prayer. 'I want you to understand clearly that . . . reading or hearing the word of God must precede pondering it and without time given to serious reflection there will be no genuine prayer.' Today he might say that these three elements are essential to any Christian life, not just for those called to monastic contemplation. To make daily times to read Scripture, and to take the trouble to learn enough about Scripture to read it as it is meant to be read, not with a naïve fundamentalist spirit, is nothing short of a radical move. To allow oneself to be challenged, as well as comforted, each day by Scripture, is to open oneself up to becoming no one's person but Christ's, no one's servant but one's neighbor's. . . . To pray each day is the culmination of reading Scripture and thinking. The two come together in a communion with the Spirit present in oneself and in one's life" (pp. 21–22).

# Scripture and the Devotional Life

Devotions are distinguished from liturgy in that they are not the public and formal prayer of the Church (the Mass, the sacraments, and the Liturgy of the Hours). A "devotion" usually refers to more than a particular prayer prayed privately (like the Hail Mary), but to a tradition among the faithful that has some structure (like the Rosary) and theme (like the passion of Christ). Devotions (like litanies and novenas) evolve historically and increase or decrease in frequency according to times in history, cultures, and individuals. The devotional life could be described as standing as a link between personal prayer and liturgy.

Devotions are "held in special esteem" by Vatican II, but "should be so drawn up that they harmonize with the liturgical seasons, accord with the sacred liturgy, are in some way derived from it, and lead the people to it . . ." (*Constitution on the Sacred Liturgy*, 13).

The renewal since Vatican II has had an important role in integrating Catholic devotions into a Christian spirituality that is clearly Scripture based. Revised devotions like the Sacred Heart devotion include catechesis and structure that explain its relationship to Scripture and use Scripture.

In many cases popular devotions have their inspiration in the truths and events recorded in Scripture. This is certainly clear in devotions like holy hours and the Way of the Cross. It may be less obvious but is no less true of others, like novenas and the Sacred Heart devotion, for example.

The following pages contain examples of the place of Scripture in the origin and practice of various devotions in the Catholic tradition: Sacred Heart devotion, the Way of the Cross, the Rosary, litanies, forty hours, holy hours, and novenas.

## Sacred Heart Devotion

Sacred Heart devotion fosters a worshipful relationship to the Person of Christ and his redeeming love, under the aspect or symbol of his heart. The *Catechism*, after explaining the image of God in the human person (355–361) and "body and soul but truly one" (362–366), goes on to say, "The spiritual tradition of the Church

also emphasizes the *heart*, in the biblical sense of the depths of one's being, where the person decides for or against God" (*CCC*, 368). It then cites Jeremiah 31:33, Deuteronomy 6:5 and 29:3, Isaiah 29:13, Ezekiel 36:26, Matthew 6:21, Luke 8:15, and Romans 5:5.

### Origins and evolution

Between AD 800 and 1000, the symbolism of Jesus' heart evolved in the venerable devotion to the humanity and wounds of Christ. Saint John Eudes (1601–1680) promoted devotion to the Sacred Heart and to the Heart of Mary, prompting Pope Pius XI to call him the father of the tradition. In apparitions to Saint Margaret Mary (1673–1675), Christ told of his concern about the indifference and coldness in the world in response to his love and asked her (among other things) to promote devotion to his heart, symbolic of his love for all. Included in these apparitions were twelve promises, several referring to the image of the heart ("I will bless every place where a picture of my heart shall be set up and honored"). The Church in her 1920 canonization implicitly approved these promises to those devoted to the Sacred Heart. The Jesuits promoted this devotion, at first through Saint Margaret Mary Alacoque's Jesuit spiritual director, Claude de la Colombiere, giving rise to the "Apostleship of Prayer" (Sacred Heart League), which popularized the Morning Offering and widely distributed the Sacred Heart badge. The "Enthronement of the Sacred Heart," a practice inspired by the promise mentioned above, is a formal acknowledge-ment of the sovereignty of the heart of Jesus over a Christian family. The "apostle" of this practice, approved by Pope Saint Pius X, was Fr. Mateo Crawley-Boevey (1875–1960), a South American Sacred Heart priest. Pope Pius XII published an encyclical in 1956 on the Sacred Heart.

### Scriptural basis

There is no evidence of specific veneration of the physical heart of Christ in Scripture. There are in Scripture, however, the key ideas that suggest and support devotion to the heart of Christ:

- **The love of God**
  The love of God for mankind is like a mother's love for her infant (see *Isaiah 49:14–15*) and like a husband's love for his wife (see *Hosea 1, 2*; *CCC*, 1604).

- **The human heart**
  The human heart, symbol of a person's deepest self, is where God has written the covenant (see *Jeremiah 31:31–34*; *CCC*, 1764–1765).

- **The love of God incarnate in Jesus**
  There are two passages in the Gospel of John that are tradition-ally cited as important parts of the scriptural foundation of the devotion to the Sacred Heart: At the feast of Tabernacles he proclaimed that "rivers of living water" will flow from within him (*John 7:38*). On the cross,

blood and water flowed from his pierced side (see *John 19:34*). With the image of flowing water, the connection was made between the promised blessings of salva-tion and the flow of blood and water from the physical lancing of the side of Christ on the cross.

## The Way of the Cross

In the devotion known as the Way of the Cross, "stations" com-memorate the stops along the *via dolorosa* (Latin: way of sorrow), Jesus' journey of about a mile from Pilate's court, the praetorium, to Calvary and the tomb. The form of this devotion common today probably originated in the practice of pilgrims visiting the Holy Land to stop and pray at various points along the way of the passion of Christ. "The Stations of the Cross developed widely along with devotion to the Passion in the 12th and 13th Centuries. The Franciscans were instrumental in this develop-ment, but it was Redemptorist, St. Alphonsus Liguori (1696–1787), who gave the devotion its modern impetus with meditations that became standard in many church-es" (John Deedy, *The Catholic Fact Book*, p. 113). Today it is common to see fourteen scenes of the passion depicted on the interior walls of a church.

Catholicism is a sacramental tradition. At the core of its prayer and ministry are seven sacraments ("outward signs, instituted by Christ, to give grace"). But even in personal and devotional prayer, "outward signs" like light, incense, gestures (upraised hands, for example), or postures (kneeling, for example) can make prayer "sacramental" instead of merely mental or verbal.

The "outward sign" of walking in a church from one station to the next, looking at a picture or image of the passion of Christ, can inspire prayer from the heart. "There is in the Way of the Cross a very incarnational symbol. As we enter into this prayer, we actually walk with Christ. Our whole body enters into the prayer. . . . We are conscious of walking with Christ, and that in the most sacred moments of his life. . . . But this walking also symbolizes what we are doing and what we want as the fruit of the prayer. We are actually walking with Christ in our lives, . . ." (Fr. Basil Pennington, *Awake in the Spirit*). At each of these fourteen points, reading words of Scripture that relate to the episode depicted can help a person "participate" in Christ's sacrifice and receive its fruits.

The following Scripture quotations, listed for each station, are from the Jerusalem Bible:

**The First Station: Jesus is condemned to death.**
"Yes, God loved the world so much that he gave his only Son, so that everyone who believes in him may not be lost but may have eternal life" (*John 3:16*).

**The Second Station: Jesus bears his cross.**
"If anyone wants to be a follower of mine, let him renounce himself and take up his cross every day and follow me" (*Luke 9:23*).

**The Third Station: Jesus falls the first time.**
"We had all gone astray like sheep, each taking his own way, and Yahweh burdened him with the sins of all of us" (*Isaiah 53:6*).

**The Fourth Station: Jesus meets his mother.**
"All you who pass this way, look and see: is any sorrow like the sorrow that afflicts me . . .?" (*Lamentations 1:12*).

**The Fifth Station: Simon of Cyrene helps Jesus carry his cross.**
"I tell you solemnly, in so far as you did this to one of the least of these brothers of mine, you did it to me" (*Matthew 25:40*).

**The Sixth Station: Veronica wipes the face of Jesus.**
"To have seen me is to have seen the Father . . ." (*John 14:9*).

**The Seventh Station: Jesus falls a second time.**
"Come to me, all you who labor and are overburdened, and I will give you rest" (*Matthew 11:28*).

**The Eighth Station: Jesus meets the women of Jerusalem.**
"Daughters of Jerusalem, do not weep for me, weep rather for yourselves and for your children" (*Luke 23:28*).

### The Ninth Station: Jesus falls a third time.
"Everyone who exalts himself will be humbled, and the man who humbles himself will be exalted" (*Luke 14:11*).

### The Tenth Station: Jesus is stripped of his garments.
"[N]one of you can be my disciple unless he gives up all his possessions" (*Luke 14:33*).

### The Eleventh Station: Jesus is nailed to the cross.
"I have come from heaven, not to do my own will, but to do the will of the one who sent me . . ." (*John 6:38*).

### The Twelfth Station: Jesus dies on the cross.
"[H]e became as men are; and being as all men are, he was humbler yet, even to accepting death, death on a cross" (*Philippians 2:7–8*).

### The Thirteenth Station: Jesus is taken down from the cross.
"Was it not ordained that the Christ should suffer and so enter into his glory?" (*Luke 24:26*).

### The Fourteenth Station: Jesus is placed in the tomb.
"[U]nless a wheat grain falls on the ground and dies, it remains only a single grain; but if it dies, it yields a rich harvest" (*John 12:24*).

## The Rosary
In their 1973 pastoral letter "Behold Your Mother," the National Council of Catholic Bishops said, "The Scriptural riches of the rosary are of permanent value" (96). In an apostolic exhortation, Pope Paul VI, calling the Rosary "a Gospel prayer," said, "[The Rosary] sets forth the mystery of Christ in the very way in which it is seen by Saint Paul in the celebrated 'hymn' of the Epistle to the Philippians—*kenosis* [self-emptying], death and exaltation (2:11). . . . By its nature the recitation of the rosary calls for a quiet rhythm and a lingering pace, helping the individual to meditate on the mysteries of the Lord's life as grasped by the heart of her who was closer to the Lord than all others" ("Devotion to the Blessed Virgin Mary," 45, 47).

In the following pages you will find a brief history of the Rosary, an explanation of the origin of the mysteries, a listing of Scriptures that underlie the mysteries, and finally suggested new ways to pray the Rosary. These suggestions might even have helped Saint Therese with this particular form of prayer: "Saint Therese of Lisieux (1873–1897) had an intense dislike for praying the rosary. She said that 'the recitation of the rosary is more difficult for me than the wearing of an instrument of penance'" (Mitch Finley, *Catholic Spiritual Classics*, p. 40).

### The history of the Rosary
The origins of the Rosary go well back into the Middle Ages. In monasteries it was the practice to allow the lay brothers (who could not read) to substitute 150 Our Fathers for the 150 psalms prayed weekly

in the Liturgy of the Hours (see Chapter 6). This practice gradually spread to the areas surrounding the monasteries, enabling the laity to participate in the Liturgy of the Hours too, using what came to be known as "the poor man's Psalter." The counting of the *"Paters"* (*pater* is Latin for father) was done on the fingers and then using pebbles in a leather pouch or knots on a cord. The beads of today's rosary evolved from these more primitive forms.

Over the course of time, a short version of the Hail Mary replaced the Lord's Prayer. (Find later in this chapter a short history of the Hail Mary.) By the eleventh century, the *Ave* (Latin for hail) had become very popular and was being prayed along with the 150 Our Fathers. Gradually the number of Our Fathers was reduced until only a few remained, along with 150 Hail Marys. Another part of the evolution of the Rosary was its division into three groups of fifty.

### The mysteries of the Rosary

At first, the Annunciation (see *Luke 1:26–38*) was the only meditation for the Rosary. Over time, other scriptural themes were introduced, even as many as 150 statements to match the 150 Hail Marys. These meditations were gradually standardized to facilitate the praying of the Rosary in common and universally. In the late 1400s, the Dominicans published "Our Lady's Psalter" with fifteen meditations or "mysteries," thirteen of which are

still used today. By 1500, the three thirds of the "poor man's Psalter" each had its own category of meditations familiar today: joyful, sorrowful, and glorious.

"[T]he Dominican rosary of 15 decades links our Lady to her Son's salvific career, from the Annunciation and the joyful events of the infancy and childhood of Jesus, through the sorrowful mysteries of His suffering and death, to His Resurrection and Ascension, and the sending of the Spirit to the apostles at Pentecost, and concluding with the Mother's reunion with her Son in the mysteries of Assumption and Coronation" (National Conference of Catholic Bishops, "Behold Your Mother," 96).

### The Scripture of the mysteries of the Rosary

Following are some samples of Scripture that underlie the mysteries. These are not only for study but also for prayer. To foster meditation, read the Scripture suggested for the various mysteries either before praying the Rosary or during it, by phrases, with the Hail Marys flowing in between them. For the assumption and the coronation—which are not biblical events, the suggested Scriptures are meditations on the themes of eternal life and glory that these two mysteries introduce. (*The Scriptural Rosary*, *Our Lady's Psalter*, and *Ten Series of Meditations on the Mysteries of the Rosary* are three standard resources for short meditations for the 150 Hail Marys of the Rosary.)

*The Joyful Mysteries*

1. The Annunciation: Isaiah 7:10–14, Luke 1:26–38
2. The Visitation: Isaiah 40:1–11, Luke 1:39–45, John 1:19–23
3. The Nativity: Micah 5:1–4, Matthew 2:1–12, Luke 2:1–20, Galatians 4:1–7
4. The Presentation: Luke 2:22–35, Hebrews 9:6–14
5. The Finding in the Temple: Luke 2:41–52, John 12:44–50, 1 Corinthians 2:6–16

*The Sorrowful Mysteries*

1. The Agony in the Garden: Matthew 26:36–46, Mark 14:32–42, Luke 22:39–46
2. The Scourging at the Pillar: Isaiah 50:5–9, Matthew 27:15–26, Mark 15:1–15
3. The Crowning with Thorns: Isaiah 52:13—53:10, Matthew 16:24–28, 27:27–31, Mark 15:16–19, Luke 23:6–11, John 19:1–7
4. The Carrying of the Cross: Mark 8:31–38, Matthew 16:20–25, Luke 23:26–32, John 19:17–22, Philippians 2:6–11
5. The Crucifixion: Mark 15:33–39, Luke 23:33–46, John 19:23–37, Acts 22:22–24, Hebrews 9:11–14

*The Glorious Mysteries*

1. The Resurrection: Matthew 28:1–10, Mark 16:1–18, Luke 24:1–12, John 20:1–10, Romans 6:1–14, 1 Corinthians 15:1–11
2. The Ascension: Matthew 28:16–20, Luke 24:44–53, Acts 1:1–11, Ephesians 2:4–7
3. The Descent of the Holy Spirit upon the Apostles: John 14:15–21, Acts 2:1–11, 4:23–31, 11:15–18

4. The Assumption of Mary: John 11:17–27, 1 Corinthians 15:20–28, 42–57, Revelation 21:1–6
5. The Coronation of Mary: Matthew 5:1–12, 2 Peter 3:10, Revelation 7:1–4, 9–12, 21:1–6

**New sets of mysteries**

In 1973 the National Conference of Catholic Bishops encouraged creativity in the use of the Rosary: "Besides the precise rosary pattern long known to Catholics, we can freely experiment. New sets of mysteries are possible. We have customarily gone from the childhood of Jesus to His Passion, bypassing the whole public life. There is rich matter here for rosary meditation. . . . Rosary vigils have already been introduced in some places, with an instructive use of readings, from the Old Testament as well as New, and with recitation of a decade or two, if not all five" (Pastoral Letter on the Blessed Virgin Mary, *Behold Your Mother*, 97).

Another possibility, instead of composing a whole new set of five mysteries, is adapting the traditional ones in order to relate the meditations of the Rosary more closely to the liturgical seasons. For example, during the Easter season (when the glorious mysteries could be given priority), the last three mysteries could be put aside and Easter appearances of the risen Christ could be inserted between the Resurrection and the Ascension.

*The Luminous Mysteries*

Pope John Paul II introduced the "mysteries of light" in 2002. The

Incarnation, the passion, and the Resurrection of Jesus Christ have been meditated upon for centuries by means of the joyful, sorrowful, and glorious mysteries. These five luminous mysteries highlight Jesus' ministry between the joyful and sorrowful mysteries (between the finding in the temple and the passion).

1. The baptism of Jesus: Matthew 3:13–17, Mark 1:9–11, Luke 3:21–22, John 1:31–34
2. The wedding feast at Cana: John 2:1–11
3. The proclamation of the coming of the Kingdom of God: Matthew 4:12–17, Mark 1:14–15, Luke 4:14–15
4. The transfiguration: Matthew 17:1–8, Mark 9:2–8, Luke 9:28–36
5. The institution of the Eucharist: Matthew 26:26–30, Mark 14:22–26, Luke 22:14–23, 1 Corinthians 10:16, 11:23–25

## Which mysteries when

"According to current practice, Monday and Thursday are dedicated to the 'joyful mysteries,' Tuesday and Friday to the 'sorrowful mysteries,' and Wednesday, Saturday and Sunday to the 'glorious mysteries.' Where might the 'mysteries of light' be inserted? If we consider that the 'glorious mysteries' are said both on Saturday and Sunday, and that Saturday has always had a special Marian flavour, the second weekly meditation on the 'joyful mysteries,' mysteries in which Mary's presence is especially pronounced, could be moved to Saturday. Thursday would then

be free for meditation on the 'mysteries of light'" (Pope John Paul II, Apostolic Letter *Rosarium Virginis Mariae*, 38).

## Merciful mysteries

The possibilities for using the beads for meditating on the life of Christ are endless. Why neglect all the material for meditation between the fifth joyful mystery and the first sorrowful mystery? The following five, for example, are inspired by the fifth petition of the Lord's prayer, "Forgive us our trespasses as we forgive those who trespass against us."

1. Jesus forgives and heals a paralyzed man (see *Matthew 9:1–8* and parallels)
2. Jesus forgives a great sinner who washed his feet (see *Luke 7:36–50*)
3. Jesus forgives a woman caught in adultery (see *John 7:53 — 8:11*)
4. Jesus forgives his executioners (see *Luke 23:34*)
5. Jesus tells the parable of the unforgiving servant: (see *Matthew 18:21–35*)

## Still more mysteries?

Here is a suggestion from Walter Kern's *New Liturgy and Old Devotions* (with slight adaptations) for updating the Rosary by composing even more sets of mysteries, opening up more of the richness of Scripture. This idea provides one set for each day of the week by adding four new sets to the traditional three. (These suggestions pre-date Pope John Paul II's Mysteries of Light.)

## Mondays: The Genesis Mysteries

1. God is infinitely perfect and happy (see *Psalm 145:1–13, 21*)
2. God creates to show his love and goodness (see *Psalm 19:1–5*)
3. God created the world and man (see *Genesis 1:1–31*)
4. God is sinned against (see *Genesis 3:1–13*)
5. God promised a redeemer (see *Genesis 3:14–16*)

## Tuesdays: Preparation for the Redeemer

1. The Israelites are chosen by God (see *Genesis 12:1–3* or *Hosea 11:1–9*)
2. God makes a covenant at Sinai (see *Exodus 19:2–9*)
3. The kings and prophets help in this plan of God (see *Psalm 132:11–18*)
4. The covenant is broken by sin again and again (see *Isaiah 5:1–7, Psalm 106*)
5. God remains faithful to the covenant (see *Psalm 105, Isaiah 49:8–18*)

## Wednesdays: The Joyful Mysteries

Already listed earlier in this chapter (see p. 296).

## Thursdays: The Doctrinal Mysteries

1. Jesus is "the way, and the truth, and the life" (*John 14:1–7*)
2. Jesus teaches us to love God with our whole being (see *Luke 10:25–37*)
3. Jesus teaches us to love and forgive (see *Matthew 5:43–48, 18:21–35*)
4. Jesus teaches love for the poor (see *Matthew 12:15–21, Luke 14:12–15*)
5. Jesus urges a loving community (see *John 15:9–17*)

## Fridays: The Sorrowful Mysteries

Already listed earlier in this chapter (see p. 296).

## Saturdays: The Glorious Mysteries

Already listed earlier in this chapter (see p. 296).

## Sundays: The Final Mysteries

1. Jesus is head of all people and creation (see *Ephesians 1:3–14*)
2. Jesus is head of the Church (see *Colossians 1:24–29, Matthew 28:16–20*)
3. Jesus is the eternal reward of the faithful (see *Colossians 1:15–23*)
4. Jesus will judge the living and the dead (see *Revelation 20:11–14, 21:1–8*)
5. Jesus gives all things to the Father (see *Ephesians 2:1–10*)

### Integrating the mysteries and the Hail Marys

"At one time there was a custom, still preserved in certain places, of adding to the name Jesus in each Hail Mary a reference to the mystery being contemplated. And this was done precisely in order to help contemplation and to make the mind and voice act in unison" (Pope Paul VI, "Marian Devotions," 46). In *New Liturgy and Old Devotions*, Walter Kern includes some samples of this practice, "adapted from a prayerbook for Byzantine-Slavonic rite Catholics." (These phrases are inserted in the middle of the Hail Mary after the word "Jesus.")

## The Joyful Mysteries

1. . . . Jesus, who was heralded by the angel. Holy Mary . . .
2. . . . Jesus, whom you carried to visit Elizabeth. Holy Mary . . .
3. . . . Jesus, who was born of you in Bethlehem. Holy Mary . . .
4. . . . Jesus, whom you presented in the temple. Holy Mary . . .
5. . . . Jesus, whom you found again in the temple. Holy Mary . . .

## The Sorrowful Mysteries

1. . . . Jesus, who suffered in agony in the garden. Holy Mary . . .
2. . . . Jesus, who was scourged for us. Holy Mary . . .
3. . . . Jesus, who was crowned with thorns. Holy Mary . . .
4. . . . Jesus, who carried the cross for us. Holy Mary . . .
5. . . . Jesus, who was crucified for us. Holy Mary . . .

## The Glorious Mysteries

1. . . . Jesus, who rose gloriously for us. Holy Mary . . .
2. . . . Jesus, who triumphantly ascended into heaven. Holy Mary . . .
3. . . . Jesus, who sent the Spirit upon the apostles. Holy Mary . . .
4. . . . Jesus, who took you into heavenly glory. Holy Mary . . .
5. . . . Jesus, who crowned you queen of all. Holy Mary . . .

## Litanies

A litany (from a Greek word meaning entreaty) is a form of prayer made up of a succession of salutations or invocations, each followed by a responsive petition, typically "have mercy on us" (when addressed to Jesus or God) or "pray for us" (when addressed to one of the saints). Among the many litanies of the Catholic Tradition are the Litany of the Saints, the Litany of the Blessed Mother, and the Litany of the Holy Name.

### The format

There are models in Scripture for the litany structure of prayer.

1. Psalm 136, for example, sings of God's everlasting love. It invites the response "[God's] love endures forever" after no less than twenty-six different proclamations, beginning with ". . . give thanks to the LORD, for he is good . . .," continuing with a catalogue of God's creation, redemption, and providence, and culminating with "O give thanks to the God of heaven . . ."

2. Likewise, in Daniel 3:52–90, the three youths, Shadrach, Meshach, and Abednego, thrown into the "furnace of blazing fire" by Nebuchadnezzar, sing the praises of God. They bless God in various ways and then, through thirty-eight invocations, call upon the various elements of nature and all the holy people of God to respond with the acclamation: ". . . to be praised and highly exalted forever . . ." and (in the second part of the canticle) ". . . to be highly praised and highly exalted forever . . ."

### Litanies of Christ

Some of the titles and invocations in these litanies are familiar from

Scripture from which some of the language and imagery comes. The following examples are taken from the Litany of the Holy Name and the Litany of the Sacred Heart. (After each invocation, the response "Have mercy on us" is made.)

1. **Phrases familiar from Scripture**
   Lamb of God, Son of the living God, Good shepherd, Sun of justice, Our way and our life, In whom the Father was well pleased, Bruised for our offenses, Desire of the everlasting hills

2. **Scriptural images and allusions**
   There are various images, some from the Old Testament and some from the New, as well as others reflecting the Church piety, assigned to Jesus. Examples include Splendor of the Father, Brightness of eternal light, Eternal wisdom, In whom dwells the fullness of divinity, Sacred temple of God, Our life and resurrection, Victim for our sins, Salvation of those who trust in you, Teacher of the Evangelists, Son of the Virgin Mary, Mighty God, God of peace, Example

## "Desire of the Everlasting Hills"

This title for Christ, included in the Litany of the Sacred Heart, is from Jacob's blessing of Joseph, the last of the patriarchs, in Genesis 49:22-26. An earlier translation of the Old Testament, the Douay Version, rendered verse 26, "The blessings of thy father are strengthened with the blessings of his fathers: until the desire of the everlasting hills should come. . . ."

Today those verses read, "Harrying and attacking,/ the archers opposed him;/ But each one's bow remained stiff,/ as their arms were unsteady,/ By the power of the Mighty one of Jacob, . . ./ The God of your father, who helps you,/ God Almighty, who blesses you,/ With the blessings of the heavens above, . . ./ The blessings of the everlasting mountains,/ the delights of the eternal hills./ May they rest on the head of Joseph,/ on the brow of the prince among his brothers" (revised NAB translation).

Why the significant differences in translations? About "Jacob's Testament" (Genesis 49:1-27), the *Collegeville Commentary* says, "The text is corrupt and parts of the poem are untranslatable, compounding the problems of interpretation." ("Corrupt" in the world of textual criticism usually means that the manuscripts used for reconstructing the original text are damaged in this place, possibly involving torn or crumbled manuscript pages, flaking ink, or worm holes, for example. For more on this topic, see "Textual Criticism" in Chapter 4.)

Bringing this phrase from the Book of Genesis and applying it to Christ is an example of the allegorizing of Scripture that was popular in the medieval period. A footnote from the old Douay translation commented on the blessings listed in verses 25 and 26 and the phrase *the desire of the everlasting hills*: "These blessings all looked forward towards Christ, called *the desire of the everlasting hills*, as being longed for, as it were, by the whole creation. Mystically, the patriarchs and prophets are called the *everlasting hills*, by reason of the eminence of their wisdom and holiness." (For more on the allegorical sense of Scripture, see Chapter 4.)

of virtues, Our refuge, Formed by the Holy Spirit in the womb of the Virgin Mother, Abode of justice and love, Most worthy of all praise, Pierced with a lance, Patient and most merciful

### The Litany of the Blessed Mother

The Litany of the Blessed Mother (or "Litany of Loreto") dates from the sixteenth century. It became popular because of its use by pilgrims coming from all over Europe to the shrine in Loreto. Still used today, it has rich images of Mary derived from Scripture as well as the Church's history and tradition.

This litany is a reflection of Marian piety at the time it was created—a piety based on the Gospel stories about Mary the mother of Jesus. ("Pray for us" is repeated after each invocation.)

## Forty Hours

The period of time in the title (and practice) of this Blessed Sacrament devotion was inspired by Scripture's description of the passion of Christ. The Blessed Sacrament is solemnly exposed in a monstrance for adoration in honor of the forty hours the body of Jesus was

---

### The Song of Songs

The love described in the "greatest of songs" has been variously interpreted: the mutual love between God and the people of God, an inspired portrayal of ideal human love, the union between Christ and the Church, and the union between Christ and the individual soul.

The revised NAB introduction to the book observes, "Throughout the liturgy, especially in the Little Office [a shortened form of the Liturgy of the Hours, once common, in honor of Mary], there is a consistent application of the Song of Songs to the Blessed Virgin Mary."

Likewise, the Litany of the Blessed Mother may also contain allusions to the Song of Songs. The attribution "Tower of David" may allude to Song of Songs 4:4 ("Your neck is like the tower of David"); it represents Mary's high perfection. "Tower of ivory" may allude to Song of Songs 7:5 ("Your neck is like a tower of ivory"); it represents her strength and stateliness. These two terms, like "House of gold," may also allude to the incarnation and Mary's role as God-bearer. "Help of Christians" may be an interpretation of Song of Songs 6:4 ("You are . . . as an army with banners").

In Catholic Tradition the "mystical rose" refers to Mary and is a common symbol of the nativity. Marian symbolism has been read into the enclosed garden of Song of Songs 4:12, 5:1, 6:2, and 6:11; in the rose references or inferences in texts like Song of Songs 2:1, Sirach 24:14, and Sirach 39:13; and in the rose itself, queen of the flowers. The mystical rose usually appears as a stylized, five-petalled rose, its five petals representing the five joyful mysteries.

The familiar emblem of Martin Luther consists of a black cross on a red heart against the Marian rose on a heavenly blue background within a gold circle, symbolizing eternity. (The "messianic rose," also known as the "rose of Sharon"–an interpretation of Songs 2:1, refers to Christ.)

believed to have been in the tomb: by tradition, nine hours on Good Friday (3 PM to midnight), twenty-four hours on Holy Saturday, and seven hours on Easter Sunday (midnight to 7 AM). This devotion was introduced by Saint Anthony Mary Zaccaria in 1527 and made popular by the promotion of the Jesuits in many countries of the world. (To make this a more practical public prayer, the Forty Hours devotion was traditionally interrupted for the night and extended over three days.)

## Holy Hours

Making a holy hour is a specific kind of keeping vigil that commemorates Jesus' agony in the garden. Like so many other devotions, it was inspired by Scripture: "So, you could not stay awake with me one hour? Stay awake and pray that you may not come into the time of trial" (*Matthew 26:40–41*).

## Novenas

A novena is a prayer or devotion with a specific intention offered nine days in a row, originating in the nine (*novem* in Latin) days of prayer in the upper room by the disciples and Mary between the Ascension of Christ (see *Acts 1:6–12*) and the coming of the Spirit (see *Acts 2:1–13*). The first community of Christians in Jerusalem is described in *Acts 1:14*: "All these [the Apostles] were constantly devoting themselves to prayer, together with certain women, including Mary the mother of Jesus, as

well as his brothers." Historically, the novena also took the form of extending through nine weeks with the devotions on a particular day each week. At one time novenas were among the most popular of the Church's devotions. There was a "novena of grace," for example, in March and a "Christmas Novena" beginning on December 16 in honor of the mystery of the Incarnation. Today the recommended (and only scriptural) novena is the one before Pentecost. Here are three suggestions for a novena prayer today:

- The traditional prayer, "Come, Holy Spirit" (which quotes Psalm 104). It can be found later in this chapter (see p. 330).

- A prayer from the Sacramentary: "God our Father, / you gave the Holy Spirit to your apostles / as they joined in prayer with Mary, the mother of Jesus. / By the help of her prayers / keep us faithful in your service / and let our words and actions be so inspired / as to bring glory to your name" (Opening Prayer, Common of the Blessed Virgin, 6).

- Saint Augustine's prayer to the Holy Spirit: "Breathe in me, O Holy Spirit, That my thoughts may all be holy. Act in me, O Holy Spirit, That my work, too, may be holy. Draw my heart, O Holy Spirit, That I love but what is holy. Strengthen me, O Holy Spirit, To defend all that is holy. Guard me, then, O Holy Spirit, That I always may be holy."

# Praying with Scripture

There is no human effort, no method, no suggestion in the following pages, more important than the Spirit of God (the Spirit who inspired the Scriptures) in praying—certainly in praying with Scripture: "Likewise the Spirit helps us in our weakness . . ." (*Romans 8:26–27*).

There are many, many resources available today to help facilitate praying with Scripture. *The Catholic Bible Study Handbook* by Jerome Kodell, O.S.B. (2001), mentioned in Chapter 4, includes several helpful bibliographies, including "Aids for Private Bible Study," "Aids for Group Bible Study," and "Aids for Praying the Bible."

The following are some examples of ways to pray with Scripture: through personal reading, group faith sharing, and Bible study groups, and by using Scripture in the devotional life.

### Personal Reading

A regular reading of Scripture that is guided in some way is more likely to bear fruit than reading with no plan, lectionary, commentary, or Scripture-based devotional.

- Reading the Scriptures assigned for the upcoming Sunday in the Lectionary would not only provide a helpful, guided, and structured reading of the Bible, but it would also help bring alive Sunday's word proclaimed at Mass.

- Lectionary-based "daily devotionals" are becoming more and more commonplace, especially in the liturgical seasons of Advent and Lent. There are many available. They are not meant to replace the reading of Scripture itself, but to offer some commentary or reflection to help the reader understand and apply the Scripture personally.

There are ideas in Chapter 4 that will help the reader choose a specific Bible (a particular Scripture translation) and possibly resources, also explained in that chapter, like commentaries, concordances, handbooks, and dictionaries. Following are three suggestions for enriching the personal reading of Scripture: using *Lectio Divina*, finding oneself in the salvation story, and answering Scripture's questions.

### Lectio Divina

*Lectio Divina* (literally, "divine reading") is a traditional Christian practice deeply ingrained in the monastic tradition, especially in Benedictine monasteries. It's a way of reading and meditating on Scripture. *Lectio Divina* is commonly left in Latin because it is such an ancient practice and has been known by this term for centuries. Calling it "spiritual reading," for example, would liken it too much to the contemporary practice of reading for insights about the spiritual life. Using the term "prayerful reading" instead of *lectio divina* would be closer to capturing its practice and its purpose.

Using the word of God, one is led by the Spirit to the highest levels of communion with God. *Lectio Divina* is summed up in the classic wording of Guigo II, a 12th-century Carthusian abbot, in his Ladder of Monks (using language from *Matthew 7:7* in the Sermon on the Mount, "search, and you will find; knock, and the door will be opened for you"): Seek in reading, find in meditating, knock in mental prayer, and it will be opened in contemplation.

## Step One: Reading

"Christian prayer tries above all to meditate on the mysteries of Christ, as in *lectio divina* or the rosary," the *Catechism* says (2708). It teaches that books, of which we have a rich supply, usually help us. The *Catechism* mentions seven types:

- Sacred Scriptures, particularly the Gospels

- holy icons

- liturgical texts of the day or season

- writings of the spiritual fathers

- works of spirituality

- the great book of creation

- history—the page on which the "today" of God is written (CCC, 2705)

Scripture, of course, is first on the list. There are many passages that many people have heard or read many times. Familiarity can be a reward of regular Scripture reading but also a danger (even "breeding contempt"). The attitude of expectation is essential, as if reading or hearing a passage for the first time. Sometimes a person has to "stare at the familiar until it becomes strange," as G. K. Chesterton once said.

## Step Two: Meditation

If the first step of *lectio divina*, reading, is an exercise of the outward senses, providing the subject for meditation, then the second step, thinking, is concerned with understanding. And silence. Vatican II's *Constitution on the Sacred Liturgy* refers to "sacred silence" (30), also called for by the *General Instruction of the Liturgy of the Hours* (202–203), which proceeds to explain its purpose: To "receive in our hearts the full resonance of the voice of the Holy Spirit," to "unite our personal prayer more closely with the word of God and the public voice of the Church," and to meditate "on some text that moves the spirit."

- "Meditation is above all a quest. The mind seeks to understand the why and how of the Christian life, in order to adhere and respond to what the Lord is asking" (CCC, 2705).

- "To meditate on what we read helps us to make it our own by confronting it with ourselves. Here, another book is opened: the book of life" (CCC, 2706).

- "Meditation engages thought, imagination, emotion, and desire. This mobilization of faculties is necessary in order to deepen our convictions of faith, prompt the conversion of our heart, and strengthen our will to follow Christ" (*CCC*, 2708).

- "This form of prayerful reflection is of great value, but Christian prayer should go further: to the knowledge of the love of the Lord Jesus, to union with him" (*CCC*, 2708).

### Step Three: Responding

The third step of *lectio divina*, responding, is concerned with desire. The *Catechism* speaks of various "forms" of prayer (2626–2643), including:

- Petition, the objects of which are (in this order) the grace of forgiveness, the quest for the kingdom, the conditions and dispositions for welcoming the kingdom, and every need

- Intercession (which is asking on behalf of another)

- Thanksgiving

- Praise

"Through his Word, God speaks to man. By words, mental or vocal, our prayer takes flesh" (*CCC*, 2700). "Even interior prayer . . . cannot neglect vocal prayer. Prayer is internalized to the extent that we become aware of him 'to whom we speak.'[3] Thus vocal prayer becomes an initial form of contemplative prayer" (*CCC*, 2704, citing Saint Teresa of Jesus).

The *General Instruction of the Liturgy of the Hours* reflects this same dynamic of reading/listening/praying when it says that prayer should accompany "the reading of Sacred Scripture so that there may be a conversation between God and man: 'we talk with God when we pray, we listen to him when we read God's words' (Saint Ambrose)" (56).

### Step Four: Contemplation

The fourth step of *lectio divina*, resting, rewards the labors of the first three steps. The *Catechism* begins its treatment of contemplative prayer by quoting Saint Teresa, "Contemplative prayer . . . in my opinion is nothing else than a close sharing between friends; it means taking time frequently to be alone with him who we know loves us[4]" (*CCC*, 2709).

- "Contemplative prayer seeks him 'whom my soul loves' (*Songs 1:7*). . . . In this inner prayer we can still meditate, but our attention is fixed on the Lord himself" (*CCC*, 2709).

- "One cannot always meditate, but one can always enter into inner prayer, independently of the conditions of health, work, or emotional state. The heart is the place of this quest and encounter, in poverty and in faith" (*CCC*, 2710).

- "Contemplative prayer is *silence*, the 'symbol of the world to come'[5] or 'silent love.'[6] Words in this kind of prayer are not speeches; they are like kindling that feeds the fire of love. In this silence, unbearable to the 'outer' man, the Father speaks to us his incarnate Word, who suffered, died, and rose; in this silence the Spirit of adoption enables us to share in the prayer of Jesus" (*CCC*, 2717, citing Saint Isaac of Nineveh and Saint John of the Cross).

## Finding Oneself in the Salvation Story

In explaining the place of Scripture in the life of the Church, Vatican II's *Constitution on Divine Revelation* says, "In the sacred books the Father who is in heaven comes lovingly to meet his children, and talks with them" (21). If we think of Scripture as the story of salvation through which God communicates with us, one way to engage the story is to find characters with whom we can identify and invite the text to speak to us. Many of the faithful have discovered their own story in Scripture. The various characters found in its pages have illumined our own lives. The following example is from a homily by Saint Gregory Nazianzen, bishop, quoted in the Office of Readings, Saturday of the fifth week of Lent. (For your reflection, the Scripture texts alluded to are interjected in the homily.)

- "If you are a Simon of Cyrene, take up your cross and follow Christ." (See *Matthew 27:32*: "As they went out, they came upon a man from Cyrene named Simon; they compelled this man to carry his cross.")

- "If you are crucified beside him like one of the thieves, now, like the good thief, acknowledge your God." (See *Luke 23:33, 39–42*: "When they came to the place that is called The Skull, they crucified Jesus there with the criminals, one on his right and one on his left . . . One of the criminals who were hanged there kept deriding him and saying, 'Are you not the Messiah? Save yourself and us!' But the other rebuked him, saying, 'Do you not fear God, since you are under the same sentence of condemnation? And we indeed have been condemned justly, for we are getting what we deserve for our deeds, but this man has done nothing wrong.' Then he said, 'Jesus, remember me when you come into your kingdom.'")

- "If you are a Joseph of Arimathea, go to the one who ordered his crucifixion, and ask for Christ's body." (See *John 19:38*: "After these things, Joseph of Arimathea, who was a disciple of Jesus, though a secret one because of his fear of the Jews, asked Pilate to let him take away the body of Jesus. Pilate gave him permission; so he came and removed his body.")

- "If you are a Nicodemus, like the man who worshiped God by night, bring spices and prepare Christ's body for burial." (See *John 19:39–40*: "Nicodemus, who had at first come to Jesus at night, also came, bringing a mixture of myrrh and aloes, weighing about a hundred pounds. They took the body of Jesus and wrapped it with the spices in linen cloths, according to the burial custom of the Jews.")

• "If you are one of the Marys, or Salome, or Joanna, weep in the early morning. Be the first to see the stone rolled back, and even the angels perhaps, and Jesus himself." (See *Luke 24:1–4, 10:* "But on the first day of the week, at early dawn, they came to the tomb, taking the spices that they had prepared. They found the stone rolled away from the tomb, but when they went in, they did not find the body. While they were perplexed about this, suddenly two men in dazzling clothes stood beside them. Now it was Mary Magdalene, Joanna, [and] Mary the mother of James . . .")

## Answering Scripture's Questions

Of course Scripture has answers to life's questions, but if there are no questions, no curiosity, of what use are answers? For some, the value of Scripture is less in the right answers it gives and more in the critical questions it poses—questions the faithful must find the courage to answer. Here are seven for starters, beginning with Herod's. (See "Rhetorical Questions" in Appendix 2, "Figures of Speech in Scripture" for these and more.)

• "John I beheaded; but who is this about whom I hear such things?" (Herod wondering about Jesus in

*Luke 9:9*; for others who wonder, the verses that follow give some answers: the story of the multiplication of the loaves, Peter's profession of faith, Jesus' transfiguration, and a prediction of the passion.)

• "What are you looking for?" (Jesus questioning John's disciples, *John 1:38.*)

• "But who do you say that I am?" (Jesus questioning his disciples, *Matthew 16:15.*)

• "You of little faith, why did you doubt?" (Jesus questioning Peter after the walking on the water, *Matthew 14:31.*)

• "Which of these three . . . was a neighbor to the man who fell into the hands of the robbers?" (Jesus questioning the scholar of the law after the Good Samaritan story, *Luke 10:36.*)

• "Do you also wish to go away?" (Jesus questioning the Twelve after the Bread of Life discourse, *John 6:67.*)

• "[D]o you love me?" (Jesus questioning Peter after his Resurrection appearance on the shore, *John 21:16.*)

• "What are you discussing with each other while you walk along?" (Jesus, during a Resurrection appearance, questioning two disciples walking to Emmaus, *Luke 24:17.*)

## Group Faith Sharing

The following simple process is suggested in the 1982 document of the United States Bishops' Committee on Priestly Life and Ministry, *Fulfilled in Your Hearing*. In a chapter called "Homiletic Method," it suggests preachers prepare with the listeners in a "Homily Preparation Group." It lists seven specific steps. This same process can be used for common reflection on Scripture, apart from homily preparation with a priest or deacon.

1. **Read the passage(s).** (15 minutes)
   In the case of preparation for Sunday Mass, the recommendation is to start with the Gospel, then turn to the Old Testament reading, then the response, and finally the New Testament reading. Any Scripture, of course, could be used in this process.
2. **Share the words.** (10 minutes) This is not merely discussion but a time for participants to "share the words or phrases which resonated and fired the imagination." This reveals the concerns, questions, and interests of those assembled.
3. **Interpret the text.** (10 minutes) This is about the "literal" sense of the text—not a literalist reading (see Chapter 4), but an understanding of what the author intended to say and what concerns were being addressed in the original audience. This is the part of the process called "exegesis," an exercise described in Chapter 4.
4. **Share the good news.** (10 minutes)
   What good news did the first

listeners hear in these accounts? What good news does the group hear? Where is God's promise, power, and influence in our personal story present in the readings?

5. **Share the challenge these words offer.** (10 minutes) Is there a sin or pain or doubt exposed by these words? Is there a conversion called for? This is an important time for personalism, not generalities.
6. **Explore the consequences.** (5 minutes)
   What difference could this make in my life? What are the possibilities? Ultimately, could the world be changed?
7. **Give thanks and praise.** (5 minutes)
   The conclusion of this process is a prayer of thanksgiving for God's saving Word.

## Bible Study Groups

Bible study groups take many forms: Some are essentially prayer groups while others are more like book clubs or discussion groups; some go through a particular book of the Bible while others are Lectionary-based, using the Scriptures of the upcoming Sunday. Each group has its merits.

A person should pay attention to the denominational character of Bible study groups: Is it sponsored by or made up of members of one particular Church? A Baptist Bible study group, for example, will be quite different from a Catholic Bible study group. This doesn't mean that a Catholic shouldn't participate in a Baptist Bible study group, but he/she should be clear that differing understandings of inspiration/inerrancy/authority of the Bible will result in different methods and ultimately different interpretations of biblical texts.

If a person wants a deeper understanding of Catholic faith, he/she should instead seek out a parish adult education program, remembering the three-fold suggestion of Vatican II's *Constitution on Divine Revelation* (25): "all the Christian faithful . . . [should] go gladly to the sacred text itself, whether in

- the sacred liturgy, which is full of the divine words; or
- in devout reading; or
- in such suitable exercises and various other helps . . ."

## Using Scripture in the Devotional Life

Devotions are treated, with examples, earlier in this chapter in a section called "Scripture and the Devotional Life." They are Scripture-based and some, like the Rosary and the Stations of the Cross, are ways of praying with Scripture.

# Praying Scripture's Prayers

In one of its summary statements about the life of the apostolic Church, the Acts of the Apostles says, "They devoted themselves to the apostles' teaching and

fellowship, to the breaking of bread and the prayers" (*Acts 2:42*; see also 4:32–37 and 5:12–16). About this passage, the *Catechism* says, "This sequence is characteristic of the Church's prayer: founded on the apostolic faith; authenticated by charity; nourished in the Eucharist" (2624). "In the first place these are prayers that the faithful hear and read in the Scriptures, but also that they make their own—especially those of the Psalms . . . The *forms of prayer* revealed in the apostolic and canonical Scriptures remain normative for Christian prayer" (2625).

## The Psalter (See CCC, 2585-2589)

The 150 psalms are the prayer book of the Church. When Christians pray the psalms, they often see images of Jesus and the Church in them. Christians must remember, however, that first of all the psalms are the prayers of the Jewish people and the Christian interpretation of a given psalm is not the first or only interpretation. See Chapter 6, "The Prayer Book of the Church," for help in understanding the psalms, using them for prayer, and overcoming the difficulties they sometimes pose.

## Other Prayers from the Old Testament

After the following lists, there are descriptions of how prayers in Scripture can shape our own prayer (using prayers of Hezekiah, Ezra, and Esther as examples).

## The "Five Books of Psalms"

Traditionally, five "books" of psalms are identified according to five doxologies (prayers or acclamations giving glory to God) that conclude each unit. Some have detected a correspondence between these five books and the five books of the Pentateuch.

1. Psalms 1-41 (ending with the doxology of Psalm 41:14)

- Correspond to the book of Genesis

- Highlight the relationship between God and human beings

2. Psalms 42-72 (ending with the doxology of Psalm 72:18-19)

- Correspond to the book of Exodus

- Highlight God's relationship to Israel

3. Psalms 73-89 (ending with the doxology of Psalm 89:53)

- Correspond to the book of Leviticus

- Highlight the sanctuary

4. Psalms 90-106 (ending with the doxology of Psalm 106:48)

- Correspond to the book of Numbers

- Highlight the earth and creation

5. Psalms 107-150 (ending with the doxology of Psalm 150—all of it)

- Correspond to the book of Deuteronomy

- Highlight the Word of God

### Old Testament canticles

The word canticle means "little song" in Latin (*canticulum*). These sacred prayers, along with the psalms, are still used today, especially in the Liturgy of the Hours. (The first list that follows is a list of the 25 canticles that are included in the Liturgy of the Hours; see Chapter 6 for when they are scheduled in the four-week Psalter.) See also CCC, 2568–2584.

- Moses' song of deliverance, Exodus 15:1–18

- Song of Moses: God's benefits to his people, Deuteronomy 32:1–12

- Song of Hannah offering up Samuel, 1 Samuel 2:1–10

- David's song, 1 Chronicles 29:10–13

- Tobit's song of praise, Tobit 13:1–8

- Tobit's song of praise (addressed to Jerusalem), Tobit 13:8–11, 13–15

- Judith's song of praise, Judith 16:2–3a, 13–15

- Solomon's prayer for wisdom, Wisdom 9:1–11

- Sirach's prayer for God's people, Sirach 36:1–5, 10–13

- Isaiah's song: Zion, city of the Messiah, Isaiah 2:2–5

- Thanksgiving song of the redeemed, Isaiah 12:1–6
- The divine vindicator, Isaiah 26:1–4, 7–9, 12
- Isaiah's song: just judgment of God, Isaiah 33:13–16
- Hezekiah's song of thanksgiving, Isaiah 38:10–20

- Isaiah's song: promise of salvation, Isaiah 40:10–17
- A new song to the Messiah and Lord, Isaiah 42:10–16
- Isaiah's song to the hidden God, Isaiah 45:15–25
- Israel renewed, Isaiah 61:10— 62:5

## A Prayer of Ezra

Ezra has been called a kind of second Moses. He was a reformer and purifier of the people during the time of the restoration after the Babylonian captivity (587-537 BC). One of his prayers is recorded in Scripture.

### The Prayer

"O my God, I am too ashamed and embarrassed to lift my face to you, my God, for our iniquities have risen higher than our heads, and our guilt has mounted up to the heavens. From the days of our ancestors to this day we have been deep in guilt, and for our iniquities we, our kings, and our priests have been handed over to the kings of the lands . . . But now for a brief moment favor has been shown by the LORD our God, who has left us a remnant, and given us a stake in his holy place, in order that he may brighten our eyes and grant us a little sustenance in our slavery. For we are slaves; yet our God has not forsaken us in our slavery, but has extended to us his steadfast love before the kings of Persia, to give us new life to set up the house of our God, to repair its ruins, and to give us a wall in Judea and Jerusalem.

And now, our God, what shall we say after this? For we have forsaken your commandments, which you commanded by your servants the prophets . . . After all that has come upon us for our evil deeds and for our great guilt, seeing that you, our God, have punished us less than our iniquities deserved and have given us such a remnant as this, shall we break your commandments . . .? O LORD, God of Israel, you are just, but we have escaped as a remnant, as is now the case. Here we are before you in our guilt, though no one can face you because of this" (*Ezra 9:6-11, 13-15*).

### The Pronouns

The pronouns in Ezra's prayer that evolve from "I" to "we" to "you" (God) illustrate an important feature of good intercessory prayer: Ezra begins with a personal statement ("O my God, I am too ashamed and embarrassed to lift my face to you . . ."), then speaks on behalf of the community (as an intercessor): "our iniquities . . . our heads . . . our guilt . . ." After this confession of sin, there is another shift in Ezra's prayer, from the guilt of the people—including his own—to the mercy and the love and the faithfulness of God: "But now for a brief moment . . ." From this point on, the prayer is all about God: "favor has been shown by the LORD our God . . . who (God) has left us a remnant, and given us a stake in his holy place . . that he may brighten our eyes . . . our God has not forsaken us . . ."

- Song of joy to the Holy City, Isaiah 66:10–14
- Lament over Zion's guilt, Jeremiah 14:17–21

- God will gather his people, Jeremiah 31:10–14
- Renewal of God's people, Ezekiel 36:24–28

## You, You, You

### King Hezekiah's Prayer

The remarkable King Hezekiah was a devout successor of David. "He did what was right in the sight of the LORD just as his ancestor David had done" (*2 Kings 18:3*). During his time, Israel's great crisis was the threat of Assyria. One of Hezekiah's prayers recorded in Scripture was offered on the occasion of the insulting threats of King Sennacherib. Instead of giving in to fear, Hezekiah (unlike some of his predecessors) presented his troubles to God. In 2 Kings 19, the king is interceding on behalf of the nation. His prayer includes an important element in the tradition of biblical prayer. It's the way he addresses God. "O LORD the God of Israel, <u>who</u> are enthroned above the cherubim, <u>you</u> are God, <u>you</u> alone, of all the kingdoms of the earth; <u>you</u> have made heaven and earth. Incline your ear, O LORD, and hear . . . ," always acknowledging God as a personal God who is known by his activity in the world (*2 Kings 19:15-16*).

### Queen Esther's Prayer

The prayer of Queen Esther, Woman of Courage, shows another example of honoring the name of God; instead of speaking immediately of her needs and her nation's crisis, she instead makes God the subject of her prayer: "<u>O my Lord</u>, you only are our king . . . <u>you, O Lord</u>, took Israel out of all the nations, and our ancestors from among all the forebears, for an everlasting inheritance, and that <u>you</u> did for them all that <u>you</u> promised . . ." (*Esther C14:1-19*). Most of Esther's prayer, in fact, "reminds" God of the divine deeds of the past. In the process, Esther is reminded of who God is.

### The Church's Prayer

The Church prays in this same tradition. The following example is from the Liturgy of the Hours, the intercessions of Holy Saturday's Morning Prayer.

Christ our savior, <u>your sorrowing Mother</u> stood by you at your death and burial,/ –in our sorrows may we share your suffering.

Christ our Lord, like the seed buried in the ground, <u>you brought forth</u> for us the harvest of grace,/ –may we die to sin and live for God.

Christ, the Good Shepherd, in death <u>you lay hidden</u> from the world,/ –teach us to love a life hidden with you in the Father.

Christ, the new Adam, <u>you entered the kingdom of death</u> to release all the just since the beginning of the world,/ –may all who lie dead in sin hear your voice and rise to life.

Christ, Son of the living God, through baptism we were buried with you,/ –risen also with you in baptism, may we walk in newness of life.

- Azariah's song, Daniel 3:26–27, 29, 34–41

- The three youths' praise of creation, Daniel 3:52–88

- Habakkuk's song of divine judgment, Habakkuk 3:2–4, 13, 15–19

### Other canticles and prayers in the Old Testament

- Deborah's song, Judges 5:2–31

- David's lament, 2 Samuel 1:19–27

- David's victory song, 2 Samuel 7:18–29

- David's deliverance song, 2 Samuel 22:2–51

- Solomon's personal prayer, 1 Kings 3:5–9

- Solomon's public prayer, 1 Kings 8:23–61 (2 Chronicles 6:14–42)

- Hezekiah's temple prayer, 2 Kings 19:15–19 (Isaiah 37:14–20)

- David's song, 1 Chronicles 16:8–36

- David's thanksgiving prayer, 1 Chronicles 29:10–19

- Ezra's prayer, Ezra 9:6–15

- Tobit's wedding night prayer, Tobit 8:5c–7

- Raguel's thanksgiving prayer, Tobit 8:15–17

- Judith's prayer, Judith 9:5–14

- People's blessing upon Judith, Judith 15:9–10

- Esther's prayer, Esther 14:1–19

- Job's pious prayer, Job 1:21

- Job's plaint, Job 3:3–26

- Job's penitential, Job 42:2–6

- Solomon's love song, Song of Songs 2:10–17

- The sage's prayer, Sirach 39:16–35 Prayer of praise, thanksgiving, Sirach 51:1–30

- Jeremiah's complaint, Jeremiah 15:10–18

- Jeremiah's vengeance prayer, Jeremiah 18:19–23

- Jeremiah's interior crisis, Jeremiah 20:7–18

- Jeremiah's praise prayer, Jeremiah 32:17–25

## New Testament Canticles

Like their Old Testament counterparts described above, New Testament canticles are a rich source of prayer. There are more New Testament canticles included in the Liturgy of the Hours (during Evening Prayer) than there had been in the past. (There is an explanation and a schedule of their use in Chapter 6.)

### The Gospel ("Evangelical") canticles
**The Canticle of Mary**
(Luke 1:46–55)
Mary's Canticle, called the "*Magnificat*" after its first word ("magnifies") in Latin, is her response to Elizabeth's greeting at the visitation. It is prayed each day by the Church as part of its Evening Prayer. (See *CCC*, 2619.)

*My soul magnifies the Lord,*
*and my spirit rejoices in God my Savior,*
*for he has looked with favor on the lowliness of his servant.*
*Surely, from now on all generations will call me blessed;*
*for the Mighty One has done great things for me,*

*and holy is his name.*
*His mercy is for those who fear him*
*from generation to generation.*
*He has shown strength with his arm;*
*he has scattered the proud in the*
*thoughts of their hearts.*
*He has brought down the powerful*
*from their thrones,*
*and lifted up the lowly;*
*he has filled the hungry with good*
*things,*
*and sent the rich away empty.*
*He has helped his servant Israel,*
*in remembrance of his mercy,*
*according to the promise he made to*
*our ancestors,*
*to Abraham and to his descendants*
*forever.*

## The Canticle of Zechariah
(Luke 1:68–79)
Zechariah's Canticle is called the *Benedictus*, its first word ("blessed") in Latin. Zechariah, the father of John the Baptist, is singing in gratitude after John's birth for God's fidelity to the messianic promise. It is prayed each day by the Church as part of its Morning Prayer.

*Blessed be the Lord God of Israel,*
*for he has looked favorably on his*
*people and redeemed them.*
*He has raised up a mighty savior for us*
*in the house of his servant David,*
*as he spoke through the mouth of his*
*holy prophets from of old,*
*that we would be saved from our*
*enemies and from the hand of all*
*who hate us.*
*Thus he has shown the mercy promised*
*to our ancestors,*
*and has remembered his holy*
*covenant,*

*the oath that he swore to our ancestor*
*Abraham,*
*to grant us that we, being rescued*
*from the hands of our enemies,*
*might serve him without fear, in*
*holiness and righteousness*
*before him all our days.*
*And you, child, will be called the*
*prophet of the Most High;*
*for you will go before the Lord to*
*prepare his ways,*
*to give knowledge of salvation to his*
*people*
*by the forgiveness of their sins.*
*By the tender mercy of our God,*
*the dawn from on high will break*
*upon us,*
*to give light to those who sit in*
*darkness and in the shadow of*
*death,*
*to guide our feet into the way*
*of peace.*

## The Canticle of Simeon
(Luke 2:29–32)
Simeon's Canticle is called the *Nunc Dimittis*, its first words ("now you may dismiss") in Latin. It is the song of the old man in the temple at the Lord's presentation, including his request for permission to die. It is prayed each day by the Church as part of its Night Prayer.

*Master, now you are dismissing your*
*servant in peace,*
*according to your word;*
*For my eyes have seen your salvation,*
*which you have prepared in the*
*presence of all peoples,*
*A light for revelation to the Gentiles*
*and for glory to your people in*
*Israel.*

## Other New Testament canticles

These canticles have also found their way into the prayer of the Church in the Liturgy of the Hours: The psalmody each day at Evening Prayer is made up of two psalms and one New Testament canticle. (For their schedule, see Chapter 6.)

1. God's Plan Fulfilled in Christ, Ephesians 1:3–10
2. Christ, Firstborn from the dead, Colossians 1:12–20
3. Song of the Paschal Mystery, Philippians 2:6–11
4. Song of the Mystery of our Faith, 1 Timothy 3:16
5. Song of the Suffering Christ, 1 Peter 2:21–24
6. Song of the Creator, and the Lamb, Revelation 4:11; 5:9, 10, 12
7. Song of Divine Judgment, Revelation 11:17–18
8. Praise of God's Power, Revelation 12:10–12
9. Song of Moses and the Lamb, Revelation 15:3–4
10. The Wedding Feast of the Lamb, Revelation 19:1–7

## Prayers in the New Testament

In many cases, the statements and acclamations below were recorded as spoken to the Lord Jesus. In every case, they can easily be borrowed and spoken as prayer today, especially in situations similar to the ones in which the statements were made originally. Some of these words have become deeply imbedded as prayers in the Catholic tradition—the angel's greeting of Mary (see *Luke 1:28*), for example, of which the *Catechism* says,

"Our prayer dares to take up this greeting to Mary with the regard God had for the lowliness of his humble servant and to exult in the joy he finds in her[7]" (*CCC*, 2676; see also *CCC*, 2623–2649).

**The Angel's Greeting** (*Luke 1:28, 42*)
"Greetings, favored one! The Lord is with you . . . Blessed are you among women . . ."

**Mary's Reply** (*Luke 1:38*)
"Here am I, the servant of the Lord; let it be with me according to your word."

**Elizabeth's Greeting** (*Luke 1:42, 45*)
"Blessed are you among women, and blessed is the fruit of your womb . . . blessed is she who believed that there would be a fulfillment of what was spoken to her by the Lord."

**Song of the Angels** (*Luke 2:14*)
"Glory to God in the highest heaven, and on earth peace among those whom he favors!"

**Temptation of Christ** (*Matthew 4:10*)
"Away with you, Satan! for it is written, 'Worship the Lord your God, and serve only him.'"

**Nathanael** (*John 1:49*)
"Rabbi, you are the Son of God! You are the King of Israel!"

**The Leper Cured** (*Luke 5:12*)
"Lord, if you choose, you can make me clean."

**The Centurion at Capernaum** (*Matthew 8:8*)
"Lord, I am not worthy to have

you come under my roof; but only speak the word, and my servant will be healed."

**The Storm on the Lake** (*Matthew 8:25*)
"Lord, save us! We are perishing!"

**Two Blind Men Cured** (*Matthew 9:27*)
"Have mercy on us, Son of David!"

**Peter on Lake Genesareth after Five Thousand Were Fed** (*Matthew 14:30*)
"Lord, save me!"

**Peter at Capernaum** (*John 6:68*)
"Lord, to whom can we go? You have the words of eternal life."

**The Canaanite Woman** (*Matthew 15:22, 25, 27*)
"Have mercy on me, Lord, Son of David . . . Lord, help me. . . . Lord, . . . even the dogs eat the crumbs that fall from their masters' table."

**Peter's Profession** (*Matthew 16:16*)
"You are the Messiah, the Son of the living God."

**Peter at the Transfiguration** (*Matthew 17:4*)
"Lord, it is good for us to be here; if you wish, I will make three dwellings here, one for you, one for Moses, and one for Elijah."

**The Man Born Blind** (*John 9:38*)
"Lord, I believe."

**Praise of Mary** (*Luke 11:27*)
"Blessed is the womb that bore you [Lord] and the breasts that nursed you!"

**The Prodigal Son** (*Luke 15:21*)
"Father, I have sinned against heaven and before you; I am no longer worthy to be called your son."

**The Apostle's Petition to the Lord** (*Luke 17:5*)
"Increase our faith!"

**As Obedient Servants** (*Luke 17:10*)
"We are worthless slaves; we have done only what we ought to have done!"

**The Tax Collector** (*Luke 18:13*)
"God, be merciful to me, a sinner!"

**A Rich Man** (*Luke 18:18*)
"Good Teacher, what must I do to inherit eternal life?"

**Martha** (*John 11:21, 22, 24, 27*)
"Lord, if you had been here, my brother would not have died. But even now I know that God will give you whatever you ask of him . . . I know that [Lazarus] will rise again in the resurrection on the last day . . . Yes, Lord, I believe that you are the Messiah, the Son of God, the one coming into the world."

**The Blind Man Near Jericho** (*Luke 18:38, 39, 41*)
"Jesus, Son of David, have mercy on me! . . . Son of David, have mercy on me! . . . Lord, let me see again."

**Zacchaeus the Tax Collector** (*Luke 19:8*)
"Look, half of my possessions, Lord, I will give to the poor; and if I have defrauded anyone of anything, I will pay back four times as much."

### Triumphant Entry Into Jerusalem
(*Matthew 21:9* and parallels)
"Hosanna to the Son of David! / Blessed is the one who comes in the name of the Lord! / Hosanna in the highest heaven!"

### The Agony in the Garden
(*Matthew 26:39* and parallels)
"My Father, if it is possible, let this cup pass from me; yet not what I want but what you want."

### First Word on the Cross
(*Luke 23:34*)
"Father, forgive them; for they do not know what they are doing."

### The Good Thief (*Luke 23:42*)
"Jesus, remember me when you come into your kingdom."

### The Death of Jesus
(*Matthew 27:46* and parallels)
"My God, my God, why have you forsaken me?"

### The Seventh Word on the Cross
(*Luke 23:46*)
"Father, into your hands I commend my spirit."

### The Disciples at Emmaus
(*Luke 24:29*)
"Stay with us, because it is almost evening and the day is now nearly over."

### Thomas (*John 20:28*)
"My Lord and my God!"

### Peter, the Shepherd
(*John 21:15, 16, 17*)
"Yes, Lord; you know that I love you . . . Yes, Lord; you know that I love you . . . Lord, you know everything; you know that I love you."

### After Peter's Release
(*Acts 4:24, 29–30*)
"Sovereign Lord, who made the heaven and the earth, the sea, and everything in them . . . grant to your servants to speak your word with all boldness, while you stretch out your hand to heal, and signs and wonders are performed through the name of your holy servant Jesus."

### Saint Stephen, Protomartyr
(*Acts 7:56, 59, 60*)
"Look, . . . I see the heavens opened and the Son of Man standing at the right hand of God! . . . Lord Jesus, receive my spirit . . . Lord, do not hold this sin against them."

### The Christians of Caesarea
(*Acts 21:14*)
"The Lord's will be done."

## Prayers in the Epistles
The following excerpts from the epistles, in their original context, were not all prayers. Some, like Romans 8:37–39, are affirmations or declarations. All can be used as prayers or models for prayer.

### Firm Resolution (*Romans 8:37–39*)
"[I]n all these things we are more than conquerors through him who loved us. For I am convinced that neither death, nor life, nor angels, nor rulers, nor things present, nor things to come, nor powers, nor height, nor depth, nor anything else in all creation, will be able to separate us from the love of God in Christ Jesus our Lord."

**317**

**Infinite Wisdom** (*Romans 11:33–36*) "O the depth of the riches and wisdom and knowledge of God! How unsearchable are his judgments and how inscrutable his ways! / 'For who has known the mind of the Lord? / Or who has been his counselor? / Or who has given a gift to him, to receive a gift in return?' / For from him and through him and to him are all things. To him be the glory forever. Amen."

**Consolation** (*2 Corinthians 1:3–4*) "Blessed be the God and Father of our Lord Jesus Christ, the Father of mercies and the God of all consolation, who consoles us in all our affliction, so that we may be able to console those who are in any affliction with the consolation with which we ourselves are consoled by God."

**The Peace of God** (*Galatians 1:3–5*) "Grace to you and peace from God our Father and the Lord Jesus Christ, who gave himself for our sins to set us free from the present evil age, according to the will of our God and Father, to whom be the glory forever and ever. Amen."

**Crucified to the World** (*Galatians 6:14*) "May I never boast of anything except the cross of our Lord Jesus Christ, by which the world has been crucified to me, and I to the world."

**The Power of God in Us** (*Ephesians 3:20–21*) "Now to him who by the power at work within us is able to accomplish abundantly far more than all we can ask or imagine, to him be glory in the church and in Christ Jesus to all generations, forever and ever. Amen."

**Glory to God** (*Philippians 4:20*) "To our God and Father be glory forever and ever. Amen."

**The King of Ages** (*1 Timothy 1:17*) "To the King of ages, immortal, invisible, the only God, be honor and glory forever and ever. Amen."

**The King of Kings** (*1 Timothy 6:15–16*) ". . . he who is the blessed and only Sovereign, the King of kings and Lord of lords. It is he alone who has immortality and dwells in unapproachable light, whom no one has ever seen or can see; to him be honor and eternal dominion. Amen."

**Birth to Salvation** (*1 Peter 1:3–5*) "Blessed be the God and Father of our Lord Jesus Christ! By his great mercy he has given us a new birth into a living hope through the resurrection of Jesus Christ from the dead, and into an inheritance that is imperishable, undefiled, and unfading, kept in heaven for you, who are being protected by the power of God through faith for a salvation ready to be revealed in the last time."

**God Glorified in Us** (*1 Peter 4:11*) ". . . so that God may be glorified in all things through Jesus Christ. To him belong the glory and the power forever and ever. Amen."

**Growth in Grace** (*2 Peter 3:18*)
"But grow in the grace and knowledge of our Lord and Savior Jesus Christ. To him be the glory both now and to the day of eternity. Amen."

## Prayers in the Book of Revelation

In a section entitled "Prayer of Praise," the *Catechism* says, "The *Revelation* of 'what must soon take place,' the *Apocalypse*, is borne along by the songs of the heavenly liturgy (see Revelation 4:8–11; 5:9–14; 7:10–12) but also by the intercession of the 'witnesses' (martyrs) (Revelation 6:10). The prophets and the saints, all those who were slain on earth for their witness to Jesus, the vast throng of those who, having come through the great tribulation, have gone before us into the Kingdom, all sing the praise and glory of him who sits on the throne, and of the Lamb (see Revelation 18:24; 19:1–8). In communion with them, the Church on earth also sings these songs with faith in the midst of trial. By means of petition and intercession, faith hopes against all hope and gives thanks to the 'Father of lights,' from whom 'every perfect gift' comes down (James 1:17)" (CCC, 2642). Why would members of the Church today not use those same prayers, like the following acclamations, proclaimed by various participants in John's vision of heavenly worship?

**The Four Living Creatures** (*Revelation 4:8*)

"Holy, holy, holy,/ the Lord God the Almighty,/ who was and is and is to come."

**All Creatures and The Universe** (*Revelation 5:13*)
"To the one seated on the throne and to the Lamb/ be blessing and honor and glory and might/ forever and ever!"

**A Huge White-Robed Crowd** (*Revelation 7:10*)
"Salvation belongs to our God who is seated on the throne, and to the Lamb!"

**Angels, Elders, and Four Living Creatures** (*Revelation 7:12*)
"Amen! Blessing and glory and wisdom/ and thanksgiving and honor/ and power and might/ be to our God forever and ever. Amen."

**One of Seven Angels and the Altar** (*Revelation 16:5, 7*)
"You are just, O Holy One, who are and were . . ./ Yes, O Lord God, the Almighty,/ your judgments are true and just!"

## Prayerful Greetings from the Epistles

There are many religious greetings in the New Testament letters. The Church draws from them for the greeting at Mass, by which the priest "signifies the presence of the Lord to the community gathered there. . . . By this Greeting and the people's response, the mystery of the Church gathered together is made manifest" (*General Instruction of the Roman Missal*, 50). There's no reason that they cannot also be used, sometimes adapted, in the domestic Church of the family and even in private prayer. (See *CCC*, 2636–2638.)

"To all God's beloved in Rome, who are called to be saints: Grace to you and peace from God our Father and the Lord Jesus Christ." (*Romans 1:7*)

"The grace of our Lord Jesus Christ be with you" (or with "your spirit"; *Romans 16:20, 1 Thessalonians 5:28, Philemon 25*)

"The grace of the Lord Jesus be with you." (*1 Corinthians 16:23*)

"My love be with all of you in Christ Jesus." (*1 Corinthians 16:24*)

"The grace of the Lord Jesus Christ, the love of God, and the communion of the Holy Spirit be with all of you." (*2 Corinthians 13:13*)

"May the grace of our Lord Jesus Christ be with your spirit, brothers and sisters. Amen." (*Galatians 6:18, Philippians 4:23*)

"Peace be to the whole community, and love with faith, from God the Father and the Lord Jesus Christ." (*Ephesians 6:23*)

"Grace be with all who have an undying love for our Lord Jesus Christ." (*Ephesians 6:24*)

"Grace to you and peace from God our Father and the Lord Jesus Christ." (*1 Corinthians 1:3, 2 Corinthians 1:2, Ephesians 1:2, Philippians 1:2, 2 Thessalonians 1:2, 1 Timothy 1:2, Philemon 3*)

"Grace to you and peace from God our Father." (*Colossians 1:2*)

"The Lord be with all of you." (*2 Thessalonians 3:16*)

"The grace of our Lord Jesus Christ be with all of you." (*2 Thessalonians 3:18*)

"Grace, mercy, and peace from God the Father and Christ Jesus our Lord." (*1 Timothy 1:2, 2 Timothy 1:2*)

"The Lord be with your spirit." (*2 Timothy 4:22*)

"Grace be with you." (*2 Timothy 4:22*)

"May grace and peace be yours in abundance in the knowledge of God and of Jesus our Lord." (*2 Peter 1:2*)

"May mercy, peace, and love be yours in abundance." (*Jude 2*)

## Pauline Gratitude Prayers for the Church

Paul's letters (and those ascribed to him) include the standard address of the day (names of the sender and addressee, and a greeting), but often with additions to describe the apostolic mission. Instead of a secular greeting, there is the wish for the spiritual gifts poured out in Christ. Usually a prayer is included that uses Christian thanksgiving formulas, sometimes integrating a blessing.

"It is the prayer of Paul, the apostle par excellence, which reveals to us how the divine solicitude for all the churches ought to inspire Christian prayer," [8] the *Catechism* says (2632). ("Solicitude" is eager, anxious concern.)

"Since Abraham, intercession—asking on behalf of another—has been characteristic of a heart attuned to God's mercy. In the age of the Church, Christian intercession participates in Christ's, as an expression of the communion of saints. In intercession, he who prays looks 'not only to his own interests, but also to the interests of others,' even to the point of praying for those who do him harm (Philippians 2:4 [9]). The first Christian communities lived this form of fellowship intensely" [10] (*CCC*, 2635–2636).

The following "gratitude prayers" are examples and models for prayer today, especially prayer for the Church, for the diocese (referred to in the phrase "all the churches" above), and for one's own parish.

1. **Romans 1:8–12**
   "First, I thank my God through Jesus Christ for all of you, because your faith is proclaimed throughout the world. For God, whom I serve with my spirit by announcing the gospel of his Son, is my witness that without ceasing I remember you always in my prayers, asking that by God's will I may somehow at last succeed in coming to you. For I am longing to see you so that I may share with you some spiritual gift to strengthen you—or rather so that we may be mutually encouraged by each other's faith, both yours and mine."

2. **1 Corinthians 1:4–9**
   "I give thanks to my God always for you because of the grace of God that has been given you in Christ Jesus, for in every way you have been enriched in him, in speech and knowledge of every kind—just as the testimony of Christ has been strengthened among you—so that you are not lacking in any spiritual gift as you wait for the revealing of our Lord Jesus Christ. He will also strengthen you to the end, so that you may be blameless on the day of our Lord Jesus Christ. God is faithful; by him you were called into the fellowship of his Son, Jesus Christ our Lord."

3. **Ephesians 1:15–23**
   "I have heard of your faith in the Lord Jesus and your love towards all the saints, and for this reason I do not cease to give thanks for you as I remember you in my prayers. I pray that the God of our Lord Jesus Christ, the Father of glory, may give you a spirit of wisdom and revelation as you come to know him, so that, with the eyes of your heart enlightened, you may know what is the hope to which he has called you, what are the riches of his glorious inheritance among the saints, and what is the immeasurable greatness of his power for us who believe, according to the

working of his great power. God put this power to work in Christ when he raised him from the dead and seated him at his right hand in the heavenly places, far above all rule and authority and power and dominion, and above every name that is named, not only in this age but also in the age to come. And he has put all things under his feet and has made him the head over all things for the church, which is his body, the fullness of him who fills all in all."

### 4. Philippians 1:3–11

"I thank my God every time I remember you, constantly praying with joy in every one of my prayers for all of you, because of your sharing in the gospel from the first day until now. I am confident of this, that the one who began a good work among you will bring it to completion by the day of Jesus Christ. It is right for me to think this way about all of you, because you hold me in your heart, for all of you share in God's grace with me, both in my imprisonment and in the defense and confirmation of the gospel. For God is my witness, how I long for all of you with the compassion of Christ Jesus. And this is my prayer, that your love may overflow more and more with knowledge and full insight to help you to determine what is best, so that in the day of Christ you may be pure and blameless, having produced the harvest

of righteousness that comes through Jesus Christ for the glory and praise of God."

### 5. Colossians 1:3–14

"In our prayers for you we always thank God, the Father of our Lord Jesus Christ, for we have heard of your faith in Christ Jesus and of the love that you have for all the saints, because of the hope laid up for you in heaven. You have heard of this hope before in the word of the truth, the gospel that has come to you. Just as it is bearing fruit and growing in the whole world, so it has been bearing fruit among yourselves from the day you heard it and truly comprehended the grace of God. This you learned from Epaphras, our beloved fellow servant. He is a faithful minister of Christ on your behalf, and he has made known to us your love in the Spirit.

"For this reason, since the day we heard it, we have not ceased praying for you and asking that you may be filled with the knowledge of God's will in all spiritual wisdom and understanding, so that you may lead lives worthy of the Lord, fully pleasing to him, as you bear fruit in every good work and as you grow in the knowledge of God. May you be made strong with all the strength that comes from his glorious power, and may you be prepared to endure everything with patience, while joyfully giving thanks to the

Father, who has enabled you to share in the inheritance of the saints in the light. He has rescued us from the power of darkness and transferred us into the kingdom of his beloved Son, in whom we have redemption, the forgiveness of sins."

6. **1 Thessalonians 1:2–10**

"We always give thanks to God for all of you and mention you in our prayers, constantly remembering before our God and Father your work of faith and labor of love and steadfastness of hope in our Lord Jesus Christ. For we know, brothers and sisters beloved by God, that he has chosen you, because our message of the gospel came to you not in word only, but also in power and in the Holy Spirit and with full conviction; just as you know what kind of people we proved to be among you for your sake. And you became imitators of us and of the Lord, for in spite of persecution you received the word with joy inspired by the Holy Spirit, so that you became an example to all the believers in Macedonia and in Achaia. For the word of the Lord has sounded forth from you not only in Macedonia and Achaia, but in every place where your faith in God has become known, so that we have no need to speak about it. For the people of those regions report about us what kind of welcome we had among you, and how you turned to God from idols,

to serve a living and true God, and to wait for his Son from heaven, whom he raised from the dead—Jesus, who rescues us from the wrath that is coming."

7. **2 Thessalonians 1:3–12**

"We must always give thanks to God for you, brothers and sisters, as is right, because your faith is growing abundantly, and the love of every one of you for one another is increasing. Therefore we ourselves boast of you among the churches of God for your steadfastness and faith during all your persecutions and the afflictions that you are enduring.

"This is evidence of the righteous judgment of God, and is intended to make you worthy of the kingdom of God, for which you are also suffering. For it is indeed just of God to repay with affliction those who afflict you, and to give relief to the afflicted as well as to us, when the Lord Jesus is revealed from heaven with his mighty angels in flaming fire, inflicting vengeance on those who do not know God and on those who do not obey the gospel of our Lord Jesus. These will suffer the punishment of eternal destruction, separated from the presence of the Lord and from the glory of his might, when he comes to be glorified by his saints and to be marveled at on that day among all who have believed, because our testimony to you was believed. To this end we

7

**Light of the Faithful**

always pray for you, asking that our God will make you worthy of his call and will fulfill by his power every good resolve and work of faith, so that the name of our Lord Jesus may be glorified in you, and you in him, according to the grace of our God and the Lord Jesus Christ."

# Blessings

"Among sacramentals, *blessings* (of persons, meals, objects, and places) come first," the *Catechism* teaches (1671). To appreciate the place and power of blessings, a review of the Catholic understanding of "sacramentals" may help: Sacramentals are "sacred signs which bear a resemblance to the sacraments. They signify effects, particularly of a spiritual nature, which are obtained through the intercession of the Church. By them [people] are disposed to receive the chief effect of the sacraments, and various occasions in life are rendered holy" [11] (CCC, 1667, quoting Vatican II's *Constitution on the Sacred Liturgy*, 60).

The *Catechism* goes on to explain that "sacramentals derive from the baptismal priesthood: every baptized person is called to be a 'blessing,' and to bless" [12] (CCC, 1669). Blessing is mentioned often in the Scriptures; for example:

• God said to Abraham, "I will bless those who bless you . . ." (*Genesis 12:3*).

• Jesus told his disciples, "[B]less those who curse you, pray for those who abuse you" (*Luke 6:28*).

• Paul wrote to the Romans, "Bless those who persecute you; bless and do not curse them" (*Romans 12:14*).

• The 1st Letter of Peter says, "Do not repay evil for evil, or abuse for abuse; but, on the contrary, repay with a blessing. It is for this that you were called—that you might inherit a blessing" (*1 Peter 3:9*).

In the following pages is a collection of blessings—a resource for enriching the prayer of the faithful with biblical blessings.

## A Sampling of Old Testament Blessings
### Mizpah blessing

Mizpah is a town in Gilead. The name is derived from a Hebrew word meaning "lookout." This blessing is from an account of the treaty between Jacob and Laban (see *Genesis 31:43–54*).

"The LORD watch between you and me, when we are absent one from the other" (*Genesis 31:49*).

### A blessing of Jacob

This is the blessing Jacob gave to Ephraim and Manasseh, his grandchildren by Joseph. Jacob considered them his own children because of the early death of his wife Rachel who bore him no more than Joseph and Benjamin.

"The God before whom my ancestors Abraham and Isaac walked, / the God who has been my shepherd all my life to this day, / the angel who has redeemed me from all harm, bless the boys; / and in them let my name be perpetuated, and the name of my ancestors Abraham and Isaac; / and let them grow into a multitude on the earth." (*Genesis 48:15–16*)

## Aaron's blessing

This priestly blessing is introduced by these two verses: "The LORD spoke to Moses, saying: Speak to Aaron and his sons, saying, Thus you shall bless the Israelites: You shall say to them, . . ." (*Numbers 6:22–23*). The text of Aaron's blessing in Numbers is followed by the following verse: "So they shall put my name on the Israelites, and I will bless them" (*Numbers 6:27*). (This blessing is also called the "Seraphic Blessing" because it became associated with Francis of Assisi—"the Seraphic Saint"—who used a form of it to bless his beloved Brother Leo on Mt. Alverno in 1224.)

"The LORD bless you and keep you; / the LORD make his face to shine upon you, and be gracious to you; / the LORD lift up his countenance upon you, and give you peace." (*Numbers 6:24–26*)

## Moses' final blessing of the people

Taken from the final words of Moses (Deuteronomy 27—33), this blessing is from a section called "Blessings for Obedience" (see *Deuteronomy 28:1–6*).

"Blessed shall you be in the city, and blessed shall you be in the field. / Blessed shall be the fruit of your womb, the fruit of your ground, and the fruit of your livestock, both the increase of your cattle and the issue of your flock. / Blessed shall be your basket and your kneading bowl. / Blessed shall you be when you come in, and blessed shall you be when you go out." (*Deuteronomy 28:3–6*)

## The blessing of Ruth by Boaz

Ruth was the Moabite daughter-in-law of Naomi, whom Ruth accompanied back to Bethlehem after proclaiming, "Do not press me to leave you or to turn back from following you! / Where you go, I will go; Where you lodge, I will lodge; / your people shall be my people, and your God my God. / Wherever you die I will die—there will I be buried" (*Ruth 1:16–17*). Upon meeting Naomi's prominent kinsman Boaz, Ruth said, "'Why have I found favor in your sight, that you should take notice of me, when I am a foreigner?' But Boaz answered her, 'All that you have done for your mother-in-law since the death of your husband has been fully told me, and how you left your father and mother and your native land and came to a people that you did not know before'" (*Ruth 2:10–11*). He then spoke the following words of blessing.

"May the LORD reward you for your deeds, and may you have a full reward from the LORD, the God of Israel, under whose wings you have come for refuge!" (*Ruth 2:12*).

### Solomon's blessing

This is Solomon's blessing of the people of Israel, following his prayer (1 Kings 8:23–53) during the dedication of the temple (see *1 Kings 8*).

"The Lord our God be with us, as he was with our ancestors; may he not leave us or abandon us, but incline our hearts to him, to walk in all his ways, and to keep his commandments, his statutes, and his ordinances, which he commanded our ancestors." (*1 Kings 8:57–58*).

## A Sampling of New Testament Blessings

"May the God of steadfastness and encouragement grant you to live in harmony with one another, in accordance with Christ Jesus, so that together you may with one voice glorify the God and Father of our Lord Jesus Christ . . . May the God of hope fill you with all joy and peace in believing, so that you may abound in hope by the power of the Holy Spirit . . . The God of peace be with all of you. Amen." (*Romans 15:5–6, 13, 33*)

"Now to God who is able to strengthen you according to my gospel and the proclamation of Jesus Christ, according to the revelation of the mystery that was kept secret for long ages but is now disclosed, and through the prophetic writings is made known to all the Gentiles, according to the command of the eternal God, to bring about the obedience of faith—to the only wise God, through Jesus Christ, to whom be the glory forever! Amen." (*Romans 16:25–27*)

"I pray that, according to the riches of his glory, he may grant that you may be strengthened in your inner being with power through his Spirit, and that Christ may dwell in your hearts through faith, as you are being rooted and grounded in love. I pray that you may have the power to comprehend, with all the saints, what is the breadth and length and height and depth, and to know the love of Christ that surpasses knowledge, so that you may be filled with all the fullness of God." (*Ephesians 3:16–19*)

"Peace be to the whole community, and love with faith, from God the Father and the Lord Jesus Christ." (*Ephesians 6:23*)

"And the peace of God, which surpasses all understanding, will guard your hearts and your minds in Christ Jesus. Finally, beloved, whatever is true, whatever is honorable, whatever is just, whatever is pure, whatever is pleasing, whatever is commendable, if there is any excellence and if there is anything worthy of praise, think about these things. Keep on doing the things that you have learned and received and heard and seen in me, and the God of peace will be with you." (*Philippians 4:7–9*)

"May the God of peace himself sanctify you entirely; and may your spirit and soul and body be kept sound and blameless at the coming of our Lord Jesus Christ." (*1 Thessalonians 5:23*)

"To this end we always pray for you, asking that our God will make you worthy of his call and will fulfill by his power every good resolve and work of faith, so that the name of our Lord Jesus may be glorified in you, and you in him, according to the grace of our God and the Lord Jesus Christ." (*2 Thessalonians 1:11–12*)

"Now may the Lord of peace himself give you peace at all times in all ways." (*2 Thessalonians 3:16*)

"Grace, mercy, and peace from God the Father and Christ Jesus our Lord." (*1 Timothy 1:2*)

"Now may the God of peace, who brought back from the dead our Lord Jesus, the great shepherd of the sheep, by the blood of the eternal covenant, make you complete in everything good so that you may do his will, working among us that which is pleasing in his sight, through Jesus Christ, to whom be the glory forever and ever. Amen." (*Hebrews 13:20–21*)

". . . the God of all grace, who has called you to his eternal glory in Christ, will himself restore, support, strengthen, and establish you. To him be the power forever and ever. Amen." (*1 Peter 5:10–11*)

"Grace, mercy, and peace will be with us from God the Father and from Jesus Christ, the Father's Son, in truth and love." (*2 John 3*)

"May mercy, peace, and love be yours in abundance." (*Jude 2*)

"Now to him who is able to keep you from falling, and to make you stand without blemish in the presence of his glory with rejoicing, to the only God our Savior, through Jesus Christ our Lord, be glory, majesty, power, and authority, before all time and now and forever. Amen." (*Jude 24—25*)

"Grace to you and peace from him who is and who was and who is to come, and from the seven spirits who are before his throne, and from Jesus Christ, the faithful witness, the firstborn of the dead, and the ruler of the kings of the earth. To him who loves us and freed us from our sins by his blood, and made us to be a kingdom, priests serving his God and Father, to him be glory and dominion forever and ever. Amen." (*Revelation 1:4–6*)

# Quoting Scripture

Committing Scripture to memory happens sometimes by choice and sometimes by accident. A person may well quote a Scripture from memory unintentionally, after becoming familiar with a passage in the course of meditation and prayer, because of a love for the inspired word and a desire to live in accord with it. Memorizing Scripture (or better, knowing it "by heart") is not an end in itself but the byproduct of prayer and love.

When discussing Saint Therese of Lisieux and her book *The Story of a Soul*, Mitch Finley writes, "Early in the book the reader may be struck with how frequently Therese quotes directly from or refers to Scripture. A quick count reveals 155 biblical references in the less than 250 pages of the English text. Therese must have steeped herself in Scripture, to be able to draw these Bible references and quotations from thin air while writing—even later when she was so seriously ill with tuberculosis. Intended or not, St. Therese of Lisieux sends a challenge to modern Catholics to spend more time with Scripture" (*Catholic Spiritual Classics*, p. 43).

The more familiar Scripture becomes, the more its history and stories, its song and its symbols, create a spiritual world in which to live; the more life is enriched and illumined by its people and themes; the more a person understands and describes life experiences in scriptural terms.

Below are four ways Scripture is already being quoted—or could be, with some effort: common prayers, personal choices, Sunday Mass readings, and the psalms of Night Prayer.

## 1. Common Prayers

Many Catholics already are able to quote Bible verses—all the while saying they can't. By praying some of our most familiar prayers, Catholics are quoting verses by

heart "accidentally," since many of our traditional prayers have their source in biblical text. Simply learning or re-learning some of the prayers of the Catholic tradition while keeping in mind their source in Scripture could have a two-fold benefit: It could build self-confidence in terms of biblical literacy as well as bring a new appreciation for the prayers themselves. Catholics would then be quoting Scripture—consciously and purposely.

### The Our Father

The Lord's Prayer is the "fundamental Christian prayer" (*CCC*, 2759), "truly the summary of the whole gospel" (Tertullian). "Run through all the words of the holy prayers [in Scripture], and I do not think that you will find anything in them that is not contained and included in the Lord's Prayer" (Saint Augustine). The Lord's Prayer appears twice in the Gospels: a shorter text in Luke 11:2–4 and a more developed form, the one adopted by the liturgical tradition of the Church, in Matthew 6:9–13. (The doxology "for thine is the kingdom . . ." was added in the sixteenth century; originally a liturgical ending, it is used during Mass with the insertion "Deliver us, O Lord . . .")

*Our Father, who art in heaven,/ hallowed be thy name;/ thy kingdom come,/ thy will be done on earth as it is in heaven./ Give us this day our daily bread;/ and forgive us our trespasses/ as we forgive those who trespass against us;/ and lead us not into temptation,/ but deliver us from evil. Amen.*

### The Hail Mary

In the early sixth century, the "*Ave*" (as it was known) consisted only of Gabriel's greeting to Mary, "Greetings, favored one! The Lord is with you" (*Luke 1:28*). Later, Elizabeth's words at the visitation were added, "Blessed are you among women, and blessed is the fruit of your womb" (*Luke 1:42*). In the thirteenth century, the word "Jesus" was added. Versions of the petition that begins "Holy Mary, Mother of God . . ." were gradually added to the ancient Hail Mary in the fourteenth and fifteenth centuries. A Dominican, Blessed Alan de la Roche (died 1475), is credited with giving the Hail Mary the form we know today so that it could be prayed publicly and universally.

*Hail, Mary, full of grace!/ The Lord is with you;/ blessed are you among women,/ and blessed is the fruit of your womb, Jesus./ Holy Mary, Mother of God,/ pray for us sinners,/ now and at the hour of our death. Amen.*

### The Glory to the Father

The Glory to the Father is sometimes called the Lesser Doxology (the Greater being the Gloria of the Mass). *Doxa* is a Greek word meaning "glory." Although the particular wording of its first part is ascribed to Saint Basil (329–379), it was probably adapted from Jewish blessings and clearly influenced by the Trinitarian baptism formula (see *Matthew 28:19*). It is said at the end of psalms in the Liturgy of the Hours.

*Glory to the Father,/ and to the Son,/ and to the Holy Spirit:/ as it was in the beginning,/ is now,/ and will be forever. Amen.*

### The Angelus

Honoring the incarnation, the *Angelus* is named for its first Latin word (*Angelus Domini*, meaning "the angel of the Lord"). Scripture citations are included below in parentheses to illustrate how much the *Angelus* is actually a mosaic of Scripture. The closing oration refers to the central truths of Christian faith: incarnation, Resurrection, redemption. Since the sixteenth century church bells have rung the *Angelus* at 6 AM, 12 noon, and 6 PM. The bells, signaling Morning Prayer, Midday Prayer, and Evening Prayer of the Liturgy of the Hours, called for the *Angelus* as a substitute for people who didn't have the luxury of going to chapel to pray the psalms. (The lines below shown in blue indicate the part prayed responsively when the *Angelus* is prayed in common.)

*The angel spoke God's message to Mary,* (see *Luke 1:28*)
*and she conceived of the Holy Spirit.* (see *Luke 1:35*)
*Hail Mary, full of grace . . . Holy Mary, Mother of God . . . .*
*"I am the lowly servant of the Lord:* (see *Luke 1:38*)
*let it be done to me according to your word."* (see *Luke 1:38*)
*Hail Mary, full of grace . . . Holy Mary, Mother of God . . . .*
*And the Word became flesh,* (John 1:14)

and lived among us. (*John 1:14*)
Hail Mary, full of grace . . . Holy
Mary, Mother of God . . . .
Pray for us, holy Mother of God,
That we may be made worthy of the
promises of Christ.
Let us pray. Lord, fill our hearts with
your grace. Once through the message of an angel you revealed to us the
incarnation of your Son; now, through
his suffering and death lead us to the
glory of his resurrection. We ask this
through Christ our Lord. Amen.

## The Jesus Prayer

This ancient Eastern Christian
contemplative prayer invokes the
name of Jesus, the only name in the
world given us by which we are to
be saved (see *Acts 4:12*; also *2:21;
9:14, 21,* for example). God has ". . .
highly exalted him/ and gave him
the name/ that is above every
name,/ so that at the name of
Jesus/ every knee should bend . . ."
(*Philippians 2:9–10*).

Developed by the Desert Fathers, it
consists of short phrases from the
Scriptures repeated mentally with
attention to God's presence until
prayer becomes one with breathing
and the Lord comes to dwell within
(see *John 14:23, Revelation 3:20*).

The most popular version combines a common early Christian
acclamation (see *Philippians 2:11, 1
Corinthians 12:3, Romans 10:9*) with
the cry of the publican, "God, be
merciful to me, a sinner!" (*Luke
18:13*), and the blind beggar, "Jesus,
Son of David, have mercy on me!"
(*Luke 18:38, 39*):

1. *Lord Jesus Christ* (breathing in)
2. *Son of God* (breathing out)
3. *have mercy* (breathing in)
4. *on me a sinner* (breathing out)

## Come, Holy Spirit

This is the simplest, most direct
prayer to the Holy Spirit in the
Catholic Tradition. It evolved in
the antiphons and hymns of every
liturgical tradition, most notably
in the Pentecost sequence. (The sequence is a hymn of joy, of varying
length and meter, sung or recited
before the Gospel on certain feasts.)
Its first two lines paraphrase the
promise of the Spirit and the
experience of Pentecost recorded
in Scripture (see *Luke 24:49; Acts
1:4–5, 8; 2:1–13*). Its verse and
response paraphrase Psalm 104:30.
Its oration is a petition that the
faithful today be allowed to experience what the first disciples did
when they received the gift of the
Holy Spirit.

Come, Holy Spirit,
    fill the hearts of your faithful
And kindle in them
    the fire of your love.
Send forth your Spirit
    and they shall be created
And you shall renew
    the face of the earth.
Let us pray. Lord, by the light of the
Holy Spirit you have taught the hearts
of your faithful. In the same Spirit help
us to relish what is right and always
rejoice in your consolation. We ask this
through Christ our Lord. Amen.

## 2. Sunday Mass Readings

Some have made a habit of taking a "word to keep" from Sunday Mass. One advantage of finding a word from Sunday lectionary readings instead of during private Scripture reading is that it may capture in some way the whole liturgy of the word. That one word, one verse, could bring along the influence of four Scripture texts—the Old Testament reading, responsorial psalm, the New Testament reading, and the Gospel—as well as a homily.

Including the responsorial psalm, there are four readings from which to choose a word at Mass. The antiphon of the psalm may be a good place to start. Every Sunday and every day of the week there's a psalm chosen to match the first reading. It includes an antiphon that's repeated several times. That brief repetition may be the start of a habit of learning more Scripture by heart.

## 3. The Psalms of Night Prayer

When the *General Instruction of the Liturgy of the Hours* explains Night Prayer and mentions that each day of the week has its own psalms assigned, it adds, "It is permissible to use the Sunday psalms instead [of those assigned to the particular day], for the convenience especially of those who may wish to say Night Prayer from memory." It's not impossible. Look in Chapter 6 to see what the psalms of Night Prayer are.

## 4. Personal Choices

More and more of the faithful are choosing to know by heart certain verses from private Scripture reading and prayer. There are lots of methods and suggested Scriptures in the sections "Praying with Scripture" and "Praying Scripture's Prayers" earlier in this chapter.

*"Thy word is a lamp unto my feet, and a light unto my path."*
(*Psalm 119:105*, King James Version)

*"Let your Word, Father, be a lamp for our feet and a light to our path, so that we may understand what you wish to teach us and follow the path your light marks out for us."*
(Psalm-prayer in the Liturgy of the Hours following Psalm 119:105–112, Evening Prayer, Saturday night, week 2)

# The Four-Fold Sense of Scripture

## A Shepherd in the Shade

The simple drawing of a shepherd sitting in the shade found on the cover and the title page of the *Catechism of the Catholic Church* has become familiar to some as the logo of the *Catechism*.

### A Spiritual Sense

As Scripture itself has both a literal sense and a spiritual sense, so too does this simple drawing, as the *Catechism* itself explains: "The design of the logo on the cover [of the *Catechism*] is adapted from a Christian tombstone in the catacombs of Domitilla in Rome, which dates from the end of the third century AD. This pastoral image, of pagan origin, was used by Christians to symbolize the rest and the happiness that the soul of the departed finds in eternal life. This image also suggests certain characteristic aspects of this Catechism: Christ, the Good Shepherd who leads and protects his faithful (the lamb) by his authority (the staff), draws them by the melodious symphony of the truth (the panpipes), and makes them lie down in the shade of the tree of life, his redeeming Cross which opens paradise."

# The Senses of Scripture

This topic is treated in Chapter 4. "According to an ancient tradition, one can distinguish between two *senses* of Scripture: the literal and the spiritual, the latter being subdivided into the allegorical, moral, and anagogical senses" (CCC, 115).

## The Four-Fold Sense of Scripture

These categories draw on an ancient tradition that, by the late thirteenth century, had constructed an elaborate system of biblical interpretation, dividing the meanings of the Old Testament texts into four senses:

1. Literal
2. Allegorical—referring to the New Testament or the Christian Church
3. Moral (tropological)—referring to the fate of the individual soul
4. Anagogical—referring to universal history and eschatology (end times)

There is a medieval verse, "The letter speaks of belief; allegory to faith; the moral how to act; anagogy our destiny." Jerusalem is a standard illustration of this scheme:

1. Literally, Jerusalem is a city.
2. Allegorically, Jerusalem is the Church.
3. Morally, Jerusalem is the soul of the believer.
4. Anagogically, Jerusalem is the heavenly city of God.

However, not all Old Testament texts were thought to have four senses. In fact, the "more-than-literal" meanings were born out of the fact that commentators couldn't come up with a literal sense that was meaningful to them.

## An Example

The following is an example of this elaborate system of biblical interpretation. It is from the writings of Pope Saint Gregory the Great (AD 540–604), the last of the Latin Fathers of the Western Church. It is from a reader by William Yarchin (*History of Biblical Interpretation*) in which the editor says, "Gregory's writings—which include hundreds of letters, an authoritative compendium of pastoral rules, reflections on the lives of the saints, and biblical commentary—had an enormous influence on the spiritual life of Western Christians and on the spiritual life of church administrators for centuries after his death. His best-known works in biblical interpretation are commentaries, one on the book of Ezekiel and one on the book of Job" (p. 86).

"By the sixth century, the figurative modes of biblical interpretation that had been worked out in more ecclesiastically contentious times were available for consistent application to the struggles of the Christian soul against moral temptation and spiritual hunger. Gregory sought to nurture his readers by first attending to the outward, literal sense of the biblical text and from there working inward to the spiritual sense through allegory, to which in turn he would give the moral meaning—thus bringing his readers back out to their own world, where they could live out what they had inwardly discovered in the text with him. His procedure is evident in his *Moralia in Job*, where he first treats the literal meaning (his phrase is 'the history' or 'the historical sense') of a passage, reviewing the passage again for the allegorical meaning and then returning once more for the tropological or moral significance hidden within the allegory. Gregory [displays] the fruits of the formative Western patristic period of biblical interpretation as exhibited in a single commentary on a single biblical book. The chart on pp. 336–337 is excerpted from *Moralia in Job*, where Gregory presents a preface to his entire commentary and treats the first five verses of Job 1. The selection contains his historical, allegorical, and tropological comments on only the second verse of Job 1, where it is recorded that Job sired seven sons and three daughters" (p. 87).

## A Contemporary Observation

The Pontifical Biblical Commission, in their 1993 publication *The Interpretation of the Bible in the Church*, comments on this kind of biblical interpretation by the fathers of the Church:

"Convinced that they are dealing with the Book of God and therefore with something of inexhaustible meaning, the fathers hold that any particular passage is open to any particular interpretation on an allegorical basis. But they also consider that others are free to offer something else, provided only that what is offered respects the analogy of faith" (III.B.2).

"The allegorical interpretation of Scripture so characteristic of patristic exegesis runs the risk of being something of an embarrassment to people today. But the experience of the Church expressed in this exegesis makes a contribution that is always useful (see *Divino Afflante Spiritu*, 31–32; *Dei Verbum*, 23). The fathers of the Church teach to read the Bible theologically, within the heart of a living tradition, with an authentic Christian spirit" (III.B.2).

## The Spiritual Application of the Bible:
## Pope Saint Gregory the Great (AD 540-604)

"The reader must realize that some things are expounded here as simple historical narrative, some things examined for the allegorical signification, and some things discussed only for their moral import—but that of course some things are explored carefully in all three ways. First we lay the foundations of historical fact; then we lift up the mind to the citadel of faith through allegory; finally through the exposition of the moral sense we dress the edifice in its colored raiment" (p. 88).

### *"There were born to him seven sons and three daughters" (Job 1:2).*

### Literal

"A large family often stirs the heart of a parent to greed. The more heirs he is blessed with, the more he is stirred to try to build a great estate. To show the holiness of mind of blessed Job, he is proclaimed and shown to have been a just man and shown again to have been the father of a large family. At the very outset of the book he is said to have been devout in offering sacrifice, and later he is reported, in his own words, to have been generous with gifts. We should recognize the great strength he was endowed with when we think how not even love for his many children could make him cling to his property.

### Allegorical

"What does the number seven stand for if not the whole of perfection? . . . These are the apostles going forth manfully to preach. When they accomplish the commands of perfection they symbolize the study life of the higher sex. This is why there were twelve of them chosen to be filled with the seven-fold grace of the spirit, for the number seven is closely related to the number twelve. The parts of the number seven (4+3) multiplied together come to twelve. Whether you take four three times or three four times, seven turns into twelve. Thus the holy apostles, who were sent to preach the three persons of God to the four corners of the world, were chosen twelve in number, so that even by their number they should symbolize the perfection they preached by their words and deeds.

"What shall we take the daughters for, if not the flock of less-gifted faithful? Even if they do not stay the course for the perfection of good works by strength and virtue, they cling tenaciously to the faith they know in the trinity. In the seven sons we see the rank of preachers, but in the three daughters the multitude of hearers.

"The three daughters can also stand for the three classes of the faithful. After the sons the daughters are named because after the courage displayed by the apostles there came three classes of the faithful in the church's life: pastors, the continent [those vowed to a religious life], and the married. This is why the prophet Ezekiel says that he heard three men were set free: Noah, Daniel, and Job [see *Ezekiel 14:14-20*]. Noah, who guided the ark through the waves, stands for the order of leaders who, while they preside over the people to set a pattern for living, govern the holy church in the midst of the breakers of temptation. Daniel, who is praised for his wonderful continence, represents the life of the ascetic who, abandoning all the things of this world, despises Babylon and lords over it in the citadel of his spirit. Job then stands for the life of the virtuous lay people in married life, who do good works with the things they possess of this world, following the path of this world to the heavenly fatherland. Since the three orders of the faithful come after the holy apostles, so it is appropriate that after the seven sons the three daughters should be mentioned.

### Tropological

"Seven sons are born for us when the seven virtues of the Holy Spirit quicken to life in us through the conception of right thinking. The prophet counts up this inner progeny that comes from the fertility of the Spirit, saying: 'The Spirit of the Lord shall rest upon him, a spirit of wisdom and understanding, a spirit of counsel and strength, a spirit of knowledge and devotion; and the spirit of the fear of the Lord shall fill him' [see *Isaiah 11:2-3*]. When wisdom, understanding, counsel, strength, knowledge, devotion and fear of the Lord spring to life for us through the coming of the Spirit, it is like the generation of a long-lived progeny in the mind, which keeps alive our noble lineage from heaven by giving us to share the love of eternity. These seven sons have three sisters in our hearts, because whatever these virtues generate is joined to the three theological virtues of hope, faith and charity. The seven sons cannot achieve the perfection of the number ten unless everything they do is done in hope, faith and charity. Because the thought of good works soon accompanies this abundance of virtues that go on before, it is rightly added: 'His wealth included seven thousand sheep and three thousand camels' (Job 1:3). We can recognize here the accuracy of the historical narrative, while still imitating the spirit what comes to our hearing through ears of the flesh. We possess seven thousand sheep when in perfect purity of heart we feed our innocent thoughts within on the long-sought food of truth. We will possess three thousand camels, if we can subdue everything lofty and twisted that is within us to the authority of faith and bow down willingly in humble longing that comes from knowledge of the trinity. We possess camels if we humbly lay down all our lofty thoughts. We surely possess camels when we turn our thoughts to compassion for our brother's weakness so that, bearing one another's burdens, we might know how to come to the aid of another's troubles [see *Galatians 6:2*]."

# Figures of Speech in Scripture

## Demosthenes

L ong, long ago in ancient Greece there were two famous Athenian orators, the celebrated Demosthenes and his rival Aeschines. Demosthenes said to his foe, "When you orate, people say, 'How well he speaks.' When I orate, they say, 'Let us march on Philip.'"

# Rousing Words

*Isaiah 50:4* declares, "The Lord GOD has given me the tongue of a teacher, / that I may know how to sustain the weary with a word." Not words, a word—a message—that will rouse them. But a word needs words, and some are more rousing than others.

## Rhetoric

Rhetoric is the art of speaking or writing effectively and / or persuasively. Rhetoric is "the deliberate exploitation of eloquence for the most persuasive effect in public speaking or in writing," according to the *Oxford Concise Dictionary of Literary Terms* (Chris Baldick, editor, 2004).

## Figures of Speech

Rhetoric uses, among other things, figures of speech to "emphasize or enliven a point," to give a special meaning, to create an effect. A figure of speech is "an expression that departs from the accepted literal sense or from the normal order of words, or in which an emphasis is produced by patterns of sound" (*Oxford Concise Dictionary of Literary Terms*). This definition includes three ways an expression qualifies as a figure of speech. All of the figures of speech in this appendix fall into one of these three categories:

- an expression that departs from the accepted literal sense

- an expression that departs from the normal order of words

- an expression in which an emphasis is produced by patterns of sound

In addition to this definition, the dictionary explains: "The ancient theory of rhetoric named and categorized dozens of figures, drawing a rough and often disputed distinction between those that extend the meaning of words [the first category in the definition above] and those that merely affect their order or their impact upon an audience [the second and third categories in the definition above]." (About the second and third categories, the dictionary mentions some of the ways that figures of speech work: by placing words in contrast to one another, by repeating words in various patterns, by changing the order or words, by [omitting] conjunctions, by assuming special modes of address, or by the repetition of sounds.)

When something especially striking and memorable is read or heard, it's probably not only because of the message itself but also because of its figurative language. Like all great literature, Scripture is a treasure trove of figurative language. How could the word not be filled with the power of words? Unfortunately, many figures of speech are lost in translation. This is especially true of figures that depend on the *sound* of words. So there are explanations in the following pages of both the modern translation as well as the original text.

# A Glossary of Figures of Speech

The definitions in this glossary rely on the scholarship of the *Oxford Concise Dictionary of Literary Terms*.

**Alliteration** (ah-lit-er-a-shun)

Alliteration is the close repetition of consonant sounds, usually at the beginning of words, as in "She sells seashells by the seashore." (The close repetition of vowel sounds is called assonance.) For these, the reader invariably needs the help of someone who knows Hebrew. Those who don't can still appreciate the commentary from those who do.

- In *1 Samuel 1:27–28*, Hannah says of Samuel, "I prayed for this child, and the Lord granted my request. Now I, in turn, give him to the Lord; as long as he lives, he shall be dedicated to the LORD" (NAB, 1970 and revised). The Hebrew words for 'requested,' 'granted,' 'give,' and 'dedicated' are all based on the same root *sa-al*. This alliterative technique, however, is lost in translation.

- *Psalm 29:3–9*: "The voice of the LORD is over the waters;/ . . . The voice of the LORD is powerful;/ the voice of the LORD is full of majesty./ The voice of the LORD breaks the cedars;/ . . . The voice of the LORD flashes forth flames of fire./ The voice of the LORD shakes the wilderness;/ . . . The voice of the LORD causes the oaks to whirl,/ and strips the forest bare . . ." (The revised NAB footnote comments, "the sevenfold repetition of the phrase imitates the sound of crashing thunder . . .") There's also an anaphora in the repetition of "the voice" (see anaphora on p. 342).

- The English translation of *Psalm 30:13a* by *The Grail* uses an alliteration of s's: "So my soul sings psalms to you unceasingly."

- *The New Jerome Biblical Commentary* points out an alliterative "call to attention" in *Isaiah 1:3*: *"sime'u samayim."* In English— with the repetition of the "h" sound—this one is not all lost on us: "Hear, O heavens . . ."

- The speakers in *Isaiah 28:9* ridicule Isaiah and use some high level sarcasm: "To whom would he impart knowledge?/ To whom would he convey the message?/ To those just weaned from milk,/ those taken from the breast?" (revised NAB) And then they mockingly imitate the prophet, with alliterative words that make him sound like a stammering child: "(For he says), 'SAU LASAU, SAU LASAU, CAU LACU, CAU LACAU, ZE'ER SHAM, ZE'ER SHAM.'" In English, of course, the alliteration is lost: "Command on command, command on command,/ rule on rule, rule on rule,/ here a little, there a little!" But even in English, the words that follow (*verse 11*) leave no doubt about the derision: "Yes, with stammering lips and in a strange language/ he will speak to this people . . ."

- *Genesis 49:19* is alliterative: *"gad dedud yegudenno . . . yagud."* English translations can only approximate rhetorical features like this: "Gad shall be raided by raiders,/ but he shall raid at their heels" (NAB, 1970 and revised) Or, "Gad, robbers rob him,/ and he, he robs and pursues them" (JB).

**Anadiplosis** (an-a-di-*plo*-sis)

"To be doubled back." Anadiplosis is the repetition of an ending phrase at the beginning of the next sentence or literary unit. (Repeated anadiplosis in a chain-like progression is called *gradatio*—which means "steps.")

- "I lift up my eyes to the hills— from where will <u>my help</u> come?/ <u>My help</u> comes from the LORD,/ who made heaven and earth" (*Psalm 121:1–2*).

- "I will turn the rivers into <u>marshes</u>,/ and the <u>marshes</u> I will dry up" (*Isaiah 42:15*, NAB, 1970 and revised).

- "What <u>I speak</u>, therefore, <u>I speak</u> just as the Father told me" (*John 12:50*).

- *The New Jerome Biblical Commentary* says this figure of speech is characteristic of *Isaiah 26*. The following, for example, are *verses 2–4, 8–9*: "Open up the gates/ to let in a nation that is just,/ one that keeps faith./ A nation of firm

purpose you keep <u>in peace</u>;/ <u>in peace</u>, for its <u>trust in you</u>./ <u>Trust in the Lord</u> forever! . . ./ Yes, for your way and your judgments, O Lord,/ we look to <u>you</u>;/ <u>Your name</u> and your title/ are the desire of <u>our souls</u>,/ <u>My soul</u> yearns for you in the night . . ." (NAB).

**Anaphora** (ah-*naph*-or-ah)

"A bringing back, repeating." The anaphora (also known as epanaphora) repeats the same word or words at the beginning of successive phrases or clauses in order to give emphasis. A similar repetition at the end is called an epiphora (also known as epistrophe). The use of anaphora and epiphora in the same sentence or passage is called a symploce.

- There is an anaphora constructed around the words "Blessed are . . ." in the eight successive phrases of the beatitudes of Matthew 5:3–10.

- The nine-fold repetition of "love" and "it" in *1 Corinthians 13:4–6* is a striking anaphora: "<u>Love is</u> patient; <u>love is</u> kind; <u>love is</u> not envious or boastful or arrogant or rude. <u>It does</u> not insist on its own way; <u>it is</u> not irritable or resentful; <u>it does</u> not rejoice in wrongdoing, but rejoices in truth."

- The repetition of the seven "I wills" in *Genesis 17:2–8* highlights God's initiative and commitment in the covenant with Abraham: "And <u>I will</u> make my covenant between me and you, and [I] <u>will</u> make you exceedingly numerous . . . <u>I will</u> make you exceedingly fruitful; and I will make nations of you, and kings shall come from you. I will establish my covenant between me and you, and your offspring after you throughout their generations, for an everlasting covenant, to be God to you and to your offspring after you. And I will give to you, and to your offspring after you, the land where you are now an alien, all the land of Canaan, for a perpetual holding; and I will be their God."

- The five "I wills" of the morning star ("Lucifer") constitute an anaphora, emphasizing the sin of Lucifer to think he was greater than God: "You said in your heart, 'I will ascend to heaven; I will raise my throne above the stars of God; I will sit on the mount of assembly . . . I will ascend to the tops of the clouds, I will make myself like the Most High.'" (Isaiah 14:12–15).

- There is an anaphora of four "fors" in 2 Timothy 3:16. In the 1970 NAB it was left out: "All Scripture is inspired of God and is useful for teaching—for re-proof, correction, and training in holiness. . . ." In the revised NAB it was restored: "All scripture is inspired by God and is useful for teaching, for refutation, for correction, and for training in righteousness . . ."

- There are ten "neither/nors" (Greek outes) in a row in Paul's outpouring in Romans 8:38–39: "For I am convinced that nei-

ther death, nor life, / nor angels, nor principalities, / nor present things, nor future things, / nor powers, nor height, nor depth, / nor any other creature will be able to separate us / from the love of God in Christ Jesus our Lord" (revised NAB).

- There is an anaphora in the repetition of "whatever is" in Philippians 4:8: "Whatever is true, whatever is honorable, whatever is just, whatever is pure, what-ever is lovely, whatever is gra-cious, if there is any excellence and if there is anything worthy of praise, think about these things" (revised NAB).

- The repetition of "any" in Philip-pians 2:1 make up an anaphora: "If there is any encouragement in Christ, any solace in love, any participation in the Spirit, any compassion and mercy, complete my joy by being of the same mind . . ." (revised NAB).

**Anastrophe** (ah-nas-tro-fee)
"A turning back." The anastrophe is an unusual word order (a "hyperbaton") that creates a word order reversed, usually of an adjective and its noun ("Working like a man possessed"; "Father all powerful") but also of a verb with its noun (Says who? Says I).

- The Word incarnate (or the devil incarnate).

- "Life eternal" is a typical New Testament expression, although you usually have to look in the Greek translations to find it. The NAB (1970) translates Romans

*5:21*, for example, ". . . as sin reigned in death, grace also might reign through justification for eternal life through Jesus Christ our Lord." In Greek, the word "life" comes first, then the adjective "eternal" (see also *John 6:54* and *17:2*).

- A people lost and forsaken.

**Antithesis** (an-*tih*-the-sis)

"Opposition." This device places a sentence—or part of it—against another to which it is opposed; a parallelism of words and ideas.

- There are six antitheses in Matthew 5:21–48. At least they are usually so called. *The New Jerome Biblical Commentary*, actually, calls them "hyphertheses" (42:29), because in them Jesus is not contradicting Mosaic law (antithetically) but going beyond it (*hyper*thetically). They are six examples of conduct demanded of the Christian disciple: about anger, adultery, divorce, oaths, love of enemies, and retaliation. Each deals with a commandment of the law introduced by "You have heard that it was said to your ancestors" (or an equivalent phrase) followed by Jesus' contrasting teaching introduced by "But I say to you." So they're called "antitheses." Three of them accept the Mosaic law but extend or deepen it (the ones about anger, adultery, and love of enemies). Three of them reject it as a standard of conduct for the disciples (the ones about divorce, oaths, and retaliation).

- There are three antitheses in the Sermon on the Mount in the course of Jesus' teaching on almsgiving, prayer, and fasting (see *Matthew 6:1–18*).

- Matthew 7:13–28 ends Jesus' Sermon on the Mount with a series of antitheses, which contrast those who obey Jesus' words and those who don't, beginning with ". . . the gate is wide and the road broad that leads to destruction, and those who enter through it are many. How narrow the gate and constricted the road that leads to life. And those who find it are few" (revised NAB).

**Apostrophe** (a-*pahss*-tro-fee)

"Turning away." The apostrophe is "a rhetorical figure in which the speaker addresses a dead or absent person, or an abstraction or inanimate object" (*Oxford Concise Dictionary of Literary Terms*).

The 1970 NAB puts the heading "Apostrophe to Jerusalem" before *Luke 13:34–35* ("O Jerusalem, Jerusalem, you slay the prophets . . .") The heading in the revised NAB simply says "The Lament over Jerusalem." Nevertheless, the two verses that follow, rhetorically speaking, are an "apostrophe," as are the similar ones in *Luke 19:41–44* that begin, "Coming within sight of the city, he wept over it and said, 'If only you had known the path to peace . . .'"

**Assonance** (*ass*-ah-nunce)

"Vowel rhyme" is the close repetition of vowel sounds, usually in stressed syllables, as in "Twinkle,

twinkle, little star" and "sweet dreams." (The close repetition of consonant sounds is called alliteration.) Enjoying the assonance in a passage depends upon knowing the original language.

A revised NAB footnote to Genesis 49:19 explains that "In Hebrew there is a certain assonance between the name Gad and the words for 'raided,' 'raiders' and 'raid.'" An effort was made to bring it into English: "Gad shall be raided by raiders,/ but he shall raid at their heels."

### Asyndeton (ah-*sin*-dah-tun)

"Not linked." This technique omits conjunctions and can convey urgency in the statement of an idea. It leaves a sentence more stark, uncluttered, without the competition of conjunctions, as in Caesar's well known "I came, I saw, I conquered" (*Veni, vidi, vici*, in Latin.) It's the opposite of "polysyndeton," which uses more conjunctions than necessary. Literary critics have observed that writers will prefer one or the other: asyndetons are more common in Shakespeare, for example, and polysyndetons in Scripture. (And Scripture scholars point out that, in Hebrew, almost every sentence opens with "and." Hebrew/ Aramaic speakers writing in Greek continued the practice.)

- "[Love] bears all things, believes all things, hopes all things, endures all things" (*1 Corinthians 13:7*).

- "And now faith, hope, and love abide, these three; and the great-

est of these is love" (*1 Corinthians 13:13*).

### Chiasmus (ky-*az*-mus)

From the Greek letter *chi* which in form resembles an X. A chiasmus is the reverse repetition of words or phrases, creating a cross parallel, as in Saint Anselm's statement, "I do not seek to understand that I may believe. I believe in order to understand." The phrases that include the words "understand" and "believe" are repeated in reverse order. By designating the words "understand," "believe," "believe," "understand" as "A-B-B-A," then writing the two sentences one above the other and connecting with one line each A and with another each B, an X or *chi* is created. It's a chiasmus. It creates an interlocking literary unit. It adds variety, as in Saint Bernard's praise of solitude, "O blessed solitude! O solitary blessedness!" It brings home the significance of the thought and makes it more memorable. And sometimes it just makes it more memorable, like the fisherman's excuse, "It's better to go fishing and think about church than go to church and think about fishing." (See synchysis below for the a different interlocking pattern of A-B-A-B.)

- In Matthew 7:12, the first part of the chiasmus is the understood "you"—You/others and them/ you: "In everything [You] do to others as you would have them do to you" (*Matthew 7:12*).

- In *Psalm 50:15b*, the X is formed by I/you and you/me: "<u>I</u> will deliver <u>you</u>, and <u>you</u> shall glorify <u>me</u>."

- Often the chiasmus is in the form of an antithesis (which introduces and emphasizes a contrast or opposition of ideas): "The <u>sabbath</u> was made for <u>humankind</u>, and not <u>humankind</u> for the <u>sabbath</u>" (*Mark 2:27*); "<u>You</u> did not choose <u>me</u> but <u>I</u> chose <u>you</u>" (*John 15:16*); "As you have used <u>us</u> to show your holiness to <u>them</u>, so use <u>them</u> to show your glory to <u>us</u>" (*Sirach 36:3*).

- Sometimes the chiasmus involves a repetition, which, together with the inverted word order, gives emphasis: "I will lead the <u>blind</u> on their <u>journey</u>; by <u>paths unknown</u> I will guide <u>them</u>" (*Isaiah 42:16*, NAB, 1970 and revised).

- A chiasmus interweaves the first two verses of *Psalm 123*: "To you I lift up my eyes, / O you who are enthroned in the heavens! (A) / As the eyes of servants / look to the hand of their master, (B) / as the eyes of a maid / to the hand of her mistress, (B) / so our eyes look to the LORD our God, / until he has mercy on us (A)."

- More than two elements can be repeated in reverse order in making a chiasmus: (A) "Jesus said to him, 'Stand up, take your mat and walk.' (B) At once the man was made well, and he took up his mat and began to walk. (C) Now that day was a sabbath. (C) So the Jews said to the man who had been cured, 'It is the sabbath; (B) it is not lawful for you to carry your mat.' But he answered them, (A) 'The man who made me well said to me, "Take up your mat and walk"'" (*John 5:8–11*).

- Luke employs a "chiastic structure" in his account of the Agony in the Garden (*22:39–46*): After an introductory verse (39) Luke has Jesus say, (A) "Pray that you may not come into the time of trial" (verse 40). Then (B) he withdraws from them, kneels and prays (see verse 41). Then Luke records (C) the content of the prayer and the resolution of Jesus (see verses 42–44). Then (B') Jesus rises from prayer and returns to the disciples (verse 45). Then Jesus repeats, (A') "Pray that you may not come into the time of trial" (verse 46).

**Ellipsis** (ee-*lip*-sus)

"Omission." An ellipsis omits some easily understood word or words in order to avoid repetition and create rapidity of narration. Ellipsis can describe several rhetorical devices—the ellipsis of conjunctions in asyndetons, for example.

- In *Jeremiah 31:10*, there is a simple ellipsis of the verb "guards": "He who scattered Israel, now gathers them together, / he guards them as a shepherd [guards] his flock" (NAB, 1970 and revised).

- In *Psalm 84:11* there is an ellipsis of "days": "Better one day in your courts / than a thousand [days] elsewhere" (revised NAB).

- The *New Jerome Biblical Commentary* points out several "elliptical phrases" in *Psalm 65*: "you prepared (the earth for the planting of) grain (with the coming of the winter rains)" (verse 10); "your tracks (left by your rain-cloud chariot) dripped (the rain that produced) lush growth" (verse 12); "the hills were clothed with (the vines that produce the wine that brings) joy" (verse 13).

- The psalmist's cry, "How long, O Lᴏʀᴅ?" (as in *Psalms 13:1* and *89:46*, for example) is elliptical for "How long, O Lᴏʀᴅ, before you act."

**Epanalepsis** (e-pan-ah-*lehp*-sus)
This is the repetition of a word or phrase that appears at the beginning of a unit at the end of that same unit. The use of epanalepsis to mark off a whole passage is called an *inclusio*.

"Rejoice in the Lord always; again I will say, Rejoice!" (*Philippians 4:4*)

**Epiphora** (e-*pih*-for-ah)
"A bringing upon." Epiphora (also known as an epistrophe) is the repetition of the same word or words at the end of successive phrases or clauses in order to give emphasis. (Repetition at the beginning is an anaphora.) When the end repetition is within words themselves (as in the third example below), it's called homoeoteleuton ("same end").

- "Do not become idolaters as some of them did, . . . We must not indulge in sexual immorality

as some of them did, . . . We must not put Christ to the test as some of them did, . . . And do not complain as some of them did . . ." (*1 Corinthians 10:7–10*).

- "When I was a child, I spoke like a child, I thought like a child, I reasoned like a child . . ." (*1 Corinthians 13:11*).

- In the creedal hymn of *1 Timothy 3:16* the six Greek verbs all end in the same sound—as they do, mostly (with the –ed and –en endings) in the revised NAB translation: "Undeniably great is the mystery of devotion, / Who was manifested in the flesh, / vindicated in the spirit, / seen by angels, / proclaimed to the Gentiles, / believed in throughout the world, / taken up in glory."

- "Vanity of vanities, says the Teacher, / vanity of vanities! All is vanity!" (*Ecclesiastes 1:1*).

**Euphemism** (*you*-fah-mizm)
"To speak well." The euphemism has been called "a strategic misrepresentation" because it substitutes a mild or acceptable or indirect expression for one that is believed to be offensively harsh or vulgar or blunt.

- "Debts" is a euphemism for sins in Matthew's version of the Lord's Prayer (see *Matthew 6:12*).

- Mary's response at the annunciation in *Luke 1:34* was "How can this be since I do not know man?" (NAB, 1970 translation.) That is a euphemism. What it really means is what the revised NAB says: "How can this be, since I have no (sexual) relations with a man?" The CEV translates it "How can this happen? I am not married!" which is itself another euphemism. It would have been considered crude and offensive for Mary to say, "I haven't had sex." And the CEV is avoiding offending its contemporary readers by not talking about premarital sex. So in this case there is a euphemism in Greek and another one in English translation.

- 1 Samuel 24 contains another passage that is a magnet for euphemisms. The KJV translation (1 Samuel 24:3) is: "And he came to the sheepcotes by the way, where was a cave; and Saul went in to cover his feet." "Cover his feet?" That's what it says in Hebrew. In English translation there is another euphemism (1 Samuel 24:4): "When he came to the sheepfolds along the way, he found a cave, which he entered to ease nature" (NAB, 1970 translation). The LB (a paraphrase) says, "Saul went into the cave to go to the bathroom." Now there's a euphemism, and an anachronism to boot. The British edition of the LB changes that to "Saul went into a cave to relieve himself." (After the American version, that's a relief.)

- The feet are sometimes used as a euphemism for sexual organs. The KJV brings it right into English, as in this euphemism within a metaphor from Isaiah 7:20: "In the same day shall the Lord shave with a razor that is hired,

namely, by them beyond the river, by the king of Assyria, the head, and the hair of the feet: and it shall also consume the beard." (The revised NAB, usually more literal, in this case drops the more acceptable Hebrew euphemism and says what they meant: "On that day the LORD shall shave with the razor hired from across the River [with the king of Assyria] the head, and the hair between the legs. It shall also shave off the beard.")

## Gradatio (grah-dah-sheo)

"Steps." A gradatio is the use of repeated anadiploses (repetition of an end at the next beginning) in a chain-like progression.

- A footnote on John 1:1–18 in the revised NAB points out this "staircase parallelism" in the first stanza of John's prologue. Notice how the last word of one phrase becomes the first word of the next: ". . . without him nothing came to be. / What came to be through him was life, / and this life was the light of the human race; / the light shines in the darkness, / and the darkness has not overcome it" (John 1:3–5).

- Romans 5:3–5 says, ". . . we even boast of our afflictions, / knowing that affliction produces endurance, / and endurance, proven character, / and proven character, hope, / and hope does not disappoint . . ." (revised NAB). It could have said (without the gradatio) something like, "With affliction comes endurance and then proven character and then hope," but the certainty of how one characteristic progressively builds on another would be less forceful.

- Also in *Romans 8:29–30*, the repetition of "predestined," "called," and "justified" is not needed for clarity, but for effect: "For those he foreknew he also <u>predestined</u> to be conformed to the image of his Son, so that he might be the firstborn among many brothers. And those he <u>predestined</u> he also <u>called</u>; and <u>those he called</u> he also <u>justified</u>; and <u>those he justified</u> he also glorified" (revised NAB).

- The staircase in *Romans 10:13–15* is in reverse order—or descending: believed/believe, hear/hear, preach/preach: "For, 'Everyone who calls on the name of the Lord shall be saved.' But how are they to call on one in whom they have not <u>believed</u>? / And how are they to <u>believe</u> in one of whom they have never <u>heard</u>? / And how are they to <u>hear</u> without someone to <u>proclaim</u> him? / And how are they to <u>proclaim</u> him unless they are sent?" (There are also four beautifully constructed rhetorical questions in this passage, as well as an anaphora in the four-fold "and how.")

The steps in *2 Peter 1:5–7* are tightly compact: "For this very reason, you must make every effort to support your <u>faith with goodness</u>, and <u>goodness with knowledge</u>, and <u>knowledge with self-control</u>, and <u>self-control with endurance</u>, and <u>endurance with godliness</u>, and <u>godliness with mutual affection</u>, and <u>mutual affection with love.</u>"

**Hyperbaton** (hy-*per*-bah-ton)
"Transposition." The hyperbaton changes the usual word order by a striking displacement of words. Most frequently a word or phrase is emphasized by placing it either at the beginning or at the end of a sentence or clause.

- In *Genesis 1:27*, the first phrase is in the expected word order, but the second and third put the prepositional phrase at the beginning instead of at the end: "So God created humankind in his image, / <u>in the image of God</u> he created them; / <u>male and female</u> he created them."

- In *Job 1:21*, the placement of "naked" as the first word in the sentence emphasizes Job's poverty and dependence on God: "<u>Naked</u> I came from my mother's womb . . ."

Likewise, in the following examples from the revised NAB, emphasis is given by moving a word or phrase from later in a sentence to the beginning:

- "<u>Complacent,</u> I once said, / 'I shall never be shaken'" (*Psalm 30:7*).

- "For <u>slaves</u> we are, but in our servitude our God has not abandoned us . . ." (*Ezra 9:9*).

- "<u>By their fruits</u> you will know them" (*Matthew 7:16*).

- "<u>Without parables</u> he did not speak to them . . ." (*Mark 4:34*).

- Verses 9 and 10 of *1 John 4*, about God's love and Christian life, have back-to-back hyperbatons (just like the Greek original): "<u>In this way</u> the love of God was revealed to us: God sent his only Son into the world so that we might have life through him. <u>In this</u> is love: not that we have loved God, but that he loved us and sent his Son as expiation for our sins." (The 1970 NAB translated these two phrases without preserving the hyperbaton, putting the words in their "proper" place: "God's love was revealed in our midst <u>in this way</u> . . . Love, then, consists <u>in this</u> . . .")

## Hyperbole (hy-*per*-bah-lee)

"Excess, exaggeration, throwing beyond." Hyperbole is an intentional, obvious overstatement or exaggeration in order to emphasize the seriousness or importance of a situation. When your mother says she's going crazy, she's probably using a hyperbole.

- "Semitic exaggeration" is a common device in Scripture. Not understanding hyperbole can lead to some novel uses of Scripture—like the minister, reacting to Catholics calling priests "father," who cited *Matthew 23:9*: "Call no one on earth your father . . ." (The 1970 NAB had a footnote on that verse: "Typical hyperbolic speech of the time. It does not reject authority in principle, but authoritarianism; not the use of titles, but the failure to acknowledge that authority exists to serve God, his anointed One, and one's neighbor.")

- Jesus employed hyperbole when he called Peter a name: "[H]e turned and said to Peter, 'Get behind me, <u>Satan</u>!'" (*Matthew 16:23*).

- Instead of warning that Jesus' saving mission would cause division, Luke has Jesus speak forcefully—and hyperbolically—when he said he came to bring division: "Do you think that I have come to bring peace to the earth? No, I tell you, but rather division" (*Luke 12:51*). Matthew records Jesus speaking in a similar vein: "For I have come to set a man against his father, / and a daughter against her mother . . .'" (*Matthew 10:35*).

- Raqa is an Aramaic word "probably meaning 'imbecile,' 'block-head,' a term of abuse" (revised NAB footnote). It's an insulting term that could be a step to anger that could be a motive for murder. Jesus taught this—using hyperbole: ". . . Whoever is angry with his brother / will be liable to judgment, / and whoever says to his brother, / 'Raqa,' will be answerable to the Sanhedrin, / and whoever says, 'You fool,' will be liable to fiery Gehenna" (*Matthew 5:22*).

- *Matthew 18:8* includes a well-known hyperbole that is extreme: "If your hand or foot causes you to stumble, <u>cut it off</u> and throw it away." One in *Luke 14:12* is more subtle: "When you give a luncheon or a dinner, <u>do not invite your friends</u> or your brothers or your relatives . . ."

- Some troublesome verses are resolved with an understanding of hyperbole. *Luke 14:26* for example: "Whoever comes to me and does not <u>hate</u> father and mother, wife and children, brothers and sisters, yes, and even life itself, cannot be my disciple." On this verse, *The Collegeville Bible Commentary* points out: "Jesus returns to the theme of family division that might come because of the gospel (see 12:51–53)." This is another literary exaggeration to stress that a disciple should not allow anyone to stand in the way of thorough commitment to Jesus, even one's closest relatives. "Hate" in this sense means "prefer less." This radical message of the cross, of course, cannot be understood to condone hatred of any kind.

### Inclusion

An inclusion is an epanalepsis, which some call by its Latin name *inclusio* (in-*clue*-zee-o). It encloses a passage within the bookends of matching phrases, stories, or scenes. It frames a passage.

- The opening and closing of Matthew's genealogy of Jesus form a very artful *inclusio* (note Jesus, David, Abraham at the beginning and Abraham, David, Messiah at the end). *Matthew 1:1:* "An account of the genealogy of <u>Jesus</u> the Messiah, the son of <u>David</u>, the son of <u>Abraham</u>." *Matthew*

*1:17:* "So all the generations from <u>Abraham</u> to David are fourteen generations; and from <u>David</u> to the deportation to Babylon, fourteen generations; and from the deportation to Babylon to the <u>Messiah</u>, fourteen generations."

- Two blindness stories in Mark, 8:22–26 and 10:46–52, are an *inclusio* that frames a picture of three passion predictions, each followed by failures of the disciples to understand and by teachings of Jesus on discipleship. In the first story of Jesus giving sight, the blind man was brought to Jesus and he was healed only in stages. In the second story, the blind man came of his own accord and received his sight immediately. They frame a literary unit whose centerpiece is the transfiguration. In the second story, Bartimaeus ends up following Jesus on the way—to Jerusalem and death. The blindness stories frame a passage designed to teach the meaning of true discipleship: the healed blind man stands in stark contrast to the disciples.

- *The New Jerome Biblical Commentary*, commenting on Luke 2:7, points out an inn/food *inclusio* in Luke: "In order to create and underline the important and symbolic value he places on the thrice-mentioned manger (2:7, 12, 16), Luke says there was no room in the inn. Although born in lowly circumstances and without hospitality, Jesus is the one who will be host to starving humanity.

Fully grown and about to lay down his life as a servant, Jesus hosts in an inn (22:11) a meal that his disciples will continue in his memory." (A manger, it should be noted in this modern day, is a feed trough for animals.) Instead of defining this as an *inclusio*, bracketing a literary unit, some scholars say instead that it's simply a flashback, calling to mind the circumstances of Jesus' destiny-revealing birth.

- Some say the temple is another *inclusio* for Saint Luke, who is unique among the Evangelists in the central role he gives to the temple in his version of the Gospel (see *Luke 2:22, 2:41, 4:9, 20:1, 21:37, 23:45*). It begins in the temple (after a four-verse prologue) and ends in the temple (24:53). Luke makes the temple an *inclusio* not only for his book but also for Jesus' life itself: from his "presentation in the temple" (2:22) as an infant to his "cleansing of the temple" (19:45) just prior to his death. (John placed the "cleansing of the temple" episode at the beginning of his book, in 2:13.) Others say that the temple is simply a theme in the Gospel of Luke, expressed through the repetition of the temple setting.

- There is an *inclusio* in Matthew *11:2–19*, formed by the word "works," in which wisdom is likened to the Messiah. The passage describes the messengers from John the Baptist in prison going to Jesus and Jesus' testimony to John. It begins, "When John heard in prison of the <u>works</u> of the Messiah . . ." It ends, "But wisdom is vindicated by her <u>works</u>" (revised NAB).

- In John's first Last Supper Discourse (*John 14:1–31*), there is an *inclusio* in verses 1 and 27: "Do not let your hearts be troubled."

- The Lectionary makes an *inclusio* in its selection of a passage from Isaiah for Wednesday of the first week of Advent: The first reading for that daily mass begins with the three words, "On this mountain . . ." (*Isaiah 25:6*) and interrupts verse 10 in the middle of a sentence after the same three words. Enclosed is a symbolic description of messianic victory and the heavenly Jerusalem.

- The last line of Matthew's version of the Gospel, "And remember, I am with you always, to the end of the age" (*Matthew 28:20*), is a conscious echo of the beginning of his Gospel where he called Jesus Emmanuel "which means 'God is with us'" (*Matthew 1:23*). Such literary touches are not *inclusios* properly speaking.

## Litotes (*light*-uh-tease)

Litotes is an understatement affirming something by denying its opposite (sometimes with a double negative, like the statement of the car company's lawyer who declared that the recalled cars were not unsafe). In everyday conversations it is not rare.

- *1 Corinthians 15:10* calls God's effective grace "not ineffective":

"[God's] grace to me has <u>not</u> been <u>ineffective</u>" (revised NAB).

- In the Greek text of *Acts 21:39* there is a litotes, which some translations bring into English: "I am a Jew of Tarsus in Cilicia, a citizen of <u>no insignificant</u> city . . ." (NASB). Paul is defending himself in Jerusalem, mentioning his hometown of Tarsus—"no insignificant city." No insignificant city? The capital of the province of Cilicia. A well-known center of culture, philosophy, and education. A city with schools outranking those in Athens and Alexandria. A city visited by Cicero, Julius Caesar, Augustus, Mark Anthony, Cleopatra. (See *The New Jerome Biblical Commentary*, 79:16–17.) No insignificant city? That's an understatement. (Some translations—like the NRSV—overlook the litotes and simply render the phrase "I am a Jew, from Tarsus in Cilicia, a citizen of an important city . . .")

- At the end of their first mission, Paul and Barnabas returned to Antioch where they reported on their work and then "spent <u>no little</u> time with the disciples" (*Acts 14:28*). This is the revised NAB's translation of "*chronon ouk oligov*" ("time not a little"), which the earlier (and less literal) NAB (1970) rendered simply "they spent some time." Seemingly insignificant rhetorical flourishes like this matter in cultured societies. Language is functional, but can be beautiful too.

- This figure is not uncommon in Luke's Acts of the Apostles. (Luke's Greek is among the most elegant in the New Testament.) In *Acts 15:2*, after some from Judea said that circumcision according to Mosaic practice was necessary for salvation, Luke says "there arose <u>no little</u> dissension and debate by Paul and Barnabas with them . . ." (revised NAB).

**Metaphor** (*met*-a-for)

A most common device, the metaphor uses an object, concept, or person to compare to another object, concept, or person as a means of explanation or elaboration. A metaphor is the simile's less-explicit relative. The simile is a stated comparison using "like" or "as." In the more literary metaphor, the comparison is implied. They stimulate the imagination of the listener or reader. There are dead metaphors that have become idioms: the arm of the chair; don't burn your bridges. (The meanings of idioms are in the dictionary; the meanings of metaphors are not.) There are mixed metaphors: "That's a can of worms that may turn around and bite you."

- Metaphors are everywhere in the Scriptures. In John 10:1–21 (The Good Shepherd passage), for example, Jesus calls himself "the good shepherd" (verses 11 and 14); the faithful are sheep. This shepherd/sheep metaphor has a history with the Jews because kings and leaders were viewed as shepherds of the people (see

*Ezekiel 34*, for example). Jesus speaks metaphorically again in this same passage, "I am the sheepgate" (*John 10:9*), referring to the gate of the place where sheep were kept at night for safety.

- The vineyard and vine are very common metaphors for Israel in the Old Testament, God being the vineyard tender or owner (see *Psalm 80:9–20; Isaiah 5:1–7, 27:2–5; Jeremiah 2:21; Ezekiel 15:2; 17:5–10; 19:10; Hosea 10:1*). Christ develops this image in speaking of God (the grower), himself (the vine), and the faithful (the branches) (*John 15:1–8*; see also *Matthew 21:33–39*; compare *Psalm 80:18, Sirach 24:17*).

- Scripture has an extensive collection of metaphors for what heaven will be like: It will be homecoming for God's orphaned children (see *John 14:2–3*); payday for the laborers (see *Matthew 20:1–16*); harvest-time for God's workers (see *Matthew 21:33–41*); a marriage feast celebrating the union of each soul with its creator (see *Matthew 22:1–14*); a wedding reception for the Church and the Lamb of God (see *Revelation 19:9*); a glorious festival for the victorious warriors of Christ (see *Revelation 7:9–17*).

- Matthew describes Jesus using the metaphor of salt and light during the Sermon on the Mount: "You are the salt of the earth . . . You are the light of the world" (*Matthew 5:13, 14*).

- Matthew records John the Baptist addressing Pharisees and Sadducees in challenging terms: "You brood of vipers!" (*Matthew 3:7*)

- The rock metaphor is plentiful in the Scriptures: "The LORD lives! Blessed be my rock . . ." (*2 Samuel 22:47*). "Trust in the LORD forever, / for in the LORD GOD / you have an everlasting rock" (*Isaiah*

## God—Our Mother

Jesus taught his disciples to pray "our Father," but there are plenty of places in the Bible that refer to God in feminine terms. *1 Peter 2:2-3* alludes to God nursing us, "Like newborn infants, long for pure spiritual milk so that by it you may grow into salvation—if indeed you have tasted that the Lord is good." Often, the Scriptures speak of God's maternal love. "As a mother comforts her child,/ so I will comfort you . . ." it says in *Isaiah 66:13*. In another place, Isaiah, using graphic feminine imagery, describes God crying out ". . . like a woman in labor,/ I will gasp and pant" (*Isaiah 42:14*). And, again in Isaiah, in one of Scripture's most tender expressions of divine love, it says, "But Zion said, 'The LORD has forsaken me,/ my Lord has forgotten me.'/ Can a woman forget her nursing child,/ or show no compassion for the child of her womb?/ Even these may forget,/ yet I will not forget you" (*49:14-15*). The prophet dresses his message in rich metaphors of childbirth and mother love. "Woe to anyone who says to a father, 'What are you begetting?'/ or to a woman, 'With what are you in labor?'" (*Isaiah 45:10*). We may not pray today, "Our mother who art in heaven . . . ," but our God's constant, mothering love always surrounds us.

26:4). "The stone that the builders rejected has become the chief cornerstone" (Peter, in *Acts 4:11* applying *Psalm 118:22* to Jesus).

- The Scriptures use metaphor in naming and calling God "Father" and in many places use a simile in comparing God to a mother (see box copy on p. 354).

- Marriage is a common scriptural metaphor for God's relationship to the faithful (and the unfaithful).

**The covenant as marriage:**
"I will espouse you to me forever:/ I will espouse you in right and in justice,/ in love and in mercy;/ I will espouse you in fidelity,/ and you shall know the LORD" (*Hosea 2:21–22*, revised NAB).

"For he who has become your husband is your Maker;/ his name is the LORD of hosts . . ./ The LORD calls you back,/ like a wife forsaken and grieved in spirit,/ A wife married in youth and then cast off, says your God. . . ./ My love shall never leave you/ nor my covenant of peace be shaken" (*Isaiah 54:5–6, 10*, revised NAB).

"No more shall men call you 'Forsaken,'/ . . . But you shall be called 'My Delight,'/ and your land 'Espoused.'/ For the LORD delights in you,/ and makes your land his spouse./ As a young man marries a virgin,/ your Builder shall marry you;/ And as a bridegroom rejoices in his bride/ so shall your God rejoice in you" (*Isaiah 62:4–5*, revised NAB).

**Idolatry as adultery:**
"I will go after my lovers; they give me my bread and my water . . ." (*Hosea 2:5*).

"But you were captivated by your own beauty, you used your renown to make yourself a harlot, and you lavished your harlotry on every passer-by, whose own you became" (*Ezekiel 16:15*, revised NAB).

**Christ as bridegroom:**
"The wedding-guests cannot mourn as long as the bridegroom is with them, can they? The days will come when the bridegroom is taken away from them, and then they will fast" (*Matthew 9:15*).

"But at midnight there was a shout, 'Look! Here is the bridegroom! Come out to meet him.'" (*Matthew 25:6*).

"John answered, '. . . You yourselves are my witnesses that I said, "I am not the Messiah, but I have been sent ahead of him." He who has the bride is the bridegroom. The friend of the bridegroom, who stands and hears him, rejoices greatly at the bridegroom's voice'" (*John 3:27–29*).

**The Church as bride:**
"For I am jealous of you with the jealousy of God, since I betrothed you to one husband to present you as a chaste virgin to Christ" (*2 Corinthians 11:1*).

"Husbands, love your wives, just as Christ loved the church and gave himself up for her, in order to make her holy . . . 'For this reason a man will leave his father and mother and be joined to his wife, and the two will become one flesh.' This is a great mystery, and I am applying it to Christ and the church" (*Ephesians 5:25–26, 31–32*).

". . . for the marriage of the Lamb has come, / and his bride has made herself ready . . ." (*Revelation 19:7*).

- In Matthew's version of the Lord's prayer (*Matthew 6:9–13*; and indirectly in *Luke 11:4*), "debts" is used metaphorically for sins (debts owed to God).

**Metonymy** (meh-*tah*-nih-me)
"Change of name." A kind of metaphor, metonymy is usually called substitution, using the name of one object or concept for that of another that's closely associated with it or of which it is a part. Usually metonymy substitutes one noun for another: cause for its effect ("Her mouth got her kicked out"), the container for the contained ("The bottle cost you your job"), a writer for the writer's work ("Lectionary Year 1 is Matthew's year"), materials for product ("Nice threads"). It can add weight and authority ("Rome has spoken"). This device adds variety and often directs attention to a significant aspect of the object that is called to mind.

- "The scepter shall not depart from Judah, / nor the ruler's staff from between his feet . . ." (*Genesis 49:10*). Scepter here means the dominion or sovereignty of Judah.

- "I gave you cleanness of teeth in all your cities, / and lack of bread in all your places, / yet you did not return to me, / says the LORD" (*Amos 4:6*). The substitution of teeth for people emphasizes the extent of their hunger.

- In the ancient world the hand was a symbol of activity, active power, or authority: "The hand of the Lord was with them, and a great number became believers and turned to the Lord" (*Acts 11:21*). References to the hand and the hands of God are very common in Scripture: *The Book of Wisdom* says, "But the souls of the righteous are in the hand of God . . ." (*3:1*). The prophet Jeremiah says, "Just like the clay in the potter's hand, so are you in my hand . . ." (*Jeremiah 18:6*). John quotes Jesus saying, "What my Father has given me is greater than all else, and no one can snatch it out of the Father's hand" (*John 10:29*). Luke says that Jesus' final words were, "Father, into your hands I commend my spirit" (*Luke 23:46*).

- "How beautiful are the feet of those who bring good news!" (*Romans 10:15*) "In Semitic fashion," a revised NAB footnote says, "the parts of the body that bring the messenger with welcome news are praised." It then mentions *Luke 11:27*, which reads, "While he was speaking, a woman from the crowd called out and said to him, 'Blessed is the womb that carried you and the breasts at which you nursed.'"

- There is a Good Friday antiphon from Morning Prayer that employs metonymy twice: "We worship your cross, O Lord, and we praise and glorify your holy resurrection, for the wood of the cross has brought joy to the world." It isn't the cross literally that is worshipped nor its wood literally that has brought the joy.

**Onomatopoeia** (on-uh-maht-uh-*pee*-ah)
This verbal sound effect uses words whose sound imitates or suggests their meaning ("hiss," "boom").

About Psalm 29:3–9, the revised NAB footnote comments, "the sevenfold repetition of ['the voice'] imitates the sound of crashing thunder . . .": "<u>The voice</u> of the LORD is over the waters;/ . . . <u>The voice</u> of the LORD is power;/ <u>the voice</u> of the LORD is splendor./ <u>The voice</u> of the LORD cracks the cedars;/ . . . <u>The voice</u> of the LORD strikes with fiery flame;/ <u>the voice</u> of the LORD rocks the desert;/ . . . <u>The voice</u> of the LORD twists the oaks/ and strips the forests bare."

**Oxymoron** (oxy-*mor*-on)
"Sharp foolishness," "pointedly foolish." An oxymoron is a compressed paradox (a seeming contradiction): Two apparently contradictory terms are put in close proximity in order to make a point (living death, cruel kindness, bittersweet, deafening quiet, conspicuous absence).

- ". . . we also boast in our sufferings . . ." (*Romans 5:3*).

- ". . . but where sin increased, grace abounded all the more . . ." (*Romans 5:20*) (inspiring the Church to sing at the Easter Vigil, "O happy fault, which gained for us so great a Redeemer!").

**Paradox** (*pair*-a-dox)
"Unbelievable." A paradox is a seeming contradiction that is resolved into truth. A paradox provokes a person to seek another sense or context in which it would be true ("You can't teach a person anything he doesn't already know"). It's been said that paradox is pervasive in the literature of Christianity, a notoriously paradoxical religion.

- "Those who find their life will lose it, and those who lose their life for my sake will find it" (*Matthew 10:39*).

- ". . . for whenever I am weak, then I am strong" (*2 Corinthians 12:10*).

- ". . . that though he was rich, yet for your sakes he became poor, so that by his poverty you might become rich" (*2 Corinthians 8:9*).

- ". . . darkness is not dark to you . . ." (*Psalm 139:12*).

- "I tell you, among those born of women no one is greater than John; yet the least in the kingdom of God is greater than he" (*Luke 7:28*).

- In the passage about the seven seals in the Book of Revelation, the wrath of the lamb is a paradox: ". . . calling to the mountains and rocks, 'Fall on us and hide us from the face of the one seated on the throne and from the <u>wrath</u> of the <u>Lamb</u> . . .'" (*Revelation 6:16*).

### Parallelism

In a parallelism the same statement is made in two different ways, or two ideas are contrasted, side-by-side, or one idea is repeated with some variation. These are very common in Hebrew poetry. (There are explanations and illustrations in Chapter 6 in a section called "The Poetry of the Psalms.")

- The parallelism in *Psalm 51:2*: "Wash me thoroughly from my iniquity,/ and cleanse me from my sin" is quoted at Mass during the preparation of the altar and the gifts, "Lord, wash away my iniquity; cleanse me from my sin."

- Another example from Psalm 51 is familiar to those praying the Liturgy of the Hours as the Invitatory, which begins each day's prayer: "O Lord, open my lips,/ and my mouth will declare your praise" (*Psalm 51:15*).

- In *Isaiah 42:10–16* there's an example of parallelism in a canticle: "Sing to the Lord a new song,/ his praise from the end of the earth! Let the sea roar and all that fills it,/ the coastlands and their inhabitants. Let the desert and its towns lift up their voice,/the villages that Kedar inhabits; let the inhabitants of Sela sing for joy,/ let them shout from the tops of the mountains./ Let them give glory to the Lord,/ and

declare his praise in the coastlands./ The Lord goes forth like a soldier,/ like a warrior he stirs up his fury; he cries out, he shouts aloud,/ he shows himself mighty against his foes./ For a long time I have held my peace,/ I have kept still and restrained myself . . ."

- There's a simple parallelism in *John 3:36*: "Whoever believes in the Son has eternal life; whoever disobeys the Son will not see life . . ."

- There are parallelisms in *1 Timothy 3:16*: "Without any doubt, the mystery of our religion is great:/ He was revealed in flesh,/ vindicated in spirit,/ seen by angels,/ proclaimed among Gentiles,/ believed in throughout the world,/ taken up in glory." These parallelisms are in a special category. *The New Jerome Biblical Commentary* calls 1 Timothy 3:16 "an early poetic formulation of the kerygma. Three pairs of phrases are arranged so as to juxtapose heavenly/spiritual and earthly events. With one exception the six Greek phrases have almost the same number of syllables" (56:35). ("*Kerygma*," a Greek word pronounced cur-*ihg*-mah, is the proclamation of the Good News, the core of which is that Jesus who died is risen and now lives among us. It's one of three terms used to describe the mission of the Church; the other two being *koinonia*—fellowship— and *diakonia*—service.) A revised NAB footnote to 1 Timothy 3:16 remarks, "It consists of three couplets in typical Hebrew balance: flesh-spirit (contrast), seen-proclaimed (complementary), world-glory (contrast)."

**Paronomasia** (par-ah-nah-*may*-zhah) Paronomasia is the technical term for a play on words. A pun. Paronomasia often depends upon how a word sounds so you have to know the language to appreciate it. Puns are usually lost in translation. When a word means one thing but sounds like a word that means something else, it can heighten the meaning of both words. Puns usually involve the use of a word with two different meanings, or similarity of meanings in two words spelled differently but pronounced the same, or two words pronounced and spelled almost the same but having different meanings ("Which witch is the witch of Endor?" "Can you hear the crashing of the symbols in the Book of Revelation?"). Puns are usually lost in translation—but not necessarily, not with a little creativity:

• Artfully, the revised NAB brings a pun from Hebrew to English in *Jeremiah 1:11–12*: "The word of the LORD came to me with the question: What do you see, Jeremiah? 'I see a branch of the watching-tree,' I replied. Then the LORD said to me: Well have you seen, for I am watching to fulfill my word." The reader can enjoy the "watching-tree" / "I am watching" pun without knowing Hebrew or needing the help of a footnote—which it supplies anyway:

"*The watching-tree*: the almond tree, which is the first to blossom in the springtime as though it had not slept. The Hebrew name contains a play on words with 'I am watching.'" The NRSV (like the KJV) translates "almond" literally: "The word of the LORD came to me, saying, 'Jeremiah, what do you see?' and I said, 'I see a branch of an almond tree.' Then the LORD said to me, 'You have seen well, for I am watching over my word to perform it.'" The translators do supply two footnotes: one for "almond tree" ("Hebrew *shaqed*") and one for "I am watching" ("Hebrew *shoqed*"). Reading the footnotes is a lot of work and takes the fun out of the pun.

Most puns, of course, require an explanation. A footnote.

• In Genesis 2:7 there is a play on words in Hebrew between *adam* ("man") and *adama* ("ground").

• In *Matthew 16:18* there is a play on the Greek words *petros* (Peter's new name) and *petra* (rock): "You are Peter (*Petros*), and on this rock (*petra*) I will build my church . . ."

• There's a nice pun in an old torn-cloak story from the days of Solomon. The prophets of Israel often used demonstrations to buttress their spoken word. Like the tenth-century prophet Ahijah who encouraged Jeroboam in his plot against the aging King Solomon: One day Jeroboam came upon the prophet Ahijah along a deserted road outside of Jerusalem. ". . . Ahijah laid hold of the new garment he was wearing and tore it into twelve pieces. He then said to Jeroboam: Take for yourself ten pieces; for thus says the LORD, the God of Israel, 'See, I am about to tear the kingdom from the hand of Solomon, and will give you ten tribes'" (*1 Kings 11:30–31*). Solomon condemned Jeroboam to death, but he fled to Egypt. When Solomon died and his son Rehoboam succeeded him, Jeroboam returned. The ten northern tribes seceded, established a separate kingdom of Israel, and made Jeroboam their king. Ahijah's prophecy was fulfilled. The pun? The Hebrew word for cloak is <u>*salma*</u>, *which* sounds a lot like the name <u>Solomon</u>. All that's left in English of this Hebrew pun is the phrase "I will tear away the kingdom from Solomon's grasp." It's a play on words because of how *salma* sounds and that's why Ahijah chose to tear a cloak instead of break a pot or divide beans or something.

- There is a play on words in *Acts 11:23*: "When [Barnabas] came and saw the <u>grace</u> of God, he <u>rejoiced</u> . . . ". The underlined words in Greek are *charin* and *echara*, from *charis* (grace) and *chairo* (rejoice).

- Puns often involved names (which, again, require the help of footnotes for those reading only in translation): "Adam again had relations with his wife, and she

gave birth to a son whom she called Seth. 'God has granted me more offspring in place of Abel,' she said, 'because Cain slew him'" (*Genesis 4:25*). A revised NAB footnote explains: "*Has granted*: Hebrew *shat*, a wordplay on the name *shet* ('Seth')."

- There is another pun on a name in *Genesis 5:28–29*: "Lamech . . . begot a son and named him <u>Noah</u>, saying, 'Out of the very ground that the Lord has put under a curse, this one shall <u>bring us relief</u> from our work and the toil of our hands.'" The pun can be understood with help from a footnote (NAB, 1970, in this case): "There is a similarity in sound between the Hebrew word *noah*, 'Noah,' and the verbal phrase *yenahamenu*, '<u>he will bring us relief</u>'; this latter refers both to the curse put on the soil because of the fall of man (see *Genesis 3:17* and following) and to Noah's success in agriculture, especially in raising grapes for wine (see *Genesis 9:20* and following)"—a "success" which eventually brings a curse on Noah's family because of his drunken stupor one night (or a few perhaps) (see *Genesis 9:20–25*).

- The Greek word *pneuma* (like the Hebrew *ruah*) means both "wind" and "spirit." There's a nice pun in *John 3:8* that plays on this double meaning that's lost in translation: "The <u>wind</u> blows where it chooses, and you hear the sound of it, but you do not know where it comes from or where it goes. So it is with everyone who is born of the <u>Spirit</u>."

## Parenthesis

The parenthesis, as a literary device, is quite different from the punctuation marks of the same name. (There were no punctuation marks in first-century Greek manuscripts). The parenthesis is a sentence or phrase (I'm sure you know this already) within a sentence that functions as an aside or narrator's comment. It can be an emotional expression so strong it needs to be said before finishing a sentence.

- "The Samaritan woman said to him, 'How is it that you, a Jew, ask a drink of me, a woman of Samaria?' (Jews do not share things in common with Samaritans.) Jesus answered her . . ." (*John 4:9–10*).

- In Genesis, the story of Tamar (38:1–30) is a kind of parenthesis (also called an interlude) within the story of Joseph.

- The "parenthetical" episode of the healing of a woman with a hemorrhage (see *Mark 5:25–34* and parallels) within the story of the raising of the daughter of Jairus (see *Mark 5:21–43*) is not an example of the literary device known as a parenthesis. It's called an intercalation—a story interrupting a related story. The inner story is usually the more important one and it informs or gives meaning to the outer story.

## Personification (per-sahn-nih-fih-*cay*-shun)

Personification attributes human and personal characteristics or qualities to what is not human—inanimate objects, animals, or concepts.

- "Let the floods clap their hands;/ let the hills sing together for joy . . ." (*Psalm 98:8*).

- "Consider the lilies of the field, how they grow; they neither toil nor spin, yet I tell you, even Solomon in all his glory was not clothed like one of these" (*Matthew 6:28–29*).

- *Job 9:8* portrays God the Father walking on the water, ". . . [God] who alone stretched out the heavens/ and trampled the waves of the Sea . . ." That's personification. When God the Son walked on water (see *Matthew 14:26*), it wasn't.

- Death is personified as a trapper in *Psalm 116:3*: "The snares of death encompassed me;/ the pangs of Sheol laid hold on me . . ."

- Sirach 24:1–27 personifies wisdom. As the NAB (1970) footnote explains, "In this chapter Wisdom speaks in the first person, describing her origin, her dwelling place in Israel, and the reward she gives her followers. As in Proverbs 8, Wisdom is described as a being who comes from God and is distinct from him. While we do not say with certainty that this description applies to a personal being, it does foreshadow the beautiful doctrine of the Word of God later developed in St. John's Gospel (John 1:1–14). In the liturgy this chapter is applied

## Ms. Wisdom

It is not uncommon for wisdom to be portrayed as a person. In the Hebrew Bible, "she" is portrayed not as an abstract virtue but as a power of God, even as a person (see *Proverbs 1:8, Sirach 1:23, Wisdom 6:12-18*). Personification was a familiar device for Israel's pagan neighbors too. The name "Sophia" is derived from the Greek word for wisdom. Christians see wisdom personified in Jesus.

Legend tells of a Roman widow named Sophia who had three daughters named Faith, Hope, and Charity. The whole family was martyred, as the story goes–the three daughters first and then "Wisdom" herself, slain as she prayed for her daughters. Her feast day was September 30.

to the Blessed Virgin because of her constant and intimate association with Christ, the Incarnate Wisdom."

• In the Book of Revelation, the new Jerusalem, the kingdom of God, is personified as a woman: "Come, I will show you the bride, the wife of the Lamb" (*Revelation 21:9*).

**Polysyndeton** (polly-*sin*-dah-tun) "Many links." The opposite of asyndeton, polysyndeton uses more conjunctions than necessary. It contributes to a deliberate and dignified style, slowing down the reader. (In contemporary usage, it's often employed to reveal the impatience of the author or speaker who thinks the list is too long.) In Scripture not all plentiful uses of conjunctions like "and" is intended for rhetorical effect.

• In *Hebrews 12:18–24*, which a revised NAB footnote calls "a remarkably beautiful passage," the last couple of verses include an effective seven-fold polysyndeton: "No, you have approached Mount Zion and the city of the living God, the heavenly Jerusalem, and countless angels in festal gathering, and the assembly of the firstborn enrolled in heaven, and God the judge of all, and the spirits of the just made perfect, and Jesus, the mediator of a new covenant, and the sprinkled blood that speaks more eloquently than that of Abel." (In the 1970 NAB translation, commas replaced the *kai's*, leaving out the original polysyndeton.)

• In *Romans 8:35*, Paul uses the polysyndeton with six successive "or's." He answers his own question "Who will separate us from the love of Christ?" with another question that includes seven wrong answers: "Will hardship, or distress, or persecution, or famine, or nakedness, or peril, or the sword?"

• In *2 Corinthians 12:10* there is a polysyndeton of "with's": "I am content with weakness, with mistreatment, with distress, with persecutions and difficulties for the sake of Christ; for when I am powerless, it is then that I am strong" (NASB).

**Prolepsis** (pro-*lehp*-suhs) "Anticipation; preconception." A prolepsis gets the jump. It's the anticipation of something that will

## And, and, and

As noted earlier, Scripture scholars point out that, in Hebrew, almost every sentence opens with "and." Hebrew/Aramaic speakers writing in Greek continued the practice (using the Greek word *kai*). In the Book of Revelation, for example, the word *kai* appears no less than 47 times in the 18 verses of Chapter 12, 51 times in the 18 verses of Chapter 13, and 55 times in the 20 verses of Chapter 14.

In some translations, most of those conjunctions are not translated because they were not intended for special effect. The KJV, however, whose translators may not have recognized this background, almost always repeat the *kai*—usually as "and" in English. In its version of Revelation 12, for example, there are 16 sentences. Fifteen of them begin with "and"–as commonly as in the original. Thirty-one of the other 32 are all brought into English, translated "and" in every case.

By comparison, the revised NAB translates Revelation 12:1-18 into 22 sentences. None of them begins with the conjunction "and." What happens to those 47 *kais*? Only 22 of them are translated as "and." Five are translated "then"; three, "but"; and one each "with," "as," and "however." One is made into a semi-colon, and 13 of them are left out and not translated at all.

It has been said that the indefiniteness of "and" interweaves with mystery such scriptural narratives as the stories of Abraham and Isaac. That's an interpretation. It was not necessarily the intent of the author.

---

appear later. It can refer to possible objections in order to counter them beforehand. It's also proleptic when a person refers to an anticipated event as though it had already happened.

Luke presents Jesus anticipating the objections that some people would have to him: "He said to them, 'Doubtless you will quote to me this proverb, "Doctor, cure yourself!" And you will say, "Do here also in your home town the things that we have heard you did at Capernaum"'" (*Luke 4:23*).

### Rhetorical Questions

Rhetorical questions are asked in order to make a point or to express surprise or indignation. The answer is built in. For example, when someone says, "Do you think I'm crazy?" it is usually best not to answer at all. The question is being asked forcefully for rhetorical effect—not in anticipation of an actual answer.

### Simile (*si*-mah-lee)

A simile is a comparison that is expressed, usually using the word "like" or "as" unlike a metaphor in which the comparison is only implied. The simile's purpose is to clarify an expression or thought.

- "See, I am sending you out like lambs into the midst of wolves" (Jesus to disciples, *Luke 10:3*).

## The Bible Has All the Questions

### God's Questions for Job

After the great misfortunes of Job, "comforters" come with their explanation for his suffering. Job rejects their case and calls on God for a response. God overwhelms Job by referring to his own omniscience and almighty power—in the form of questions: "Gird up your loins, like a man;/ I will question you, and you shall declare to me." (*Job 38:3*)

"Where were you when I laid the foundation of the earth?" (*Job 38:4*)

"Have you commanded the morning since your days began,/ and caused the dawn to know its place,/ so that it might take hold of the skirts of the earth,/ . . .?" (*Job 38:12*)

"Have the gates of death been revealed to you,/ or have you seen the gates of deep darkness?" (*Job 38:17*)

"Have you entered the storehouses of the snow,/ or have you seen the storehouses of the hail . . .?" (*Job 38:22*)

"Can you bind the chains of the Pleiades,/ or loose the cords of Orion?" (*Job 38:31*)

"Do you know the ordinances of the heavens?/ Can you establish their rule on the earth?" (*Job 38:33*)

"Can you send forth the lightnings . . .?" (*Job 38:35*)

"Do you know when the mountain goats give birth?/ Do you observe the calving of the deer?/ Can you number the months that they fulfill,/ and do you know the time when they give birth . . .?" (*Job 39:1-2*)

"Do you give the horse its might?/ Do you clothe its neck with mane?" (*Job 39:19*)

"Is it by your wisdom that the hawk soars,/ and spreads its wings towards the south?" (*Job 39:26*)

God reaches a crescendo with a final question: "Shall a fault-finder contend with the Almighty?/ Anyone who argues with God must respond." (*Job 40:2*). Job answered none of them, and all of them: "See, I am of small account; what shall I answer you?/ I lay my hand on my mouth" (*Job 40:4*).

### Questions of Jesus

The Evangelists put many questions in the mouth of Jesus, who is described as asking questions even in childhood: "After three days [Mary and Joseph] found him in the temple, sitting in the midst of the teachers, listening to them and asking them questions . . ." (*Luke 2:46*). The following are some of the well-known questions of Jesus.

"What are you looking for?" (to John's disciples, *John 1:38*)

"But, who do you say that I am?" (to his disciples, *Matthew 16:15*)

"[W]hy did you doubt?" (to Peter after the walking on the water, *Matthew 14:31*)

"Do you also wish to go away?" (to the Twelve after the Bread of Life Discourse, *John 6:67*)

"[D]o you love me?" (to Peter after Jesus' post-Resurrection appearance at the Sea of Tiberias, *John 21:16*)

"Which of these three . . . was a neighbor to the man who fell into the hands of the robbers?" (to the scholar of the law after the story of the Good Samaritan, *Luke 10:36*)

### Other Questions in Scripture

From Genesis to the letters of the New Testament, Scripture builds life lessons and answers into questions:

"Where are you?" "Who told you that you were naked?" (God questioning Adam in the beginning, *Genesis 3:9, 11*)

"Can a woman forget her nursing child?" (A profession of God's love, *Isaiah 49:15*)

"[I]f the LORD is with us, why then has all this happened to us?" (Gideon's response, not without cynicism, to the angel who had greeted him, "The Lord is with you, you mighty warrior" *Judges 6:13*)

"What are human beings that you are mindful of them . . . ?" (*Psalm 8:5*)

"What shall I return to the LORD/ for all his bounty to me?" (*Psalm 116:12*)

"What is truth?" (Pilate to Jesus before the scourging, *John 18:38*)

"If God is for us, who is against us?" asks Paul in *Romans 8:31*, one question among seven that are actually all one.

- The book of Hosea ends with eight similes, six of them describing Israel, sandwiched between two describing God: "I will be like the dew to Israel;/ he shall blossom like the lily,/ he shall strike root like the forests of Lebanon./ His shoots shall spread out;/ his beauty shall be like the olive tree,/ and his fragrance like that of Lebanon. . . ./ they shall blossom like the vine,/ their fragrance shall be like the wine of Lebanon . . ./ I am like an evergreen cypress . . ." (*Hosea 14:6–9*).

- In the Praise of Israel's Ancestors (44:1—50:24), Sirach piles up eleven similes (50:6–10) in extolling Simon the priest, son of Jochanan, likening the priest to star, full moon, sun, rainbow, spring blossoms, lily, trees, fire of incense, gold vessel, olive tree, and cypress tree. Quite a man. That list is like a litany.

- There is an extended simile in *Psalm 17:9–12*: ". . . my deadly enemies . . . surround me./ . . . like a lion eager to tear,/ . . ."

- *Psalm 42:1* compares longing of a deer to the human soul: "As a deer longs for flowing streams,/ so my soul longs for you, O God."

- Luke describes Jesus comparing the people of his generation to children: "They are like children sitting in the marketplace. . ." (*Luke 7:32*).

**365**

**Soliloquy** (so-*lih*-lo-kwee)
A soliloquy is the act of speaking while alone or as if alone and is a way to reveal a character's thoughts to the reader or listener.

Before the destruction of Sodom and Gomorrah (see *Genesis 19:1–29*), there is an account of Abraham interceding for Sodom (*Genesis 18:16–33*). It begins, "Then the men set out from there, and they looked toward Sodom; and Abraham went with them to set them on their way. The Lord said, 'Shall I hide from Abraham what I am about to do, seeing that Abraham shall become a great and mighty nation, and all the nations of the earth shall be blessed in him? . . .'" The Lord reflecting on whether or not he will hide his plans from Abraham is a soliloquy.

**Symploce** (*sim*-plo-see)
"Intertwining, combination." Symploce is the simultaneous use of anaphora and epiphora (the repetition of both beginnings and endings in successive phrases or clauses).

• "Are they Hebrews? So am I. Are they Israelites? So am I. Are they descendants of Abraham? So am I" (*2 Corinthians 11:22*).

• "Lord, Lord, did we not prophesy in your name, and cast out demons in your name, and do many deeds of power in your name?" (*Matthew 7:22*).

• "Whoever loves father or mother more than me is not worthy of me; and whoever loves son or daughter more than me is not worthy of me; and whoever does not take up the cross and follow me is not worthy of me" (*Matthew 10:37–38*).

**Synchysis** (sin-*key*-sis)
Synchysis is an interlocked order of words in the pattern of A-B-A-B, as in "What you see is what you get." (See chiasmus for the related interlocking pattern of A-B-B-A.)

• The words "poor"/"rich" and "poverty"/"rich" form a synchysis in *2 Corinthians 8:9*: ". . . for your sake he became poor/ although he was rich, so that by his poverty/ you might become rich" (revised NAB).

• *Luke 19:40* is from the Palm Sunday episode of Jesus' entry into Jerusalem. "These"/"stones" and "silent"/"shout out" are in the pattern of a synchysis: "I tell you, if these were silent, the stones would shout out" ("these" referring to Jesus' disciples).

• The simple synchysis in *Romans 5:20* highlights the power of grace over sin: "Where sin increased, grace overflowed all the more . . ." (revised NAB translation). The NKJV reflects the original even closer, "Where sin abounded, grace abounded much more;" likewise the NIV: "Where sin increased, grace increased all the more . . ."

**Synecdoche** (sih-*neck*-dah-key)
The synecdoche is a specific and simple kind of metonymy (substitution): It substitutes a part for the whole ("Keep your nose out of

this"). This rhetorical device usually stresses an important feature of the object ("They took her keys away, now she has no wheels.") The synecdoche makes a phrase more vivid, adding interest while directing attention to a significant part of the object that is called to mind.

- Body parts commonly represent, by synecdoche, a person or person's character—the foot for

example: ". . . guide our feet into the way of peace" (*Luke 1:79*); "And he has put all things under his feet and has made him the head over all things for the church" (*Ephesians 1:22*).

- "I have sinned by betraying innocent blood" (*Matthew 27:3*).

- "From oppression and violence he redeems their life;/ for precious is their blood in his sight" (*Psalm 72:14*).

# Words & Phrases with Scriptural Origin or Allusion

## "Unless I . . .
## Put My Finger
### in the
## Mark of the Nails"

In American Sign Language, the name "Jesus" is signed by touching with the middle finger of the right hand, pointing down, the palm of the left hand, then touching with the middle finger of the left hand the palm of the right. This significant gesture is an allusion to the story of Jesus' Easter appearance, which Thomas could not at first believe (see *John 20:24–29*).

# Translations

In the following glossary, not all entries are exact translations of Scripture verses.

1. **Some are quotations still familiar in today's translations**
   "The love of money is the root of all evil" (*1 Timothy 6:10*) is fairly universal.
2. **Some are from older translations that are no longer used today**
   ". . . [Y]ou are dust and to dust you shall return" (*Genesis 3:19*) has become, in typical contemporary and exact translations (like the 1970 NAB), ". . . you are dirt / and to dirt you shall return." You probably won't hear that version on Ash Wednesday.
3. **Some are Scriptural paraphrases or allusions**
   They merely make reference to events or personages in the Bible ("the patience of Job"). They are not direct translations but their frequent use has made them familiar, such as phrases like "the apple of your eye" and "all things to all men."

# Allusions in Titles

They're everywhere. Seek and ye shall find. The following phrases that are used as titles in literature are only a small taste of what is out there.

1. *Giants in the Earth*
   This phrase is taken from *Genesis 6:4*, according to the KJV translation: "There were giants in the earth in those days; and also after that, when the sons of God came in unto the daughters of men, and they bare children to them, the same became mighty men which were of old, men of renown." (The 1970 NAB leaves the Hebrew word for "giant"—*nephilim*—untranslated: "At that time the Nephilim appeared on earth [as well as later], after the sons of heaven had intercourse with the daughters of man, who bore them sons. They were the heroes of old, the men of renown.")
2. *The Seventh Seal*
   This term is an allusion to *Revelation 5:1*: "Then I saw in the right hand of the one seated on the throne a scroll written on the inside and on the back, sealed with seven seals."
3. *The Grapes of Wrath*
   This phrase is an allusion to the winepress image of *Revelation 14:19–20*, which teaches about the harvest of the earth and the impending doom of the ungodly. It was used by John Steinbeck as the title of a 1939 novel and occurs in the first stanza of "The Battle Hymn of the Republic"—"He is trampling out the vintage where the grapes of wrath are stored."
4. *Chariots of Fire*
   The name of this Hollywood film refers to the "ascension"

of Elijah: "As they [Elijah and Elisha] continued walking and talking, a chariot of fire and horses of fire separated the two of them, and Elijah ascended in a whirlwind into heaven" (*2 Kings 2:11*).

5. *East of Eden*

After Cain slew his brother Abel, he was exiled: "Then Cain went away from the presence of the LORD, and settled in the land of Nod, east of Eden" (*Genesis 4:16*). John Steinbeck took that term "east of Eden" as the title for a novel about conflict between brothers in which he says, "Two stories haunted us and followed us from the beginning, . . . the story of original sin and the story of Cain and Abel. And I don't understand them at all, but I feel them in myself."

6. *The Skin of our Teeth*

This phrase—and the name of Thornton Wilder's 1942 play—comes from the King James Version of *Job 19:20*: "My bone cleaveth to my skin and to my flesh, and I am escaped with the skin of my teeth."

7. *Lilies of the Field*

This phrase comes from the KJV rendering of *Matthew 6:28–29*: "Consider the lilies of the field, how they grow; they toil not, neither do they spin: And yet I say unto you, That even Solomon in all his glory was not arrayed like one of these." (The revised NAB is slightly less specific, "Learn from the way the wild flowers grow.")

8. *The Sun Also Rises*

The *Book of Ecclesiastes* begins "Vanity of vanities! All things are vanity!" and proceeds to lament life's emptiness and futility, "The sun also ariseth, and the sun goeth down" (according to the KJV). Ernest Hemingway used it as the title of a 1926 novel.

9. *Lord of the Flies*

"Lord of the flies" is a translation of the Hebrew *Ba'alzevuv*, which is a slightly mis-transliterated form of the name of a foreign god. The change of just one letter—probably purposely—changed the translation from "Prince Baal" to "Lord of the Flies." For his 1954 novel, fraught with symbolism, William Golding used it deftly as the title (see p. 372).

10. *A Laodicean*

This term, referring to a timid, indecisive person, indifferent toward religion, was borrowed by Thomas Hardy as the title of a novel. Laodicea is one of the seven Churches of the Book of Revelation, the one to whom "the Amen, the faithful and true witness, the source of God's creation" said, "I know your works; you are neither cold nor hot. I wish that you were either cold or hot. So, because you are lukewarm, and neither cold nor hot, I am about to spit you out of my mouth" (*Revelation 3:15–16*).

11. *Stranger in a Strange Land*

Robert Heinlein chose this

## *The Lord of the Flies* or Every Letter Counts

The only difference between the names Beelzebub and Beelzebul is that last letter. "Beelzebub" is what we used to hear at Mass from time to time, when the older translations of Scripture were used. It's still heard in literal and traditionalist translations today. But it's "Beelzebul" in the revised NAB.

First, the Old Testament background—a story from 2 Kings 1: "Ahaziah had fallen through the lattice in his upper chamber in Samaria, and lay injured; so he sent messengers, telling them, 'Go, inquire of Baalzebub, the god of Ekron, whether I shall recover from this injury.' But the angel of the LORD said to Elijah the Tishbite, 'Get up, go to meet the messengers of the king of Samaria, and say to them, 'Is it because there is no God in Israel that you are going to inquire of Baalzebub, the god of Ekron?' Now therefore thus says the LORD, 'You shall not leave the bed to which you have gone, but you will surely die.'" ("Baalzebub" is the Hebrew form of the Greek "Beelzebub.")

But some experts through the years have said that "Baalzebub" (which translates "lord of the flies") was a mis-transliteration into Hebrew of Baalzebul (which translates "Prince Baal"—a bona fide god of the neighbors). That's so derisive it's hard to believe that it wasn't intentional (like calling somebody's tour de force a tour de farce).

When that name comes up in the New Testament (as in Matthew 10:25 and in the Jesus/Beelzebul controversy in Luke 11:14-23), the best New Testament manuscripts today support the "correct" transliteration (and forget the sarcasm).

That's why the reader finds "Beelzebul" in the revised NAB and "Beelzebub" in the likes of the NKJV and NIV (which acknowledge in footnotes the evidence of the more ancient "l" ending, even while keeping the traditional translation of the old KJV). Familiarity and tradition sometimes carry the day. The CEV doesn't make a choice, but translates (interprets) the "B" word in Matthew 10:25 as "Satan."

It was that probable old Jewish pun about the lord of the flies, plus later likenesses to the Aramaic *beeldebaba* ("enemy"), that made that old name one of the nicknames of the devil, appropriate for one devoted to demoralization, destruction, and decay. It is certain that the scriptural "lord of the flies" inspired William Golding in his choice for a title for his 1954 novel.

phrase in 1961 for what became his best-known novel. It's from Exodus 2:22 and a passage in which Moses explains the name Gershom that he gave to his son born in Midian when he was taking refuge there from the pharaoh. It was the King James Version of the Bible (as usual) that made that phrase memorable.

12. *Four Horsemen of the Apocalypse*

There are "Four Horsemen of the Apocalypse" released (on the earth and in literature), one at a time, as the first four seals of the seven seals on the scroll are broken in Revelation 6:1–8. This is its description of the fourth horse and horseman: "I looked and there was a pale green horse! Its rider's name was Death, and Hades followed with him; they were given authority over a fourth of the earth, to kill with sword, famine, and pestilence, and by the wild animals of the earth" (*Revelation 6:8*). Katherine Anne Porter alludes to the fourth horse and rider in the title of a short story set in the influenza epidemic of 1918, *Pale Horse Pale Rider. The Four Horsemen of the Apocalypse* is also the title of a 1918 novel by Vicente Blasco Ibanez.

13. *The Way of All Flesh*
This common phrase referring to human mortality, including demise and burial, has roots in the Bible. See Joshua 23:14 and 1 King 2:2, for example, but don't expect those exact words. It was in the old Catholic Douay-Rheims Bible that this phrase first appeared, in 1609. It is also the title of a 1903 novel by Samuel Butler.

# Glossary

Some of these terms do not appear in all translations.

### Abomination of desolation
("desolating sacrilege") An abominable thing, an idol, a pollution; quoting Jesus (*Matthew 24:15*)

### Abraham's bosom
("to be with Abraham") The rest of the blessed in death, alluding to Luke 16:22, and the custom of a friend reclining on one's bosom, as John on Jesus'

### Abyss
("a great abyss fixed," "a great chasm") An unsurmountable barrier, alluding to Lazarus and Dives (*Luke 16:26*)

### Adam's ale
Water (the only drink in Eden)

### Adam's apple
The remnant of Adam's sin, a piece of the forbidden fruit stuck in his throat

### The Adversary
("opponent") The devil (*1 Peter 5:8*)

### Agur's wish
"Give me neither poverty nor riches" comes from *Proverbs 30:8*—in a section of proverbs entitled "The Words of Agur" (an unknown person)

### Ahithophel
A treacherous counselor and friend. This man was David's adviser, but joined the revolt of Absalom, advising him "like the oracle of God" (*2 Samuel 16:20–23*)

### All things to all people
Indispensable; the effort to relate to all; what Saint Paul said of himself (see *1 Corinthians 9:22*)

### Alpha and Omega
("the beginning and the end") The beginning and the end; a biblical reference to a divine title, being actually the first and last letters of the Greek alphabet (*Revelation 1:8*)

**Apple of one's eye**

("apple of the eye") Something or someone precious (*Psalm 17:8*)

**Armageddon**

("Harmaged'on") A slaughter, or great battle; according to Revelation 16:16, the site of the last great battle on judgment day; geographically, the mountainous district near Megiddo

**Ashes to ashes, dust to dust**

Complete finality; an old English burial service phrase, alluding to the creation of humans from the dust of the ground (see *Genesis 2:7*). See also ". . . you are dust and to dust you shall return" (*Genesis 3:19*)

**Babel**

All-out confusion, unintelligibility; allusion to the confusion of tongues at Babel (see *Genesis 11:1–9*)

**Balm**

("Is there no balm in Gilead?"), balm being comfort ". . . Why then has the health of my poor people not been restored?" (*Jeremiah 8:22*)

**Benjamin**

The youngest, a favorite; allusion to Jacob's youngest son of this name (see *Genesis 35:18*)

**Benjamin's portion**

(or mess) The largest; allusion to Joseph's banquet for his brothers in Egypt, and the fact that Benjamin's share was five times the others (see *Genesis 43:34*)

**Beulah Land**

A paradise, promised land, far away dream-come-true land; *Isaiah 62:4* reference to Israel being called not "Desolate" but "Married" ("Beulah" in Hebrew)

**Bird**

("A little bird told me.") A caution against speaking privately what one would not want known publicly (see *Ecclesiastes 10:20*)

**Birthright**

(to sell one's birthright for a mess of pottage) To exchange one's heritage for a trifle; alluding to Esau selling his birthright for Jacob's pottage (see *Genesis 25:29–34*)

**Blind leading the blind**

("blind guides of the blind") Allusion to *Matthew 15:14*, Jesus confronting the Pharisees

**Bosom friend**

(". . . it used to . . . lie in his bosom, and it was like a daughter to him.") In *2 Samuel 12:3*, Nathan tells David a parable in which he describes a poor man's ewe lamb in those terms; see also Lazarus on Abraham's bosom (see *Luke 16:22*) and John on Jesus' (see *John 13:25*) in some translations

**Bowing the knee to Rimmon**

Temporizing; knowingly doing wrong in order to save face; allusion to *2 Kings 5:18*: Naaman the Syrian getting Elisha's permission to worship Rimmon when with his master he visited the house of Rimmon

**Bread**

("Asks for bread, will get a stone.") Spoken of a rebuff, a denied request; from *Matthew 7:9* where Jesus teaches about the power of prayer

**Bread**

(break bread) Eat together; perhaps also what today's Catholics call the Eucharist (see *Acts 2:44–47*)

**Bread**

(cast one's bread upon the water; send out your bread upon the water) ". . . for after many days you will get it back . . ." (*Ecclesiastes 11:1*). Be adventuresome, take a chance, be generous, don't expect immediate recognition (The waters of the ocean sometimes bear lost treasures to the shore)

**Bricks**

(to make bricks without straw) Trying to do a job without ability or materials; allusion to Hebrew forced labor under Egyptian task-masters (see *Exodus 5:6–14*)

**Build on sand**

Working with poor planning or unsure beginning; from a parable of Jesus (see *Matthew 7:24–27*)

**Burden**

("Borne the burden of the day and the scorching heat.") To do all the hard work; the complaint of those in Jesus' parable who got paid no more than those who came on at the eleventh hour (*Matthew 20:1–16*)

**Cain**

(the curse [brand, mark] of Cain) Said of one with nowhere to go or no place to call his or her own; the stigma of murder; blood guilt that

cannot be expiated; it's an allusion to God's mark of protection so no one would exact blood vengeance on Cain after his murder of Abel (see *Genesis 4:1–16*)

**Calf**

("Kill the fatted calf.") Let's celebrate. To welcome with the best; allusion to the parable of the prodigal son (*Luke 15:1–32*)

**Charity**

("charity begins at home") In *1 Timothy 5:4* the author teaches how adult children must bear responsibility for the care of their widowed mother

**Citizens of no mean city**

("a citizen of an important city") A recommendation because of back-ground; quoting Paul who referred to Tarsus as he solicited a hearing in Jerusalem (*Acts 21:39*)

**Clay feet**

A surprising flaw in one esteemed; from the clay feet of the image in Nebuchadnezzar's dream (*Daniel 2:31-33*) and an allusion to the standard composition of ancient idols.

**Cloud of witnesses**

Quoting Hebrews 12:1, the refer-ence to the witness of the faith of the ancients

**Coals**

("Heap coals of fire on their heads") Using kindness to melt another's animosity; turning the other cheek; repaying good for evil: an effective reproach (*Proverbs 25:21, 22*; also see *Romans 12:20*)

**Come to pass**

(take place) Happen; a phrase made popular by old translations of Christ's words regarding what would happen before the end (see *Matthew 24:6*)

**Cover a multitude of sins**

A compensating virtue; a pleasing cover of good over the bad that can't be seen. Quoting the author of 1 Peter 4:8 when he spoke of love, the ultimate virtue

**Crumbs from the rich man's table**

("what fell from the rich man's table") A pittance for the poor; a phrase from a parable of Christ: all that Lazarus said he wanted from Dives (*Luke 16:19–31*)

**Cup**

("Let this cup pass from me.") May I not have to go through this; from Christ's agony in the garden (*Matthew 26:39*)

**Cup**

("My cup runneth over; my cup overflows.") I am richly blessed (*Psalm 23:5*)

**Dan**

(from Dan to Beersheba) From one end (of the kingdom) to the other; coast to coast; all over. These two cities were the farthest north and south in Israel

**Dead**

(". . . let the dead bury their own dead.") Against temporizing; quoting *Matthew 8:22*—the conditions for following Jesus. Let bygones be bygones. Break with the past

**De profundis**

(Latin: out of the depths) Said of a bitter cry; first words of the Latin translation of Psalm 130; common in burial services

**Delilah**

("There is no leaping from Delilah's lap into Abraham's bosom.") One cannot live and die in grave sin and expect salvation. Referring to the lovely betrayer of Samson (*Judges 16*), and to the patriarch whose bosom represented reward and rest (see *Luke 16:22*)

**Doubting Thomas**

A skeptic; Thomas doubted when told of the Resurrected Christ (see *John 20:24–29*)

**Eat, drink, and be merry**

(". . . eat, and drink, and enjoy . . .") In *Ecclesiastes 8:15* it is pessimistically recommended to enjoy life while we have it, since this is the best we can do in the world. In *Isaiah 22:13*, in another context, there is a similar phrase, with the added "for tomorrow we die"

**Eleventh hour**

Just in time; an allusion to the day laborers parable Matthew 20:1–16, and the ones hired last

**Entertain an angel unawares**

From Hebrews 13:2, an exhortation on hospitality; see also Genesis 18:1 –15, the story of the three visitors to Abraham who were actually angels (the story that provided the imagery for Rublev's Trinity icon)

**Eye for an eye, tooth for a tooth**
The *Lex Talionis* (law of reciprocal punishment in kind: see *Deuteronomy 19:21*)

**Eye of a needle**
A difficult task, if not a human impossibility; from *Matthew 19:24*: "It is easier for a camel to go through . . ."

**Flesh**
(remembering the fleshpots of Egypt) Fantasizing over, glorifying the (perceived) good things of the past when they are no longer available (see *Exodus 16:3*)

**Fly in the ointment**
(". . . one bungler destroys much good.") A little thing that spoils everything, or at least detracts from its attractiveness (*Ecclesiastes 9:18*)

**Forbidden fruit**
Anything stolen, but especially illicit love; alluding to the fruit stolen by the first humans in the garden

**Fruit**
("By their fruits you shall know them.") Judging by one's actions, not words; results, not intentions; from Matthew 12:33 (also translated ". . . the tree is known by its fruit.") where Jesus exposes the legalistic, externalized perversion of religion by some of the Pharisees

**Gall and wormwood**
Extremely distasteful, a bitter pill; quoting Lamentations 3:18–19

**Gird your loins**
Roll up your sleeves; hitch up your figurative belt for vigorous action;

common biblical exhortation (see *1 Kings 18:46*; *Job 38:3*; *Jeremiah 1:17*; *1 Peter 1:13*)

**Giving**
("It is more blessed to give than to receive.") Words of Jesus, although not in the Gospels; Luke describes Paul as ending his farewell address to the elders of Ephesus by recalling these words of Jesus (*Acts 20:35*)

**Giving up the ghost**
(only in the King James Version) Death; expression used by Job (see *Job 14:10*), by the psalmist (see *Psalm 31:6*; *Luke 23:46*), and by John for Jesus' death (see *John 19:30*), for example

**Gladden**
(to gladden the hearts of men; "to gladden the human heart") An allusion to *Psalm 104:15*; the purpose of the gift of wine

**Glory**
(in his glory) In one's natural, truest element; Jesus was seen in his glory only in Transfiguration (see *Mark 9:2–10*); used of those who are at their best, in their natural habitat, doing what is their destiny

**Goads**
(to kick against the goad) Competing against odds, especially authority or fate, or in Saul's case, grace (see *Acts 9:5*)

**Good Samaritan**
A good neighbor, helper of the distressed; alluding to Jesus' parable involving the priest, the Levite, and the Samaritan (see *Luke 10:30–37*)

## Grapes of wrath

Potential recipients of just punishment; used by John Steinbeck as the title of a novel and occurring in the first stanza of the "Battle Hymn of the Republic"; allusion to the winepress image of Revelation 14:19–20 which teaches about the harvest of the earth and the impending doom of the ungodly

## Greater love than this no one has

("No one has greater love than this") From Jesus' last discourse (*John 14—17*, specifically *15:13*), where he teaches about the extent to which love will take the followers: martyrdom for the beloved; applied to the unbloody martyrdom of unrecognized service, especially when agape (sacrificial/ divine love) and philia ("brotherly"/sisterly love) are united in one person

## Green wood

("For if they do this when the wood is green [innocent], what will happen when it is dry [wicked]?") Quoting Jesus meeting the Jerusalem women on the way of the cross (*Luke 23:31*)

## Handwriting on the wall

The all but obvious being revealed; the announcement of the imminent fulfillment of some doom. At Belshazzar's party, it was right there on the wall: "God has numbered the days of your kingdom and brought it to an end" (*Daniel 5:26*)

## Hewers of wood and drawers of water

Drudges; humble workers; quoting *Deuteronomy 29:10* ("... those who

### "Grim Reaper?"

One of the common personifications of death is a man holding a scythe. A reaper. A *grim* reaper. *Revelation 14:14-20* is the inspiration, providing a vivid picture: "Then I looked, and there was a white cloud, and seated on the cloud was one like the Son of Man, with a gold crown on his head, and a sharp sickle in his hand! Another angel came out of the temple, calling with a loud voice to the one who sat on the cloud, 'Use your sickle and reap, for the hour to reap has come, because harvest of the earth is fully ripe.'"

*Another* angel (reaper) soon comes into the picture, and the metaphor mixes grapes in with the wheat–grapes of *wrath*, we say today, although the Scripture never does, any more than it calls the reaper "grim." It does describe "the great wine press of the wrath of God'" (*Revelation 14:19*). No "grim reaper" and no "grapes of wrath," but a grim and wrathful scene, with plenty of reaping and grapes that *are* mentioned. In fact, *described*. In more detail than we need.

cut your wood and those who draw your water") where Moses, in his final discourse, is summoning all Israel, from least to greatest, to a renewal of the covenant. In Joshua 9:21 it is also used as a phrase for the slaves of the community

## House built on rock

Someone or something with a sure foundation; allusion to Jesus' parable on the practice of religion (see *Matthew 7:24–27*)

**House divided**

When some said that Jesus was casting out devils by the power of the prince of devils (see *Luke 11:14 –23*), Jesus said that Satan in that case would be divided against himself, and that such a house divided falls; but God's kingdom lasts

**Howling wilderness**

Suggesting dreariness and savagery (wind and wild beasts); from Moses' song of deliverance (see *Deuteronomy 32:10*)

**Jacob's ladder**

Steps that are high and steep; also "jacob" for a ladder; an allusion to the ladder of Jacob's dream on which God's messengers were going up and down (see *Genesis 28:12*); the flaw in a stocking where only the ladder-like threads crossing from side to side are left

**Jeremiad**

A doleful complaint, lamentation. Jeremiah contains warnings of disaster for Israel. His words reveal his own inner conflicts and personal feelings about God and his job (see *Jeremiah 15:10–21, 18:18–23, 20:7–18*)

**Jericho**

Used to give a specific name to an indefinite place; allusion to the "Remain at Jericho until your beards have grown" story in *2 Samuel 10:1–5* (in other words, "Stay away for a while")

**Jeroboam**

One who is of great promise, but who ends up in perversion; allusion to the mighty man of valor.

"He will give Israel up because of the sins of Jeroboam, which he sinned and which he caused Israel to commit" (*1 Kings 14:16*)

**Jeroboam, Rehoboam**

The first king of Israel and the first king of Judah

**Jesse tree**

A genealogical tree, sometimes taking the form of a vine (sometimes arising from Jesse himself, recumbent), or a branched candlestick, tracing the ancestry of Jesus (if in a window, a "Jesse window"); from *Isaiah 11:1*, "A shoot . . . from the stump of Jesse"

**Jezebel**

(a painted Jezebel) A depraved and seductive person; a flaunting woman, bold in manner and morally questionable; said about ninth-century BC Phoenician wife of King Ahab of Israel who fostered worship of other gods in Israel and who arranged the murder of Naboth (see *1 Kings 16:31–32, 18:1 –19:3, 21; 2 Kings 9:7–37*)

**Job**

Personification of patience, poverty (see *Book of Job*)

**Job's comforter**

An ineffectual empathizer or pretender who only worsens the situation; Job's friends concluded that he must have somehow caused his own grief (see *Job 16:2*)

**Jonathan's arrows**

A warning, not meant to hurt; allusion to 1 Samuel 20:18–23 and the story of the arrows Jonathan shot to signal to David according to a prearranged code

## Jordan
(bathing seven times in the Jordan) A remedy; an action (sacramental), not necessarily understood, and not therapeutic in itself, but efficacious; alluding to the directions Elisha gave Naaman the Syrian to heal his leprosy (see *2 Kings 5:1–27*)

## Jordan
(crossing Jordan; Jordan passed) Dying; like the mythical River Styx, the Jordan formed the boundary of the Promised Land, and crossing it ended the journey in the wilderness ("the world"; *Joshua 1:1–2*)

## Joseph
One unsuccessfully seduced, unwavering in constancy; allusion to the wife of Potiphar trying to seduce Joseph (see *Genesis 39*)

## Jot or tittle
(not one jot or tittle) The absolute minimum, the smallest possible amount or degree. Alluding to Jesus referring to letter of the law, which would not pass away until the laws were fulfilled (see *Matthew 5:18*). In older translations, "one letter" was more literally rendered "jot," which is from the Latin jota, which is from the Greek iota, which is the ninth—and smallest—letter of the Greek alphabet. Hence the saying "not one iota." Tittle is rendered "one stroke of a letter." It is an old name for the diacritical marks used in Hebrew, marks that furnished a vowel sound for a word; hence, not even a letter

## Kedar's tents
This world; unpeaceful and nomadic; allusion to Psalm 120:5, the cry of one longing for peace and a home (Kedar, in Genesis 25:15, a nomad)

## Kill the fatted calf
Prepare to celebrate! Especially, warm hospitality for a homecoming; the father gave these instructions upon the return of the prodigal son (see *Luke 15:23*)

## Kiss of Judas
Pretended affection; betrayal; an obvious reference to Judas and Jesus (see *Matthew 26:49*)

## Labor of love
Work engaged in because of affection for, or desire to please another; probably alluding to Paul (see *1 Thessalonians 1:3*) and the Letter to the Hebrews (see *Hebrews 6:10*) where the believers are commended for the way they live

## Laborer is worth his wage
(". . . laborers deserve to be paid.") Be fair. With these words Jesus assured the seventy-two he was sending on mission that they could "remain in the same house, eating and drinking whatever they provide" (*Luke 10:7*)

## Land of the living
Life; a phrase Jeremiah used in quoting his enemy's evil intents (Jeremiah 11:19); also meaning that while still here ". . . I shall see the goodness of the Lord in the land of the living" (*Psalm 27:13*)

### Land of (flowing with) milk and honey

Paradisal; heaven; in Exodus 3:8, this was the phrase used to describe the destiny of the enslaved Hebrews whom Moses was called to lead (see also *Joel 2:18–29*)

### Laodicean

One indifferent about religion, because the Christians of that city in the Book of Revelation were indifferent about their religion (see *Revelation 3:14–18*)

### Lazar

Victim of a repulsive disease; any poor beggar; from Lazarus, the leper who lay daily at the rich man's gate, a story Jesus told (see *Luke 16:19–31*)

### Legion

("My name is Legion.") Many; hydra-headed; more than one would want or guess; it was the name given by the Gerasene demoniac in *Mark 5:9*

### Leopard changing its spots

An impossibility; this is how Jeremiah described the ability of disgraced Jerusalem to change from evil to good (see *Jeremiah 13:23*)

### Light

(to hide your light under a bushel basket) Modesty, to the point of "depriving" others; concealing abilities or merit; from Christ's Sermon on the Mount (*Matthew 5:14–16*)

### [The] lines have fallen for me in pleasant places

"The boundary lines have fallen for me in pleasant places; I have a goodly heritage" (*Psalm 16:6*), meaning the lines drawn for the portion of a tribe

### (The) lion shall lie down with the lamb

("The wolf and the lamb shall feed together.") Harmony; quoting *Isaiah 65:25* and the prophesy of a new world

### Lip service

Just talk; from Jesus' discussions with some Pharisees (see *Matthew 15:8*; see also *Isaiah 29:13*)

### Live by the sword, die by the sword

Harm set, harm get. Jesus' use is recorded in Matthew 26:52, Mark 14:47, Luke 22:49–51, John 18:10–11, when he was being arrested and a follower drew a sword (In the Gospel according to John, it was Peter)

### Loaves

(with an eye to loaves and fish) Poor motive; camouflaged desire for material gain; allusion to Jesus' teaching and feeding the multitude, and his knowledge of their motive (*John 6:26*)

### [The] Lord loves a cheerful giver

So says Paul as he teaches stewardship and generosity (see *2 Corinthians 9:7*)

### Lord of Creation

Human; an allusion to the divine gift to humanity of care over the world (*Genesis 1:28–29*)

### [The] love of money is the root of all evil

According to Paul (see *1 Timothy 6:10*)

### Magdalene

A reformatory for prostitutes; allusion to the great sinner of Luke 8:1–3, falsely identified with Mary of Magdala, out of whom Jesus cast seven devils

**Magnificat**

Mary's song of praise: "My soul magnifies (*magnificat*) the Lord . . ." (*Luke 1:46–55*)

**Mammon of righteousness**

Money; an old translation of Luke 16:9 in which Jesus is counseling on the right use of this world's goods

**Man proposes, God disposes**

("The human mind plans the way, but the LORD directs the steps.") The scriptural version of this ancient proverb is in *Proverbs 16:9*

**Many are called but few are chosen**

A warning about the need for ongoing conversion and growth, especially in the face of apathy and self-assurance; the last line of Jesus' wedding banquet parable (see *Matthew 22:1–14*)

**Mark of the beast**

Anything so designated is branded evil, unorthodox, from Revelation 16:2 and 19:20, and the references to the personification or focus of evil in the world

**Maudlin**

Sickeningly sentimental; the word is derived from from Mary Magdalene (see *Luke 8:1–3*), whose face and eyes according to some medieval artists had that kind of look

**Miserere (or *misericord*)**

The underside of a folding choir stall seat, called this because in its folded-up position it is comfortable for the aged in a kneeling position;

named from the Latin title (first word) of Psalm 51, David's prayer of repentance

**Money**

(". . . the love of money is a root of all kinds of evil") see *Timothy 6:10*

**Mouths**

(out of the mouths of babes) "Out of the mouths of infants . . . you have prepared praise for yourself" (*Matthew 21:16*); see *Psalm 8:2*

**Naboth's vineyard**

A vulnerable holding; another's possession that one could take; Ahab did take Naboth's (see *1 Kings 21*)

**Name**

(". . . their name lives on.") Popular memorial saying; from the famous "Hymn in Honor of Our Ancestors" in *Sirach 44:14*

**Nazareth**

("Can anything good come from Nazareth?") A skeptical observation; doubting greatness because of humble origin, as Nathanael was skeptical about Christ (*John 1:46*); in the time of Christ, Nazareth was understood to be small and unimportant

**New Jerusalem**

Paradise; heaven; allusion to John's vision of the new creation (see *Revelation 21*)

**New wine in new skins**

Brand new, not a re-make; in Matthew 9:17, Jesus expounds on the need for a recreated spirit, not just a remodeled religion

**Nimrod**

A distinguished, daring hunter; Nimrod was "a mighty hunter before the LORD" (*Genesis 10:9*)

**No respecter of persons**

(". . . God shows no partiality.") Indiscriminate, ignoring distinctions; quoting Saint Peter (*Acts 10:34*, old translation) explaining that God doesn't play favorites

**No rest for the wicked**

Isaiah's observation (Latin: *Nemo malus felix*, No bad man is happy)

**Nod**

(land of nod) The place of Cain's banishment; "East of Eden"— means "wandering." "Land of Nod" for sleep is a pun (and misinterpretation) only possible in English

**Nothing new under the sun**

(Latin: *Nil novi sub sole*); from *Ecclesiastes 1:9*, "What has been is what will be, and what has been done is what will be done; there is nothing new under the sun"

**Numbered**

("Your days are numbered.") Doom saying; what Daniel saw in the handwriting on the wall, "God has numbered the days of your kingdom and brought it to an end" (*Daniel 5:26*)

**Nunc dimittis**

To receive (or sing) one's *nunc dimittis* is to receive permission for a leave-taking, and to take satisfaction in a leave-taking; from the opening words of Simeon on the occasion of the presentation of the child Jesus, "Master, you are now dismissing your servant in peace . . ." (*Luke 2:29*)

**Olive shoots**

A lighthearted term for one's children; the psalmist (see *Psalm 128:3*) calls them that, and the wife a fruitful vine

**Ox**

("You shall not muzzle an ox while it is treading out the grain.") Do not begrudge a laborer his little compensation; quoting *Deuteronomy 25:4* and applying it to the laborer and the privileges that could be allowed him regarding the circumstances and products of his work (see Paul's use, *1 Corinthians 9:9, 1 Timothy 5:18*)

**Patience of Job**

Maximum long-suffering and forbearance; from the Book of Job, though no particular line in it speaks exactly those words

**Patmos**

A hermitage; exile; in *Revelation 1:9* it says John retired or was exiled there.

**Pearls**

(". . . do not throw your pearls before swine . . .") Giving what is precious to the unappreciative; to waste; allusion to *Matthew 7:6*— Jesus' acknowledgment that the Good News will not be accepted by all, and that responsibility for this belongs to the one who "tramples them underfoot"

**Philistine**

A boorish, uncultured person; Israelite neighbor and long-standing enemy. Their name came to be used because they believed in Canaanite religion and because they stole the ark of the covenant

**Physician, heal thyself**
("Doctor, cure yourself!") The advice, recorded by Saint Luke (*Luke 4:23*), for those who should take the advice they give, *Medice, cura te ipsum*

**Plow**
("... put a hand to the plow ...") Commencing in earnest; quoting *Luke 9:62*, where Jesus preaches the cost of discipleship, and the temptation to temporize

**Poor as Job**
The man dispossessed through the devil's testings (see *Book of Job*)

**Poor as Lazarus**
A beggar by this name lay daily at the gate of the rich Dives (see *Luke 16:19–31*)

**Potters' field**
A cemetery for the poor; originally the land in the infamous Valley of Hinnom (Gehenna) called Ha•kel'•da•ma (Field of Blood, *Acts 1:19*) which was bought with Judas's betrayal money (*Matthew 27:7*) as a cemetery for foreigners. Called "Potter's field" possibly because it was once used for clay or because it was where potsherds were discarded (see *Jeremiah 19*), the land being good for nothing else

**Prodigal son**
The wastrel who returns, repentant, after dissipation; from a parable in which Jesus taught about the nature of God (see *Luke 15:11–32*)

**Promised land**
The place of one's dreams, referring originally to Canaan, promised to Abraham by God (see *Exodus 12:25, Deuteronomy 9:28*)

**[A] Prophet is not without honor, except in his native place**
Admiration and fame is greater the farther one is from home; proverbial in the Scriptures (see *Matthew 13:57; Mark 6:6*)

**Race**
("The race is not to the swift, nor the battle to the strong.") Adapting *Ecclesiastes 9:11*

**Raise Cain**
Raise a ruckus, make noise, cause trouble; an allusion to Cain who murdered his brother (Genesis 4)

**Reed**
(a bruised reed) Unstable, in a weakened condition, untrustworthy; allusion to Egypt as an ally for the Jews against Assyria (see *2 Kings 18:21; Isaiah 36:6*)

**Reed shaken in the wind**
One who goes where the wind goes; Jesus, said John the Baptist was not one, but that he was a man with firm conviction (see *Matthew 11:7*)

**Render unto Caesar what is Caesar's (and unto God what is God's)**
Referring to Jesus' quote allowing the just claims of the state; from a discussion on tribute to the emperor, "Give to the emperor the things that are the emperor's, and to God the things that are God's" (*Mark 12:17*)

### Return one's vomit

Backsliding; return to sin; 2 Peter 2:22 cites a dog's disgusting habit (see also *Proverbs 26:11*)

### Right mind

(in one's right mind) Sane; serenity following agitation; this is how the townsfolk found a demoniac whom Jesus had exorcized (see *Mark 5:15*—old translation)

### Root of the matter

Basic issue; quintessence; Job (see *Job 19:28*) wondered if the problems cause was within him

### Sackcloth and ashes

Penitence, strictly speaking; common scripturally (see *Matthew 11:21*)

### Saint Peter's fingers

The fingers of a thief ("A thief has a fish hook on every finger."), alluding to the fish Peter caught that had a coin in its mouth (*Matthew 17:24–27*)

### Saint Stephen's loaves

Stones; allusion to the stoning of Saint Stephen (see *Acts 7:54–60*)

### Salt

(covenant of salt) An unbreakable bond; from 2 Chronicles 13:5, referring to God's covenant with Israel; salt being a symbol of incorruption and perpetuity

### Salt of the earth

Good people, for their sanctifying effect on others, "preservers of civilization"; used by Jesus of his disciples in the Sermon on the Mount, "You are the salt of the earth" (*Matthew 5:13*)

### Samson

An exceptionally strong person; referring to the Hebrew hero (see *Judges 13–16*)

### Sanctum sanctorum

A private place, holy ground, intimacy; Latin for "holy of holies," properly the inner chamber of the Jewish temple entered only by the high priest on the high feast of atonement.

### [Is] Saul also among the prophets?

Of one who now espouses a cause or idea he hitherto assailed; *1 Samuel 10:9–12* tells of the origin of this proverb. It may have been used of another Saul (or is it Paul?) in *Acts 9:21*

### Scapegoat

An innocent one bearing responsibility for the guilty; one paying the price for another; from the Old Testament atonement ritual (see *Leviticus 16*) in which two goats were brought to the temple: One was sacrificed to the Lord, the other "heard" the confession of the high priest and was taken into the wilderness with the transferred sins of the people

### See how the land lies

To check out; make preliminary investigations; to test the water; an old translation of *Numbers 13:16* ("reconnoiter"), where Moses is readying to enter Canaan

### Semitic

Pertaining to those thought to be descendants of Shem, the eldest son of Noah (Genesis 10), that is, the Jews, Arabs, Assyrians, Aramaeans, and others

## Seventh Heaven

This one isn't exactly in Scripture, but it's close (within four heavens). In *2 Corinthians 12:2-4*, Paul (carefully speaking of himself in the third person) reflects on the origin of what he knows: "I know a person in Christ who fourteen years ago was caught up to the third heaven—whether in the body or out of the body I do not know; God knows. And I know that such a person . . . was caught up into Paradise and heard things that are not to be told, that no mortal is permitted to repeat."

Ancient blueprints of the cosmos depicted a multi-leveled universe. There is a lot of speculation in Jewish literature from the period between the Old and New Testaments about the number of heavens (or levels of heaven). Apocalyptic literature (see Chapter 2) commonly proposed seven heavens (so if you're in seventh heaven, it doesn't get any better than this). There is a testament of Levi that proposes three, with God, in the third heaven. Paul was writing out of this tradition.

### Seventy is the sum of our years

("The days of our life are seventy years, or perhaps eighty, if we are strong") Our allotted span, our natural life; frequently used scripturally (*Psalm 90:10*)

### Shake off the dust from your feet

Leave an inhospitable place; implying judgment, or at least determination and finality; alluding to Jesus' advice to disciples in the event they were not received well (see *Mark 6:11*; *Luke 9:5*)

### Sheep

(". . . he will separate . . . as a shepherd separates the sheep from the goats.") The good from the bad; alluding to the last judgment (*Matthew 25:32*)

### Shibboleth

A catchword, slogan or test word; the criterion for distinguishing insiders from outsiders. Differences in the pronunciation of this word's initial sound betrayed rival tribal affinities and became the basis for discovering and exterminating outsiders (see *Judges 12:4–6*)

### Simony

Buying and selling sacred things and Church offices; from the magician Simon Magus's offer to buy the power to bestow the Holy Spirit (see *Acts 8:18*)

### Skin

(by the skin of one's teeth) Just barely; Job thus described his hold on life (see *Job 19:20*)

### Slow to anger

How Nehemiah, for example, describes God (see *Nehemiah 9:17*); equanimity

### Sounding brass or tinkling cymbal

(". . . noisy gong or a clanging cymbal") A lot of talk; words without sense; from a traditional translation of *1 Corinthians 13:1*, Paul's description of a person who has many gifts and does great things but doesn't have love

### Sow

("As you sow, so shall you reap.") This old translation of part of *Galatians 6:7* is from an exhortation of Saint Paul that the community of Christ live out their faith and never "grow weary in doing what is right, for we will reap at harvest time, if we do not give up" (*Galatians 6:9*)

### Sow the wind, reap the whirlwind

Causing trouble, and getting more than you bargained for; starting something you can't finish; so Hosea fumes (see *Hosea 8:7*) about Israel's perversity

### Spare the rod and spoil the child

("Those who spare the rod hate their children . . .") It's folly to allow childish faults to go unreproved; an allusion to *Proverbs 13:24*

### Spirit

(". . . the spirit indeed is willing, but the flesh is weak.") The will is strong but there is no power to execute it. It is the caution of Jesus from *Matthew 26:41*, human nature being what it is

### Stars in their courses

Destiny; alluding to Judges 5:20: The enemy of Sisera in battle

### Still, small voice

(". . . and after the fire a sound of sheer silence.") The sound of God's presence; an allusion to *1 Kings 19:12*, the sound Elijah finally heard by which he found God after not finding God in the earthquake and the fire

### Stolen sweets are always sweeter

Illegality charms, making such ill-gotten gains the more palatable; an old translation of an Old Testament proverb (see *Proverbs 9:17*)

### Stone

(". . . be the first to throw a stone . . .") To lead in fault-finding; quoting Jesus' challenge to the crowd in his defense of the woman caught in adultery (*John 8:7*)

### Straight and narrow

Path of virtue; probably alluding to Matthew 7:14 where Jesus describes the path to eternal life

### Strain

(". . . you strain out a gnat but swallow a camel!") Fussing about peccadilloes while committing serious offenses; not allowing a small point, all the while blithely accepting a difficult one. From *Matthew 23:24*, and the practice of straining wine; in this instance Jesus is criticizing Pharisees

### Stranger in a strange land

A foreigner, or feeling like one. This is an allusion to the explanation Moses gave for the name ("Gershom") he bestowed on his son born in Midian when he was taking refuge there from the pharaoh (see *Exodus 2:22*); it was the King James Version of the Bible (as usual) that made this phrase memorable

### Strength

(to go from strength to strength) To improve work, reputation, and so on; so the psalmist proclaims the progress of the just (see *Psalm 84:7*)

### Suffer fools gladly

Be patient, because you have the consolation of knowing that you are wise. Quoting one old translation of 2 Corinthians 11:19, where Paul acknowledges factions in the

community, and teaches that the
good will stand out by contrast

## Sun

("... do not let the sun go down on
your anger ...") Quoting *Ephesians
4:26*; a verse from one of Saint
Paul's passages on daily conduct
in the community of faith

## Sweat

(by the sweat of your brow) By
hard manual labor; the injunction
of God to Adam after the fall (see
*Genesis 3:19*)

## Sweating blood

Anxiety, if not anguish; a scribal
addition to Luke's story of Christ's
experience in the garden the night
before his death (see *Luke 22:44*)

## Swords

("... they shall beat their swords
into plowshares ...") Changing
from war-mongering to peace-
seeking (quoting *Isaiah 2:4*; see also
*Micah 4:3*)

## Taking your life in your hands

Risking your life; a scriptural
expression (see Jephthah in *Judges
12:3*; David in *1 Samuel 19:5*; Job
in *Job 13:14*)

## Talent

Gift, ability; reference to Jesus'
parable of Matthew 25:14–30; this
was the name of a weight or large
sum of money in the ancient world

## Teeth set on edge

Grating; experience difficulty or
revulsion. When Jeremiah (31:29)
and Ezekiel (18:2) teach about
the consequences of sin and our
personal responsibility for it, they

quote a proverb with this phrase

## Tell it not in Gath

"Don't publicize this, lest my enemies rejoice." "Don't tell anybody
or they'll laugh at me"; based on
David (*2 Samuel 1:20*) lamenting
the death of Saul, aware that the
Philistines (in Gath) would rejoice

## Thirty pieces of silver

Blood money; the price for a
slave's manumission; a bribe; Judas
Iscariot's payment for betraying
Christ (see *Matthew 27:3*)

## Thorn in the flesh

God used this phrase in describing
for Moses the inhabitants of
Canaan, should they be allowed
to remain after the Hebrews took
over (see *Numbers 33:55*). However,
it usually alludes to Saint Paul's
reference to some personal cross of
his, "... a thorn was given to me in
the flesh ..." (*2 Corinthians 12:7*)

## Tongue, a two-edged sword

When words wound, as in an
argument cutting both ways,
addressing both the pro and the
con; alluding to Hebrews 4:12
describing the word of God; also
Revelation 1:16 and the sword out
of the mouth of the Son of Man,
with one edge to convict, the other
to redeem

## Touch-me-not

Name given to an impatiens plant,
from the post-Resurrection words
of the Lord to Mary Magdalene in
John 20:17, "Do not hold on to me"
(in Latin, *Noli me tangere*)

## Tried and found wanting

Or "... you have been weighed on

the scales and found wanting . . .";
tested and proven false; translations of a phrase from Daniel's
interpretation of Belshazzar's
dream (*Daniel 5:27*)

### Turn the other cheek

Advice against retaliation, and an
allusion to Jesus' mandate to love
one's enemy (see *Luke 6:29*)

### In the twinkling of an eye

Quickly; this is how Saint Paul
describes how quickly the bodies
of believers who are alive at the
end of the world will be changed
(see *1 Corinthians 15:52*)

### Uriah (letter of Uriah)

A treacherous message; a death
warrant in the guise of a friendly
letter; alluding to the letter by
David to General Joab that Uriah
should be sent to the front (see *2
Samuel 11:15*)

### Vanity of vanities, all is vanity

The opening words of the book of
Ecclesiastes (1:2); "vanity" being
fruitlessness; the sense being,
"Everything people do is in vain"

### A voice crying in the wilderness

Prophetic voice, precursive word
and warning; John the Evangelist
thus described John the Baptist
(see *John 1:23*)

### [The] Wages of sin is death

Sin results in death; so Paul teaches
(see *Romans 6:23*)

### Wars and rumors of wars

Bad news; Jesus cautions that these
are not signs of an imminent end
(see *Matthew 24:6*)

### Washing one's hands

To back out of, to disdain responsibility after initial involvement;
especially to declare someone
innocent and to declare oneself not
responsible for what others do to
him, alluding to Pilate with Jesus'
death on his hands (see *Matthew
27:24*)

### [The] Way of all flesh

To die, including demise and
burial; a common phrase with roots
in the Bible. See Joshua 23:14 and
1 King 2:2, for example, but don't
expect those exact words. It was
in the old Catholic Douay-Rheims
(not the King James Bible, for a
change) that this phrase first
appeared, in 1609

### Weathercock (weathervane)

A person always changing his
mind; one not living up to his own
words. A weather vane in the form
of a rooster; it was a medieval
tradition to adorn church steeples
with this symbol of Saint Peter; an
allusion to Saint Peter's denial of
Christ after Christ predicted it (see
*Matthew 26:31–35, 69–75*)

### Widow's cruse

Any small supply that—managed
well, or merely spent—becomes
adequate and apparently inexhaustible; from Elisha's miracle
with the cruse (or cruet) of oil
(see *2 Kings 4:1–7*)

### Widow's mite

A small amount at great sacrifice;
the offering praised by Christ (see
*Mark 12:42*)

## Wine

("Good wine gladdens a person's heart.") This Latin phrase (*Bonum vinum laetificat cor hominis*) makes a proverb of *Psalm 104:15*: ". . . and wine (God's providence) to gladden the human heart . . ." (see also *Judges 9:13*)

## Wings of the wind

Swiftly; alluding to *Psalm 18:10*, "He rode on a cherub, and flew; / he came swiftly upon the wings of the wind"; describing divine mobility

## Wisdom of Solomon

Proverbial wisdom; great wisdom. Referring to the Hebrew king; see Solomon's prayer for wisdom (see *Wisdom 9:1-12*). Jesus recalled that the Queen of the South came to hear the wisdom of Solomon, and was said to have proclaimed that "something greater than Solomon is here" (*Luke 11:31*).

## Wise as serpents, gentle as doves

Referring to the advice that Matthew's Jesus gives to his disciples; a modern translation renders this as "clever" and "innocent," pointing to two virtues that are not mutually exclusive (see *Matthew 10:16*)

## Work

("If any would not work, neither should he eat.") This is the KJV translation of *2 Thessalonians 3:10*, advice that the author gave about how to treat those who sit around waiting for the end time and don't go on with their daily responsibilities—advice that has become the basis for the so-called work ethic

## You are dust, and to dust you shall return

God's words to Adam (see *Genesis 3:19*); also Ezekiel 28:18 refers to returning to ashes (dust); an option for the wording for the Ash Wednesday conferral of ashes

## Youth renewed like the eagle's

From Psalm 103:5, and the ancient belief that every ten years an eagle would fly into the "fiery regions," thence to the ocean depths, and then rise, molted, to a new life like the phoenix rising

# A History of the Translation of Scripture into English

## Saint Jerome
### and the Lion

The lion is a common feature of story and legend, especially to illustrate the effect of kindness, and the transforming power of gratitude. The following is a Christian version of *Androcles and the Lion*.

*Once a lion entered a schoolroom in which Jerome was teaching, and lifted one of its paws. Although the disciples all fled, Jerome noticed that the paw was wounded, and proceeded to extract a thorn from it and dressed the wound. The grateful lion stayed at the side of its benefactor.*

That is why the saint is commonly depicted accompanied by a lion. It is not surprising that this story's setting is a schoolroom. Jerome spent much time there. No less than Saint Augustine said of him, "If Jerome doesn't know, nobody does, or ever did." A prodigious scholar, Jerome's ultimate work was translating the entire Bible into Latin (the Vulgate), the Old Testament from Hebrew and the New from Greek. The Council of Trent, having called for its revision, declared it the authentic text for the Church.

# The History

The reference works for the information in this outline are *Background to the Bible* by Richard Murphy, O.P.; *The Bible in Translation, Ancient and English Versions* by Bruce Metzger; and *The Complete Guide to Bible Versions*, by Philip Comfort.

In the pages that follow, the history of English Bible translations is divided into six eras. ("OT" and "NT" refer to Old Testament and New Testament.)

1. Before 1382: Saint Augustine to Wycliffe
2. 1382–1525: Wycliffe to Tyndale
3. 1525–1611: Tyndale to the King James Version
4. 1611–1902: The KJV to The Twentieth Century NT
5. 1902–1982: Modern Translations
6. Since 1982: New Revisions

(The *Catechism* does not mention "Protestant Bibles" in either of its two direct exhortations to the faithful to read the Bible—paragraphs 133 and 2653, since there is no need to emphasize this distinction.)

## 1. Before 1382: Saint Augustine to Wycliffe

- **In the sixth century**, Pope Saint Gregory the Great commissioned a party of forty monks under the leadership of Augustine (later known as Augustine of Canterbury) to bring Christianity to Britain. With the faith, these missionaries brought the Bible.

- **English translations** of portions of the Bible followed, notably by Saint Augustine (around 600), Saint Wilfred (around 670), Caedmon (in song, around 670), the Venerable Bede (Saint John's Gospel, the final passages of which he dictated from his death bed, in 735), and King Alfred (901).

- **Other fragmentary evidence also remains**, like the Lindisfarne Gospels (also known as the *Book of Durham*, and *The Gospels of St. Cuthbert*), an inter-linear translation of the gospel by the monks of Lindisfarne, dated around 950. They took a copy of the Gospels and printed Anglo-Saxon equivalents above the lines (like a "crib"). This work, now in the British Museum, is the nearest surviving "Bible" handwritten in Anglo-Saxon. It probably borrowed heavily from a now non-existent work of the Venerable Bede from around 700.

- **"Old English" or Anglo-Saxon** (400s/800s–1150) is the English of this period: the original pre-Norman Germanic stock of English used from the fifth century (or eighth, according to some) to the twelfth century. It is the language of the epic poem *Beowulf* of the early eighth century. The oldest extant Old English translation of the gospel is the tenth-century *Wessex Gospels*.

- **Before the flourishing of Middle English** (1150–1475) and the age of Chaucer (1340–1400), there is no evidence of English translations of significant portions of the

Bible. There was, in the 1300s, a metrical translation of the psalms into English was done by William of Shoreham and another by Blessed Richard Rolle (first of the great fourteenth century English mystics).

### 2. 1382-1525: Wycliffe to Tyndale

These were the years when large portions of the Bible, especially the New Testament, were coming out in translation. In the millennium (more or less) between Saint Jerome (331–420) and Wycliffe (about 1329–1384), Jerome's Latin translation was the Vulgate, and Latin was the dominant language of scholarship. With the Renaissance came a resurgence of interest in the study of the classics, including the Greek and Hebrew languages. Now scholars were reading the New Testament in its original Greek for the first time in nearly one thousand years. By 1500, Greek was being taught at Oxford.

- **1382, John Wycliffe** (NT, 1380) (1330–1384), controversial cleric and ex-priest, the "morning star of the Reformation," is credited with the first translation of the entire Bible into English from Latin (the Vulgate). It remained unprinted, however, until 1850. The major part of the Old Testament was done by an associate, Nicholas of Hereford. (In the midst of Catholic-Protestant polemics, it was often repeated that it took a Protestant to produce the first English Bible. The much earlier tradition and translations mentioned above, of which we have only fragmentary remains, should not be ignored.)

- **1388, John Purvey**, a close associate of Wycliffe, produced a revision of Wycliffe's Bible, which, in less than a century, replaced it. It has been pointed out that the prologue in Purvey's edition of the Wycliffe Bible "deserved Thomas More's characterization as heretical." It was traditional to construe the hierarchy's opposition to Wycliffe's translation, and others, as a desire to keep the Bible from the people. As a matter of fact, vernacular translations could enjoy Church approval, as stated by the provincial council of Oxford in 1408. (An historic example would be the ninth-century Slavonic translation by SS. Cyril and Methodius.) It should be remembered that there was more to the early Bible translations than the word of God: The circulation of English Bibles, both in England and on the continent, included the circulation of heretical propaganda, most blatantly in the notes that accompanied the translation.

### 3. 1525-1611: Tyndale to the King James Version

This was the next great era for English translations of the Bible. Although there were translations coming into use in the Mother Church (like Bishop John Fisher's penitential psalms in 1505), it was the Reformation movement that generated the chain of translations that led to the King James Bible of 1611.

This period includes the so-called Elizabethan Age, named after the reign of Queen Elizabeth, 1558–1603. This was a great age of English literature, in both prose and poetry, and the greatest age of drama. Among others it included Marlowe, Sidney, Spenser, Shakespeare, Raleigh, and Ben Jonson.

- **1525, Tyndale's Bible** was the first printed English New Testament, to which were later added the Pentateuch (1530) and various Old Testament parts. Its translator was William Tyndale (1490–1536), "The Father of the English Bible," an ex-Augustinian monk, and an Oxford student of the Scriptures in Greek and Hebrew. It was not embraced by the hierarchy in England because of its strident anti-Catholic notes and its theological slant (it was quickly noticed, for example, that the new translation used the terms "congregation," "overseer," and "elder," instead of "church," "bishop," and "priest"). These were finer points, however, compared with what brought the wrath of Henry VIII: the arbitrary omission of *1 Peter 2:13–14* ("For the Lord's sake accept the authority of every human institution, whether of the emperor as supreme, or of governors, as sent by him . . ."). In 1536, Tyndale was arrested and put to death by the emperor, Charles V, thus becoming a Protestant martyr. (His final revision of the New Testament, published in 1535, gained more acceptance

since by that time Henry VIII had broken with Rome.) It has been estimated that 80% of the King James Bible's New Testament is Tyndale's work.

- **1537, Coverdale's Bible**, referring to Miles Coverdale, an associate of Tyndale, who published the first complete English Bible, based largely on Tyndale's translation of the New Testament with a makeshift rendering of most of the Old Testament from other secondary sources. It was the first English Bible printed in England.

- **1537, Matthew's Bible**. Thomas Matthew, a pseudonym for a Tyndale assistant (and an ex-priest) named John Rogers, collated apparently unpublished Old Testament translations of Tyndale's and parts of Coverdale's work and published the first authorized Bible, beginning an evolution that culminated in the Authorized Version (AV) in 1611 (the "King James Bible"). Many of his "notes" were indecent and objectionable, often abusive of the Church, its teaching and clergy. The regrettable banning and burning of Bibles (not to mention translators) needs to be understood in the context of the regrettable propaganda ("notes") that became the nasty habit of the day. For a sample: Matthew's "note" on 1 Peter 3:7 suggests that if a "wyfe" be not obedient and helpful to her husband, he should endeavor "to beate the feare of God into her heade, that therby she maye be compelled to learne her dutie, and to do it."

- **1538, The Great Bible**, so called because of its size (9" by 15") and costliness, was a revision of Matthew's Bible and other earlier translations, including the Vulgate. Printed for distribution throughout England, it was the first English Bible authorized for public use. (Its psalter was used in the *Book of Common Prayer*.)

- **1539, Taverner's Bible** was a translation by the Greek scholar Richard Taverner. It was an independent work; that is, it stood apart from the tradition culminating in the Authorized Version ("King James Bible").

- **1560, The Geneva Bible** (NT, 1557) was a translation by English Protestant exiles in Geneva during Mary Tudor's Catholic restoration (1553–1558). It was a revision of Tyndale and the Great Bible, with the influence of the great textual scholar, Theodore Beza. It was very popular and became the Bible of the commoner, in part simply because it was small and moderately priced. Some 200 editions are known. (It was also the Bible of Shakespeare, Bunyan, and the Puritans, and the first Bible printed in roman type instead of black letter, with the verses designated, and with explanatory words and phrases set in italics.) Many leaders in the Church of England, while recognizing its superior style and scholarship, were not accepting of it because of its

Calvinist preface and notes (which were also predictably anti-Catholic). A comment on the Geneva Bible by Richard T.A. Murphy, O.P., in *Background to the Bible*, recognizes a sad part of the story of "the English-ing of the Bible": "It is unfortunate that while the text itself had improved, the notes that accompanied it had not. The notes attacked clerical celibacy, the sacraments, the Roman Catholic Church, and the pope. One can scarcely believe that such abuse was included in the Bible, but this was the mental fare of many sixteenth and seventeenth century Bible readers. It explains to some extent the instinctive hostility some have felt toward the Church of Rome and its leader, the pope. Such notes are unthinkable today in the *Common Bible* which has, since Vatican II, become a happy reality."

- **1568, The Bishops' Bible**, with contributions by most Anglican bishops, was the answer by the hierarchy of the Church of England to the popular but bitterly sectarian Geneva Bible (which had revealed the inadequacy of the Great Bible, and which the Bishop's Bible never replaced in the hearts of the people). A revision of the Great Bible and the second authorized version in English, it served as the working basis for the King James Bible, which finally superseded it in 1611.

- **1609, Douay-Rheims** (NT, 1582). This translation from the Vulgate, with careful comparisons to original Hebrew and Greek, was by English Catholic scholars, mainly Gregory Martin (d. 1582) in France. The NT translation was carried out at Rheims in 1582, the Old Testament at Douay in 1609 (it was done in two towns because of the move of English College where the work was done). It was an effort for accuracy more than literary style. Its "Latinisms," common in the English writing of the day, made it archaic for later generations. "The Vulgate was chosen as a basis of translation instead of Hebrew and Greek for several reasons. Textual criticism as we know it was then non-existent; the collection and collation of manuscripts had only just begun. The Vulgate had also been given primacy of place by the Council of Trent (1545–1563) and therefore had authority. Its antiquity was a genuine asset, and it was closer by far to the originals than some of the manuscripts used by the sixteenth century reformers. For all its Latinisms, the Douay-Rheims translation was accurate, and no instances of deliberate perversion or twisting of the text can be shown. And it is not as if Latinisms were everywhere; long passages of the work are not at all unusual in diction. It was, in fact, so good that the translators of the King James Version made extensive use of it." (Richard T.A.

Murphy, O.P., *Background to the Bible*, p. 90)

- **1611, Authorized Version** (AV, or KJV; the so-called King James Bible). The Authorized Version was commissioned by King James I (hence its more common title). It came at the request for a Bible more accurate than previous translations. King James (who had an amateur's interest in Bible translation) approved, knowing that the Bishops' Bible had never enjoyed the success of the Geneva Bible, whose notes he considered seditious. Fifty scholars were instructed to use the Bishops' Bible as their basic version as long as it was faithful to the original text, but to use the translations of Tyndale, Matthew, Coverdale, the Great Bible, and the Geneva Bible, as well as the Catholic translation done at Rheims in 1582. (It was also to be printed without marginal notes!) As respectfully stated in its preface, "We never thought from the beginning that we should need to make a new translation, nor yet to make of a bad one a good one . . . but to make a good one better, or out of many good ones one principal good one." In a word, it took the best of the rest, and far surpassed them. As is well known, it became the standard and has been through much revision over the years. With its noble simplicity, its turns of phrase, melodious rhythm and cadence, it has been called the noblest monument of English prose. Its Elizabethan English (sixteenth-seventeenth century), gracious in style and majestic in language, is complicated by today's standards. It included the Apocrypha (deuterocanonical books), placing them at the end of the Old Testament and deeming them of lesser importance. It also includes the doxology ("for thine is the kingdom . . .") in Matthew 6:13, a verse scholars now recognize to be the addition of a scribe and not appearing in the older and better manuscripts (hence its omission in modern translations like the *New International Version*, the *New Century Version*, and the *Contemporary English Version*). It is written at a twelfth-grade reading level.

### 4. 1611-1902: The KJV to the Twentieth Century NT

Around 1630, a fifth-century manuscript containing the entire New Testament (called *Codex Alexandrinus*) was brought to England. This was an earlier text than the King James translators had available.

- **1750 and 1763, Challoner's Bible** (NT, 1749 and 1752) was a revised version, by a Bishop Challoner (1691–1781), of the English translation of the Douay-Rheims (a century ahead of its Protestant counterpart, the King James Bible, which was revised in 1885). It was, for all intents and purposes, "the Catholic Bible" (for English speakers) until the mid-twentieth century.

Among other nineteenth-century finds, a manuscript (*Codex Sinaiticus*) was discovered by German scholar Tischendorf (1815-1874), offering translators a manuscript from around 350 that was earlier and better than previously available. In 1850, a manuscript from the Vatican's library (*Codex Vaticanus*) became available. Dated 325, it offered a more accurate and reliable witness of Scripture's original texts than had been available before.

- **1885, Revised Version** (RV) (NT, 1881). The RV was the first serious revision of the Authorized ("King James") Version, after 250 years of use. It was based on (and required by) the enormous volume of discovery and scholarship of the nineteenth century that had provided far more reliable original-language texts and greater knowledge of the meaning of Hebrew and Greek words. (In the New Testament alone there were about 30,000 changes, 5,000 of them because of better Greek texts.)

- **1901, American Standard Edition of the Revised Version** (ASV) was a U.S.-published, revised rendition of the RV, required for two reasons: Not only was American usage departing significantly from British English, but textual scholarship had already come far enough to provide a much better text base than the 1885 RV had. It is commonly called the "American Revised Version" and was generally regarded as superior to the 1885 British version. However, neither the RV nor the ASV

## The Gideon Bible

The "Gideon Bible" is the Bible (New King James translation) placed in various public places by the Gideons, a non-sectarian evangelical group of Christians who have made it their mission to distribute the Bible and encourage its use. Lay people from various denominations, often business and professional men, their primary goal is "winning people for Christ," with Bible distribution being their principal means. Gideons began when two traveling men, strangers to each other, met in a Wisconsin hotel in the fall of 1898. As they began to share evening devotions, they decided to form an association, taking the name Gideon (from the story in Judges 6 and 7), the leader of a small group of men dedicated to God through whom God accomplished great things. Their Bible distribution program (typically in the hotel and motels rooms, and to individuals like members of the armed forces) is financed primarily through the support of evangelical churches.

replaced the established KJV in church and private use.

### 5. 1902–1982: Modern Translations

- **1902, The Twentieth Century New Testament**, first in a family of new translations, departs from the traditional Elizabethan English (as in the King James Bible) in favor of fresh renderings in a more common idiom. This change was prompted by early-twentieth-century discoveries of a *"koine"* (common) form of Greek, in which most of the New Testament was written. Traditional scholarship had supposed that Bible Greek was the formal, literary language of Greek poetry and tragedy. If "common" was the language in which the Bible was written, so should the English be in which it is translated.

- **1903, The New Testament in Modern Speech**. The English scholar Richard Weymouth translated a modern speech version of the New Testament that was well received and went through several editions and printings.

- **1924, Moffat** (NT, 1913). The great Scottish scholar, James Moffat, did a new translation of the Bible in modern English ("as one would render any piece of contemporary Hellenistic prose"). This brilliant and independent work was based on what we now know to be a very defective Greek New Testament.

- **1935, The Complete Bible, An American Translation** (NT, 1923). Edgar Goodspeed, a New Testament professor at the University of Chicago, was critical of modern-style translations and so did his own. The "Chicago Bible" (a New Testament) appeared in 1923 and was the earliest American modern-speech translation. The *Complete Bible* (produced by others) followed in 1935 and was judged by *The Jerome Biblical Commentary* "both scientifically and stylistically a superior effort and in many ways the best complete Bible available as of early 1968" (69:164).

- **1941, Confraternity Revision of the NT** (CCD). Like the Protestant RSV of 1952 and the NEB of 1970, the Catholic CCD Bible answered the call for a Bible for the twentieth century. The Bishops' Committee for the Confraternity of Christian Doctrine (hence "CCD") authorized this revision of the Rheims-Challoner New Testament. Its style was relatively modern, but still large amounts of Bible English (thou, behold) were preserved. The Douay-Challoner Old Testament was abandoned with the 1943 publication of *Divino Afflante Spiritu*, Pope Pius XII's encyclical encouraging vernacular translations from the original languages.

- **1944, Knox**. The need for a Douay-Rheims-Challoner update in Great Britain was filled by Father Ronald Knox, the eminent convert and classics scholar from Oxford. A rendering from the Latin, it was a complete break from "Bible English" and was more appreciated in literary circles than biblical. Its lively New Testament, especially the Pauline epistles, has been called masterful.

> A new enthusiasm for modern translations of the Bible came with the end of World War II, a seedtime for translations that were published through the course of the next decades.

- **1952, The Revised Standard Version** (RSV) (NT, 1946) is a modern American rendering (at a tenth-grade reading level) of the English Bible in the King James tradition. By far the best in its day, the RSV is probably the last Bible in the Tyndale/KJV tradition. Demand for the RSV came for these two reasons: First, the Revised Versions (both British and American) had a reputation for accuracy, but also for being "wooden," translating words with greater care for accuracy than for context, following even the Greek word order regardless of the English result ("unidiomatic"). Second, there had been important manuscript discoveries in the 1930s and 1940s. As its preface says, "The RSV is not a new translation in the language of today. It is not a paraphrase which aims at striking idioms." Since it preserves the KJV language as much as possible, much Bible English (thou, behold) still remains (although it exchanged "who" for "which" in reference to persons, "know" for "wot" and "knew" for "wist"). It surprisingly changed the KJV's "Lord" to "Jehovah" in the Old Testament. The well-received RSV became a standard for many Protestants —notable exceptions being scandalized fundamentalists and conservative evangelicals who debated over changes like "young woman" for "virgin" in Isaiah 7:14, for example.

- **1958, New Testament in Modern English** (Phillips). The British vicar J.B. Phillips carried modern idiomatic translation even beyond Goodspeed's. This very readable version is so lively that it becomes almost a paraphrase, making Paul's letters "sound as if they'd just come through the mail."

- **1961, The New World Translation** (NT, 1950) is only noted here as a warning about reliability. Prepared by the Jehovah's Witnesses (Watchtower Bible and Tract Society), it's probably the only modern translation driven by doctrinal views instead of the text itself. There is no textual reason, for example, for translating the New Testament "Lord" as "Jehovah."

- **1965, Amplified Bible.** Since the RSV had been condemned as unfaithful by a majority of American conservatives, translations like this one were done to provide them with an acceptable updated Bible. (See its descendants, the 1971 New American Standard Bible and the 1978 New International Version, below.)

- **1966, The Jerusalem Bible** (JB). In 1955, French Dominicans of the Ecole Biblique in Jerusalem published a new, excellent translation from the original languages into French. It was immediately recognized as one of the greatest achievements of a reborn Catholic biblical scholarship and a response to the invitation of the 1943 encyclical *Divino Afflante Spiritu*. A free translation, it has been praised for its extensive introductions and footnotes (the most scholarly and comprehensive of any English Bible to that

point, and strictly related to the text) that offer help with difficult passages and background information where geography or cultural details need to be clarified. Uniquely, it uses "Yahweh" as God's name in the Old Testament. It was translated (along with its invaluable notes) into English in 1966. In 1985 a revision of the JB was done.

- **1968, New Confraternity Bible** (New CCD). With the 1943 encyclical calling for recourse to the original languages, the old CCD revision of the Douay-Challoner was abandoned, and a new translation of the whole Bible was commissioned by the Episcopal Committee. The old CCD project, like its Protestant counterpart, the RSV, boldly undertook the revision of a sacrosanct tradition and translation. The New CCD (not unlike the Protestant NEB) used new concepts and tools in both style and scholarship. It avoided Bible English, eliminating all "thou" forms, for example, and using contractions. (Most of its Old Testament came out in three volumes in 1952, 1955, and 1961.)

- **1970, The New English Bible** (NEB) (NT, 1961). The Church of Scotland (in 1946, the same year the RSV's New Testament was published) proposed a fresh translation in modern idiom (which will be highly British, of course) of the original languages—not a revision of any previous translation and not a

literal translation. This was different in theory and practice. A
dramatic breakthrough, the NEB
was experimental, producing
phrasings never published before,
and is praised by some for
ingenuity, and criticized by others for the same reason (see for
example its rendering of John 1:1:
"When all things began, the Word
already was"). Its British English
includes "cairn" for "heap,"
"corn" for "wheat," and "thirty
pounds" for "300 denarii." Its
revision (changing its distinctive
nature) was published in 1989.

- **1970, The New American Bible**
(NAB), published by members of
the Catholic Biblical Association
as the successor of the Confraternity Bible translated from the
Vulgate, is the first English Bible
from the Catholic Church translated from the original texts. It's
a highly regarded work of some
fifty scholars, adhering strictly to
the rules of biblical criticism. In
the functional equivalent category, and at an eleventh-grade
reading level, it walks the middle
ground between literal fidelity
and readability. One notable
change was the use of proper
names derived from the Hebrew
instead of the Latin ("Isaiah" for
"Isaias" and "Elijah" for "Elias,"
for example). Another change
was to name biblical books to
agree with the more proper usage
of the Protestant Bible ("Chronicles" for "Paralipomenon,"
"Sirach" for "Ecclesiasticus," and
"Revelation" for "Apocalypse,"

for example). It's a respecter of
tradition, leaving Isaiah 7:14 as
"virgin," for example. Its New
Testament was hastened somewhat for use in the new Lectionary following Vatican II and the
need was soon apparent for its revision (which was done by 1987).
Furthermore, the distinctively
contemporary sound of the NAB,
when read liturgically, revealed
the need for a more traditional
and formal translation.

- **1971, The Living Bible** (NT,
1966). Kenneth Taylor's huge success uses the ASV as a working
text and rephrases (paraphrases)
into modern speech that anyone,
including children, can understand ("expanding where necessary"). "The Way," as it was originally called, along with its earlier
New Testament, "Reach Out,"
is very readable (eighth-grade
reading level) of course, but is
criticized for being too interpretive. Its theological orientation
is conservative and evangelistic.
(Tyndale House Publishers is
Taylor's creation—originally for
publishing The Living Bible.)

- **1971, New American Standard
Bible** (NAS). Like the RSV of
1952, the NAS was based on the
ASV of 1901, which was a tower-
ing and very accurate work of
scholarship, but was slipping
in popularity. A conservative
evangelistic group sought to
revive it with the goal of a literal
translation in fluent, readable
(eleventh-grade reading level),
and current English (a literary

goal that still suffers for the sake of the literal). This process began with the 1965 Amplified Bible and culminated with the 1978 New International Version (see below). The NAS claims the ASV lineage, but is in fact a different translation to satisfy conservative Protestant congregations. Note, for example, the absence of the Apocrypha and the capitalization of all pronouns referring to God and all Old Testament references thought to be messianic.

- **1973, The Common Bible** is an RSV translation (including Apocrypha, excluding any polemical notes), published with international Catholic, Orthodox, and Protestant endorsement.

- **1976, Good News Bible: Today's English Version** (TEV) (NT, 1966). This is an American Protestant counterpart of the 1970 NEB (the completely new British translation in modern English). Very affordable and heavily marketed, it has been embraced by millions as an idiomatic version in modern and simple English, in a style purposely chosen for the elementary age reading level. (Its popular New Testament was called "Good News for Modern Man.") The translation principle, unlike the RSV's a generation before, is dynamic equivalent, standing somewhere between Phillips and the NEB. Often a virtual paraphrase (in "newspaper English"), it's better for private reading than for study. It was revised in the 1980s.

- **1978, The New International Version** (NIV) (NT, 1973). Since 1987, this reliable and readable Bible has outsold the King James Version, which had been the bestseller for centuries. Now a standard for both private reading and public proclamation in English-speaking countries, it is the fruit of more than a hundred scholars from English-speaking countries around the world with, as they say, "a high view of Scripture." Designed for conservative evangelical Protestants, it uses a vocabulary common to all English speakers (with a seventh-grade reading level) and strives for a balance between a literal rendering and a paraphrase. It is very successful in fulfilling the goals of major translations since the RSV: the contextualizing the meaning of words, modifying sentence structure, and eliminating archaic pronouns and verb forms. (Its goals did not include eliminating gender-specific language.) It emphasizes the messianic meaning of certain Old Testament texts (for example, still translating Isaiah 7:14 "virgin," contrary to the best scholarly opinion).

## 6. Since 1982: Revisions of Versions

This era of new revisions more than new translations was prompted by knowledge of still older manuscripts, advances in Biblical linguistics, and continuing evolution of preferred English usage.

- **1982, The New King James Version** (NKJV) is a formal

equivalence translation in the literal tradition of the AV, but with contemporary American English replacing Elizabethan (thees and thous and other archaic words). In its efforts to salvage some of the lyricism of Elizabethan English (at an eighth-grade reading level), this translation satisfies the nostalgia of those familiar with the KJV. Its Old Testament messianic passages are clearly influenced by Christian theology. Its New Testament, depending on the Greek text that it does, forfeits the best modern text criticism.

- **1985, The New Jerusalem Bible** (NJB), a revision of the 1966 *Jerusalem Bible*, is based on the 1973 French edition and includes an improved text and updated footnotes (and reflects the new sensitivity to inclusive language).

- **1986, The New American Bible**, with revised NT (revised NAB). After an original 1970 content-centered translation, this revision reflects (intentionally) a more form-centered approach. Typical of many, many changes, for example, is *Matthew 5:18*: "of this much I assure you," now is revised to "Amen, I say to you." According to some, this change is "a deliberate step backward," of the worst "formal equivalence." (Likewise, the 1989 REB is less idiomatic than the 1970 NEB it revises.) The revision, with the goal of communicating to "ordinary educated people," also reflects a greater gender inclusivity and "a

dignity" more suitable for public reading (liturgical use).

- **1986, The New Century Bible**, with a conservative, evangelistic theological orientation, is published in two editions. "The Everyday Bible" is for adults and is a simple, functional equivalent translation for those with a limited vocabulary. The "International Children's Version" uses shorter, uncomplicated sentences and vocabulary at a third-grade reading level.

- **1989, The Revised English Bible** (REB). This extensive revision of the popular British NEB of 1970 was needed to keep the English current and the text up-to-date with modern scholarship. Although something of a disappointment (reverting to more traditional language and exegesis than the NEB), it still remains the foremost dynamic equivalence in English translation. More inclusive language is used and the thees and thous that had been retained in prayers are now completely abandoned. Some say it is "more restrained" in its paraphrasing tendencies (thinking better, for example, of *John 1:1*: "When all things began, the Word already was," has become "In the beginning the Word already was").

- **1990, The New Revised Standard Version** (NRSV) is the authorized revision of the 1952 RSV, which was a revision of the 1901 ASV, which embodied earlier revisions of the 1611 KJV. (It's the text of the Oxford Annotated study Bible.) It eliminates male-oriented language (where the original text is inclusive—"brothers and sisters" instead of "brethren," for example) and abandons the thees and thous that had been retained in prayers. Despite attacks on the RSV's translation of Isaiah 7:14, the NRSV keeps "young woman" (which had replaced "virgin"). In 1991 the NRSV (with deutero-canonicals included between the two testaments) was approved by the American bishops for Catholic use in the U.S. In 1992 it published a Catholic edition that, uniquely, included the deutero-canonicals in their proper order among the other Old Testament books (as all Catholic Bibles always have).

- **1992, Today's English Version** (second edition), a new edition of the 1976 TEV, eliminates exclusive language. It is the translation used in the *Precious Moments* Bible.

- **1993, The Message** (NT) is a contemporary idiomatic English paraphrase of the New Testament, psalms, and some other Old Testament books.

- **1994, Contemporary English Version** (CEV) (NT, 1991). This is a youth-oriented, dynamic equivalent translation.

- **1996, The New Living Translation**. This revision of the very popular The Living Bible (1967, 1971) is in the dynamic equivalent family.

# Comparing Translations

These are various translations of the Lord's Prayer (see *Luke 11:2–4*).

## Lindisfarne Gospels, about 950

*This translation is in Old English (or "Anglo-Saxon"), the original pre-Norman Germanic stock of English used from the fifth century (or eighth, according to some) to the twelfth century. It is the language of the epic poem Beowulf of the early eighth century.*

Fader gehalgad sie noma oin tocymaeo ic oin hlaf userne dae-ghuaemlice sel us eghuelc daege fgef us synna usra gif faestlice aec pe fgefaes eghuelc scyldge us fgef ne usic onlaed ou in costunge.

## Wycliffe Bible, 1382

*This translation is in Middle English, the language of the period from about 1150 to 1475 (which includes Geoffrey Chaucher, 1340-1400).*

Fadir, halewid be thi name. Thi kyngdom come to. Zyue to vs to day oure eche dayes breed. And forzyue to vs oure synnes, as and we forzyuen to each owynge to vs. And leed not vs in to temptacioun.

## Tyndale New Testament, 1525

*This translation is in early Modern English, post-1475 (which includes the works of Shakespeare, 1564-1616).*

Oure father which arte in heve, halowed be thy name. Lett thy kyngdom come. Thy will, be fulfil-let, even in erth as it is in heven. Oure dayly breed geve us this daye. And forgeve vs oure synnes:

for even we forgeve every man that traspaseth vs, and ledde vs not into temptacio, Butt delliver vs from evyll Amen.

### Coverdale Bible, 1537

O oure father which art in heauen, halowed be thy name. Thy kyngdome come. Thy wil be fulfilled vpon earth, as it is in heauen. Geue vs this daye oure daylie bred. And forgeue vs oure synnes, for we also forgeue all them that are detters vnto vs. And lede vs not in to temptacion, but delyuer vs from euell.

### Matthew's Bible, 1537

O oure father which arte in heauen, halowed be thy name. Thy kyngdome come. Thy will be fulfylled, eucn in erth as it is in heauen. Oure dayly breed geue vs euermore. And forgeue vs our synnes: For euen we forgeue euery man yt treaspaseth vs. And leade vs not into temptacion. But delyuer vs from euyll.

### The Great Bible, 1538

O oure father which are in heauen, halowed be thy name. Thy kyngdome come. Thy will be fulfylled, eue in erth also as it is in heaue. Oure dayly breed geue vs thys daye. And forgeue vs our synnes; For eue we forgeue euery man that treaspaseth vs. And Leade vs not ito temptacyon. But delyuer vs from euyll.

### Geneva Bible, 1560

Our Father, we art in heaue, halowed be thy Name: Thy kingdome come: Ut thy wil be done eue

in earth, as it is in heavuen: Our daily bread giue vs for the day: And forgiue vs our sinnes: for euen we forgiue euerie man that is indetted to vs: And lead vs not into temptation: but deliuer vs from euil.

### Bishop's Bible, 1568

O our father which art in heauen, halowed be thy name, thy Kyngdome come, thy wyll be fulfylled, euen in earth also, as it is in heaven. Our dayly breade geue vs this day. And forgeue vs our synnes: Foe euen we forgeue euery man that trespasseth vs. And leade vs not into temptation, but delyuer vs from euyll.

### Rheims New Testament, 1582

Father, sanctified be thy name. Thy kingdom come, Our daily bread giue vs this day, and forgiue vs our sinnes, for because our selues also doe forgiue euery one that is in debt to vs. And lead vs not into temptation.

### King James Bible, 1611

Our Father which art in heaven, Hallowed be thy name. Thy kingdom come. Thy will be done, as in heaven, so in earth. Give us day by day our daily bread. And forgive us our sins; for we also forgive every one that is indebted to us. And lead us not into temptation; but deliver us from evil.

### Revised Version, 1881

Father, Hallowed be thy name. Thy kingdom come. Give us day by day our daily bread. And forgive us our sins; for we ourselves also forgive

every one that is indebted to us.
And bring us not into temptation.

### American Standard Edition of the Revised Version, 1901

Father, Hallowed be thy name. Thy kingdom come. Give us day by day our daily bread. And forgive us our sins; for we ourselves also forgive every one that is indebted to us. And bring us not into temptation.

### Revised Standard Version, 1946

Father, hallowed be thy name. Thy kingdom come. Give us each day our daily bread; and forgive us our sins, for we ourselves forgive every one who is indebted to us; and lead us not into temptation.

### The New English Bible, 1961

Father, thy name be hallowed; Thy kingdom come. Give us each day our daily bread. And forgive us our sins, for we too forgive all who have done us wrong. And do not bring us to the test.

### The Jerusalem Bible, 1966

Father, may your name be held holy, Your kingdom come; give us each day our daily bread, and forgive us our sins, for we ourselves forgive each one who is in debt to us. And do not put us to the test.

### Today's English Version, 1966

Father, may your name be kept holy, May your Kingdom come. Give us day by day the food we need. Forgive us our sins, for we forgive everyone who has done us wrong. And do not bring us to hard testing.

### The New American Bible, 1970

Father, hallowed be your name, your kingdom come. Give us each day our daily bread. Forgive us our sins for we too forgive all who do us wrong; and subject us not to the trial.

### New International Version, 1978

Father, hallowed be your name, your kingdom come. Give us each day our daily bread. Forgive us our sins, for we also forgive everyone who sins against us. And lead us not into temptation.

### The New King James Version, 1982

Our Father in heaven, Hallowed be Your name. Your kingdom come. Your will be done On earth as it is in heaven. Give us day by day our daily bread. And forgive us our sins, For we also forgive everyone who is indebted to us. And do not lead us into temptation, but deliver us from the evil one.

### The New Century Bible, 1986

Father, may your name always be kept holy. May your kingdom come. Give us the food we need for each day. Forgive us for our sins, because we forgive everyone who has done wrong to us. And do not cause us to be tempted.

### The New American Bible, revised, 1986

Father, hallowed be your name, your kingdom come. Give us each day our daily bread and forgive us our sins for we ourselves forgive everyone in debt to us, and do not subject us to the final test.

## New Revised Standard Version, 1990

Father, hallowed be your name. Your kingdom come. Give us each day our daily bread. And forgive us our sins, for we ourselves forgive everyone indebted to us. And do not bring us to the time of trial.

## Contemporary English Version, 1991

Father, help us to honor your name. Come and set up your kingdom. Give us each day the food we need. Forgive our sins, as we forgive everyone who has done wrong to us. And keep us from being tempted.

## The Message, 1993

Father, reveal who you are. Set the world right. Keep us alive with three square meals. Keep us forgiven with you and forgiving others. Keep us safe from ourselves and the Devil.

## New Living Translation, 1996

Father, may your name be honored. May your Kingdom come soon. Give us our food day by day. And forgive us our sins—just as we forgive those who have sinned against us. And don't let us yield to temptation.

# ENDNOTES

## Chapter 1
[1] Second Vatican Council, *Dogmatic Constitution on Divine Revelation (Dei Verbum)* (DV), no. 2.
[2] Cf. *Gen* 9:16; *Lk* 21:24; *DV* 3.
[3] *DV* 7; cf. *Mt* 28:19–20; *Mk* 16:15.
[4] St. Augustine, *En. in Ps.* 103, 4, 1: PL 37, 1378; cf. *Ps* 104; *Jn* 1:1.
[5] St. Bernard, *S. missus est hom.* 4, 11: PL 183, 86.
[6] *DV* 8 § 3; cf. *Col* 3:16.
[7] *DV* 7 § 2
[8] Cf. *Rev* 22:17; *John* 10:7, 8.
[9] *DV* 12 § 2.
[10] *DV* 10 § 3.

## Chapter 2
[1] *LG* 2.
[2] Cf. *DV* 8 § 3.

## Chapter 3
[1] Cf. *2 Cor* 3:14; *Jn* 5:39, 46.
[2] *DV* 17; cf. *Rom* 1:16.
[3] St. Thérèse of Lisieux, *ms. autob.* A 83v.
[4] *DV* 18.
[5] *SCh* 345, 480.
[6] *LG* 2.
[7] Cf. *2 Cor* 3:14–16.
[8] Cf. *1 Pet* 3:21.
[9] *Jn* 6:32; cf. *1 Cor* 10:1–6.

## Chapter 4
[1] Origen, *Hom. in Lev.* 5, 5: PG 12, 454D.
[2] Cf. John Paul II, *DeV* 46.

## Chapter 5
[1] Cf. Second Vatican Council, *Constitution on the Sacred Liturgy (Sacrosanctum Concilium)* (SC), no. 35.
[2] GDC, no. 51.
[3] *LG* 2
[4] Cf. *Lectionary for Mass.* English translation of the Second *Editio-Typica* (1981) #24 prepared by International Commission on English in the Liturgy.
[5] Cf. *On Catechesis in Our Time*, 1979, #48; also, *Sharing the Light of Faith*, 1981, p. 54.
[6] Cf. *Rom* 10:9; *1 Cor* 15:3–5, etc.
[7] *Catech. illum.* 4, 12: PG 33, 521–524.
[8] *Didache* 8, 2: SCh 248, 174.
[9] *Apostolic Constitutions*, 7, 24, 1: PG 1, 1016.
[10] *Titus* 2:13; cf. *Roman Missal* 22, Embolism after the Lord's Prayer.
[11] St. Augustine, *Ep.* 130, 12, 22: PL 33, 503.
[12] Cf. *Lectionary for Mass.* English translation of the Second *Editio-Typica* (1981) #24 prepared by International Commission on English in the Liturgy.

## Chapter 6

[1]Cf. *Mk* 12:29–31

## Chapter 7

[1]*DV* 21.
[2]*Ps* 119:105; cf. *Isa* 50:4.
[3]St. Teresa of Jesus, *The Way of Perfection* 26,9 in *The Collected Works of St. Teresa of Avila*, tr. K. Kavanaugh, OCD, and O. Rodriguez, OCD (Washington DC: Institute of Carmelite Studies, 1980), II, 136.
[4]St. Teresa of Jesus, *The Book of Her Life*, 8, 5 in *The Collected Works of St. Teresa of Avila*, tr. K. Kavanaugh, OCD, and O. Rodriguez, OCD (Washington DC: Institute of Carmelite Studies, 1976,) I, 67.
[5]Cf. St. Isaac of Nineveh, *Tract.*

*myst.* 66.
[6]St. John of the Cross, *Maxims and Counsels*, 53 in *The Collected Works of St. John of the Cross*, tr. K. Kavanaugh, OCD, and O. Rodriguez, OCD (Washington DC: Institute of Carmelite Studies, 1979), 678.
[7]Cf. *Lk* 1:48; *Zeph* 3:17b.
[8]Cf. *Rom* 10:1; *Eph* 1:16–23; *Phil* 1:9–11; *Col* 1:3–6; 4:3–4, 12.
[9]cf. *Acts* 7:60; *Lk* 23:28, 34
[10]Cf. *Acts* 12:5; 20:36; 21:5; 2 *Cor* 9:14.
[11]*SC* 60; cf. CIC, can. 1166; CCEO, can. 867.
[12]Cf. *Gen* 12:2; *Lk* 6:28; *Rom* 12:14; 1 *Pet* 3:9.

# INDEX

Psalms, 248–253; celebrating the special
character of Friday, 269, 270; celebrating
the special character of Sunday, 268, 269;
division of, 264; exclusion of verses, 264,
265; for particular days, 259; for particular
hours, 259; in the office, 260–262; musical
character, 252; of Evening Prayer, 267;
of Morning Prayer, 266; of Night Prayer,
267; of the Steps, 263; poetry in the, 253;
repetition of, 263, 264; the prayer book of
Jesus, 249; the prayer of the assembly, 249,
250; the spiritual sense, 250–252; the title
of, 265; the voice of Christ, 251; who they
address, 253
Psalter, 248, 251, 259, 309
pseudonymous, 35

## Q

Quadratus, 64
Quasimodo Sunday, 176
Qumran, 56

## R

rapture, 151, 152
Reconciliation, 219–222
reconciling both testaments, 75, 76
redaction criticism, 44
Responsory, 277, 278
Resurrection, 14, 30, 32, 47, 79, 80, 91, 109, 110,
198, 246, 247
resuscitations, 108
Revelation, 9, 11, 14, 28, 74; see also Divine
Revelation
Rite of Christian Initiation of Adults, 3
rock, the, 86
Rosary, the, 294–299

## S

sacramentals, 222–227; anointing, 223; ashes,
224; candles, 224, 225; incense, 225, 226;
palms, 226, 227; water, 227
sacraments, 218, 220, 221
Sacred, Heart, 235, 291, 292, 300; Scripture, 4,
11, 14, 17, 18, 27, 51, 73, 75, 147, 176, 286;
Synod, 28; Tripod, 17
Saint Augustine, 12, 45, 284, 286, 287
Saint Gregory Nazianzen, 87
Saint Gregory the Great, 87
Saint Hippolytus, 146
Saint Irenaeus, 9, 15, 67
Saint Jerome, 55, 65, 116, 122
Saint John (the Evangelist), 15, 28, 81
Saint Justin, 177
Saint Luke, 42
Saint Paul, 12, 14, 39, 80
Saint Polycarp, 15
Saint Theodore the Studite, 87
salvation, 8, 11, 73, 78, 92; history, 30
Samaria, 37
Samuel, 38
sanctus, the, 213
Scripture, allegorical sense, 143; anagogical
sense, 144; contextual, 148; four-fold sense
of, 334; interpretation, 137–156; literal sense,
142; moral sense, 144; pneumatic
(spiritual), 145; psychic (inner), 145;
quoting out of context, 148; readings in the
Liturgy of the Hours, 274–277; somatic
(literal), 145; spiritual sense, 143; the fuller
sense, 144, 145; translation of, 115–136; why
pray with it, 288–290
Scripture translation, content-centered, 122;
form-centered, 122; punctuation, 136, 137;
readability, 132; word-for-word, 128, 130
Semitic causative, 130
Septuagint, 55, 115, 116
sermon, 63
Sermon on the Mount, 89